M

GRE®
FOR
DUMMIES®
A Wiley Brand

8th Edition

GRE®

FOR DUMMIES®
A Wiley Brand

8th Edition

by Ron Woldoff, MBA, MIS
Founder, National Test Prep
with Joe Kraynak

FOR
DUMMIES®
A Wiley Brand

GRE® For Dummies® 8th Edition

Published by
John Wiley & Sons, Inc.
111 River Street
Hoboken, NJ 07030-5774
www.wiley.com

For general information on our other products and services, please contact our Customer Care Department within the U.S. at 877-762-2974, outside the U.S. at 317-572-3993, or fax 317-572-4002. For technical support, please visit www.wiley.com/techsupport.

Wiley publishes in a variety of print and electronic formats and by print-on-demand. Some material included with standard print versions of this book may not be included in e-books or in print-on-demand. If this book refers to media such as a CD or DVD that is not included in the version you purchased, you may download this material at http://booksupport.wiley.com. For more information about Wiley products, visit www.wiley.com.

Library of Congress Control Number: 2014948536

ISBN 978-1-118-91164-8 (pbk); ISBN 978-1-118-91148-8 (ebk); ISBN 978-1-118-91171-6 (ebk)

Manufactured in the United States of America

10 9 8 7 6 5 4

Contents at a Glance

Table of Contents

Introduction

Welcome to *GRE For Dummies*, 8th Edition. Don't take the dummies thing personally — you're obviously no dummy. You made it through high school with high enough grades and test scores to get into college. You then graduated to join the elite group of approximately 30 percent of U.S. citizens who hold bachelor's degrees, and some of you already have advanced degrees. And now you're ready to go further.

Between you and your goal is the GRE: a test designed solely to challenge your ability to remember everything you've forgotten since high school — material you haven't touched in years. To clear this hurdle, all you really need is a refresher course. This book is your refresher course plus; it goes beyond rehashing what you've learned (and forgotten) by providing valuable strategies and tips for answering questions efficiently and correctly. You also find plenty of examples, practice questions, and practice tests to hone your skills, identify subject areas you need to work on a little more, and build your confidence for test day.

Like a personal guide, this book reveals the ins and outs of the GRE and secret passageways to reaching your goal: admittance to the grad school of your choice and perhaps a scholarship to help pay your way. The purpose of this book is to provide the skills and strategies that you need to score well on the GRE. Period. You can walk out of your local library with 20 books on the GRE, but that won't help you. Who has time to read all that? In your hands is a concise, complete reference containing everything that you need for the exam. If you need a fast, effective guide to acing the GRE, you're holding the right book.

About This Book

In *GRE For Dummies*, 8th Edition, I cover all the basic math and verbal concepts and introduce GRE-type questions for practice. I also show you how to approach each type of question, spot the traps built into the questions, and master the tricks that help you avoid those traps.

To earn a top score on the GRE, you must achieve two goals:

- ✔ **Primary goal: Master everything the test covers.** Read through the whole book. No matter how well you know a topic, you can learn strategies and common traps, and you need to make sure you have the knowledge and skills to handle each section at the GRE level. That you should work on your weakest sections is true, but you need to be ready for anything the GRE may ask you. The exam measures your overall and top skill levels, so building on your strengths is just as important as improving your weakest subject areas.

- ✔ **Secondary goal: Strengthen your weak subject areas.** Turn to specific sections for targeted information. The organization of this book makes it easy to find the types of math questions you always have trouble with, suggestions for answering Reading Comprehension questions without having finished the passage, and tricks for acing the sentence-based questions.

Not only is this book simple and straightforward enough if you're rusty with the GRE math and verbal topics, but it's also detailed and sophisticated enough to deliver the high-level guidance to help you earn truly excellent scores.

As you read through the book, you'll notice that some words have a style all their own. Each GRE vocabulary word in this text appears in **this** special font, followed directly by its meaning. A good way to learn a new vocabulary word is to encounter it in regular text and see what it means along with how it's used. In this way, these pages serve as a combination lesson: You learn the topic of the pages and some vocab at the same time.

Foolish Assumptions

This book is intended to help you prepare for the GRE. I assume that you're in at least one of these three stages of your GRE planning:

✔ You've already scheduled the GRE, or are about to, and you need some preparation before taking it.

✔ You have to take the GRE for acceptance into the graduate program at your preferred school.

✔ You're considering a graduate program or school that requires the GRE as part of the application process and want to know what the exam is all about.

Icons Used in This Book

Although everything included in this book is valuable, some tidbits call for special attention. Look for the following icons to quickly spot the most important information in each chapter.

This icon marks practice questions that are relevant to the subject matter being covered. After explaining a concept, I usually follow with an example question to show you how it's done.

This icon indicates little bits of wisdom to make your GRE experience go more smoothly and improve your success.

This icon marks key points to remember while you're working the GRE questions, especially anything that's likely to surprise you on the test. By knowing what to expect, you become better able to handle it.

This icon marks GRE traps and common student mistakes. Discovering these traps before test day is better than being ensnared in them when taking the test.

Beyond the Book

This book is packed with information to help you perform well on the GRE, but you can find even more online, including the following:

✔ **Cheat Sheet:** At www.dummies.com/extras/gre, you'll find last-minute details that you'll want to have at your fingertips, including a rundown of what to expect when you take the GRE, a list of what to bring with you and what to leave at home on test day, tips for taking the computerized exam, and pointers for answering multiple-choice questions.

✔ **Bonus content:** Additional articles take you beyond what's covered in the book to boost your GRE success. At www.dummies.com/extras/gre, you can find information on how to master the Verbal and Quantitative sections, pointers on writing the essays, advice on deciding whether to retake the exam, and tips for getting in test mode on the big day.

✔ **400 GRE vocabulary flashcards:** Stock your mental word bank and boost your verbal reasoning score by mastering the meanings of 400 words that make frequent appearances on the GRE. These appear online at studyandprep.dummies.com.

✔ **Nearly 500 practice questions:** You'll find hundreds of GRE-type questions online to help you build your competence and confidence. You can focus on areas where you need more practice and verify that you're up to speed in other areas. You can answer the questions through untimed and timed quizzes, so you can work at your own speed and gain experience working under pressure. Find these at studyandprep.dummies.com.

To gain access to the online practice, all you have to do is register. Just follow these simple steps:

1. **Find your PIN code.**

   • **Print-book users:** If you purchased a hard copy of this book, turn to the inside front cover of this book to find your PIN.

   • **E-book users:** If you purchased this book as an e-book, you can get your PIN by registering your e-book at www.dummies.com/go/getaccess. Simply select your book from the drop-down menu, fill in your personal information, and then answer the security question to verify your purchase. You'll then receive an email with your PIN.

2. **Go to studyandprep.dummies.com.**

3. **Click on *GRE For Dummies*, 8th Edition.**

4. **Enter your PIN.**

5. **Follow the instructions to create an account and establish your own login information.**

Now you're ready to go! You can come back to the online program as often as you want — simply log on with the username and password you created during your initial login. No need to enter the PIN a second time.

If you have trouble with your PIN or can't find it, contact Wiley Product Technical Support at 877-762-2974 or go to http://support.wiley.com.

Where to Go from Here

You can approach this book in three ways:

✔ **Read it from beginning to end.** For most readers, I recommend this approach. Although prepping to take the GRE isn't a linear process, I present topics from easy to challenging, so they build on each other as you progress through the chapters. I start by providing a feel for the test-taking experience so you know what to expect when that day rolls around. I continue by providing guidance for each section of the exam — verbal reasoning, quantitative reasoning, and the writing of analytical essays. Practice exams follow, and I wrap things up with some Part of Tens chapters that will stick with you long after you're done with this book.

- ✔ **Skip around.** Each chapter is a stand-alone lesson on a specific GRE-related topic. If your study time is limited, skip around to focus on areas where you need the most guidance. For example, you can skip to Chapter 6 to hone your skills at answering argument analysis questions, or skip to Chapter 10 to brush up on geometry. Another strategy is to take one of the sample tests to evaluate your skills and identify areas of weakness and then use that information to develop your plan of attack.

- ✔ **Use it as a reference book.** Whenever you need information and advice on a specific GRE topic or skill, simply flip to the chapter or section that contains the information and guidance you need. *GRE For Dummies* offers a refresher course on every topic and skill you need to master to succeed on the GRE.

As you work your way through the book, I recommend you create flashcards to note key concepts and strategies to get the most out of your review. The flashcards will serve as a handy reference while you review your notes.

I've been helping GRE students beat the test for years, so not only do I know students' common questions and mistakes, but I also know how to make the math and verbal questions easier for you to answer. This book distills my tricks and secrets, which I'm pleased to share with you. Your success, after all, is why we're both here.

Part I
Getting Started with the GRE

In this part . . .

- ✔ Get the details about signing up for the GRE, what's on the exam, and how your score is calculated.

- ✔ Figure out how to schedule your study time in advance of test day and get some pointers if you're retaking the exam.

- ✔ Know what you need to do to prepare for the exam (beyond studying) and find out what to expect on test day.

Chapter 1

Knowing What to Expect with the GRE

In This Chapter

▶ Fitting the GRE into your schedule

▶ Deconstructing the GRE to better understand what's on it

▶ Grasping the scoring system

▶ Looking forward to intermissions

*O*ne of the easiest ways to reduce your test anxiety and optimize your performance on the GRE is to become familiar with it. Knowing what to expect gives you less to think about and fret over come test day so you can focus on what really matters — the test itself.

In this chapter, I encourage you to schedule your exam early so you can get a time slot that works for you. I also discuss the GRE's structure and scoring system so you can build your strategies around them. With this guidance, you're better equipped to avoid surprises that may throw you off your game.

Signing Up for the GRE

In most parts of the world, the GRE is a computer-based test, which makes it easier to administer to individual test-takers. Sign up early so you can choose the day, time, and place that work best for you. If you're a morning person who's sharpest at sunrise, you can schedule the test for early morning; if you're a night owl who tends to sleep in, you can opt for late morning or early afternoon. Actual time slot availability varies according to the testing center, but you have more days and times to choose from than you do with paper-and-pencil tests, such as the LSAT and SAT.

The paper and computer versions of the GRE are slightly different. For example, the paper version has 25 questions per section, while the computer version has only 20. Don't worry too much about the differences; your only option will most likely be to take the computer version.

To sign up for the GRE, see the current *GRE Information and Registration Bulletin* (available through most college admissions offices), register online at www.ets.org, or register via phone by calling 800-473-2255. You can also check the GRE testing center locations and available time slots at www.ets.org.

To help you get in the right mindset, take the practice tests at the same time of day you plan on taking the real thing. (Check out the practice tests in Chapters 16, 18, and 20.) I've had students use this strategy to become accustomed to the effects that their *circadian rhythms* (hunger and nap patterns) have on their test-taking abilities. If you're used to eating or relaxing at a certain time each day, make sure these tendencies don't sneak up on you during the exam. As I discuss in greater detail throughout this book, one of your goals is to make the GRE as familiar as possible, or rather, to make the test-taking experience as less *un*familiar as possible. (See Chapter 3 for more on how to prepare for the GRE.)

Because the computerized GRE is administered to individual test-takers, testing centers tend to have few seats, and those seats fill up quickly during peak admission deadline months (April and November). If you're planning to take the GRE around these months (to get your test scores in on time), schedule your test early and secure your ideal time slot. You can always reschedule, but the last thing you need is an inconvenient time or location. One of my students waited until the last minute to schedule his exam, and he had to drive from Phoenix to Tucson (approximately 120 miles) to take his GRE and get his scores in on time. He called me during his drive to review math formulas, but this wasn't an ideal way to ramp up for the test.

Breaking the GRE into Manageable Pieces

Standardized tests tend to convey a sense of gloom and doom. Telling someone you have to take the SAT, ACT, or GRE usually elicits the same facial expression as saying that you need to have your wisdom teeth pulled. However, breaking the GRE down into its component parts makes it more manageable and less threatening.

Table 1-1 provides a quick overview of what's on the exam. The essays are always first, but the multiple-choice sections may be in any order.

Table 1-1	GRE Breakdown by Section (Computer-Based)	
Section	*Number of Questions*	*Time Allotted*
Analyze an Issue	1 essay	30 minutes
Analyze an Argument	1 essay	30 minutes
Verbal Section	20 questions	30 minutes
Math (Quantitative) Section	20 questions	35 minutes
Verbal Section	20 questions	30 minutes
Math (Quantitative) Section	20 questions	35 minutes
Discreetly Unscored Math or Verbal Section (may be earlier in the exam)	20 questions	30 or 35 minutes

At close to four hours long, the GRE challenges your stamina as much as your ability to answer the questions. No matter how solid your math and verbal skills are, you must maintain the concentration and focus needed to do well for four hours, which isn't easy on a challenging task such as the GRE. You can build your test-taking stamina by practicing in four-hour stretches and taking multiple timed practice tests.

The GRE includes one unscored Math or Verbal section in addition to the scored sections. So you actually have three Math *or* three Verbal sections, with one of those sections unscored. This unscored section neither helps nor hurts your score. The GRE may indicate that the section is unscored, but usually it doesn't, so be sure to work all of the sections to the best of your ability.

Unlike other computer-based tests (such as the GMAT and TOEFL), the GRE allows you to skip questions and return to them later, as long as you're still in the section. When you reach the end of a section, the GRE displays a review screen that indicates any unanswered questions. If you have time remaining in the section, return to these questions and answer them as well as you can. This feature is nice because you can knock out all the easy questions before spending time on the hard ones. (See Chapter 2 for tips on managing your time during the exam.)

In each section, the questions are worth the same number of points, and within that section, they don't become more or less difficult based on your performance. However, on the computer version of the exam, your performance on the Math or Verbal section determines the overall difficulty level of the *next* Math or Verbal section. For example, if you do extremely well on the first Math section, the GRE makes the second Math section harder. Even if you don't get many questions right in the second Math section, your score may be higher than the score of someone who answers more easier questions correctly, because GRE scoring accommodates for the difficulty level of the questions.

So exactly what types of questions and how many of each type can you expect to run into on the GRE? Check out Table 1-2 for the answers.

Table 1-2	GRE Breakdown by Question Type
Type of Question	*Approximate Number of Questions*
Per Math Section (20 questions each)	
Multiple-choice with exactly one correct answer	6
Multiple-choice with one or more correct answers	2
Fill-in-the-blank with the correct answer	2
Data Interpretation (based on graphs)	3
Quantitative Comparisons	7
Per Verbal Section (20 questions each)	
Text Completion	6
Sentence Equivalence	4
Argument Analysis	2
Reading Comprehension	8

These question types are mixed throughout their respective sections, so you may encounter them in any order. Sometimes the software groups similar questions at the beginning or the end. For example, if you're halfway through a Verbal section and haven't seen a Text Completion question, you soon will.

Scoring Max: 340 and 6

With the GRE, you receive three separate scores: Verbal, Math, and Analytical Writing. Although you get your unofficial Verbal and Math scores immediately after taking the test (as explained in the following section), you must wait 10 to 15 days to get your Analytical Writing score in the mail. The following sections explain in depth some important scoring details you may want to know.

Understanding how the scoring breaks down

On the GRE, you can score a maximum of 340 points on the multiple-choice and 6 points on the essays. Here's the scoring range for each of the three sections:

- **Verbal:** The Verbal score ranges from 130 to 170 in 1-point increments. You get 130 points if you answer just one question, which accounts for about 80 percent of a job well done. It doesn't help much, though: You need to score as well as or better than most of the other people who took the test to improve your chances of being admitted to the school of your choice. Refer to the chapters in Part II for the lowdown on the Verbal sections.

- **Math:** The Math score also ranges from 130 to 170 in 1-point increments. Flip to Part III for more on the Math sections.

- **Analytical Writing:** You get 1 to 6 points per essay, with 6 being the highest. Each essay is graded separately, first by a trained evaluator and then by a computerized essay-grading system. Your score for that essay is the average of the two. If the two scores are very different, then another human grader steps in, and your score for that essay is the average of the two human scores. Finally, the scores of your two essays are averaged for your Analytical Writing score of 1 to 6. Essay responses that are blank or off-topic receive a score of 0. You can discover more information about the essays in Part IV. (The paper version of the GRE essay is scored only by people, not the computerized system.)

So in essence, if you perfectly ace the Verbal and Math sections, you get 170 points for each, for a total of 340. If you're perfect on the two essays, you can get an essay score of 6. The three scores are separate: You get a Math score and a Verbal score, each from 130 to 170 in 1-point increments, and an Analytical Writing score of 0 to 6, in half-point increments.

On the multiple-choice questions, you earn points only for completely correct answers. If the question requires two or more answers, you have to get all the answers correct; you don't get partial credit for a partially correct answer. However, you don't lose any points for wrong answers, so guessing behooves you. See "Playing the guessing game," later in this chapter, for more on this.

Calculating your score

Within each section, each question counts exactly the same toward your score. An easy question is worth exactly the same as a hard question. Because you can move back and forth within each section, a good strategy is to skip around and answer all the easy questions first; then go back and work the hard questions. Quite simply, in each section, the more questions you get right, the higher your score for that section.

When you complete a practice test from Part V, you can easily estimate your Math and Verbal scores. For the Math score, count the math questions you answered correctly and then add 130 to that number. Because the GRE has 40 math questions (two sections with 20 questions each), this method gives you an approximate score from 130 to 170. You can find your Verbal score the exact same way, because the GRE also has 40 Verbal questions.

The way that the computer version of the GRE calculates your scores is slightly more complicated. It takes into account the difficulty levels of the second Math and Verbal sections, weighing the scores accordingly. For example, if you do very well on the first Math section, the second Math section will be more difficult. In this second section, you may not answer as many questions correctly, but you'll have a higher score, because the GRE accounts for the increased difficulty level. However, within any section, each question counts exactly the same toward your score. The exams in this book, however, have no such adaptive mechanism, so for these, you can approximate your score by counting the correct answers.

Figuring out how your scores measure up

If you score a perfect 340 or something close to it, you know you did well. If you score a 260, you know you bombed. But what if you score something in between? Did you pass? Did you fail? What do you make of your score? Well, you can't really tell much about your score out of context. There's no pass or fail, no A, B, C, D, F — but there is a percentile ranking. To download the complete percentile table, visit www.ets.org, click GRE Tests, and search for "percentile ranking." Here are some highlights:

- ✔ A raw score of 165 is typically a 95th percentile ranking in the Verbal and a 91st percentile ranking in the Math.

- ✔ A raw score of 160 is typically an 84th percentile ranking in the Verbal and a 78th percentile ranking in the Math.

Basically, with a range of 40 points, each point counts for a lot. How well you do is relative to how well the other people taking the test perform and the requirements of the graduate program you're applying to. What's most important is that you score high enough to get accepted into the program you have your heart set on. Once you're in your program, the GRE score doesn't matter.

Your GRE score is only one part of the total application package. If you have a good undergraduate GPA, a strong résumé, and relevant work experience, you may not need as high of a GRE score. On the other hand, a stellar GRE score can compensate for your weak areas.

Playing the guessing game

The GRE doesn't penalize you by deducting points for incorrect answers, so

- ✔ If you don't know the answer, rule out as many obviously incorrect choices as possible and then guess from the remaining choices.

- ✔ Finish the section, even if you must take wild guesses near the end. Wrong answers count the same as not answering a question, so guessing on questions that you would otherwise have left blank can only help your score, not hurt it.

Seeing or canceling your scores

Immediately after finishing the GRE, you have the option of either seeing or canceling your Verbal and Math scores. Unfortunately, you don't get to see your scores first. If you *think* you had a bad day, you can cancel, and your scores are neither reported to the schools nor shown to you. However, the schools are notified that you canceled your test. If you choose to see your score, you see it — minus the essay scores — right away.

How much do the schools care about canceled scores? Probably not much, especially if a top GRE score (from when you retake the test 21 days later) follows the notice of cancellation. If you really want to know the impact of a canceled score, check with the admissions office of your target school. Each school weighs canceled scores differently. See Chapter 2 for more about what to do after canceling your GRE score.

Taking advantage of the ScoreSelect option

At the end of the test, you have the option of choosing which test scores to send to your target schools, assuming that you've taken the GRE more than once (within five years). You can send the most recent scores, scores from the past, or all your test scores. However, you can't pick and choose sections from different testing dates. For example, if today's Verbal score rocked but last fall's Math score was outstanding, you can't select only those sections — you have to select the scores from one entire test. Choose to send the scores from today's test, last fall's test, or all your tests.

Gimme a Break! GRE Intermissions

The GRE provides an optional ten-minute break after the third section of the exam. However, don't expect to have the entire time to yourself: Part of that time is for checking in and out while the proctors go through their security procedures to ensure that you're not bringing in any materials to cheat with. The ten-minute intermission is timed by the computer, which resumes the test whether you're seated or not. You probably have five minutes to do your business, which leaves little time to grab a bite if you're hungry. Plan accordingly with snacks and water in your locker so that during your actual five minutes, you can refresh yourself without having to scramble.

Make sure your packed snacks are light and nutritious. Sugar makes you high for a few minutes and then brings you way down. Something heavy, like beef jerky, makes you drowsy. You don't want to crash right in the middle of a quadratic equation. Take a handful of peanuts, some trail mix, or something light that isn't going to send all the blood from your brain down to your stomach for digestion.

Between other sections of the test, you get a one-minute break — just enough time to stand up and stretch a bit. You don't have time to leave your seat and come back before the test resumes. If you absolutely, positively must use the restroom and leave the computer during the test, just remember that the clock keeps ticking.

Recognizing the importance of test prep

Stories abound about how someone's friend's cousin's roommate took the GRE cold (with no preparation) and aced it. This story may be true on a very rare occasion, but you hear only the success stories. Those test-takers who took the test unprepared and bombed it don't brag about the outcome. As an instructor, however, I hear those other stories all the time.

The GRE doesn't test your intelligence; it tests how prepared you are for the test. I'd put my money on a prepared dunce over an unprepared genius every single time. Dramatically raising a test-taker's score, say from the 30th percentile to the 90th percentile ranking, is something I do every day before breakfast, and it's what I do for you through this book. Being prepared means knowing what to expect on the test and in the questions, which means that the first time you calculate a fraction of a circle had better not be on the actual GRE. Make your mistakes *here,* in practice, *not* on the test.

Chapter 2

Owning the GRE: Strategies for Success

The GRE isn't an IQ test. Nor is it a measure of your worth as a human being or a predictor of your ultimate success in life. The GRE is designed to assess your ability to excel in grad school by sizing you up in three areas:

- **Work ethic:** How hard you're willing and able to work to achieve an academic goal — in this case, performing well on the GRE — determines your work ethic. Graduate schools consider this to be a measure of how hard you'll work in their programs.

- **Study skills:** To do well on the GRE, you must master some basic study skills and be able to process and retain new information.

- **Test-taking ability:** Your test-taking ability is your ability to perform well on a test, under pressure, which is a separate ability from being able to answer the questions. Exams are an essential part of grad school, so you need to prove that you can take a test without folding under pressure.

This book can't help you in the first area; that's all you. As a study guide, however, this book shapes you up in the second and third areas, enabling you to study more effectively and efficiently and improve your overall test-taking skills. By knowing the material and taking the practice tests, you establish a foundation for doing well on the GRE.

This chapter is designed to take your study skills and test-taking ability to the next level. To beat the GRE at its game, you need to maximize the use of your time, focus on key areas, and apply strategies to answer the questions quickly and correctly. This chapter shows you how to do all these things and provides you with a Plan B — what to do if things don't go so well the first time.

Making the Best Use of Your Time

As soon as you decide to take the GRE, the clock starts ticking. You have only so much time to study, so much time to practice, and suddenly so little time before the exam is tomorrow morning. The good news: I've taken many students down this road, with great results, and here I've distilled the best of the success strategies. The following sections show you how to optimize your study and practice time so you can answer the test questions more efficiently.

Budgeting your time for studying

As an undergrad, you may have mastered the fine art of cramming the night before an exam, but that doesn't work on the GRE. This test is based less on memorization and more on skills, which take time to develop. Give yourself plenty of time to absorb all the material you need to study. Here's what I recommend in terms of total time, the amount of that time you spend working through this book, and the amount of time to set aside per day:

- ✔ **Six to 12 weeks of total preparation:** Give yourself plenty of time to work through this book, take practice tests, and review areas where you need extra preparation. Six to eight weeks works well for most people, but more time is generally better. At 12 weeks, you can do extremely well, but after 12 weeks, most people get burned out or lose interest, and they forget things they learned early on.

- ✔ **Three to four weeks on this book:** Working through this book takes about three weeks, not including the practice tests. The practice tests should each take 2.5 hours (no essays) or 3.5 hours (with essays), plus another hour or two to review the answer explanations.

- ✔ **One to three hours per day, five or six days per week:** Pace yourself. I've seen too many students burn themselves out from trying to master the whole test in three days. Your brain needs time to process all this new information and be ready to absorb more.

If you have only a couple weeks to study, mark your weakest subject areas in the table of contents at the beginning of this book and work through those chapters or sections first. If you're not sure about your weakest subject areas, take one of the practice tests in the book or use the practice questions online at `learn.dummies.com` to find out.

This book provides broad coverage of everything you're likely to encounter on the test, but if taking the practice tests reveals weaknesses in certain areas, you may need to consult additional resources to improve your understanding and skills.

Prioritize your study time and schedule daily review sessions. Otherwise, other activities and responsibilities are likely to clutter your day and push study time off your to-do list.

Budgeting your time for practice

Just because you know a subject inside and out doesn't mean you can ace a test on it. Test-taking requires a completely separate skill set. Start taking practice tests at least two weeks prior to your scheduled GRE so you have time to hone your skills, learn from your mistakes, and strengthen your weak areas.

Your proficiency with the test itself is as important as your math and verbal skills for attaining a top GRE score. As you take the practice tests, don't focus exclusively on errors you made in answering specific questions. Spend time evaluating your testing performance. What kinds of mistakes do you make two hours into the exam? Do you still try as hard at the end as you do in the beginning? Do you misread the questions or make simple math mistakes? Do you fall for traps?

In addition to working the practice tests in this book, I recommend working the free computer-based practice tests that Educational Testing Service (ETS) provides at `www.ets.org`. See Chapter 3 for details.

Beating the clock: Time management tips

Taking the GRE is a little like playing *Beat the Clock*. The computer provides you with a stop-watch — an on-screen clock — to time each section. Your goal is to answer as many questions correctly as quickly as possible before the clock ticks down to 0:00. You have the option of hiding the on-screen clock, but I don't recommend this. Instead, make the on-screen timer familiar and comfortable (or rather, less *un*comfortable) by using a stopwatch while doing homework and practice tests. Practicing with a stopwatch is part of preparing for the test-taking experience.

The clock changes from hours:minutes to minutes:seconds during the last five minutes; this, of course, means hustle time.

Don't obsess over giving each question a specific number of seconds, but do know when to give up and come back to a question later. As long as you haven't exited a section, you can return to questions in that section. Simply click Review, click the question you want to return to, and then click Go to Question. You can also mark a question for review so it's flagged on the Review Screen. Just keep in mind that while you're on the Review Screen, the clock still ticks. (See Chapter 3 for more about the computer version of the test.)

Within each section, each question carries the same weight; easier ones are worth just as much as harder ones. A good strategy is to note on your scratch paper a question that you can't answer quickly so you can answer as many of the easy questions as possible and go back to the harder ones at the end.

Answer *every* question, even if you have to make a wild guess. You're not penalized for incorrect answers, so you may as well try. See Chapter 1 for info on how the exam is scored.

Repeating the Test

Upon completing the exam, you have the option of accepting and seeing your scores immediately or canceling the results if you're convinced you did poorly. If you cancel the results, you have two choices: Retake the test or choose another career path. Most people choose to retake.

Most test-takers who repeat the exam tend to do *much* better the second time. It's as if there's no better way to prepare for the GRE than taking the GRE. Of course, you want to avoid having to take the test a second time, but if the first round doesn't go so well, don't lose hope. Also, be sure to schedule your GRE a month before your school needs the scores. That way, if you do have to retake it, you'll still meet the application deadline. Also, just knowing you have a second chance helps ease your nerves in the first round.

If you think you underperformed on the GRE, consider the following when deciding whether to retake it and when preparing to retake the exam:

- **Am I repeating the test to get a certain minimum qualifying score?** If you have your heart set on a particular graduate school that requires a minimum GRE score, you may not need to take the test again and again until you get that score. Talk to the admissions folks at the school you want to attend. They weigh the GRE score along with your GPA, résumé, and personal interests and have some flexibility when making their decision; if your score is close to the target, they may just let you in. I see it happen all the time.

- **Am I willing to study twice as hard, or am I already burned out?** If you put your heart and soul into studying for the exam the first time, you may be too burned out (or ***enervated***) to take on another round of study and practice. After all, scores don't magically go up by themselves; improvement requires effort.

✔ **What types of mistakes did I make on the first test?** If you made mistakes because of a lack of familiarity with either the test format (you didn't understand what to do when faced with a Quantitative Comparison question) or substance (you didn't know the vocabulary words or were baffled by the geometry problems), you're a good candidate for repeating the test. If you know what you did wrong, you can mend your ways and improve your score. This is one purpose of taking and reviewing the practice tests.

After taking the actual GRE, you don't get to review the correct and incorrect answer choices. However, you can get a good sense of the types of mistakes that you're likely to make by going through the practice tests in this book and reviewing your wrong answers afterward.

✔ **Was there something beyond my control?** Maybe your nerves were acting up on the first exam, you were feeling ill, or you didn't get enough sleep the night before. In that case, by all means repeat the exam. You're bound to feel better the next time. If the test was administered poorly or in a room full of distractions, you really should consider a retake. (See the later section "Reporting Test Administration Abnormalities" for details.)

✔ **Did I choke?** This happens all the time, especially on the essays at the beginning. Or you could panic on a thorny math question, spending several minutes and frazzling yourself for the rest of the test. Fortunately, choking doesn't usually happen again. Almost every test-taker I've seen choke does phenomenally better on the next try.

✔ **Did I run out of steam?** Stamina is a key factor of success on the four-hour GRE. If you don't practice writing the essays when taking the practice tests, you won't be prepared for the extra hour of work before the Math and Verbal sections. Also, because you're amped on test day, you're likely to crash faster than usual. Knowing what to expect and preparing for it could boost your score on a retest.

✔ **Am I eligible to retake the GRE?** You can take the GRE only once per 21-day period and no more than five times per rolling 12 months. If you try to take the test more often than that, you won't be stopped from registering for or taking the test, but your scores won't be reported.

Can repeating the exam hurt you? Typically, no. Most schools consider only your highest score. Find out from the individual schools you're interested in whether that's their policy; it isn't the same for every school. If you're on the borderline, or if several students are vying for one spot, sometimes having taken the exam repeatedly can hurt you (especially if your most recent score took a nosedive). On the other hand, an admissions counselor who sees several exams with ascending scores may be impressed that you stuck to it and kept trying, even if your score rose only slightly. In general, if you're willing to invest the study time and effort and take the repeat exam seriously, go for it.

All your test scores for the past five years are part of your record, but you can choose which scores to send using the ScoreSelect option, as I explain in Chapter 1. For example, if you did great in October but not so well in April, you can tell ETS to ignore the April *debacle* (a sudden collapse, a rout) and send just the October scores. (If you cancel a score and later have second thoughts about that cancellation, you can reinstate the canceled score up to 60 days after the test date. The service costs $30. Reinstatement takes up to two weeks.)

Reporting Test Administration Abnormalities

Your test isn't actually administered by ETS. It's administered by a company licensed by ETS, and the company is required to adhere to certain standards. If something irregular occurred during the test that you believe negatively affected your score, call the ETS complaint line at 866-756-7346. You have seven days to register a complaint, so don't delay.

One of my students was seated and ready to begin the GRE, only to have the test start time delayed an hour! On top of that, a lot of noise was coming from the next room — definitely an unwarranted distraction. If something like this happens to you, you can petition to have your score withheld and for the opportunity to take the GRE again at no charge.

Using Old Scores

What if you took the GRE a long time ago when you thought you were going to grad school and then opted to take a job or start a family instead? Well, if it was within the past five years, you're in luck (assuming you scored well). The GRE folks make the scores reportable for up to five years. That means that if you're pleased with your old score, you can send it right along to the school of your choice and say *adios* to this book right here and now. However, if you took the test more than five years ago, you have to take it again.

You can retake the test and perhaps improve your score, but until that score's fifth birthday, it remains part of your GRE record.

Chapter 3

Gearing Up for Exam Day

In This Chapter

▶ Having everything you need for exam day

▶ Brushing up on the testing center's rules and regulations

▶ Staying in tiptop test-taking shape

▶ Rehearsing with a computerized sample test

*O*n the day of the exam, there's no such thing as a pleasant surprise. Any surprise that you experience is just going to throw you off your game, stress you out, deplete your energy, and draw your focus away from what really matters — performing your best on the GRE. Surprises can also make you so late that you actually miss your scheduled test time.

The goal of this chapter is to help you avoid nasty surprises so you know exactly what to expect on the day of the test. This way, you can focus on the GRE in a more relaxed and confident frame of mind. Confidence comes from being prepared; if you're prepared, you're more confident.

Gathering Your Stuff the Night Before

Give yourself one less distraction the morning of the exam by figuring out where the testing center and parking facilities are and getting your stuff together the night before. The test is stressful in itself, and the last thing you need is to forget something important or spend the morning in a frantic search for the testing center or a parking space.

Here's what you need:

- ✔ **Authorization voucher from Educational Testing Service (ETS):** If you pay with a method other than a credit/debit card or have a disability or require certain testing accommodations, ETS provides an *authorization voucher.* Not everyone gets this voucher, but if you do, be sure to bring it with you on the day of the test.

- ✔ **Comfortable clothes:** Dress in layers. Testing centers can be warm or, more typically, cold. Sitting there for hours shivering won't help your performance. Dress in layers so you can be comfortable regardless of how they run the A/C.

- ✔ **Map or directions:** Know in advance where you're going. Drive to the testing center a few days prior to your scheduled test day to check out how long the drive is, where to park, how much parking costs, and so on. If you're taking public transportation, find out where and when you need to board the bus or train, how long the ride is, how much it costs, and where you get off.

One student had to take the test at a center in the middle of a downtown area. She had checked out the area on a Saturday, when the streets were empty and parking was ample. On the day of the test, Monday morning, the streets were jammed and all the parking was taken. Naturally, she became stressed out before her exam, and this affected her performance. She could have avoided this situation if she'd planned extra drive time for the rush-hour traffic and found alternate places to park.

✔ **Photo ID:** You must have identification with three key elements:

  • A recognizable photo

  • The name you registered for the test under

  • Your signature

Usually, a driver's license, passport, employee ID, or military ID does the trick. A student ID alone isn't enough (although it works as a second form of ID in case something's unclear on your first form of ID). Note that a Social Security card or a credit card isn't acceptable identification.

✔ **Water and a snack:** Bring a bottle of water and a light snack, such as an energy bar or a granola bar. Avoid snacks high in sugar, simple carbohydrates, or fats.

If you're wondering whether you need to bring scratch paper, pencils, a calculator, or anything like that, proceed to the next section.

Knowing What Not to Bring

Just as important as knowing what to bring to the testing center is knowing what not to bring. Leave these items at home, in your car, or at the door:

✔ **Books and notes:** Forget about last-minute studying. You aren't allowed to take books or notes into the testing center. Besides, if you don't know the material by that time, cramming won't help and may hurt. (One of my students almost had his test score nullified because during his break, he picked up his test-prep book that was in his testing center locker. Fortunately, he didn't *open* the book, so he was allowed to keep his test score.)

✔ **Calculator:** You aren't allowed to use your own calculator, but an on-screen calculator is available during the math sections of the exam. One nice thing about the on-screen calculator is that it features a button that transfers the number from the calculator field to the answer space. Your handheld calculator won't do that.

✔ **Friends for support:** Leave your friends at home. ETS frowns on visitors. However, having a friend drop you off and pick you up isn't a bad idea, especially if parking is likely to be a problem, such as at a downtown testing center.

✔ **Phones and other electronics:** Mobile electronic devices, including smartphones, are strictly prohibited. You can bring these to the testing center, but they must stay in a locker while you're taking the GRE. And because you can't use these devices during the test, don't use them while taking practice tests.

✔ **Scratch paper:** You aren't allowed to bring in your own scratch paper; the testing center provides it for you. If you run low during the test, request more from the proctor during the one-minute breaks between sections. Although you have plenty of room to do calculations and scribbling, your scratch paper stays at the testing center when you're done.

The testing center provides lockers for test-takers to store their belongings, so if you bring a purse or backpack, you'll have a secure place to keep it.

Handling unique circumstances

If you have a special circumstance or need, the GRE powers-that-be are usually very accommodating, as long as you give them a heads-up. For example, if you have a learning disability, you may be able to get additional testing time. Following is a brief list of special circumstances and how to obtain assistance for each:

✔ **Learning disabilities:** These disabilities refer to attention deficit hyperactivity disorder (ADHD), dyslexia, and other related or similar conditions. To find out whether you qualify for accommodations or a disabilities waiver of any sort, contact ETS Disability Services, Educational Testing Service, P.O. Box 6054, Princeton, NJ 08541-6054; phone 866-387-8602 (toll free) or 609-771-7780 (Monday–Friday 8:30 a.m. to 5:00 p.m. Eastern Time), TTY 609-771-7714, fax 609-771-7165; website www.ets.org/gre, email stassd@ets.org. Qualifying for accommodations is an involved process that takes time and may require significant effort on your part to gather the required documentation. If you have a qualifying disability, act sooner rather than later to find out what's required and when you need to submit your request and documentation.

✔ **Physical disabilities:** ETS tries to accommodate everyone. Folks who need special arrangements can get Braille or large-print exams, have test-readers or recorders, work with interpreters, and so on. You can get the scoop about what ETS considers to be disabilities and how the disabilities can change the way you take the GRE in the *Supplement for Test Takers with Disabilities.* This publication contains information, registration procedures, and other useful forms for individuals with physical disabilities. To get this publication, send a request to ETS Disability Services, P.O. Box 6054, Princeton, NJ 08541-6054. Or better yet, head to www.ets.org/gre and click the Test Takers with Disabilities or Health-Related Needs link. Voilà! All the info you need to know, along with contact information if you have questions or concerns.

✔ **Financial difficulties:** Until you ace the GRE, get into a top-notch graduate school, and come out ready to make your first million, you may have a rough time paying for the exam. However, fee waivers are available. Note that the waiver applies only to the actual GRE fee, not to miscellaneous fees such as the test-disclosure service, hand-grading service, and so on. Your college counselor can help you obtain and fill out the appropriate request forms. (If you're not currently in college, a counselor or financial aid specialist at a nearby college or university may still be glad to help you. Just call for an appointment.)

Training Physically and Mentally for Test Day

Taking an intense four-hour exam is challenging both mentally and physically. Most people aren't used to concentrating at this level for such a long time. To meet the challenge, your brain needs a good supply of oxygen and nutrients, and it gets those from an active, healthy, and alert body that consumes nutritious foods and beverages. The following sections provide guidance on whipping your body into shape for test day.

Staying active

You can't just be a bookworm for the year before the exam. You need to stay active. Exercise helps all parts of the body and leads to clearer thinking by increasing oxygen to the brain, so get moving! You don't need to train for a marathon. Walking, swimming, jogging, yoga, Pilates, basketball, and even active video games get your body in motion and increase overall health and circulation.

Eating well

Certain foods and beverages affect your cognitive ability, so avoid highly processed foods and foods high in sugar, starch, or fat. These foods tend to make you feel sluggish or result in brief highs followed by prolonged crashes. Lean more toward veggies, especially green, leafy veggies, and foods that are high in protein. When it comes to carbohydrates, opt for complex over simple. Complex carbohydrates are typically in fresh fruits, veggies, and whole-grain products. Simple carbohydrates (to be avoided) are in candy, soda, anything made with white flour, and most junk foods, including chips. And forget those energy drinks that combine huge amounts of caffeine and sugar to get you to a state of heightened tension.

If you plan on taking an energy drink or anything unusual on the day of the test, here's the best advice I can offer: Try it out on a practice test first. If the drink gives you the jitters or upsets your stomach, you won't want to discover this on the day of the exam.

Relaxing

Relaxation comes in many different forms for people. Some folks are relaxed when they're with friends; some read books and play music; and some do yoga, meditate, or paint. The only requirement when choosing what relaxation tool to use is making sure your brain isn't running 100 miles an hour. The whole purpose of relaxation is to give your brain a rest. So find a relaxing activity you enjoy, thank your brain by telling it to take some time off, and recharge.

Relaxation isn't a luxury — it's a requirement for both a well-balanced life and success on the GRE. You're a multifaceted human, not a work-and-study automaton. Check out the free online article at www.dummies.com/extras/gre for some hands-on ways to relax before the test.

I've seen students who are so overextended and overachieving that they stress themselves out for the test. They have trouble concentrating, get panic attacks, and generally exhaust themselves. One sure sign of the mix of panic and exhaustion is the tendency to overanalyze simple questions. If you can't accept a simple, correct answer because you're sure there must be more to it, then it's time to take a break from studying.

Test-Driving the Computerized Version

You take the exam entirely on the computer. But even the most basic software has a learning curve, and you don't want to wait till test day to learn how the software works. Nor do you want to risk making a mistake that kills your score — such as getting stuck on a question because you forgot that you can go back to it.

To gain some experience with the computerized GRE, take it for a test drive using the free Powerprep II software that ETS offers for both Macs and PCs. At the time of this writing, the software features two actual GRE computer-based practice tests for you to become accustomed to the format of the computer-based test.

To download and install the most recent version of the software, go to www.ets.org/gre, click Prepare for the Test, click POWERPREP Software, and carefully follow the on-screen directions.

If you have trouble with the installation, return to the GRE site, click the link to view frequently asked questions about the Powerprep II software, and then click the Downloading/Installation link. This takes you to a page with solutions to the most common problems. Note, too, that the software activates all the computer security precautions, but it's not likely that the file will harm your computer.

When you run the software, it displays the Introduction to the Computer-based GRE revised General Test page in your default web browser. This opening page contains several tabs for accessing an overview of the test; guidance on preparing for the test; details about the Analytical Writing, Verbal Reasoning, and Quantitative Reasoning sections of the test; and details about test scores. Scroll down to the section "Practicing for the Test," click the Start Practicing Now button, and then scroll to the bottom of the resulting page and click Continue. This launches the practice test, which gives you access to a test preview tool and a timed and untimed practice test. Choose the desired practice test option and click Start Test.

The test appears just as it will on test day, with a title page and introduction. Keep clicking Continue in the upper-right corner of the screen until you reach the General Test Information. Read the information and click Continue to proceed. Use the buttons in the upper-right corner of the screen to navigate the test. Most of the buttons are self-explanatory, but these deserve special attention:

- ✔ **Mark:** Mark enables you to flag the question for review. The Review screen shows marked questions with a check mark next to them so you can easily pick them out from the rest of the questions in the list.

- ✔ **Review:** Review displays a list of questions you can return to. Click the question you want to go back to and then click the Go To Question button. You can then review the question and change your answer if desired.

- ✔ **Exit Section:** This button ends the section and saves your essay or answers so you can proceed to the next section. After you click this button, you can't go back to change answers or return to unanswered questions in the section.

- ✔ **Quit Test:** This button ends the test prematurely, canceling your scores. You usually want to avoid this button, especially during the actual test — unless, of course, you really want to stop and cancel your scores.

Take the computerized sample test not only to get a feel for the content and format of the questions but also to become accustomed to selecting answers and using the buttons to navigate. A day or two prior to the actual test, take the computerized practice test again to reorient yourself with the buttons.

For additional practice, head to `learn.dummies.com`, where you can access six computer-based practice exams in a slightly different format. And for even more practice, check out *1,001 GRE Practice Questions For Dummies* (Wiley).

Bringing the GRE into Your Comfort Zone

Panicking about the GRE is counterproductive. You want to enter the testing center feeling confident and relaxed. That means bringing the GRE into your comfort zone. Working through this book and taking the practice tests, both on paper and on a computer, can bring you very close to that goal, but having the right mindset is also useful. The following sections put the GRE in the proper perspective and serve to remind you of just how prepared you really are.

Getting familiar with subject matter and questions

The GRE focuses on a specific range of core concepts and presents questions in a fairly predictable format. Surprises are unlikely, especially if you're prepared and know what to expect. After you've successfully completed this book, you'll have the knowledge and experience needed to do great on the test. You gain even more familiarity with the test questions and format by taking the computerized GRE sample tests.

A little self-affirmation goes a long way. In the days leading up to the test and on test day, remind yourself just how fully prepared you are. The GRE is designed to be challenging, but your preparation brings confidence. You've done all you can to prepare, and this is an opportunity to prove yourself and put into play all the time and effort you invested in gearing up for the challenge.

Understanding that the GRE is only one of many admissions requirements

Although your performance on the GRE is an important qualification for admission into the graduate school and program of your choice, it's not the only factor that admissions departments consider. Your work experience, GPA, extracurricular activities (including volunteer work), and other factors that define you are also important parts of your application. Of course, you should do your very best on the test, but remind yourself that this isn't a do-or-die situation. Worst case, retake the exam. I've had plenty of students forget one of the key points I taught them in class and make a mistake on the day of the test. Next time around, they aced the exam.

Part II
Tackling the Verbal Section One Word at a Time

5 types of answer choices to steer clear of

- ✔ Beware of "always," "never," and other absolutes; these choices are almost always wrong.

- ✔ Avoid answer choices that contain information that's irrelevant to the argument.

- ✔ Look for unbiased and tone-neutral answer choices. Choices that seem emotional or opinionated are generally wrong.

- ✔ Avoid picking an answer just because it's true; the correct choice answers the question.

- ✔ Don't be tempted by answers that do the opposite of what the question asks for.

 Check out additional tips for mastering the Verbal section of the GRE in the free article at www.dummies.com/extras/gre.

In this part . . .

- ✔ Discover how to complete sentences when you need to fill in a word or choose two words that retain a sentence's meaning.

- ✔ Understand the topics and question types you'll encounter with the Reading Comprehension passages.

- ✔ Find out what to look for in Argument Analysis questions and how to deconstruct the argument to reach the correct answer.

- ✔ Brush up on GRE-level vocabulary and review roots, prefixes, and suffixes.

Chapter 4

Making Sense of Sentences: Text Completion and Sentence Equivalence

....

In This Chapter

▶ Learning about the Text Completion and Sentence Equivalence questions

▶ Establishing an effective strategy for identifying the correct answer

▶ Attacking questions confidently with a three-step approach

▶ Tackling the more-challenging questions

....

Text Completion and Sentence Equivalence questions hold all the clues you need to answer these questions correctly. By using key strategies and avoiding common mistakes, you can breeze through these questions and rack up points in a hurry. If you find the vocabulary is slowing you down, turn to Chapter 7 to brush up on words that you're likely to encounter and their definitions.

Grasping Text Completion and Sentence Equivalence Questions

Because Text Completion and Sentence Equivalence questions are so similar, the strategy is the same for both:

✔ **Text Completion:** A Text Completion question consists of a sentence or paragraph with one, two, or three blank spaces for a missing word(s) or phrase(s). Following the sentence or paragraph are choices for filling in the blank(s): five choices if the sentence has only one blank or three choices for each blank if the sentence has two or three blanks. Your job is to choose the most suitable word or words. Although all the answers may sound okay in the sentence, only one is correct for each blank. If the text contains more than one blank, you don't get partial credit for choosing only one correct word.

✔ **Sentence Equivalence:** A Sentence Equivalence question consists of a single sentence with exactly one word missing and six answer choices. You're required to select the two words that fit the sentence and mean the same thing, and, as with the Text Completion questions, you don't get partial credit for choosing only one of the correct words.

The following at-a-glance table shows you what to expect from the variations of Text Completion and Sentence Equivalence questions. Don't worry about mixing this up: On the GRE, the numbers of blanks and choices for the Text Completion questions are obvious, and Sentence Equivalence questions with too few or too many answers selected are marked "Incomplete" in the review screen following the Verbal section, which means you can go back and correct them with the time remaining on the section.

Question Type	Blanks	Choices per Blank	Choose Total
Text Completion	3	3	3
	2	3	2
	1	5	1
Sentence Equivalence	1	6	2

The questions are always preceded by directions, such as "For each blank, select one entry" or "Select two answer choices." Also, the one-answer questions allow you to select only one answer, and the two-answer questions allow you to select more than one.

The following example of a Text Completion question shows how all answer choices appear to fit perfectly but only two specific words actually make logical sense.

Directions: For each blank, select one entry from the corresponding column of choices. Fill all blanks in the way that best completes the text.

Frustrated at having to spend the entire weekend studying for the GRE instead of going hiking, Faye (i) _____ her book out the window with such (ii) _____ that it soared high into the sky, prompting three of her neighbors to capture it on video and post it on YouTube.

Blank (i)	Blank (ii)
Ⓐ tossed	Ⓓ ferocity
Ⓑ hurled	Ⓔ glee
Ⓒ pitched	Ⓕ gentleness

The key word in this example is *frustrated,* which conveys a strong negative emotion. Choices **(B)** and **(D)**, *hurled* and *ferocity,* are the only choices that support such a negative emotion. Note that this is a single, two-part question. You may select any of the three answer choices for each blank, but you must choose *both* correct answers to earn credit for the question.

The following example of a Sentence Equivalence question shows how all six answer choices appear to fit within the sentence structure, but only two answers actually support the meaning of the sentence.

Directions: Select the two answer choices that, when used to complete the sentence, fit the meaning of the sentence as a whole and produce two completed sentences that are alike in meaning.

Well-prepared and ready to take on the GRE, Billy _____ the test and made his family proud.

[A] aced

[B] missed

[C] passed

[D] held

[E] took

[F] knew

The sentence suggests that Billy did well on the GRE. The best words to convey GRE success are *aced* and *passed*, making Choices **(A)** and **(C)** the correct answers. Again, you must select both of these correct answers to earn credit for the question.

Developing Your Skills for Finding the Correct Answers

Text Completion and Sentence Equivalence questions are designed to measure three core proficiencies: interpreting the sentence; using vocabulary properly; and recognizing irony, figures of speech, and formal diction. By understanding what the test-makers are looking for, you significantly improve your chances of correctly answering their questions.

The following sections give you an overview of these three proficiencies and how you can spot the correct answers. These proficiencies always lead you to the correct answer and, with practice, are easy to apply.

Interpreting the sentence

Interpreting a sentence consists of determining its meaning in the absence of the missing words. By knowing the meaning of the sentence prior to looking at the possible answers, you can quickly eliminate choices that don't make sense. This technique is the single most important skill for working these verbal questions, and the GRE-makers have fun trying to trick you. No worries, though — this section (and the rest of the chapter) is packed with methods for interpreting sentences.

To interpret a sentence, read it carefully using keywords to understand the overall meaning that the sentence conveys. Check out the following Sentence Equivalence example to see what I mean.

Directions: Select the two answer choices that, when used to complete the sentence, fit the meaning as a whole and produce two completed sentences that are alike in meaning.

The bags were so heavy that we could _____ lift them.

[A] easily

[B] hardly

[C] fully

[D] nearly

[E] barely

[F] effortlessly

Even without the missing word, you can construe the meaning of the sentence. The phrase so *heavy* tells you that these bags are difficult or impossible to lift. After realizing this, you can immediately eliminate *easily* and *effortlessly.* The words *fully* and *nearly* are a little tougher to ignore, but they really don't make sense either. The correct answers are Choices **(B),** *hardly,* and **(E),** *barely.*

Using vocabulary properly

After interpreting the sentence, the next step is to pick the right word. Proper usage helps determine this. *Usage* is the customary manner of using particular words.

 To pick the correct word, think of how each answer choice sounds in the context of the sentence, as if you're speaking the sentence. Consider whether the word in the sentence makes sense or sounds a little odd. (To brush up on vocabulary and strategies for approaching unknown words, check out Chapter 7.)

 Directions: For each blank, select one entry from the corresponding column of choices. Fill all blanks in the way that best completes the text.

The lights _____ when the engineer hit the kill switch.

Ⓐ died
Ⓑ went out
Ⓒ discontinued
Ⓓ ended
Ⓔ stopped

Each word choice supports the sentence meaning, but only *one* is properly used. Although the sentence does use the word *kill,* lights don't die, stop, discontinue, or end — they go out. The correct answer is Choice **(B).**

Recognizing irony, figures of speech, and formal diction

Even if the answer choices support the sentence meaning, nuances in the meaning of words can separate wrong answers from right ones. Examine answer choices for skepticism, doubt, uncertainty, and emotional connotations that just don't fit.

 Consider the tone of the sentence: Is it positive or negative? Pleased or disappointed? This high-level perspective can help you find words that convey the correct meaning.

Directions: Select the two answer choices that, when used to complete the sentence, fit the meaning of the sentence as a whole and produce two completed sentences that are alike in meaning.

I'm _____ that you performed so well on the GRE; I knew you could do it!

- A ecstatic
- B stunned
- C thrilled
- D shocked
- E dumbfounded
- F bewildered

All the choices suggest that you did better than expected, but *stunned, shocked, dumbfounded,* and *bewildered* imply that your friend thought you would tank. However, she knew you would do great, probably because you used *GRE For Dummies* to prepare for the test. The second half of the sentence doesn't convey doubt ("I knew you could do it!"), so the correct answers are Choices **(A)** and **(C)**.

Attacking the Question Head-On

Whether you're faced with Text Completion or Sentence Equivalence questions, your battle plan is the same: Attack each question with confidence. Hesitation and doubt can waste time and make you talk yourself out of the right answer. Instead, use this three-step strategy:

1. **Read and interpret the sentence without looking at the answer choices.**

2. **Fill the blanks with your own words.**

3. **Eliminate answer choices that don't match your words.**

The following sections explain these steps in detail.

Read and interpret the sentence without looking at the answer choices

When working Text Completion and Sentence Equivalence questions, your first step is to interpret the sentence. If you know what the sentence is saying, you have a better understanding of the words that best fill the blanks. Although this first step seems obvious, many test-takers skip it.

While interpreting the sentence, don't look at the answer choices! Each puzzling answer choice not only completes the sentence but also gives the sentence a very different meaning. Trying out answer choices before interpreting the sentence turns an easy question into a hard one and shifts your focus away from the sentence itself. Instead, read the sentence carefully and figure out what it's trying to say.

To avoid involuntarily glancing at the answer choices, hide them with your hand or the scratch paper provided. Doing so allows you to ponder the sentence's meaning without being distracted by the answer choices. Right there, your Verbal score just jumped 10 points. Easy, right? Hold your scratch paper right up on the computer screen. (You're not working math now, anyway.) Silly? Yes. Effective? Absolutely. My students tell me it's a lifesaver.

The following example illustrates the different meanings that a sentence can convey, using different words in the blanks. If you first try out all the answer choices, it becomes impossible to tell what the sentence is actually saying, so they're not shown here yet.

Having been coerced by his kids into seeing *The LEGO Movie*, Andy was (i) _____, although the movie surprisingly turned out to be (ii) _____.

First, interpret what the sentence is trying to say. The word *although* in the middle of the sentence tells you that the two phrases have different meanings — that the words in those blanks should be opposite, or close to it. *Although* is an example of a transition word, which can function as a valuable clue. (See the later section "Identify transition words and use them to get the gist of the phrases" for more on this.)

Ask yourself the following questions: Was Andy eager or reluctant? Was *The LEGO Movie* surprisingly lame or good? That he needed *coercion* tells you that Andy didn't want to go, so he was *reluctant,* and he probably expected the movie to bomb. Then he was *surprised,* so the movie was probably pretty good. This is how you tell what the sentence is trying to say.

Fill in the blanks with your own words

The next step to answering the Text Completion and Sentence Equivalence questions is to think of your own words to fill in the blanks. Your words don't have to be perfect — you're not writing the sentence — but they do have to support the meaning of the sentence and, by extension, the meanings of the missing words themselves. By using this technique, you know exactly what to look for and can eliminate some answer choices (which is the following step). Right now, you're still covering up the answer choices with your scratch paper.

Pretend you're saying this sentence to someone in a conversation. Even though you may arrange the sentence differently, your keywords will match the missing words in the question.

Having been coerced by his kids into seeing *The LEGO Movie*, Andy was *reluctant,* although the movie surprisingly turned out to be, *well . . . awesome.*

You already know that Andy wasn't looking forward to the movie, but the movie surprisingly was good.

Your fill-in-the-blank word choice doesn't have to fit perfectly; it just needs to convey the meaning.

Eliminate answer choices that don't match your words

The last step to answering Text Completion and Sentence Equivalence questions is to look at the answer choices. Now that you know what the sentence is saying, the right answers are obvious.

Here's the example question again, this time with the answer choices provided.

Directions: For each blank, select one entry from the corresponding column of choices. Fill all blanks in the way that best completes the text.

Having been coerced by his kids into seeing *The LEGO Movie*, Andy was (i) _____, although the movie surprisingly turned out to be (ii) _____.

Blank (i)	Blank (ii)
Ⓐ thrilled	Ⓓ lousy
Ⓑ excited	Ⓔ subpar
Ⓒ hesitant	Ⓕ a blast

Compare the answer choices, one at a time, to the words you already came up with on your own (*reluctant* and *awesome*). Cross *thrilled* and *excited* off the first list, because they have nothing to do with *reluctant*. Similarly, *lousy* and *subpar* are far from *awesome*. The correct answers are Choices **(C)**, *hesitant*, and **(F)**, *a blast*, which both match your predictions and make sense when you read the sentence.

Text Completion and Sentence Equivalence questions can be challenging, so if you get stuck, don't use up a lot of time and energy trying to arrive at the right answers. Instead, cut your losses: Eliminate obviously wrong answer choices, make an educated guess, mark the question for review (so you can return to it later if you have time), and move on.

These verbal questions should take you less than a minute each, saving you valuable time for the more time-consuming Reading Comprehension questions. (For info on the GRE Reading Comprehension questions, head over to Chapter 5.)

Interpreting Trickier Sentences

If every Text Completion and Sentence Equivalence question were as easy as the preceding examples, everyone would get a perfect 170 on the Verbal section (those who have this book, anyway), and testing would be pointless. However, actual GRE questions can be more challenging to interpret. When you come across these sentences, start with the three basic strategies mentioned earlier and build on them with these three steps:

1. **Identify transition words and use them to get the gist of the phrases.**

2. **Break the sentence into smaller pieces.**

3. **Check one word blank at a time to eliminate answer choices.**

The following sections delve further into these steps.

Identify transition words and use them to get the gist of the phrases

Transition words exist in almost all GRE Text Completion and Sentence Equivalence questions and serve as valuable clues to interpreting the meaning of a sentence. (*Transition words* connect two ideas in a sentence or paragraph and tell you whether the two ideas in the sentence agree or contradict one another.) Transition words help you decipher the meaning of a sentence with key words missing.

For example, changing the transition word in the following sentence completely alters its meaning:

> *Although* he ran as fast as he could, Eric _____ the bus.

The transition word *although*, indicating contrast, tells you that Eric missed the bus. Consider the same sentence with a different transition word:

> *Because* he ran as fast as he could, Eric _____ the bus.

The transition word *because*, indicating cause and effect, tells you that Eric caught the bus.

With a little practice, transition words become easy to identify and use to your advantage. They're helpful when breaking the sentence into pieces (which is the next step) and are used frequently in the Analytical Writing portion of the GRE. (See the chapters in Part IV for more on the Analytical Writing essays.)

Common transition words include the following:

although	and	because	but
despite	either/or	however	in spite of
moreover	nonetheless	therefore	or

The English language has hundreds of transition words. Fortunately, you don't need to memorize them, but you do need to be able to spot them.

Transition words can be divided into two categories: *same direction* and *change direction*. Same-direction transition words — *and, because, moreover,* and *therefore* — indicate that the phrase that follows will build on or continue in the same direction as what has been stated. Change-direction transition words — *although, but, despite, however, in spite of,* and *nonetheless* — indicate that what follows is likely to contradict what has been or is about to be stated.

In the example sentence with Eric and the bus, changing the transition word *although* to *because* changes the entire meaning of the sentence. Note that the transition word isn't always between the phrases. In this next example, use the transition word to help interpret the sentence.

Although she usually was of a (i) _____ nature, Patty was (ii) _____ when the history professor assigned a paper due the day after spring break.

The transition word *although* tells you that Patty's usual nature is different from the way she felt when receiving her assignment. (And it's too early for answer choices — that's why they're not shown here.)

Break the sentence into smaller pieces

Some sentences are so long and convoluted that you can't make much sense of them. To handle tricky questions, break the sentence into pieces to simplify the interpretation before adding your own words. The simplest way to do this is to separate the phrases, usually indicated by commas.

Continuing with the example from the previous section, break the sentence into the two following parts:

Patty was _____ when the history professor assigned a paper.

Although she usually was of a _____ nature,

In smaller pieces, the gist of this sentence is easier to discern. One phrase describes how Patty felt when receiving the assignment, and the other phrase describes how she usually feels. You know from the transition word *although* that the words are probably dissimilar in meaning. You can also figure out that the first blank needs a word like *happy,* and the second blank, with an opposite meaning indicated by *although,* needs a word like *annoyed.*

Check one word blank at a time to eliminate answer choices

Although many of these questions feature one word blank, some Text Completion questions have two or three blanks. You may not always be able to match all the blanks, especially on the more difficult questions. After you think of your own words to go in the blanks, the best strategy is to eliminate the answer choices one word at a time. So even if you're unable to match all the words, you can still eliminate a few wrong answer choices and select from a smaller group of answers.

Directions: For each blank, select one entry from the corresponding column of choices. Fill all blanks in the way that best completes the text.

Although she usually was of a (i) _____ nature, Patty was (ii) _____ when the history professor assigned a paper due the day after spring break.

Blank (i)	Blank (ii)
Ⓐ frugal	Ⓓ enigmatic
Ⓑ keen	Ⓔ lugubrious
Ⓒ cheerful	Ⓕ ebullient

Now look at the answer choices and eliminate those that don't match the words you used to fill the blanks (*happy* and *annoyed*). Start with the first blank.

Using your first word clue, *happy,* which word from the first column of choices best describes Patty's nature? *Frugal* doesn't fit based solely on its meaning (economical), and it has no opposite in the second column. *Keen* really doesn't fit based simply on usage (described in the earlier section "Using vocabulary properly"). *Cheerful* seems to be the right choice for the first blank.

In the second column, *enigmatic* means mysterious or cryptic, which doesn't match *annoyed.* If you don't know what *lugubrious* and *ebullient* mean, you can guess that *lugubrious* is heavy and *ebullient* means upbeat, based on how the words sound. (*Ebullient* means very happy, and *lugubrious* means sad. Flip to Chapter 7 for a lot more vocabulary.) Anyway, the transition word *although* rules out *ebullient* because it's too similar to the first answer choice, *cheerful,* so *lugubrious* fills the second blank. The correct answers are Choices **(C)** and **(E)**.

Getting Your Hands Dirty with Practice Questions

You're ready to tackle some practice Text Completion and Sentence Equivalence questions to get a better grasp of how to solve them using all the tools described in this chapter.

Text Completion questions

Directions: For each blank, select one entry from the corresponding column of choices. Fill all blanks in the way that best completes the text.

1. As a public relations specialist, Susan realizes the importance of treating even the most exasperating tourists with kindness and _____.

Ⓐ etiquette
Ⓑ realism
Ⓒ patience
Ⓓ compassion
Ⓔ honesty

First, ask yourself, "What's important when dealing with exasperated tourists?" A public relations specialist would need to be polite. The first word choice, *etiquette,* looks good, but you don't treat someone with etiquette. (***Etiquette*** is a system of rules for manners.) Cross that word off the list. You don't show exasperated tourists *compassion,* either. Gone. *Honesty* won't help. Gone! *Realism* isn't even close. Gone! Through logic and elimination, the correct answer is Choice **(C).**

2. Enabled by his (i) _____ and unimpeded by any sense of (ii) _____, Henry reached the end of the Ironman Triathlon.

Blank (i)	Blank (ii)
Ⓐ knowhow	Ⓓ weariness
Ⓑ appetite	Ⓔ courage
Ⓒ stamina	Ⓕ power

What's one thing that helps and another that hinders a triathlete? *Strength* and *fatigue* are good choices. In the first column, you can rule out *knowhow.* Either of the remaining words, *appetite* (in the sense of desire) and *stamina,* could fit, but stamina is more closely related to strength. In the second blank, you look for a word like *fatigue,* and *weariness* is clearly the closest match. Correct answers: Choices **(C)** and **(D).**

3. Although dismayed by the pejorative comments made about her inappropriate dress at the diplomatic function, Judy (i) _____ her tears and showed only the most calm and (ii) _____ visage to her critics.

Blank (i)	Blank (ii)
Ⓐ suppressed	Ⓓ incensed
Ⓑ monitored	Ⓔ articulate
Ⓒ succumbed to	Ⓕ placid

If Judy had a calm and (something) *visage* (a form of the word *vision;* a countenance, or facial expression), the (something) must go hand in hand with *calm.* Although the second word doesn't have to be an exact synonym, it can't be an antonym, either. Look for a word that means calm. *Placid* means calm and tranquil, as you may know from the root *plac,* meaning peace (as in *placate*). Check the remaining two choices in the second column: *Incensed* means upset, burning mad (think of burning incense); *articulate* means well-spoken. Her visage (or facial expression) wouldn't be well-spoken, although Judy herself may be, so cross off *articulate*. *Placid* is therefore best for the second word, so now find something suitable for the first word. *Monitoring* or *succumbing to* (giving in to) her tears is unlikely to make Judy appear calm and placid, but suppressing her tears will. The correct answers are Choices **(A)** and **(F).**

4. There are those writers who carp and (i) _____ about the depressed state of our economy. However, many people insist that such writers don't speak for the common man (or woman) who believes in the (ii) _____ of the nation and the (iii) _____ of its future.

Blank (i)	Blank (ii)	Blank (iii)
Ⓐ laud	Ⓓ resilience	Ⓖ morbidity
Ⓑ grouse	Ⓔ chaos	Ⓗ security
Ⓒ ponder	Ⓕ generosity	Ⓘ lampoon

Try to predict the words that fit into the blanks. Here, you can predict that the first word must be something bad (because the writers are *carping,* or griping, about a depressed economy). The word *however* cues you that the next two words are going to be more optimistic. In the first column, look for a word with a negative connotation; neither *laud* (to praise, as in ap*plaud*) nor *ponder* (as in *wonder*) meet that requirement. Only *grouse* (meaning to complain or grumble) fits with *carp.* In the second column, you can rule out *chaos* (confusion and disorganization), because it's not positive, and *generosity* (charitableness), because that's not necessarily going to help turn around a depressed economy. *Resilience* (the ability to recover) is the best choice there. As for the third word, *lampoon* means to ridicule (think of the satirical magazine *National Lampoon*), and *morbidity* (desperation) conveys a very negative tone, so you can eliminate those choices and choose *security,* which describes a positive state for a future. Correct answers are Choices **(B), (D),** and **(H).**

5. Although often writing of (i) _____ activities, Emily Dickinson possessed the faculty of creating an eclectic group of characters ranging from the reticent to the epitome of (ii) _____.

Blank (i)	Blank (ii)
Ⓐ mundane	Ⓓ stoicism
Ⓑ egregious	Ⓔ effrontery
Ⓒ commensurate	Ⓕ taciturnity

If you know that *reticent* means shy and holding back, you can predict that the second blank must be the opposite of that, something bold and forward. *Effrontery* is shameless boldness and audacity. You have effrontery when you ask your boss for a raise right after he or she chews you out for bungling a project and costing the company money. *Effrontery* is the only word that fits the second blank. *Taciturnity* is the noun form of the word *taciturn*, meaning quiet, not talkative, not forward. *Stoicism* is not showing feelings or pain.

The transition word *although* tells you that the first blank must be the opposite of *eclectic,* which means from multiple sources or, in this case, diverse. *Mundane* means common, which is a good opposite of eclectic. Mundane activities are day-to-day tasks, nothing exciting like winning a lottery or visiting Antarctica. *Egregious* means terrible or flagrant. An egregious mistake is right out there for the world to see, not nearly the opposite of eclectic, so you can eliminate it. *Commensurate* means equivalent to or proportionate (your score on this section is commensurate with your vocabulary); again, this word isn't an opposite of eclectic, so cross it off the list. The correct answers are Choices **(A)** and **(E)**.

6. Unwilling to be labeled _____, Gwenette slowly and meticulously double-checked each fact before expounding upon her theory to her colleagues at the convention.

Ⓐ precipitate
Ⓑ meticulous
Ⓒ loquacious
Ⓓ efficacious
Ⓔ painstaking

First, break the sentence into two parts at the comma. Using the word *unwilling* in the first part, you know that the second part is going to be the opposite meaning of the word required to complete the first part. Now work from the second part back. The gist of the second part is that Gwenette is being careful, so now all you need to do is find the one word in the list that's closest to meaning careless.

The key here is pure vocabulary, but if you don't have a clue what any of the words mean, don't get stuck on it — just guess and go.

Precipitate means overly quick, leaping before looking. This word is a perfect fit. Correct answer: Choice **(A).**

If you don't want to be labeled precipitate, confirm your answer by eliminating the four other choices. *Loquacious* means overly talkative, something Gwenette doesn't want to be labeled as, but that has little relevance to preparing her theory. *Meticulous* and *painstaking* mean careful with detail, paying close attention, so they're both the opposite of what you're looking for. *Efficacious* means efficient and effective, which Gwenette *does* want to be labeled.

Even if you don't know the exact meaning of the words, you can judge whether they generally fit. If you're not sure of an answer choice, confirm it after eliminating the other answer choices.

Sentence Equivalence questions

Directions: Select the two answer choices that, when used to complete the sentence, fit the meaning as a whole and produce two completed sentences that are alike in meaning.

7. A successful business-process _____ designed to streamline existing operations will, by its nature, also support the company's strategic planning.

   [A] reaction

   [B] management

   [C] plan

   [D] initiative

   [E] supply chain

   [F] method

Is this business-process thing a new event or ongoing? That it's designed to affect "existing operations" tells you that it doesn't currently exist and is therefore new. Look for words that suggest an early phase of development. *Reaction* obviously doesn't fit. *Management* and *supply chain* are business-sounding words that don't suggest anything new. *Method* also isn't distinctly new (a method could have been around for a while). The words *plan* and *initiative* suggest something in the early stages of development. The correct answers are Choices **(C)** and **(D)**.

8. The sea tortoise, though lumbering and slow on land, can move with _____ speed and agility in water.

   [A] surprising

   [B] actual

   [C] according

   [D] defiant

   [E] unexpected

   [F] unequivocal

If the tortoise is lumbering and slow on land, wouldn't you expect it to be slow in water, too? The crocodile, for example, is fast and nimble in either environment. In this sentence, however, the transition word *though* tells you that the tortoise's speed and agility in water is a surprise. The words *actual, according, defiant,* and *unequivocal* (straightforward) don't suggest any sort of surprise. The correct answers are Choices **(A)** and **(E)**.

9. Ironically, the speaker _____ the very point he had stood up to make and hurriedly sat down, hoping no one had caught his solecism.

   A prognosticated

   B divulged

   C refuted

   D countered

   E duplicated

   F ferreted out

A **solecism** is an inconsistency, such as a mistake. From the context of the sentence, you can gather that a solecism is something negative because the speaker hoped no one had noticed it.

To **refute** is to disprove or show to be false. To **counter** is to contradict. It'd be **ironic** (the opposite of what's expected) if the speaker disproved or contradicted the very point he stood up to make. Therefore, the correct answers are Choices **(C)** and **(D)**.

Take a moment to go through the other words to increase your vocabulary. To **prognosticate** is to predict. *Pro-* means before, *gnos* means knowledge, and *-ate* means to make. To **prognosticate** is to "make knowledge before," to predict.

If you picked *prognosticated,* you probably fell for the trap of looking only at the answer choices and not inserting them in the sentence. Yes, something ironic is the opposite of what's expected, and a prognostication is nearly opposite of a summation, but that answer doesn't fit the sentence. Be sure to take your time and look at the sentence with each answer choice. The Sentence Equivalence section isn't a place to try to save a few seconds.

The second choice, **divulge,** means to reveal. Though this word seems to fit, it doesn't support the intended meaning of the sentence. To divulge the very information you stand up to say isn't ironic; it's normal.

The second-to-last choice, **duplicated,** may have caused the speaker to feel embarrassed enough to sit down, but it wouldn't be as much of a solecism as refuting or countering the point he stood up to make, and there's no close match for *duplicate* among the other answer choices. Finally, to **ferret out** is to search diligently, as a detective ferrets out clues to help his client. You ferret out the tips and traps scattered throughout these explanations to remember them.

10. Dismayed by the _____ evidence available to her, the defense attorney spent her own money to hire a private investigator to acquire additional evidence.

    A dearth of

    B scanty

    C vestigial

    D immense

    E concrete

    F impartial

Predict words to fit in the blanks. If the attorney is dismayed by the evidence and hires an investigator to get *more* evidence, she must not have had much evidence to begin with. You can predict that the first word means not very much. **Scanty** means barely sufficient, and a **dearth of** is a lack of, which are the only two choices that fit the blank. So the correct answers are Choices **(A)** and **(B)**.

As for the remaining words, *vestigial* means functionless after much of the original has disappeared; for example, the tailbone of humans is a vestigial tail. *Immense* means large, just the opposite of what you want. *Concrete,* in this context, means irrefutable; again, the opposite of what you want. *Impartial* evidence is neutral, neither good nor bad, which has nothing to do with the amount of evidence.

11. Rather than be decadent, the actor adopted an _____ lifestyle to help him focus on the professional side of his work.

    A austere

    B anachronous

    C ascetic

    D assiduous

    E abject

    F avarice

The actor could have adopted any kind of lifestyle, but look for words that indicate the opposite of decadent. *Austere* and *ascetic* both describe one who practices self-denial, so these words fit. The correct answers are Choices **(A)** and **(C)**.

As for the remaining words, *anachronous* describes something out of the proper time, such as if Robin Hood had carried a flashlight. *Avarice* refers to a desire to hoard wealth, so that's definitely out. *Assiduous* means hardworking, which may also describe the actor, but you need a word that's the opposite of decadent. *Abject* means miserable or wretched, which would fit, but it has no close match among the other answer choices.

12. One who postures as completely fearless is unsurprisingly likely to drop the pretense and show a(n) _____ face.

    A artless

    B contentious

    C craven

    D deferent

    E mealymouthed

    F pusillanimous

If someone has a pretense of fearlessness, then behind it is a sense of cowardice. The words *craven* and *pusillanimous* both mean cowardly, so the correct answers are Choices **(C)** and **(F)**.

Artless means honest and natural, which may be the face behind a pretense, but the sentence describes fearlessness. *Contentious* describes someone willing to stand up for himself, which may be this posturing person, but it, too, wouldn't be behind a pretense of fearlessness. *Deferent* means giving in out of respect for another, and *mealymouthed* means insincere, which may refer to the pretense but wouldn't be behind it.

13. Inspired by their leader's tirade, the protestors took it upon themselves to continue the _____.

    A diatribe

    B diffidence

    C harangue

    D hyperbole

    E euphemism

    F equivocation

A *tirade* is a bitter verbal attack, so the protestors could only continue with their own tirades. *Diatribe* and *harangue* are synonyms for *tirade,* making the correct answers Choices **(A)** and **(C)**.

Diffidence refers to a lack of confidence. *Hyperbole* is an exaggeration, *euphemism* is the use of gentle words in place of offensive language, and *equivocation* is the use of intentionally vague language.

14. The welfare system, designed to help those who are _____, is in need of reform.

    A indigent

    B mendacious

    C mendicant

    D misanthropic

    E morose

    F quiescent

The welfare system was designed to help those who are poor or destitute. *Indigent* and *mendicant* are synonyms for *destitute,* making the correct answers Choices **(A)** and **(C)**.

Mendacious means dishonest, *misanthropic* means antisocial, *morose* means sullen, and *quiescent* means at rest.

15. As a rule, the company hires only _____ engineers, believing years of experience tend to jade engineers, blinding them to new ideas.

    A felicitous

    B fledgling

    C gregarious

    D insensible

    E ingenuous

    F neophyte

If the company wants only inexperienced engineers, then the engineers would have to be beginners or novices. *Fledgling* and *neophyte* fit this meaning, making the correct answers Choices **(B)** and **(F)**.

Felicitous means suitable or appropriate, which may be true of the desired engineers but doesn't support the sentence's purpose of hiring novices. *Gregarious* means sociable and outgoing, which is also possibly true of the new hires but doesn't support the sentence's purpose. *Insensible* means unresponsive. *Ingenuous* means naive and trusting, which is close, but a company wouldn't necessarily look to hire someone who is naive.

16. Many _____ social media hacks continue to aver countless half-truths, despite ample evidence to the contrary.

    A dissonant

    B doctrinaire

    C dogmatic

    D ebullient

    E eclectic

    F erudite

Aver means to declare something to be true. If these hacks declare half-truths to be true despite the contrary evidence, then they're ignoring the evidence. *Doctrinaire* and *dogmatic* fit this meaning, making the correct answers Choices **(B)** and **(C)**.

Dissonant means ill-fitting, which may be true of the hacks but doesn't address their aversion to the evidence. *Ebullient* means buoyant in disposition, which also doesn't fit. *Eclectic* means derived from various sources, and *erudite* means educated.

17. The buffalo, once _____ to this area, has been hunted nearly to extinction.

    A endemic

    B indigenous

    C quintessential

    D truculent

    E veracious

    F viable

The buffalo must have originated and lived in the area. *Endemic* and *indigenous* fit this meaning, making the correct answers Choices **(A)** and **(B)**.

Quintessential refers to a perfect state, *truculent* means displaying poor behavior, *veracious* means truthful and accurate, and *viable* means practical.

18. The _____ spares no time for conciliatory gestures.

    A churl

    B cohort

    C consummate

    D contrite

    E coy

    F curmudgeon

Conciliatory refers to an effort to bring peace, as in the word *reconcile*. The sentence is talking about a person, because the pronoun *who* can refer only to a person, never a thing.

What kind of person would be too impatient to reconcile with those around him? One who is ill-tempered, such as a *churl* or a *curmudgeon*. The correct answers are Choices **(A)** and **(F)**.

A *cohort* is a group of people with something in common. *Consummate* means complete and perfect, certainly not the case here. *Contrite* refers to one who is filled with sorrow for a wrongdoing, and *coy* means shy or modest.

19. A talent for easy conversation can help one build relationships, but too much can make one appear _____ and have the opposite effect.

    A abstruse

    B garrulous

    C loquacious

    D lachrymose

    E ponderous

    F recondite

If too much conversation can be bad, then find words that mean too talkative. *Garrulous* and *loquacious* refer to one who talks to the point of being meddlesome, so Choices **(B)** and **(C)** are the correct answers.

Abstruse and *recondite* refer to one who isn't easily understood, and they wouldn't necessarily be the bad effect of talking too much. *Lachrymose* means tearful, which is certainly not the case here. *Ponderous* refers to one who is dull or moves slowly.

20. Beneath the _____, the man is something else entirely.

    A disingenuousness

    B divergence

    C exculpation

    D superciliousness

    E superfluity

    F veneer

If the man puts up a false front, *disingenuousness* and *veneer* both accurately describe this person. The correct answers are Choices **(A)** and **(F)**.

Divergence refers to straying away from the main point of a discussion. *Exculpation* means no longer considered guilty. *Superciliousness* would be on someone who is disdained and scorned. *Superfluity* refers to someone or something that's extraneous.

Chapter 5

Extracting Meaning from Text: Reading Comprehension

. . . .

In This Chapter

▶ Approaching the Reading Comprehension passages

▶ Learning tips and tricks designed to save you time

. . . .

Reading Comprehension questions on the GRE comprise about half of the Verbal questions and therefore about half of your Verbal score. Each question concerns a single passage that is sort of like a graduate-level journal article on a science, social sciences, or humanities topic that you've probably never considered before and never will again.

Each Verbal section contains about four Reading Comprehension passages, each with one to four questions. The computer screen is split, with the passage on the left and a question on the right. You get the questions one at a time while the passage stays in place.

This chapter introduces the three Reading Comprehension question formats, presents strategies for identifying the correct answers quickly, and provides some sample passages along with questions and their answers so you know what to expect on the test.

All Reading Comprehension questions are based directly on what's in the passage. To answer the questions, you don't need to know anything about the subject beyond what's in the passage. In fact, if you're familiar with the subject, be careful not to mix your own knowledge with what you read.

Recognizing the Three Reading Comprehension Question Formats

Being familiar with the question formats for the Reading Comprehension section enables you to field the questions more confidently, because you know what to expect. The GRE presents each question in one of the following three formats:

✔ Multiple-choice: Choose one answer

✔ Multiple-choice: Choose one or more answers

✔ Sentence-selection

The following sections describe each question format in greater detail and provide an example of each format based on the following short passage from *Food Allergies For Dummies* by Robert A. Wood, MD, with Joe Kraynak (Wiley):

Anaphylaxis resulting in death is relatively uncommon among children and young adults, because their cardiovascular systems are so resilient. This does not mean, however, that younger people are immune to severe anaphylaxis. Anaphylaxis in younger people typically results in breathing difficulty — a constricted or blocked airway that causes a fatal or near fatal reaction. In a fatal reaction, the heart stops only because the body eventually runs out of oxygen.

Multiple-choice questions: Choose one answer

The following format is the traditional multiple-choice question. You get five answers to choose from, and only one is correct.

Based on the passage, how common is anaphylaxis in older adults?

Ⓐ Very common

Ⓑ Relatively uncommon

Ⓒ About as frequent as in the general population

Ⓓ Nonexistent

Ⓔ Not stated in the passage

You pick one and only one answer. In this case, the correct answer is Choice **(E)**, because the passage doesn't mention older adults.

Multiple-choice questions: Choose one or more answers

The next question format is a spin on the traditional multiple-choice question. Three choices follow the question, and one, two, or all three of them are correct. You must pick *all* of the correct choices and no incorrect choices to receive credit for your answer. You don't receive partial credit for picking only some of the correct answers. The GRE treats a partially answered question as a wrong answer.

When anaphylaxis in a child or young adult is fatal, what happens? Consider each of the three choices separately and select all that apply.

A Heart stops.

B Airway is blocked or constricted.

C Body runs out of oxygen.

You pick all answers that are correct. In this case, all the answer choices — Choices **(A)**, **(B)**, and **(C)** — are correct.

You can quickly tell whether to select only one answer or up to three answers by looking at the instruction that accompanies the question: The GRE always instructs you whether to choose *one* or *all answers that apply*.

Sentence-selection questions: Choose a sentence from the passage

In sentence-selection questions, the GRE presents a description or question followed by instructions to click the sentence in the passage that most closely matches the description or answers the question. Clicking any part of the sentence selects the entire sentence.

Choose the sentence in the passage that parents of young children are likely to find most reassuring.

In the passage, you click the answer sentence, and it highlights on the screen, like this:

Anaphylaxis resulting in death is relatively uncommon among children and young adults, because their cardiovascular systems are so resilient. This does not mean, however, that younger people are immune to severe anaphylaxis. Anaphylaxis in younger people typically results in breathing difficulty — a constricted or blocked airway that causes a fatal or near fatal reaction. In a fatal reaction, the heart stops only because the body eventually runs out of oxygen.

Developing Strategies for Success

Reading Comprehension questions can be the most time-consuming questions of the Verbal section. The best way to ace these questions is to master and use strategies for quickly reading the passages, identifying key facts called for in the questions, and drawing inferences based on subtle implications. The following sections explain four useful strategies for effectively and efficiently arriving at the correct answers (and avoiding incorrect answers).

Using the context as your road map

For a science or humanities passage, read the passage lightly and create a mental grid that gives you a general idea of where the key information is and what is going on in the passage. This helps you figure out where to find the information as you begin to answer questions. Remember: Don't sweat the details (yet). After reading a question, you can quickly revisit the passage to locate the details for answering the question correctly.

Usually, the first paragraph is an introduction, telling you what the passage is about (the main idea). Subsequent paragraphs (the body of the passage) provide details to support or develop the topic stated in the first paragraph. As you read each body paragraph, ask yourself what its purpose is and how it supports the main idea. Asking these questions gives you a clearer idea of what the related details are and where they're located in the passage.

Don't use the road-map strategy for social sciences questions, which tend to be based less on facts and more on what can be determined from the facts. As I explain later in the section "The social sciences passage," you want to read these passages more carefully so you have the information needed to draw correct inferences.

Sometimes the entire passage is one giant paragraph. Don't let that deter you from using this strategy. Look for where one idea ends and another begins and treat that as where the paragraphs should be separated. This can help you map the details as you would for a passage that is actually in separate paragraphs.

Grasping the gist of the passage

Understanding the main idea of the passage is the key to establishing the context of the paragraphs within. The main idea is typically the basis of one of the questions. If you can briefly sum up the gist of the passage, then you've not only developed a contextual understanding of the passage but also answered one of the questions.

Using keywords strategically

Reading Comprehension passages and questions often contain keywords that act as valuable clues in identifying correct answers and eliminating wrong ones. For example, say a particular passage is all about successful international adoption; you're asked to choose the best title for the passage from the following choices:

Ⓐ Trends in International Adoption

Ⓑ Children at Risk

Ⓒ Analyzing the Child Psyche

Ⓓ Overcoming the Challenges of International Adoptions

Ⓔ What Makes a Good Parent

In this case, both Choices (A) and (D) mention international adoption, but of these two answers, only Choice **(D)** suggests a title leading to a *successful* adoption.

Avoiding traps

The folks who write the GRE are a tricky lot. They dangle wrong but tempting answers in front of you, hoping you take the bait. By recognizing common traps (and the natural tendency to make assumptions), you have a better chance of avoiding those traps. Here's what to watch for:

- **Unmentioned facts:** Answer choices may contain facts that aren't mentioned in the passage. The answer strikes you as correct because it's a true statement, but if that fact isn't mentioned in the passage, it's not a correct answer.

- **Half-truths:** Answer choices may contain information that's only partly accurate or not even mentioned in the passage. Before choosing an answer, make sure it's 100 percent accurate based on the passage.

- **Your own knowledge:** If you're like most people, you add detail based on your own knowledge and expertise from other things that you've read. Sometimes, these details tempt you to choose an answer that's correct based on what you know but incorrect according to the passage. Be careful not to add your own knowledge to what's in the passage.

- **Subtle distinctions:** When a question includes words like *mostly, best, primarily,* or *primary,* watch out. Most of the answers are probably correct to some degree, but only one answer is the *most* correct.

- **Judgment statements:** A judgment or value statement declares that something's right or wrong or better or worse, as in "Cats make better pets than dogs" or "People should stay out of other people's business." These statements may be tempting choices because the human mind likes to draw conclusions. However, value statements are almost never correct answers.

Acing the Three Commonly Tested Reading Comprehension Passages

Reading Comprehension passages are based on biological or physical sciences, social sciences, and the humanities. Each of the following sections explains one of the passage types; presents a passage of that type along with sample questions, answers, and explanations to get you up to speed; and provides additional guidance and tips for successfully answering each question.

The biological and physical science passage

A biological or physical science passage is straightforward, giving you the scoop on how stellar dust is affected by gravity, how to build a suspension bridge, how molecular theory applies, and so on. Although the passage may be difficult to get through (because it's full of facts and data on an unfamiliar subject), this type of passage can be the easiest because it has so few traps and tricks.

When approaching biological and physical science passages, don't get hung up on the scientific terminology. You usually don't need to know the meaning of all the scientific terms a passage throws at you in order to answer the questions correctly. However, these terms may function as keywords to help you locate the answers within the passage even if you don't know what the terms mean.

You can answer most biological or physical science questions directly from the facts provided in the passage itself.

Here's a science passage for you to practice on. Don't forget to check the introduction paragraph for the overall gist of the passage and to look for the high-level contribution of each paragraph. If you know each paragraph's purpose, you can quickly find the details when you need them.

Microbiological activity clearly affects the mechanical strength of leaves. Although it cannot be denied that with most species the loss of mechanical strength is the result of both invertebrate feeding and microbiological breakdown, the example of *Fagus sylvatica* illustrates loss without any sign of invertebrate attack being evident. *Fagus* shows little sign of invertebrate attack even after being exposed for eight months in either a lake or stream environment, but results of the rolling fragmentation experiment show that loss of mechanical strength, even in this apparently resistant species, is considerable.

Most species appear to exhibit a higher rate of degradation in the stream environment than in the lake. This is perhaps most clearly shown in the case of *Alnus*. Examination of the type of destruction suggests that the cause for the greater loss of material in the stream-processed leaves is a combination of both biological and mechanical degradation. The leaves exhibit an angular fragmentation, which is characteristic of mechanical damage, rather than the rounded holes typical of the attack by large particle feeders or the skeletal vein pattern produced by microbial degradation and small particle feeders. As the leaves become less strong, the fluid forces acting on the stream nylon cages cause successively greater fragmentation.

Mechanical fragmentation, like biological breakdown, is to some extent influenced by leaf structure and form. In some leaves with a strong midrib, the lamina breaks up, but the pieces remain attached by means of the midrib. One type of leaf may break cleanly, whereas another tears off and is easily destroyed after the tissues are weakened by microbial attack.

In most species, the mechanical breakdown will take the form of gradual attrition at the margins. If the energy of the environment is sufficiently high, brittle species may be broken across the midrib, something that rarely happens with more pliable leaves. The result of attrition is that where the areas of the whole leaves follow a normal distribution, a bimodal distribution is produced, one peak composed mainly of the fragmented pieces, the other of the larger remains.

To test the theory that a thin leaf has only half the chance of a thick one for entering the fossil record, all other things being equal, Ferguson (1971) cut discs of fresh leaves from 11 species of leaves, each with a different thickness, and rotated them with sand and water in a revolving drum. Each run lasted 100 hours and was repeated three times, but even after this treatment, all species showed little sign of wear. It therefore seems unlikely that leaf thickness alone, without substantial microbial preconditioning, contributes much to the probability that a leaf will enter a depositional environment in a recognizable form. The results of experiments with whole fresh leaves show that they are more resistant to fragmentation than leaves exposed to microbiological attack. Unless the leaf is exceptionally large or small, leaf size and thickness are not likely to be as critical in determining the preservation potential of a leaf type as the rate of microbiological degradation.

1. Which of the following would be the best title for the passage?

   Ⓐ Why Leaves Disintegrate

   Ⓑ An Analysis of Leaf Structure and Composition

   Ⓒ Comparing Lakes and Streams

   Ⓓ The Purpose of Particle Feeders

   Ⓔ How Leaves' Mechanical Strength Is Affected by Microbiological Activity

Note that because the passage is talking primarily about leaves, that word needs to be in the title, which eliminates Choices (C) and (D) right off. Choice (A) is too broad; other causes of disintegration may exist that the passage doesn't mention. Choice (B) is too specific. The passage mentions leaf structure, but that topic isn't its primary focus. Correct answer: Choice **(E)**.

2. Which of the following is mentioned as a reason for leaf degradation in streams? Consider each of the three choices separately and select all that apply.

   Ⓐ Mechanical damage

   Ⓑ Biological degradation

   Ⓒ Large particle feeders

The second paragraph of the passage tells you that "loss of material in stream-processed leaves is a combination of biological and mechanical degradation." Choice (C) is incorrect because the passage specifically states that the pattern of holes is contrary to that of large particle feeders. The correct answers are Choices **(A)** and **(B)**.

3. The conclusion that the author reached from Ferguson's revolving drum experiment was that

   Ⓐ Leaf thickness is only a contributing factor to leaf fragmentation.

   Ⓑ Leaves submerged in water degrade more rapidly than leaves deposited in mud or silt.

   Ⓒ Leaves with a strong midrib deteriorate less than leaves without such a midrib.

   Ⓓ Microbial attack is exacerbated by high temperatures.

   Ⓔ Bimodal distribution reduces leaf attrition.

The middle of the last paragraph tells you that leaf thickness *alone* is unlikely to affect the final form of the leaf. You probably need to reread that sentence a few times to understand it, but a detail or fact question is the type of question you should be sure to answer correctly. Choice (B) introduces facts not discussed in the passage; the passage didn't talk of leaves in mud or silt. Choice (C) is mentioned in the passage but not in Ferguson's experiments.

Nothing about high temperatures appears in the passage, which eliminates Choice (D). (***Exacerbated*** means made worse.) Choice (E) sounds pretentious and pompous — and nice and scientific — but has nothing to do with Ferguson. To answer this question correctly, you need to return to the passage to look up Ferguson specifically, not merely rely on your memory of the passage as a whole. Correct answer: Choice (**A**).

Be careful to answer *only* what the question is asking. Answer-choice traps include statements that are true but don't answer the question.

4. The tone of the passage is

   Ⓐ Persuasive

   Ⓑ Biased

   Ⓒ Objective

   Ⓓ Argumentative

   Ⓔ Disparaging

The passage is hardly persuasive; it isn't really trying to change your opinion on an issue. It objectively presents scientific facts and experimental evidence. Because you know the gist of the passage and the context of each paragraph, the answer is obvious. Correct answer: Choice (**C**).

5. Select the sentence that explains the form of mechanical breakdown of most species of leaves.

   Keywords come in handy in answering this question. The first and only place *mechanical breakdown* is mentioned is in the first sentence of the fourth paragraph. Correct answer: "In most species, the mechanical breakdown will take the form of gradual attrition at the margins."

6. The author is most likely addressing this passage to

   Ⓐ Gardeners

   Ⓑ Botanists

   Ⓒ Paleontologists

   Ⓓ Biologists

   Ⓔ Epidemiologists

The most important clue in the question is *most likely.* You know the passage is about plants, so you can eliminate Choice (E), *epidemiologists* (people who study transmittable diseases). You can also eliminate Choice (A), gardeners, because they're more interested in growing plants than in watching them decompose. Choice (D) is tempting because biologists study life, but they study both plant and animal life and usually investigate decomposition only from the perspective of other living things involved in the process; they're not likely to investigate the mechanical degradation of leaves. Botanists, Choice (B), who focus exclusively on plants in any sort of scientific way, are a good choice, but they tend to focus more on living plants and species than the breakdown of plant material. This passage is most relevant to paleontologists, who study plant fossils and may use the information to help determine the age and habitat of deceased organisms. The key lies in the last paragraph, which mentions the "fossil record." The correct answer is Choice **(C)**.

The social sciences passage

The GRE usually includes at least one social sciences passage. It may be about history, psychology, business, or a variety of other topics. In other words, the term *social sciences* is broad enough to include whatever the test-makers want it to include. Because social sciences passages offer a perspective on a subject that you may already be familiar with, you can use your understanding of the subject as a backdrop to make the passage easier to read and understand.

Within each section, you can work the passages in any order. If you find that you prefer a social sciences passage over a biological or physical science passage, you can skip the other passages and work the passage you prefer first.

Be sure not to use your own knowledge of the subject to answer the questions. *Everything* you need to answer the questions is in the passage, and your outside knowledge may differ from what the questions ask.

In many ways, a social sciences passage is nearly the opposite of a biological or physical science passage. The questions deal more with inferences and less with explicitly stated facts. Therefore, you must read the passage carefully, trying to understand not only what's stated but also what's implied. Take some time to think about what you're reading.

The questions that follow a social sciences passage may not be as straightforward as those for a biological or physical science passage. You may not be able to go back to a specific line and pick out a single fact. Instead, these questions require that you understand the big picture or comprehend what the author meant but didn't come right out and say. You may be asked why an author included a particular example or explanation.

Here's a social sciences passage for you to practice on. Though you need to read the passage more carefully, the underlying strategy is the same: Look for the gist of the passage, usually in the first paragraph, and identify the purpose of each paragraph thereafter. You'll still need to revisit these paragraphs to find details, so knowing where the details are located is easier and more useful than memorizing them.

Multinational corporations frequently encounter impediments in their attempts to explain to politicians, human rights groups, and (perhaps most importantly) their consumer base why they do business with, and even seek closer business ties to, countries whose human rights records are considered heinous by United States standards. The CEOs propound that in the business trenches, the issue of human rights must effectively be detached from the wider spectrum of free trade. Discussion of the uneasy alliance between trade and human rights has trickled down from the boardrooms of large multinational corporations to the consumer on the street who, given the wide variety of products available to him, is eager to show support for human rights by boycotting the products of a company he feels does not do enough to help its overseas workers. International human rights organizations also are pressuring the multinationals to push for more humane working conditions in other countries and to, in effect, develop a code of business conduct that must be adhered to if the American company is to continue working with the overseas partner.

The president, in drawing up a plan for what he calls the "economic architecture of our times," wants economists, business leaders, and human rights groups to work together to develop a set of principles that the foreign partners of United States corporations will voluntarily embrace. Human rights activists, incensed at the nebulous plans for implementing such rules, charge that their agenda is being given low priority by the State Department. The president vociferously denies their charges, arguing that each situation is approached on its merits without prejudice, and hopes that all the groups can work together to develop principles based on empirical research rather than political fiat, emphasizing that the businesses with experience in the field must initiate the process of developing such guidelines. Business leaders, while paying lip service to the concept of these principles, fight stealthily against their formal endorsement because they fear such "voluntary" concepts may someday be given the force of law. Few business leaders have forgotten the Sullivan Principles, in which a set of voluntary rules regarding business conduct with South Africa (giving benefits to workers and banning apartheid in the companies that worked with U.S. partners) became legislation.

7. Which of the following best states the central idea of the passage?

   Ⓐ Politicians are quixotic in their assessment of the priorities of the State Department.

   Ⓑ Multinational corporations have little if any influence on the domestic policies of their overseas partners.

   Ⓒ Voluntary principles that are turned into law are unconstitutional.

   Ⓓ Disagreement exists between the desires of human rights activists to improve the working conditions of overseas workers and the pragmatic approach taken by the corporations.

   Ⓔ It is inappropriate to expect foreign corporations to adhere to American standards.

In Choice (A), the word *quixotic* means idealistic or impractical. The word comes from the fictional character Don Quixote, who tilted at windmills. (*Tilting* refers to a knight on horseback tilting his joust toward a target for the purpose of attack.) Although the president in this passage may not be realistic in his assessment of State Department policies, his belief isn't the main idea of the passage.

Choice (E) is a value judgment. An answer that passes judgment, saying something is right or wrong, better or worse, or more or less appropriate (as in this case), is almost never the correct answer.

The main idea of any passage is usually stated in the first sentence or two. The first sentence of this passage touches on the difficulties that corporations have in explaining their business ties with certain countries to politicians, human rights groups, and consumers. From this statement, you may infer that those groups disagree with the policies of the corporations. Correct answer: Choice **(D)**.

Just because a statement is true doesn't necessarily mean it's the correct answer to the question, especially a main idea question. The answer choices are often true statements, or at least plausible ones.

8. According to the passage, the president wants the voluntary principles to be initiated by businesses rather than by politicians or human rights activists because

   Ⓐ Businesses have empirical experience in the field and thus know what the conditions are and how they may/should be remedied.

   Ⓑ Businesses make profits from the labor of the workers and thus have a moral obligation to improve their employees' working conditions.

   Ⓒ Workers will not accept principles drawn up by politicians whom they distrust but may agree to principles created by the corporations that pay them.

   Ⓓ Foreign nations are distrustful of U.S. political intervention and are more likely to accept suggestions from multinational corporations.

   Ⓔ Political activist groups have concerns that are too dramatically different from those of the corporations for the groups to be able to work together.

Choices (B), (C), (D), and (E) assume facts not in evidence, as lawyers say. Although you personally may believe the statements in these answer choices to be true, they don't answer the specific question.

When a question begins with the words *according to the passage,* you need to go back to the passage and find the answer. *Empirical* is a keyword here, and it's buried in the middle of the second paragraph.

Find the word and read the sentence, and you've found the answer: "The president vociferously denies their charges, arguing that each situation is approached on its merits without prejudice, and hopes that all the groups can work together to develop principles based on *empirical research* rather than political fiat, emphasizing that the *businesses with experience in the field must initiate the process* of developing such guidelines." You don't even need to know what ***empirical*** (derived from observation or experiment) means. Correct answer: Choice **(A).**

9. Select the sentence that describes the human rights activists' response to the president's plan.

   The passage contains only one mention of *human rights activists,* and it appears in the second sentence of the first paragraph. So the correct answer is "Human rights activists, incensed at the nebulous plans for implementing such rules, charge that their agenda is being given low priority by the State Department."

10. Which of the following is a reason the author mentions the boycott of a corporation's products by its customers? Consider each of the three choices separately and select all that apply.

    A To show the difficulties that arise when corporations attempt to become involved in politics

    B To suggest the possibility of failure of any plan that does not account for the customer's perspective

    C To indicate the pressures that are on the multinational corporations

    Choice (A) makes a valid point. Difficulties may arise when corporations attempt to become involved in politics. However, the passage doesn't give that as a reason for a boycott, so Choice (A) is wrong. Choice (B) seems logical because a company that ignores its customers will probably fail. The passage mentions corporate communications with customers in the first sentence but not the customer's perspective, so Choice (B) is wrong. Choice (C) is also true, because according to the passage, multinational corporations run the risk of alienating any group and thus inciting a boycott, which is a reason given by the passage. Correct answer: Choice **(C).**

If you're familiar with international marketing and politics, don't let your knowledge interfere with your ability to correctly answer the questions. If you know for sure that the passage is dead wrong, it doesn't matter: On the GRE, the passage knows all, so go with what the passage says.

11. Which of the following statements about the Sullivan Principles can best be inferred from the passage?

    Ⓐ They had a detrimental effect on the profits of those corporations doing business with South Africa.

    Ⓑ They represented an improper alliance between political and business groups.

    Ⓒ They placed the needs of the foreign workers over those of the domestic workers whose jobs would therefore be in jeopardy.

    Ⓓ They will be used as a model to create future voluntary business guidelines.

    Ⓔ They will have a chilling effect on future adoption of voluntary guidelines.

Choice (A) is the major trap here. Perhaps you assumed that because the companies seem to dislike the Sullivan Principles, they hurt company profits. However, the passage says nothing about profits. Maybe the companies still made good profits but objected to the Sullivan Principles, well, on principle. The companies just may not have wanted governmental intervention, even if profits weren't decreased.

Two keywords/phrases can help you answer this question: *Sullivan Principles* tells you to look at the end of the final paragraph where these principles are first mentioned. The word *chilling* in Choice (E) means "to cause fear." The second-to-last sentence, just before the sentence about the Sullivan Principles, states that business leaders "*fear* such 'voluntary' concepts may someday be given the force of law." Because business leaders fear that the adoption of voluntary guidelines will lead to forced legislation, the Sullivan Principles will have a chilling effect on the future adoption of voluntary guidelines. The correct answer is Choice **(E)**.

To answer this question correctly, you need to understand not only the sentence about the Sullivan Principles but also the sentence before it. An inference question like this one usually means you have to read at least two statements and make a conclusion from them; you can't just go back to one specific sentence or phrase of the passage and get the answer.

The humanities passage

A humanities passage may be about art, music, philosophy, drama, or literature. It typically places its subject in a positive light, especially if it's about a person who was a pioneer in his or her field, such as the first African American astronaut or the first female doctor. Use this to your advantage: If someone is worthy of mention historically or in a Reading Comprehension passage, then he or she must have been an amazing person or done something truly noteworthy. Use this sense of admiration from the author to create the context in which to frame the passage.

The humanities passages seem to be the most down-to-earth of the lot. They're easy to read, informative, and can even be enjoyable. Too bad they're rare. The approach is the same, though: Look for the gist of the passage in a few words and establish a context for the whole story and each paragraph. You can always go back for the details later.

Although the humanities passages don't require meticulous reading, the questions are another matter. The questions following a humanities passage often require you to get into the mind of the author in order to read between the lines and make inferences. While you're reading a passage about a particular person, for example, you're supposed to ascertain not just what the person accomplished but why she worked toward her goals and what mark she hoped to leave on the world.

Here's an example of a typical humanities passage, taken from *LSAT For Dummies* by Amy Hackney Blackwell (Wiley), about someone you've probably never heard of before but will still enjoy reading about.

Junzaburou Nishiwaki, a 20th-century Japanese poet, scholar, and translator, spent his career working to introduce Japanese readers to European and American writing and to break his country out of its literary insularity. He was interested in European culture all his life. Born to a wealthy family in rural Niigata prefecture in 1894, Nishiwaki spent his youth aspiring to be a painter and traveled to Tokyo in 1911 to study fused Japanese and European artistic traditions. After his father died in 1913, Nishiwaki studied economics at Keio University, but his real love was English literature. After graduating, he worked for several years as a reporter at the English-language *Japan Times* and as a teacher at Keio University.

Nishiwaki finally received the opportunity to concentrate on English literature in 1922, when Keio University sent him to Oxford University for three years. He spent this time reading literature in Old and Middle English and classical Greek and Latin. He became fluent in English, French, German, Latin, and Greek. While he was in England, Roaring Twenties modernism caught his eye, and the works of writers such as James Joyce, Ezra Pound, and T. S. Eliot were crucially important to his literary development. In 1925, Nishiwaki published his first book, *Spectrum,* a volume of poems written in English. He explained that English offered him much more freedom of expression than traditional Japanese poetic language.

Nishiwaki returned to Keio University in 1925 and became a professor of English literature, teaching linguistics, Old and Middle English, and the history of English literature. He remained active in modernist and avant-garde literary circles. In 1933 he published *Ambarvalia,* his first volume of poetry written in Japanese; this collection of surrealist verse ranged far and wide through European geography and history and included Japanese translations of Catullus, Sophocles, and Shakespeare. Angered by the Japanese government's fascist policies, Nishiwaki refused to write poetry during the Second World War. He spent the war years writing a dissertation on ancient Germanic literature.

After the war, Nishiwaki resumed his poetic pursuits and in 1947 published *Tabibito kaerazu,* in which he abandoned modernist language and returned to a classical Japanese poetic style but with his own postmodernist touch, incorporating both Eastern and Western literary traditions. In 1953, Nishiwaki published *Kindai no guuwa,* which critics consider his most poetically mature work. He spent his last years producing works of such writers as D. H. Lawrence, James Joyce, T. S. Eliot, Stéphane Mallarmé, Shakespeare, and Chaucer. Nishiwaki retired from Keio University in 1962, though he continued to teach and write poetry. Before his death in 1982, he received numerous honors and awards; he was appointed to the Japanese Academy of Arts and Sciences, named a Person of Cultural Merit, and nominated for the Nobel Prize by Ezra Pound. Critics today consider Nishiwaki to have exercised more influence on younger poets than any other Japanese poet since 1945.

12. Which one of the following most accurately states the main idea of the passage?

   Ⓐ Nishiwaki was a Japanese poet who rebelled against the strictures of his country's government and protested its policies toward Europe during World War II.

   Ⓑ Nishiwaki was a Japanese poet and literary critic who embraced European literature as a way of rebelling against the constraints of his family and traditional Japanese culture.

   Ⓒ Nishiwaki was a Japanese poet and professor who spent his life trying to convince young Japanese students that European literary forms were superior to Japanese poetic styles.

   Ⓓ Nishiwaki was a Japanese poet and linguist who throughout his life chose to write in English rather than Japanese.

   Ⓔ Nishiwaki was a Japanese poet and scholar who spent his life specializing in European literature, which proved tremendously influential to his own work.

A process of elimination reveals the correct answer. Choice (A) is wrong: Though Nishiwaki did protest against his country's fascist policies during World War II, this fact isn't the main idea of the passage. Choice (B) is flat-out wrong: Although the first paragraph discusses Nishiwaki's departure from family and his country's literary insularity, the word *rebelling* is too harsh. Choice (C) is also wrong: The passage doesn't say that he tried to convince his students one way or the other. Choice (D) is wrong: The passage states only that his first book was in English and many others were in Japanese. Correct answer: Choice **(E).**

13. The author's attitude toward Nishiwaki's life and career can be best described as

    Ⓐ Scholarly interest in the life and works of a significant literary figure

    Ⓑ Mild surprise at Nishiwaki's choosing to write poetry in a language foreign to him

    Ⓒ Open admiration for Nishiwaki's ability to function in several languages

    Ⓓ Skepticism toward Nishiwaki's motives in refusing to write poetry during the Second World War

    Ⓔ Envy of Nishiwaki's success in publishing and academia

    Choices (B), (D), and (E) are wrong because the passage doesn't reflect surprise, skepticism, or envy. Choices (A) and (C) remain, but you can eliminate Choice (C): The passage is objective, not admiring, and Nishiwaki's multilingual ability is a supporting detail to his accomplishments. The correct answer is Choice **(A)**.

14. The primary function of the first paragraph is to

    Ⓐ Describe Nishiwaki's brief study of painting.

    Ⓑ Introduce Nishiwaki and his lifelong interest in European culture.

    Ⓒ Summarize Nishiwaki's contribution to Japanese literature.

    Ⓓ Explain why a Japanese man chose to specialize in English literature.

    Ⓔ Analyze European contributions to Japanese culture at the start of the 20th century.

    After rereading the first paragraph, you know that in a nutshell it introduces Nishiwaki as one who worked to bridge the literature gap separating Japan from Europe and America. It also summarizes Nishiwaki's interest in art through college and his early career years afterward. Most importantly, the first paragraph sets the stage for the rest of the essay. Armed with this perspective, only one possible answer remains: Choice **(B)**.

15. Select the sentence in the passage that explains why Nishiwaki stopped writing poetry during World War II.

    Like most select-a-sentence questions, look for the correct sentence buried in the passage. Correct answer: "Angered by the Japanese government's fascist policies, Nishiwaki refused to write poetry during the Second World War."

16. The passage is primarily concerned with

    Ⓐ Comparing Nishiwaki's poetry to that of other Japanese poets of the 20th century

    Ⓑ Discussing the role of the avant-garde movement in Nishiwaki's writing

    Ⓒ Providing a brief biography of Nishiwaki that explains the significance of his work

    Ⓓ Explaining why writers can benefit from studying literature from other countries

    Ⓔ Describing the transformation in Japanese poetic style during the post-war period

    The keywords in this question are *primarily concerned with*. The passage may suggest some of the points listed, but its *primary concern* is more explicit. Choice (A) is wrong because the author doesn't mention the work of other Japanese poets. Choice (B) is wrong because although the avant-garde movement was influential to Nishiwaki's writing, this point is hardly the primary concern. Choice (C) looks about right, but check the others just in case. Choice (D) is wrong because the author doesn't mention the benefits of studying foreign literature. Choice (E) is wrong because the passage doesn't mention changes in Japanese poetic style after the war. Correct answer: Choice **(C)**.

17. According to the passage, which one of the following types of literature did *not* greatly interest Nishiwaki? Consider each of the three choices separately and select all that apply.

    A Old and Middle English literature such as *Beowulf* and *The Canterbury Tales*

    B Classical Greek works such as *Antigone*

    C Classical Japanese literature such as *The Tale of Genji*

    From the first paragraph, you know that Nishiwaki's real love was English literature. From the second paragraph, you know that Nishiwaki spent his time at Oxford reading Old and Middle English and classical Greek and Latin. However, even though he may have had some interest in Japanese literature, it didn't *greatly* interest him as the question states. Only one correct answer: Choice **(C)**.

18. Select the sentence that explains why Nishiwaki chose to write his first published poems in English.

    Though many sentences in the passage mention Nishiwaki's interest in English literature, in only one sentence does the passage provide Nishiwaki's explanation of why he chose to write his first published poems in English. Correct answer: "He explained that English offered him much more freedom of expression than traditional Japanese poetic language."

Chapter 6

Analyzing the Argument Questions

In This Chapter

▶ Tackling Argument Analysis questions step-by-step

▶ Reading the passage analytically

▶ Discovering what the question is asking for

▶ Thinking up your own answer before choosing one

▶ Picking the correct answer by the process of elimination

*Y*ou've probably heard the expression "you can't believe everything you hear." That's what argument analysis is all about: challenging arguments that you read in books, magazines, newspapers, and on the web; examining assertions that you see on the nightly news; and questioning claims that you hear from politicians, not to mention sales pitches. Graduate schools expect you not only to read with understanding but also to scrutinize information and arguments and sort out what's supported by the facts and what isn't.

An *Argument Analysis question* asks you to determine whether the argument may have a flaw or a weakness. This chapter reveals what to look for in the argument and in the question and answer choices that follow it. This chapter also explains how to deconstruct an argument to determine whether it's logically sound and well supported.

 When taking the GRE, expect two Argument Analysis questions in each Verbal section. An Argument Analysis question consists of a short passage and a single question. Arguments are easy to spot because they present a plan or a conclusion based on a set of facts. In this chapter, you find out how to deconstruct the argument or plan based on those very facts.

Use this five-step approach to tackle an Argument Analysis question:

1. **Skip the answer choices.**

2. **Read the question and understand what it's asking you to do.**

3. **Read the passage, keeping an eye out for information you need to answer the question.**

4. **Answer the question in your own words.**

5. **Compare each answer choice to your answer and pick the closest one.**

This chapter leads you through this five-step process and either transforms you into a critical thinker or makes you more of one.

Skipping the Answer Choices

First, don't look at the answer choices. Avoiding the choices *facilitates* (eases) your ability to follow the argument, because the answer choices clutter your brain and muddle your thinking with *superfluous* (nonessential) information. Then, with a solid understanding of the argument, you can more easily spot any irrelevant answer choices to rule them out.

Knowing What to Look for in the Question

Still without looking at the answer choices, read and understand the question so you know what to look for in the passage. The question typically asks you to pick the choice that does one of the following:

- ✔ Most seriously weakens the argument
- ✔ Best supports the argument
- ✔ Draws the most reasonable conclusion from the passage
- ✔ Identifies the assumption that must be true for the argument to be true
- ✔ Most accurately represents the premise on which the argument is based

The questions may not use the actual wording provided here; for example, instead of asking which choice most seriously *weakens* the argument, a question may ask which choice most effectively **undermines** (weakens) the argument. Don't get hung up on the wording — just be sure to understand what the question is looking for.

Reading the Passage with a Critical Eye

Now, knowing what the question is looking for, you're better equipped to *actively read* — read with a purpose. Instead of just reading the words, active and critical readers go in asking questions, such as "How is the conclusion drawn?" "What would strengthen this argument?" "What would weaken this argument?" and "What's the author assuming?" Having read the question first, you can take this critical reading step because you know what to look for.

While actively reading, you ask these questions and more, helping you gain a deeper understanding of the material and improve your retention. On the GRE, however, active reading is guided, because the exam gives you the *one* question to answer, and you read it before reading the argument.

The following sections provide guidance on what to look for in a passage when answering different types of Argument Analysis questions.

Identifying the premise and conclusion

Think of a logical argument as an if-then statement: The *if* part is the premise, and the *then* part is the conclusion. When reading an argument, break it down into these two parts:

- ✔ **Premise:** The premise (the *if* part) is facts or reasons that support the conclusion, including observations, statistics, reasonable generalizations, and anecdotes.
- ✔ **Conclusion:** The conclusion (the *then* part), which is based on the premise, is the argument's main point or assertion.

After identifying the premise and conclusion, you have what you need to begin your argument analysis, as I explain in the next few sections. Consider the following passage:

A strong selling point for charter schools has been that they are cost-effective. Because charter schools receive no public funding, they have to innovate ways to reduce costs. The current bill would give public funding to charter schools. If the bill passes, charter schools will no longer have an incentive to innovate to reduce costs and will therefore no longer strive to be cost-effective.

To reduce this argument to an if-then statement, you may come up with something like this:

 ✔ **Premise (if):** If public funding is made available to charter schools,

 ✔ **Conclusion (then):** then they will no longer strive to be cost-effective.

This single, simple restatement of the argument helps you evaluate the answer choices without having to reread the entire passage.

Look for the following words to identify the conclusion: *then, therefore, thus, hence, so, consequently, as a result,* and *in conclusion.* However, don't rely solely on these words; they may be implied rather than stated.

Finding the hidden assumption

An *assumption* is a claim that the passage makes without stating it directly. The assumption is based on the premise and suggests that the argument has only one reasonable conclusion. When asked to identify an assumption, look for the answer choice that *must* be true for the argument to be true. Ask yourself, "Does this have to be true for the argument to work?" If your answer is *yes,* you've most likely found the right choice, but read through the other choices just to be sure.

Unfortunately, identifying an assumption by just looking at the passage is difficult, because you're looking for something that's missing — it's *not* there. What you look for is a logical gap in the passage, typically between the premise and the conclusion. The question may say something like this:

 ✔ Which of the following is an assumption . . .?

 ✔ . . . relies on which of the following assumptions?

 ✔ . . . is based on which of the following assumptions?

Here's an example for finding a hidden assumption in a passage:

  Employees in the sales department have had special training and perform better than employees in other departments. The special training, therefore, should be given to the employees in the other departments in order to improve performance of the company overall.

First, identify the premise and conclusion, the parts of the if-then statement:

 ✔ **Premise (if):** Sales employees have had special training and perform better than other employees.

 ✔ **Conclusion (then):** Give the special training to the other employees, and the company will improve overall.

Between the premise and the conclusion is the assumption that the improved performance in the sales department is a direct result of the special training. This isn't stated, but you can infer it.

For this plan to work, the assumption has to be true. If the improved performance of the sales department were from something *other* than the special training it received, then the plan to improve overall company performance is based on a false premise. (Of course, you could also argue that the special training given to sales personnel might not be effective in improving performance in other departments.)

potting weaknesses in supporting details

...guments contain supporting details, such as facts, statistics, examples, or expert opinions. When you encounter a question that asks you to identify the statement that undermines or supports the argument, you need to evaluate supporting details first in the premise and then in the answer choices. As you read the passage, look for weaknesses or inaccuracies in the supporting details as well as in the conclusion drawn from them.

To choose the answer choice that weakens an argument, look for the choice that highlights the disconnect in the passage between the supporting details and the conclusion.

According to the USDA, ethanol production will consume about 40 percent of this year's corn harvest, so this corn will be used for fuel instead of food. With global drought and weather-related food shortages occurring in countries all over the world and the drastic reduction of corn supplied for food, prices for cereal, meat, and other staples are likely to soar in the U.S., while people in many poorer countries will go hungry. To make up for the diversion of the corn supply, the lifting of the federal government's mandates that require gasoline producers to include a certain minimum percentage of corn-based ethanol in their products has become a moral imperative.

When you read a passage that's packed with details like this, jot them down on your scratch paper followed by the conclusion:

- ✔ **Premises:** 40 percent of corn is used to produce fuel instead of food; global drought; rising global food prices.
- ✔ **Conclusion:** Federal mandates on ethanol use must be lifted.

If the question asks you to choose a statement that best undermines the argument, examine the choices to find the one that does the best job of showing that one or more of the supporting details isn't responsible for what's stated in the conclusion. For example, if the global drought affected other foods but not corn, and if enough corn exists for both the ethanol production *and* the existing food chain, then the plan to use 40 percent of corn for fuel wouldn't really affect the price of food.

On the other hand, if the question asks you to choose the statement that adds the best support for the argument, look for the choice that most effectively supports the conclusion that lifting the federal government's mandates on ethanol use would increase the availability of food for human consumption. For example, pointing out that there is no substitute for corn in the food chain and that corn production is insufficient even *without* the 40 percent skim would support the assertion that ethanol production will contribute to food shortages and price increases.

Exploring common logical fallacies

Arguments may seem logical and fair on the surface but actually be **fallacious** (erroneous, flawed). The following sections reveal some of the more common logical fallacies you're likely to find on the exam. By spotting these, you identify weaknesses in arguments and gather the knowledge required to determine which statements best support or refute the argument.

Circular reasoning: It is what it is

In *circular reasoning,* a premise supports a premise or a conclusion supports a conclusion. For example, a statement such as "The United States is the greatest country in the world, because no other country comes close" is an example of circular reasoning — trying to support the conclusion with another conclusion. Another example is "Most dentists prefer this toothpaste because four out of five dentists prefer it," which is supporting a premise with a premise; in this case, the conclusion merely restates the premise.

Logical fallacies you won't see

Just as important as knowing what to look for is knowing what *not* to look for. Though you may encounter these fallacies in day-to-day life, don't waste your time looking for these in the GRE answer choices.

✔ **Ad hominem:** Latin for "to the man," an *ad hominem* argument attacks the person instead of what the person says. For example, if an investment advisor comes on the news and says that investors should buy gold as a hedge against inflation and another analyst replies, "You don't even have a bachelor's degree in economics," the second analyst is arguing *ad hominem* by attacking the person and not the advice to buy gold.

✔ **Red herring:** A *red herring* is any attempt to stray from the issue. For example, suppose two people are discussing the pros and cons of nuclear energy, and one person says something like, "Sure, nuclear energy is a clean, efficient source of power, but the atomic bomb has the potential of wiping out entire cities." This red herring takes the debate in an entirely different direction, shifting the focus from nuclear power to nuclear warfare.

✔ **Straw man fallacy:** The *straw man fallacy* intentionally distorts the opponent's position and then attacks the distorted position instead of attacking what the person actually said. Suppose two politicians are discussing the state budget. The first politician says, "By combining these three health agencies, the state can save 25 percent in funding annually." The second politician replies, "Slashing funding for healthcare actually costs more money than it saves." The second politician has committed the straw man fallacy by misrepresenting the first politician's position and then attacking it.

✔ **Either/or fallacy:** The *either/or fallacy,* sometimes called a *false dilemma* or *black-and-white thinking,* presents two options as the only available ones, even though neither option may be correct and other options may exist. Suppose a committee is discussing the future of its parent-teacher organization, and one of the committee members says, "If we decide to stop fundraising, we may as well not have a parent-teacher organization." The either/or fallacy here is based on the premise that the sole function of a parent-teacher organization is to raise money for the schools, when in fact other functions exist, such as increasing levels of volunteerism and improving communication between parents and schools.

You won't see circular reasoning in the passage, but it may appear in the answer choices, especially when the question asks you to choose a statement that supports an argument. Watch out for answer choices that restate information already in the argument. These answers are wrong because restating an argument doesn't make it true.

Erroneous cause-and-effect arguments

An erroneous cause-and-effect argument assumes that because one event followed another, the first event caused the second event. For example, suppose that you've been taking the same multivitamin every day for years. One day, you take a new multivitamin, and you are just full of energy. Your productivity at work triples, and you set a new record at the gym. Did this new multivitamin bring this energy? One might think so, but you don't know for sure that the new vitamin caused the effect (your energy). Maybe something else caused it. If you also got plenty of rest, ate a great breakfast, and drank an extra coffee, maybe all that extra energy *wasn't* from the new multivitamin.

Sweeping generalizations

A *sweeping generalization* applies a general rule to a specific case; someone may suppose that a plan that works in one context will certainly work in another. For example, someone may argue that because the addition of sharp-turn warning signs to roads in Town X reduced the rate of accidents, adding these signs to the roads in Town Y will surely have the same effect. This argument uses a sweeping generalization by assuming that the roads in the two towns are similar. To weaken this argument, the correct answer choice may suggest that Town X has lots of curvy mountain roads, while Town Y has only straight, flat roads. Because sharp-turn warning signs don't make straight roads safer, this new information weakens the argument.

Answering the Question in Your Own Words

After you have a clear understanding of the argument's premise and conclusion, answer the question in your own words, giving the answer choices less power to lead you astray. Fortunately, the question serves as your focal point. For example, if the question asks you to identify the assumption, you needn't waste time considering whether the argument commits a logical fallacy or evaluating evidence that may support or undermine the argument — you focus solely on the assumption.

Following are the different question types and what you need to ask yourself and answer before looking at the answer choices:

- ✔ **Weakening the argument:** What new information that's not in the argument would weaken it? Does the argument commit a logical fallacy? If so, which one?

- ✔ **Strengthening the argument:** What new information that's not in the argument would strengthen it?

- ✔ **Identifying the assumption:** What assumption does the author make that, if proven untrue, would render the conclusion false?

- ✔ **Identifying the inference:** Based on the supporting details, what point is the author trying to make?

- ✔ **Choosing the best conclusion:** What is the author's stand on this issue?

Don't review the answer choices before answering the question in your own words. Just as with the Text Completion and Sentence Equivalence questions I discuss in Chapter 4, if you read the choices first, they'll distract you from understanding the passage and the question.

Eliminating Wrong Answers to Find the Right One

Like the other Verbal questions on the GRE, answering the Argument Analysis questions means eliminating the obviously wrong answers and working with what's left. After you've answered the question yourself, look at each answer choice and eliminate those that don't match your own answer. The following sections show you how to eliminate wrong answers and also highlight some common traps to avoid.

Leveraging the process of elimination

GRE developers are a tricky bunch. They seem to take pleasure in intentionally misleading test-takers. To defend yourself against such *chicanery* (trickery intended to deceive), brush up on these common traps.

Beware of "always," "never," and other absolutes

Absolute answers — those containing the words *always, never, must, all,* or *none* — are almost always wrong, so you can flag them for elimination more quickly than the other choices. You may not always be able to eliminate answer choices that contain absolutes, but this strategy works often enough to narrow your choices if you're stuck.

Dodge the decoys

An answer choice may contain information that's irrelevant to the argument. If you're not sure of what you're looking for, you may get stuck evaluating the extra information. Avoid this trap by answering the question yourself before looking at the answer choices — this makes any of these irrelevant answers easier to spot.

Stay dispassionate

Correct answer choices are usually unbiased and tone-neutral. The premise is based on facts, not feelings. If an answer choice seems emotional or opinionated, it's probably a prime candidate for elimination.

Avoid picking an answer just because it's true

Don't choose an answer just because it's true. Plenty of answer choices are true but don't answer the question. When you see an answer choice that's true, make sure it answers the question.

Don't be tempted by opposites

If you're asked to weaken or support the argument, the answer choices almost always contain at least one statement that does the exact opposite. It may make sense because it contains the elements that you're looking for, but make sure it goes in the right direction. If you're strengthening an argument, for example, this trap answer will fit perfectly but actually weaken the argument.

Testing your skills

Here's a sample question to test your skills, followed by the best approach for choosing the right answer.

Recent test scores released by Washington D.C.'s department of education show a four-point drop in reading proficiency in its elementary schools from the previous year to 44.5 percent. Math proficiency dropped five points to 43.4 percent. Washington D.C.'s public school system is obviously failing in its mission to improve academic success.

The argument that Washington D.C.'s public school system is failing to improve academic success is based on which of the following assumptions?

Based on the guidelines in this chapter, here's how to approach this question:

1. **Cover the answer choices with your scratch paper.**

   I show the answer choices for this question later in this section.

2. **Read the question to discover your mission.**

   What's the assumption upon which the argument is based?

3. **Read the passage to identify the premise and conclusion (if-then).**

   If test scores have dropped, *then* Washington D.C.'s public school system is failing.

4. **Answer the question in your own words.**

   The assumption is that these test scores accurately reflect a school system's progress in achieving academic success.

5. **Compare each answer choice to your answer and pick the closest one.**

The question asks, "The argument that Washington D.C.'s public school system is failing to improve academic success is based on which of the following assumptions?" Here are the answer choices:

Ⓐ Washington D.C.'s public school system doesn't have sufficient funding to improve test scores.

Ⓑ Proficiency rates are the same at the middle- and high-school levels.

Ⓒ Private schools and charter schools had significantly higher test scores.

Ⓓ Test scores are an accurate measure of academic success.

Ⓔ The school has increased focus to improving its athletic program.

Now analyze each choice, one by one:

Choice (A) is wrong because funding is outside the scope of the argument.

Choice (B) is wrong because it simply further discusses proficiency rates but doesn't address the assumption that the tests are a valid measure of success.

Choice (C) is wrong because the success of other schools has nothing to do with the failure of the school system in question.

Choice (D) is correct because if test scores weren't an accurate indication of academic success, this argument would be false.

Choice (E) is wrong because other programs are out of scope of the argument.

The correct answer is Choice **(D),** and you know it's correct because you answered the question yourself before looking at the answer choices.

Trying other examples

Now that you know the overall approach, try your hand at a few more Argument Analysis questions.

For healthcare and health insurance to become less expensive, the federal government first needs to implement cost-control measures in the healthcare industry. Tort reform is the obvious place to start. The costs of medical malpractice insurance and lawsuits are skyrocketing, and medical professionals simply increase the cost of their services to keep pace. Tort reform would significantly reduce the number of frivolous malpractice claims, limit the damage awarded to plaintiffs, and reduce the cost of malpractice insurance. Healthcare providers and insurance companies could then pass the savings along to consumers. Until some sort of tort reform effectively addresses this issue, healthcare will continue to be expensive regardless of whether people are paying out of pocket or through a government-administered program.

1. Which of the following statements most accurately identifies the assumption that must be true for the argument to be true?

Ⓐ Medical insurance will increase the cost of healthcare services.

Ⓑ Medical insurance costs are rising.

Ⓒ The costs of medical malpractice lawsuits and insurance represent a significant portion of healthcare costs.

Ⓓ Providers are responsible for the high healthcare costs.

Ⓔ Tort reform would reduce medical malpractice litigation and limit damages awarded to plaintiffs.

The question asks for the assumption on which the argument is based, and the assumption lies between the premise and the conclusion. Rephrase the argument as an if-then statement, and you get something like this: "If we have tort reform, then health services will cost less." Examine the answer choices to find the one that lies between the premise and conclusion. You can instantly rule out Choice (E), because it merely repeats the definition of tort reform from the passage. Rule out Choices (A) and (D), because nothing in the passage suggests that insurance or providers have an effect on the cost of healthcare services. Rule out Choice (B), which may be true but doesn't touch on the premise. That leaves Choice (C), the assumption that medical malpractice lawsuits and insurance contribute significantly to the cost of health services. If this isn't true, then tort reform is unlikely to significantly reduce costs for consumers. Correct answer: Choice **(C).**

While many government reformists seek to curb the influence of corporate lobbying on Capitol Hill, the issue of insider trading continues to fly under the radar. Currently, no law prevents members of Congress from trading shares of stock based on what they know about legislative acts that could benefit or harm any given industry or company. Likewise, no law prevents a member of Congress from voting on legislation that would likely affect the share price of a company in which the member is currently invested. As a result, congressional votes may be influenced less by what is right and best for the country and more by the potential effect those votes may have on the performance of a Congress member's investment portfolio. To encourage Congress to do what's best for constituents rather than what's best for their investment portfolios, Congress needs to close the loopholes that exempt members of Congress from the insider trading rules and regulations, thus making it less tempting for members of Congress to shift their priorities away from the good of the nation.

2. Which of the following statements, if true, most supports the position that Congress needs to vote for the good of the country rather than for the enhancement of their investment portfolios?

Ⓐ In two months, a top energy-policy adviser nearly doubled his $3,500 investment in a renewable-energy firm after the senator for whom he worked helped pass a 30 percent tax credit for companies in the solar-energy business.

Ⓑ Members of Congress tend to favor investments in the private sector over U.S. Government bonds.

Ⓒ In 2009, a bill that would have reduced trucking regulation and supported the trucking industry, thus reducing costs for consumer goods and bolstering the ailing economy, was voted down by Congress. It was later revealed that this bill would have adversely affected the railway industry, in which many members of Congress are vested.

Ⓓ Three members of Congress introduced the Stop Trading on Congressional Knowledge Act, or STOCK Act (H.R. 682), in March 2009, to bar federal employees, including members of Congress and their staff, from cashing in on non-public information they receive in their official capacities.

Ⓔ A 2004 study revealed that U.S. senators' stock trades performed, on average, 12.3 percent better than the market average and 6 percent better than professional investment portfolio manager averages.

Choice (A), an example of an unusually high return, shows the unfair advantage that members of Congress have over the average investor but doesn't support the point of the argument that Congress needs to shift its priorities. Choice (B) is tempting, but it doesn't really make the case that members of Congress have skewed priorities. Choice (C) looks good, as it points out how members of Congress place the value of their investments over the good of the country. You can rule out Choice (D), because an act to prohibit an action isn't proof that the action has occurred. You can also rule out Choice (E), because other reasons for the U.S. senators' good performance are possible. It could be that senators are savvier investors or can afford better portfolio managers. Correct answer: Choice **(C).**

Chapter 7

Expanding Your Vocabulary to Boost Your Score

In This Chapter

▶ Looking for clues in prefixes, suffixes, and roots

▶ Reviewing vocabulary words found on the GRE

You can't get around it: You absolutely must know vocabulary to do well on the GRE. Regardless of your conversational expertise, the GRE tests your grasp of commonly used academic vocabulary words. Many of the words used on the GRE probably aren't words you use on a daily basis, but you've most likely heard them somewhere before. You can't know for certain which words are going to appear on the test, but the odds are good that you'll see some of the vocab words presented in this chapter.

Mastering new vocabulary words is more than just reading this chapter. You need to make it part of your daily practice. Study daily. Revisit the words you think you already know. Knowing as many vocabulary words as possible helps immensely with the Verbal section. You can also improve your vocabulary by reading novels, articles, and so on.

This chapter helps you get a firmer grasp on vocabulary words used on the GRE. I provide a detailed discussion of prefixes, suffixes, and roots, which can help you significantly improve your vocabulary. I also provide a long list of common vocabulary words that you need to know. For additional vocabulary review, visit learn.dummies.com, where you'll find flashcards to test your knowledge.

Brushing Up on Prefixes, Suffixes, and Roots

Mastering prefixes, suffixes, and roots can bump up your Verbal score significantly. Although prefixes and suffixes abound, the ones in the following sections are the most common. Take the time to memorize them.

If English isn't your first language, vocabulary may be the hardest part of the exam for you. Using roots, prefixes, and suffixes to determine a word's meaning can help you greatly.

Prefixes

A *prefix* is one or more letters at the beginning of a word that alters its meaning. For example, if a feat is *possible,* then you can do it. With a simple prefix, you can change that feat to *im*possible, and you can't do it. Knowing that in this case *im-* means not, you can narrow down the possible meanings of a word starting with *im-,* such as *impermeable.* Whatever the word is, the *im-* usually stands for not. (Because *permeate* means to pass through, **impermeable** means not capable of being passed through.) Following are the most common prefixes you need to know with several related examples:

- ✔ *a-/an-* = **not or without:** Someone *amoral* is without morals or conscience; someone *atypical* isn't typical or normal. Someone *apathetic* is uncaring or without feeling, like most test-takers by the time they finish the GRE and are leaving the exam room. ("The world is going to end tomorrow? Who cares? I'm going to bed.") Similarly, an *anaerobic* environment is without oxygen (like the testing center feels when a killer question leaves you gasping for air). *Anarchy* is without rule or government (like a classroom when a substitute teacher is in for the day).

- ✔ *ante-* = **before:** When the clock reads 5 a.m., the *a.m.* stands for *ante meridiem,* which means before the middle of the day. *Antebellum* means before the war. Tara in *Gone with the Wind* was an antebellum mansion, built before the Civil War. *Antediluvian* literally means before the flood, before Noah's deluge. Figuratively, it means very old; if you call your mother *antediluvian,* you mean that she's been around since before the flood. (It's a great word to use as an insult because almost no one knows what it means and you can get away with it.)

- ✔ *ben-/bon-* = **good:** A *benefit* is something that has a good result, an advantage. Someone *benevolent* is good and kind; when you have a date, a benevolent father lets you take his new car rather than your old clunker. *Bon voyage* means have a good voyage; a *bon vivant* is a person who lives the good life.

- ✔ *contra-* = **against:** A medical treatment that's *contraindicated* for a certain condition is something that would make the condition worse, not better. *Contravene,* which means to deny or oppose, is from the Latin *venir* (to come) and *contra* (against).

- ✔ *de-* = **down from, away from (to put down):** To *descend* or *depart* is to go down from or away from. To *denounce* is to put down or to speak badly of, as in *denouncing* those hogs who chow down all the pizza before you get to the party.

  Many unknown words on the GRE that start with *de-* mean to put down in the sense of to criticize or bad-mouth. Here are just a few: demean, denounce, denigrate, derogate, deprecate, and decry.

- ✔ *eu-* = **good:** A *eulogy* is a good speech, usually given for the dearly departed at a funeral. A *euphemism* is a good way of saying something or a polite expression, like saying that someone has passed away rather than calling her worm meat.

- ✔ *ex-* = **out of, away from:** An *exit* is literally out of or away from *it* — *ex*-it. (The word *exit* is probably one of the most logical words around.) To *extricate* is to get out of something. You can extricate yourself from an argument by pretending to faint, basking in all the sympathy as you're carried away. To *exculpate* is to let off the hook — literally to make away from guilt. *Culp* means guilt. When the president of the Hellenic Council wants to know who plastered the dean's house, you can claim that you and your sorority sisters aren't *culpable.*

- ✔ *im-/in-* = **not:** Something *impossible* isn't possible — it just can't happen. Someone *immortal* isn't going to die but will live forever, because *mortal* means able to die. Someone *implacable* isn't able to be calmed down, because *placate* means to ease one's anger. Similarly, something *inappropriate* isn't appropriate, because *appropriate* means proper. Someone *inept* isn't adept, meaning she's not skillful. Someone who's *insolvent* has no money and is bankrupt, like most students after four years of college.

Note that *im-* can also mean into (*immerse* means to put into), inside (*innate* means something born inside of you), or beginning (the *initial* letters of your name are the beginning letters), but those meanings aren't as common on the GRE. First, think of *im-* or *in-* as meaning not; if that doesn't seem appropriate, switch to Plan B and see whether *im-* or *in-* can mean into, inside, or beginning; use the context of the question to make your determination.

- **ne-/mal-** = **bad:** Something *negative* is bad, like a negative attitude. Someone *nefarious* is full of bad, or wicked and evil; you may read about a nefarious wizard in a fantasy novel. Something *malicious* also is full of bad, or wicked and harmful, such as a malicious rumor.

- **post-** = **after:** When the clock reads 5 p.m., the *p.m.* stands for *post meridiem,* which means after the middle of the day. Something *postmortem* occurs after death. A postmortem exam is an autopsy.

Eponymous words

An *eponym* is a word derived from the name of a person. For example, the cardigan sweater got its name from the Earl of Cardigan. Here are a few eponyms to add to your GRE vocabulary:

- **bowdlerize:** To omit indecent words or phrases in a book or piece of writing (you bowdlerize a love letter before you let your roommate read it). In 1818, Dr. Thomas Bowdler, an English physician, published a ten-volume edition of Shakespeare's plays called *The Family Shakespeare.* He left out all the dirty parts. For example, instead of "Out, damn'd spot!" the line reads, "Out, crimson spot!"

- **boycott:** You'd think that Mr. Boycott started the practice of boycotting, wouldn't you? Just the opposite: He was the victim of the first boycott. Charles Boycott was a retired English army captain who refused to lower rents to his farmer tenants after a few bad harvests and was accused of exploiting the poor. The locals harassed him, stealing his crops and refusing to sell his products in their stores, until he was hounded out of the county. Today, when you refuse to have anything to do with someone, you're said to boycott him or her.

- **draconian:** Extremely harsh and severe. When you tell your professor that dropping your grade one whole letter just because you turned in a report one day late is truly draconian, you're harking all the way back to about 620 BC. Draco was an Athenian who wrote a code of laws that made nearly every crime punishable by death, even laziness and, uh, urinating in public. The word *draconian* came to describe any laws that are too cruel or strict.

- **maverick:** An individualist; an unconventional person. Samuel Maverick, who lived during the 1800s, was a Texas rancher whose unbranded cattle roamed free. Maverick's neighbors refused to hand back his strays, claiming that because they were unbranded, he had no proof they were his. The word eventually came to be used to describe people

or ideas that are unconventional, independent, or defiant.

- **quisling:** A traitor. Vidkun Quisling was a Norwegian politician who turned traitor in World War II, siding with Hitler. He was executed by a firing squad at the end of the war, but his name lives on to torment GRE-takers.

- **simony:** The buying or selling of religious or sacred objects or privileges. Simon Magus (who's often described as a reformed wizard) offered St. Peter and St. John money to give him their religious abilities. *Simony* was especially popular in the Middle Ages, when people sold pardons, indulgences, and the like.

Bonus! You probably already know the following words, but did you know they're also eponyms?

- **diesel:** A type of engine, named for Rudolf Diesel, a German engineer.

- **mausoleum:** A large tomb or memorial, named for King Mausolus, King of Calia in ancient Greece about 370 BC.

- **nicotine:** The addictive stuff in tobacco, named for French diplomat Jean Nicot.

- **quixotic:** A word used to describe a person who's excessively chivalrous, romantic, impractical, and impulsive, like the character Don Quixote in Cervantes's novel *The Ingenious Gentleman Don Quixote of La Mancha.*

- **saxophone:** A musical instrument, invented by and named after Adolphe Sax, a Belgian musician of the early to mid-1800s.

- **shrapnel:** Fragments thrown out by a shell or a bomb, invented in 1802 by Lt. Gen. Henry Shrapnel, an English army officer.

- **silhouette:** Profile or shadow of a face, named after Étienne de Silhouette, a French finance minister.

Suffixes

A *suffix* is usually three or four letters at the end of a word that give the word a specific inflection or changes its type, such as from a verb to an adjective; for example, to transform the verb *study* into the adjective *studious*, you change the *y* to *i* and add the suffix *-ous*. Following are the most common suffixes you need to know with several related examples:

- ✔ *-ate* = **to make:** To *duplicate* is to make double. To *renovate* is to make new again (*nov* means new). To *placate* is to make peaceful or calm (*plac* means peace or calm).

- ✔ *-ette* = **little:** A *cigarette* is a little cigar. A *dinette* table is a little dining table. A *coquette* is a little flirt (literally, a little chicken, but that doesn't sound as pretty).

- ✔ *-illo* = **little:** An *armadillo* is a little armored animal. A *peccadillo* is a little sin. (Do you speak Spanish? If so, then you probably know that *pecar* translates as "to sin" in English.)

- ✔ *-ify (-efy)* = **to make:** To *beautify* is to make beautiful. To *ossify* is to make bone. (If you break your wrist, it takes weeks to ossify again, or for the bone to regenerate.) To *deify* is to make into a deity, a god. To *liquefy* is to turn a solid into a liquid.

- ✔ *-ist* = **a person:** A *typist* is a person who types. A *pugilist* is a person who fights, a boxer (*pug* means war or fight). A *pacifist* is a person who believes in peace, a noncombatant (*pac* means peace or calm).

- ✔ *-ity* = **a noun suffix that doesn't actually mean anything; it just turns a word into a noun:** *Jollity* is the noun form of jolly. *Serenity* is the noun form of serene. *Timidity* is the noun form of timid.

- ✔ *-ize* = **to make:** To *alphabetize* is to make alphabetical. To *immunize* is to make immune. To *ostracize* is to make separate from the group, or to shun.

- ✔ *-ous* = **full of (very):** Someone *joyous* is full of joy. Someone *amorous* is full of *amour*, or love. Someone *pulchritudinous* is full of beauty and, therefore, beautiful.

Roots

A *root* is the core part of a word that gives the word its basic meaning. Recognizing a common root helps you discern the meaning of an unfamiliar word. For example, knowing that *ver* means truth, as in *verify*, you can recognize that the unfamiliar word *aver* has something to do with truth. *Aver* means to hold true or affirm the truth. Following are the most common roots that you need to know with several related examples:

- ✔ *ambu* = **walk, move:** In a hospital, patients are either bedridden (they can't move) or *ambulatory* (they can walk and move about). A *somnambulist* is a sleepwalker. *Som-* means sleep, *-ist* is a person, and *ambu* is to walk or move.

- ✔ *andro* = **man:** An *android* is a robot shaped like a man. Someone *androgynous* exhibits both male (*andro*) and female (*gyn*) characteristics (literally, he/she is full of man and woman).

- ✔ *anthro* = **human or mankind:** *Anthropology* is the study of humans (not just a particular gender but humans in general). A *misanthrope* hates humans (an equal-opportunity hater: He or she hates both men and women alike.)

- ✔ *bellu, belli* = **war, fight:** If you're *belligerent*, you're ready to fight — in fact, you're downright hostile. An *antebellum* mansion is one that was created before the Civil War. (Remember that *ante-* means before.)

- **cred = trust or belief:** Something *incredible* is unbelievable, such as the excuse "I would've picked you up on time, sweetheart, but there was a 75-car pileup on the freeway." Saying something is *incredible* is like saying, "I can't believe it!" If you're *credulous,* you're trusting and *naive* (literally, full of trust).

  Be careful not to confuse the words *credible* and *credulous.* Something *credible* is trustable or believable. A credible excuse can get you out of trouble if you turn a paper in late. *Credulous,* on the other hand, means full of trust, naive, or gullible. The more credulous your professor is, the less credible that excuse needs to be. Furthermore, if you're *incredulous,* then you doubt something is true.

- **gnos = knowledge:** A doctor shows his or her knowledge by making a *diagnosis* (analysis of the situation) or a *prognosis* (prediction about the future of the illness). An *agnostic* is a person who doesn't know whether a god exists. Differentiate an agnostic from an atheist: An *atheist* is literally without god, a person who believes there's no god. An *agnostic* is without knowledge of whether a god exists.

- **greg = group, herd:** A *congregation* is a group or herd of people. A *gregarious* person likes to be part of a group — he or she is sociable. To *segregate* is literally to make away from the group. (*Se-* means apart or away from, as in *separate, sever, sequester,* and *seclusion.*)

- **gyn = woman:** A *gynecologist* is a physician who treats women. A *misogynist* is a person who hates women.

- **loq, log, loc, lix = speech or talk:** Someone *loquacious* talks a lot. (That person is literally full of talk.) A *dialogue* is talk or conversation between two or more people. *Elocution* is proper speech. A *prolix* person is very talkative. (Literally, he or she engages in big, or much, talk.)

- **luc, lum, lus = light, clear:** Something *luminous* is shiny and full of light. Ask the teacher to *elucidate* something you don't understand (literally, to make clear). *Lustrous* hair reflects the light and is sleek and glossy.

- **meta = beyond, after:** A *metamorphosis* is a change of shape beyond the present shape.

- **morph = shape:** Something *amorphous* is without shape. *Morphology* is the study of shape. ("Yes, of course, I take my studies seriously. I spent all weekend on *morphology* at the beach.")

- **mut = change:** The Teenage Mutant Ninja Turtles *mutated,* or changed, from mild-mannered turtles to pizza-gobbling crime fighters. Something *immutable* isn't changeable; it remains constant. Don't confuse *mut* (change) with *mute* (silent).

- **pac = peace, calm:** Why do you give a baby a *pacifier?* To calm him or her down. To get its name, the *Pacific* Ocean must have appeared calm at the time it was discovered.

- **path = feeling:** Something *pathetic* arouses feeling or pity. To *sympathize* is to share the feelings (literally, to make the same feeling). *Antipathy* is a dislike — literally, a feeling against. For example, no matter how much the moron apologizes, you still may harbor antipathy toward the cad who parked right behind you and blocked you in, making you late for a date and having all sorts of unfortunate romantic repercussions.

- **phon = sound:** *Phonics* helps you to sound out words. *Cacophony* is bad sound; *euphony* is good sound. *Homophones* are words that sound the same, such as *red* and *read.*

- **plac = peace, calm:** To *placate* someone is to calm him or her down or to make peace with that person. You placate your irate sweetheart, for example, by sending a dozen roses. Someone *implacable* is someone you aren't able to calm down — or someone really stubborn. If those roses don't do the trick, for example, your sweetheart is too implacable to placate.

All in a day's work, labor, toil, pursuit, grind . . .

One way you can improve your vocabulary quickly is to group words with similar meanings — remembering five or ten for the price of one. If you can remember *harbinger,* you can remember *prescient.*

✔ I'm *looking forward* to this:

auguries	presage
bode	prescient
harbinger	prognosis
portent	prognosticate

✔ You have to keep your sense of *humor:*

badinage	mirth
japing	puckish
jocose	ribald
jocular	risible
jollity	twit
levity	wag

✔ It's a *sad* day when you don't know your vocabulary:

bereft	lugubrious
despondent	plaintive
doleful	maudlin
dour	melancholic
jeremiad	saturnine
lachrymose	Weltschmerz

✔ That's easy for you to *say:*

declaim	prolix
exhort	raconteur
persiflage	stentorian
philippic	tergiversate
pontificate	voluble

✔ Just how *boring* is this vocabulary?

banal	prosaic
bromide	somniferous
ennui	soporific
hackneyed	tedious
listless	trite
platitude	vapid

✔ It takes a lot of *guts* to know these words:

audacity	intrepid
doughty	redoubtable
effrontery	uncowed
impudent	undaunted

✔ Hip, hip, hooray! Words of *praise:*

accolade	obsequious
encomium	paean
eulogy	panegyric
extol	plaudits
kudos	sycophant
laud	toady

✔ Are you sick to *death* of vocabulary?

cadaver	morbid
demise	noxious
dirge	obsequies
elegy	valetudinarian
insalubrious	wan

✔ *pro* = **big, much:** *Profuse* apologies are big, or much — in essence, a *lot* of apologies. A *pro*lific writer produces a great deal of written material.

Pro has two additional meanings less commonly used on the GRE. It can mean before, as in "A *prologue* comes before a play." Similarly, to *prognosticate* is to make knowledge before, or to predict. A *prognosticator* is a fortuneteller. *Pro* can also mean for. Someone who is *pro* freedom of speech is in favor of freedom of speech. Someone with a *proclivity* toward a certain activity is for that activity or has a natural tendency toward it.

✔ *pug* = **war, fight:** Someone *pugnacious* is ready to fight. A *pugilist* is a person who likes to fight, such as a professional boxer. Did you ever see those big sticks that Marines train with in hand-to-hand combat — the ones that look like cotton swabs with a thyroid condition? Those are called *pugil sticks.*

- **scien = knowledge:** A *scientist* is a person with knowledge. Someone *prescient* has forethought or knowledge ahead of time — for example, a prognosticator. (A fortuneteller, remember?) After you study these roots, you'll be closer to being *omniscient* — all knowing.

- **somn = sleep:** If you have *insomnia,* you can't sleep. (The prefix *in-* means not.)

- **son = sound:** A *sonic* boom breaks the sound barrier. *Dissonance* is clashing sounds. A *sonorous* voice has a good sound.

- **sop = sleep:** A glass of warm milk is a *soporific.* So is a boring professor.

Memorizing the GRE's Most Common Vocabulary Words

This section features the most commonly occurring words on the GRE. Besides reviewing the words and their definitions in this section, I recommend using an online dictionary while practicing the Verbal section of the GRE. When you get stuck on a word, you can look it up.

As you review these words, pay attention to the word parts (prefixes, suffixes, and roots) from the lists earlier in this chapter. Try covering up the definitions and discerning the word meanings from these parts. You can also make notecards and highlight the word parts. With practice, interpreting new words becomes much easier.

- **aberrant:** Abnormal; different from the accepted norm

- **abeyance:** State of suspension; temporary inaction

- **abstemious:** Characterized by a state of self-denial, particularly in the area of food or drink

- **abstruse:** Difficult to comprehend

- **acquiescent:** Agreeing without protest

- **acrid:** Bitter; harsh

- **acrimonious:** Bitter in temper, manner, and speech

- **acumen:** Keenness; quickness of intellectual insight

- **admonition:** A gentle reproof

- **affront:** To deliberately offend, as with a gesture

- **aggrandize:** To widen in scope or make bigger or greater

- **aggregate:** Amounting to a whole

- **allay:** To reduce the intensity of

- **amalgamate:** To mix or blend together in a homogenous body

- **ameliorate:** To make better or improve

- **anachronous:** Out of place in time

- **anecdote:** A short account of an interesting incident

- **archipelago:** A large group of islands

- **articulate:** Well-spoken, eloquent

- *artifice:* Cleverness or skill
- *artless:* Without deceit or cunning; sincere
- *ascetic:* Given to severe self-denial; practicing excessive abstinence
- *assiduous:* Persistent, unceasing
- *astute:* Keen; wise
- *audacious:* Fearless, bold
- *austere:* Unadorned; severely simple
- *avarice:* Extreme greed characterized by the hoarding of riches
- *aver:* To declare or profess
- *banal:* Trite; commonplace
- *base:* That on which something is built or established; also used to describe a person lacking in moral fiber or kindness
- *beset:* To surround, as in an attack
- *blatant:* Very obvious, offensively loud, or coarsely conspicuous
- *bolster:* To support; to reinforce
- *bombastic:* Using inflated language; pompous
- *boon:* A timely benefit; a blessing
- *brevity:* Briefness or conciseness
- *browbeat:* To intimidate in an overbearing manner
- *bumptious:* Offensively self-assertive; pushy
- *bungle:* To perform clumsily or inadequately; botch
- *burgeon:* To grow forth; to send out buds
- *cacophony:* A disagreeable, harsh, or discordant sound or tone
- *callous:* Insensitive; indifferent
- *calumniate:* To make false and malicious statements about; to slander
- *candor:* The quality of being open and sincere
- *carp:* To complain unreasonably
- *chaos:* A state of disorder and confusion
- *chicanery:* Trickery, deception, especially through the use of words and questionable logic
- *churl:* A rude, boorish, or surly person
- *coda:* Concluding section of a musical or literary piece; something that summarizes
- *codify:* To assemble related laws or principles into a systematic collection
- *cognizant:* Aware; taking notice
- *cohort:* A companion or associate
- *colloquial:* Pertaining to common speech
- *commensurate:* Corresponding in amount, quality, or degree
- *complacency:* A feeling of quiet security; satisfaction

- *conciliatory:* A state of seeking to reconcile or make peace
- *concrete:* Actual, irrefutable, as in concrete evidence
- *confidante:* One to whom secrets are confided
- *congruous:* Appropriate or fitting
- *consternation:* Unsettling dismay or amazement
- *consummate:* To bring to completion
- *contentious:* Quarrelsome
- *contrite:* Penitent, apologetic
- *contumacious:* Rebellious
- *corroborate:* To make more certain; confirm
- *countenance:* Appearance, especially the look or expression of the face
- *counter:* To go against or attempt to undermine an action
- *counterpart:* A person or thing resembling or complementing another
- *craven:* Cowardly
- *credulity:* Willingness to behave or trust too readily
- *cronyism:* The practice of favoring one's friends, especially in political appointments
- *curmudgeon:* An ill-tempered person
- *cursory:* Hasty, superficial, as of a review of something
- *dearth:* An inadequate supply; scarcity; lack
- *debacle:* A complete collapse or failure
- *decorum:* Orderliness and good taste in manners
- *deferent:* A state of giving in out of respect for another person
- *deleterious:* Hurtful, morally or physically
- *delineate:* To represent by sketch or diagram; to describe precisely in words
- *depravity:* The state of being morally bad or evil
- *deride:* To ridicule; to make fun of
- *derision:* Ridicule
- *derivative:* Something obtained or developed from a source
- *desultory:* Aimless; haphazard
- *diatribe:* Bitter or malicious criticism
- *didactic:* For the purpose of teaching
- *diffidence:* Lacking confidence
- *dilatory:* Causing delay
- *disconcert:* To disturb the composure of
- *discretion:* The power to act according to one's own judgment; the quality of being discreet
- *disingenuous:* Insincere, phony
- *disquiet:* Lack of calm, peace, or ease

- **dissemble:** To disguise or pretend in order to deceive or mislead
- **dissolution:** Breaking up of a union of persons
- **dissonant:** Out of harmony, incongruous
- **divergent:** Deviating from a certain course
- **divest:** To strip; to deprive, often in terms of property
- **divulge:** To tell or make known, generally of something secret or private
- **doctrinaire:** A person who's fanatical about enforcing a certain principle, regardless of its practicality
- **dogmatic:** Forceful and unwavering, allowing no room for interpretation or dissent
- **doldrums:** A state of inactivity or low spirits
- **dubious:** Doubtful
- **dupe:** Someone who's easily fooled; to fool someone
- **duplicity:** Deceitfulness
- **ebullient:** Showing great enthusiasm or exhilaration
- **eclectic:** Drawn from multiple sources or based on multiple styles
- **efficacious:** Capable of producing the intended result
- **efficacy:** Power to produce an intended effect
- **effrontery:** Shameless boldness; impudence
- **egregious:** Seriously bad or wrong
- **egress:** Exit
- **elegy:** A poem lamenting the dead
- **elicit:** To extract (usually information, a reaction, or an emotional response) without the use of force; to learn through discussion
- **elitism:** Consciousness or pride in belonging to a select group
- **embellish:** To beautify or enhance with additional features or information
- **empirical:** Proven by observed occurrence or existence
- **emulate:** Imitate
- **endemic:** Characteristic of a specific place or culture
- **enervate:** To weaken
- **engender:** To produce or to make something come into existence
- **enigmatic:** Mysterious, perplexing
- **ennui:** Boredom
- **ephemeral:** Short-lived; fleeting
- **equable:** Free from many changes or variations
- **equanimity:** Evenness of mind or temper
- **equivocal:** Ambiguous
- **equivocate:** To use ambiguous or unclear expressions, usually to avoid commitment or to mislead
- **eradicate:** To destroy completely

- *erudite:* Very well-educated

- *eschew:* To keep clear of, avoid

- *esoteric:* Hard to understand; known only by a few

- *euphemism:* A nicer way of saying something that's likely to make people feel uncomfortable

- *exacerbate:* To make sharper or more severe; to make worse

- *exculpate:* To free from blame

- *exigency:* Urgent situation

- *expatiate:* To speak or write at some length on a given topic or theme

- *expiation:* The means by which atonement or reparation is made

- *extenuating:* The state of explaining or justifying in order to lessen the seriousness of an action; for example, extenuating circumstances may lessen the punishment for a crime

- *extirpate:* To root out; to eradicate

- *extrapolation:* To infer an unknown from something that's known

- *facetious:* Not intended to be taken seriously

- *facilitate:* To make easier

- *fallacious:* Illogical

- *fatuous:* Idiotic

- *felicitous:* Appropriate or suitable for the situation or circumstances

- *ferret out:* To track down, discover

- *fervor:* Ardor or intensity of feeling

- *fledgling:* Inexperienced

- *foment:* To instigate or encourage negative behavior, such as violence

- *forestall:* To prevent by taking action in advance

- *fortification:* The act of strengthening or protecting

- *frugal:* Thrifty

- *fulminate:* To cause to explode; to detonate

- *fumble:* To feel or grope about clumsily

- *gaffe:* A social blunder; faux pas

- *gainsay:* To contradict or oppose

- *garrulous:* Prone to trivial talking

- *generosity:* The state of giving freely

- *germane:* Relevant

- *goad:* To urge on

- *grandiloquent:* Speaking or expressing oneself in a lofty style, often to the point of being pompous or bombastic

- *grandstand:* To conduct oneself or perform showily in an attempt to impress onlookers

- *gregarious:* Sociable; outgoing
- *grouse:* To complain or grumble
- *guileless:* Without deceit
- *gullible:* Easily deceived
- *halcyon:* Calm
- *haphazard:* Characterized by a lack of order or planning
- *harangue:* A tirade
- *harbinger:* Anything or anyone who makes known the coming of a person or future event; an omen
- *hedge:* A barrier or boundary; an act of preventing complete loss of a bet or investment
- *heresy:* Opinion or doctrine subversive of settled or accepted beliefs
- *homogeneous:* Of the same kind
- *hyperbole:* Exaggeration or overstatement
- *iconoclast:* A person who attacks and destroys religious images or accepted beliefs or traditions
- *ignominious:* Shameful, disgraceful
- *immense:* Very large
- *impartial:* Objective, open-minded
- *impecunious:* Having no money; broke
- *impede:* To hinder; to block
- *impenitent:* Not feeling regret about one's sins
- *imperious:* Domineering, overbearing; urgent
- *imperturbable:* Calm
- *impervious:* Impenetrable
- *impetuous:* Impulsive
- *implicit:* Implied
- *importune:* To harass with persistent demands
- *impugn:* To challenge as false with arguments or accusations
- *inadvertently:* Unintentionally
- *inane:* A nicer word for describing someone or something as stupid or idiotic
- *incensed:* Angered
- *inchoate:* Recently begun, not fully developed or organized
- *inconstant:* Changeable; fickle; variable
- *indigenous:* Originating in a particular place or region
- *indigent:* Lacking necessities, such as food, clothing, and shelter
- *indolence:* Laziness
- *ineffable:* Incapable of being expressed in words; unutterable
- *inert:* Inactive; lacking power to move or react

- *inexorable:* Not subject to change; not able to be persuaded or convinced
- *ingenuous:* Innocent, sincere
- *ingratiating:* Charming, agreeable
- *innocuous:* Harmless
- *insensible:* Incapable of perceiving or feeling
- *insinuate:* To suggest or hint slyly
- *insipid:* Bland
- *insouciant:* Free from worry or concern; carefree
- *intimation:* Something indicated or made known indirectly
- *intrepid:* Fearless and bold
- *inure:* To harden or toughen by use, exercise, or exposure
- *invidious:* Showing or feeling envy
- *irascible:* Easily angered
- *ironic:* To convey the opposite of an expression's literal meaning
- *itinerant:* Traveling from place to place
- *jingoism:* Professing one's patriotism loudly and excessively, often used in terms of having an aggressive foreign policy
- *killjoy:* A person who spoils the joy or pleasure of others
- *laconic:* Brief and to the point; concise
- *lampoon:* To make fun of; to mock or ridicule
- *latent:* Dormant
- *laud:* To praise
- *laudable:* Praiseworthy
- *licentious:* Unrestrained by laws or rules, especially those related to sexuality
- *liken:* To represent as similar to someone or something
- *loquacious:* Talkative
- *lucid:* Easily understood; clear
- *lugubrious:* Gloomy, depressing
- *magnanimity:* Generosity
- *malingerer:* One who feigns illness to escape duty
- *malleable:* Pliant; able to be reshaped
- *masticate:* To chew or reduce to a pulp
- *maverick:* Rebel; nonconformist
- *mealy mouthed:* Insincere, deceitful
- *mediocrity:* The state or quality of being barely adequate
- *mendacious:* Untruthful, deceitful
- *mendicant:* A beggar or homeless person
- *metamorphosis:* Change of form

- **meticulous:** Very thorough and precise
- **misanthrope:** One who hates people
- **mitigate:** To lessen in intensity; to appease
- **modicum:** A small amount
- **mollify:** To soothe
- **morbidity:** Related to illness or disease, especially the prevalence of illness in a certain population or geographical area
- **mordant:** Sarcastic, harsh
- **moribund:** Near death or extinction
- **morose:** Ill-humored; sullen
- **mundane:** Ordinary; dull
- **myopic:** Shortsighted or narrow-minded
- **narcissism:** Excessive fascination with oneself
- **nefarious:** Extremely wicked
- **negate:** To cancel out; to nullify
- **neophyte:** Beginner
- **nepotism:** Favoritism shown on the basis of family relationship
- **obdurate:** Stubborn
- **obfuscate:** To darken or conceal
- **obsequious:** Servile; ready to serve
- **obviate:** To make unnecessary
- **odious:** Hateful
- **officious:** Aggressively authoritative in offering help or advice, especially when dealing with trivial matters
- **onus:** Burden
- **opprobrium:** Infamy that results from shameful behavior
- **oscillate:** To waver or switch between different positions or beliefs
- **ostentation:** A display of vanity; showiness
- **painstaking:** Characterized by being very careful and diligent
- **palpable:** Readily seen, heard, or perceived
- **panache:** A grand or flamboyant manner or style
- **parable:** A short story designed to teach a lesson
- **paragon:** Model of perfection
- **parsimonious:** Sparing in spending of money; stingy
- **partisan:** One-sided; committed to one party
- **pathos:** Having a quality that rouses emotion or sympathy
- **paucity:** Scarcity, insufficiency
- **pejorative:** Having a disparaging or derogatory effect

- ✔ *penchant:* Strong inclination
- ✔ *penurious:* Excessively sparing in the use of money; extremely stingy
- ✔ *perennial:* Something long-lasting
- ✔ *perfidy:* Treachery, betrayal
- ✔ *permeable:* Penetrable; porous
- ✔ *pernicious:* Tending to kill or hurt
- ✔ *pervasive:* Spread throughout
- ✔ *phlegmatic:* Not easily roused to feeling or emotion
- ✔ *pious:* Religious
- ✔ *placate:* To soothe; to bring from a hostile state to a calm one
- ✔ *placid:* Peaceful
- ✔ *platitude:* Trite or commonplace statement
- ✔ *plethora:* Excess; abundance
- ✔ *plumb:* To make vertical; to reach the deepest point
- ✔ *polarize:* To divide into sharply opposing factions
- ✔ *pompous:* Ostentatiously lofty or arrogant
- ✔ *ponder:* To consider something thoroughly and thoughtfully
- ✔ *ponderous:* Massive, awkward, unwieldy
- ✔ *porous:* Full of holes; spongy, absorbent
- ✔ *portend:* Foretell
- ✔ *poseur:* A person who attempts to impress others by assuming a manner other than his true one
- ✔ *pragmatic:* Practical
- ✔ *precarious:* Hazardous, perilous
- ✔ *precipitate:* To hasten the occurrence of
- ✔ *precocious:* Mature beyond one's age, typically in respect to mental abilities, talents, or skills
- ✔ *preeminent:* A step above others; distinguished, renowned
- ✔ *prescience:* Knowledge of events before they happen
- ✔ *presentiment:* A feeling or impression that something is about to happen
- ✔ *prevaricate:* To use ambiguous language for the purpose of deceiving
- ✔ *proclivity:* Natural inclination
- ✔ *prodigal:* Wasteful or lavish
- ✔ *prodigious:* Immense
- ✔ *prodigy:* A person, usually a child, having extraordinary talent
- ✔ *profound:* Deep, significant
- ✔ *prognosticate:* To predict something in the future
- ✔ *proliferate:* To grow rapidly

- *propensity:* Natural inclination
- *prophetic:* Ability to predict the future
- *propitious:* Presenting favorable conditions
- *prosaic:* Commonplace or dull
- *protean:* Changeable in shape or form
- *prudence:* Cautious wisdom
- *puerile:* Childish
- *pugnacious:* Quarrelsome or combative
- *pungent:* Stinging; sharp in taste or smell
- *pusillanimous:* Cowardly; fainthearted
- *qualms:* Misgivings; uneasy fears
- *quibble:* Minor objection or complaint
- *quiescence:* Being quiet or still; inactivity
- *quintessential:* The perfect representation of something
- *quixotic:* Idealistic; romantic to a ridiculous degree
- *recant:* To formally withdraw a statement
- *recidivism:* The tendency toward repeated or habitual relapse
- *recondite:* Beyond ordinary knowledge or understanding; profound
- *redress:* To set right by compensation or punishment
- *refutation:* An act of disproving a statement or charge
- *refute:* To disprove
- *repose:* The state of being at rest
- *reprobate:* A sinful and depraved person
- *repudiate:* To refuse to have anything to do with
- *rescind:* To repeal, revoke, or void
- *resilience:* The ability to recover from a setback
- *respite:* Interval of rest
- *restive:* Impatient or stubborn
- *reticent:* Reluctant or inclined to silence
- *reverent:* Respectful
- *rhetoric:* The art of effective communication
- *rout:* To drive out; to stampede
- *rueful:* Causing sorrow or pity
- *ruminate:* To chew over and over again; to think over, ponder
- *sagacious:* Wise
- *salacious:* Lustful; sexually indecent
- *salubrious:* Healthful

✔ *sanction:* To approve; in legal circles, a law that enacts a penalty for disobedience or a reward for obedience

✔ *sanguine:* Cheerfully confident; optimistic; bloody, ruddy, or reddish (What's bloody about cheerfulness? Rosy cheeks!)

✔ *satiate:* To satisfy or fulfill the appetite or desire of

✔ *savor:* To enjoy fully

✔ *scanty:* Scarce in quantity or amount

✔ *secrete:* To hide away

✔ *security:* Safety

✔ *sedulous:* Persistent in effort or endeavor

✔ *seethe:* To be in a state of excitement or agitation

✔ *seminal:* Influencing future developments

✔ *shard:* Fragment

✔ *shirk:* To avoid

✔ *shoddy:* Not genuine; inferior

✔ *sinuous:* Curving in and out

✔ *skeptic:* Doubter

✔ *skepticism:* Doubt or disbelief

✔ *skittish:* Lively; restless

✔ *slander:* Defamation

✔ *slothful:* Slow-moving, lazy

✔ *solecism:* A minor mistake in grammar or usage; a breach of good manners

✔ *solicitous:* Worried or concerned; eager to receive approval from others

✔ *sonorous:* Loud, deep, or resonant, as a sound

✔ *soporific:* Causing sleep

✔ *spate:* A sudden, almost overwhelming outpouring

✔ *specious:* Seemingly reasonable but incorrect

✔ *spendthrift:* Someone who wastes money

✔ *spurious:* Not genuine

✔ *stentorian:* Extremely loud

✔ *stigma:* A token of disgrace

✔ *stint:* A period of time (noun); to be thrifty (verb)

✔ *stipulate:* To make specific conditions

✔ *stoic:* Lacking in emotional response, especially in the face of pain or adversity

✔ *stolid:* Dull; impassive

✔ *stratify:* To form or place in layers

✔ *striated:* Marked with parallel bands

✔ *strut:* A pompous walk

- *sublime:* Supreme or outstanding; elevated
- *subterfuge:* Evasion
- *supercilious:* Showing careless contempt; arrogant
- *superfluous:* More than what's needed
- *supersede:* To replace or supplant
- *supine:* Lying on one's back face upward
- *sybarite:* A person devoted to luxury and pleasure
- *sycophant:* A self-seeking, servile flatterer
- *tacit:* Understood
- *taciturn:* Stern; silent
- *tangential:* Only slightly connected or related
- *tantamount:* Equivalent in significance, effect, or value
- *tawdry:* Showy, in a cheap way
- *temerity:* Recklessness
- *tempestuous:* Stormy; impassioned
- *tenacious:* Holding fast
- *tendentious:* Having or showing a definite tendency, bias, or purpose
- *tenuous:* Thin; slim
- *tepid:* Lukewarm
- *thrall:* A state of being enslaved or held captive physically, mentally, or morally
- *thwart:* To frustrate
- *tilt:* To lean forward, as if to attack
- *timidity:* Lacking in self-assurance or courage
- *tirade:* A long, passionate speech against something
- *titillate:* To excite or arouse
- *titular:* Holding a position in name (title) only without the power, responsibility, and so forth that usually comes with that position
- *torpid:* Dull; sluggish; inactive
- *tortuous:* Abounding in irregular bends or turns
- *tractable:* Docile, easily controlled or shaped
- *transgression:* Violation; sin
- *transience:* A temporary state
- *transmute:* To change
- *transparent:* Easily detected
- *transpire:* To happen, to be revealed
- *trepidation:* Nervous feeling; fear
- *truculence:* Ferocity
- *truculent:* Harsh, brutal

- ✔ *turgid:* Inflated, overblown, or pompous; literally swollen to the point of being firm
- ✔ *tutelage:* The act of training or being under instruction
- ✔ *tyro:* Beginner, novice
- ✔ *ubiquitous:* Being present everywhere
- ✔ *umbrage:* Sense of having been injured
- ✔ *unassuaged:* Not soothed or relieved
- ✔ *uncouth:* Clumsy; rude
- ✔ *undermine:* To weaken or derail
- ✔ *unerringly:* Without fail
- ✔ *ungainly:* Awkward; clumsy
- ✔ *unison:* Complete accord
- ✔ *unruly:* Disobedient
- ✔ *untenable:* Indefensible
- ✔ *upbraid:* To reproach as deserving blame
- ✔ *urbanity:* Refined courtesy or politeness
- ✔ *vacillate:* To waver; to fluctuate
- ✔ *vagabond:* Wanderer
- ✔ *vainglorious:* Excessive; pretentious
- ✔ *valorous:* Courageous
- ✔ *vantage:* Position giving advantage
- ✔ *vapid:* Having lost quality and flavor; dull; lifeless
- ✔ *variegated:* Many-colored
- ✔ *vehement:* Forceful
- ✔ *veneer:* A thin covering to improve the appearance of something
- ✔ *venerate:* To look upon with deep respect
- ✔ *veracious:* Truthful
- ✔ *verbiage:* Use of many words
- ✔ *verbose:* Wordy
- ✔ *vestigial:* Occurring or persisting as a rudimentary or degenerate structure
- ✔ *viable:* Capable of living or succeeding
- ✔ *vicissitude:* Change of condition or circumstances, generally of fortune
- ✔ *virtuosity:* Having the character or ability of an expert
- ✔ *virulence:* Intense sharpness of anger; intensity
- ✔ *visage:* Face, especially in terms of its features or expression
- ✔ *viscous:* Sticky; gluey
- ✔ *vituperate:* Overwhelm with wordy abuse
- ✔ *vociferous:* Making a loud outcry
- ✔ *volatile:* Changeable, explosive

- **volition:** A willful choice or decision
- **voluble:** Fluent; talkative
- **warranted:** Justified
- **wary:** Very cautious
- **welter:** Turmoil (noun); to roll, tumble, or toss about (verb)
- **whet:** To sharpen or stimulate
- **whimsical:** Fanciful
- **whorl:** A circular or spiral arrangement
- **winsome:** Attractive, charming
- **wreak:** Inflict
- **writhe:** Twist
- **yore:** Time past
- **zealot:** Fanatic
- **zeitgeist:** Intellectual and moral tendencies of any age

As you study for the exam and encounter words throughout the days leading up to test day, create your own vocabulary list, complete with the definition of each word. Consider maintaining your list on quizlet.com, where you can make your own vocabulary lists and digital flashcards for free to practice on your computer or cellphone. And don't overlook low-tech vocabulary-building tools and techniques. Several studies suggest that memory is better when students handwrite their notes (and by extension, flashcards) instead of typing them. Reading or writing interesting example sentences that provide context is useful, too, because sentences tend to be more memorable than words in isolation. Although digital flashcards allow learning by rote, handwritten notes and flashcards and other low-tech techniques improve memory by encoding information in multiple ways and connecting new information to what you already know. Using multiple techniques, including repetition, makes the information more likely to stick and become a part of your working vocabulary.

Finding GRE vocab words in literature

Question: What do the GRE and *Moby Dick* have in common?

Answer: They both feature the following vocabulary words:

antediluvian	fastidious	omnipotent
blunder	fathom	precipice
cadge	floundering	prodigious
conflagration	heinous	ruefully
depict	incensed	sagacious
descry	incredulous	superficial
disparaging	indiscriminate	tyro
dogged	inert	voracious
effulgent	leviathan	wretched

Part III
High School Math and Beyond: Math You Thought You'd Never Need Again

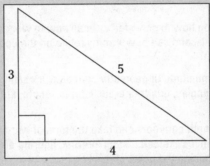

In this part . . .

✔ Review the order of operations, units of measurement, and basic operations with decimals, fractions, percentages, and ratios.

✔ Brush up on how to solve for x, recall how to work with roots and radicals, and see how x and y relate on the coordinate plane.

✔ Master a multitude of geometry concepts, including lines and angles, triangles, quadrilaterals, circles, length, area, and volume.

✔ See how math concepts can take the form of word problems with objectives like calculating interest, figuring out probability, and determining the order of things.

✔ Strengthen your knowledge of statistics and practice drawing conclusions from tables and graphs.

✔ Become familiar with Quantative Comparison questions and get strategies for answering these questions quickly and correctly.

Chapter 8

Brushing Up on Basic Arithmetic

●●

In This Chapter

▶ Working with whole numbers, including factors, multiples, and prime numbers

▶ Making calculations easier with the distributive, associative, and commutative properties

▶ Using parts of numbers, including decimals, fractions, and percentages

▶ Mastering ratios

▶ Practicing a few simple math problems

●●

This chapter may take you back . . . all the way to middle school. Although many of the basic math concepts covered in this chapter are fairly easy, you may not have used them in a long time, and you do need a firm grasp of them for the Quantitative sections of the GRE. Fortunately, you've been exposed to these concepts before, so this is a refresher.

This chapter covers most of the basic arithmetic concepts featured on the GRE, including whole numbers, units of measurement, decimals, fractions, percentages, and ratios. After reading this chapter and practicing the concepts described within, you'll be armed and ready for any basic math question the GRE throws at you.

Knowing Integers, Factors, and Multiples

GRE math questions may use some unfamiliar math terminology when referring to values. For example, a question may state, "x is an integer" or "x is a factor of 21." You're expected to know the meaning of these terms:

✔ **Integers:** Any whole number, positive or negative, is an integer. Zero is neither positive nor negative, but it's considered an integer. Examples of integers include –3, –2, –1, 0, 1, 2, and 3.

✔ **Real numbers:** Any number that goes on the number line, whether positive or negative, is considered a real number. This includes every fraction (in which the number on the bottom is *not* zero), decimal, and whole number, along with π, zero, and the square root of any positive number.

✔ **Non-real numbers:** Any number that can't exist in real math and therefore isn't on the number line is a non-real number. Mathematics has several types of non-real numbers, but you need to know about only two for the GRE:

  • The square root of a negative number (see Chapter 9)

  • Any number divided by zero

✔ **Factors:** Any integer that you get from dividing an integer by another integer is a factor. For example, if you divide 15 by 5, you get 3, so 3 is a factor of 15; 5 is also a factor of 15. Note that every integer is a factor of itself and that 1 is a factor of every number. For example, 1 and 15 are both factors of 15.

- ✔ **Multiples:** Any integer you get from multiplying an integer by another integer is a *multiple*. Multiples of 3 begin with 3, 6, 9, 12, and 15, and they go on forever. Every integer is a multiple of itself.

- ✔ **Prime numbers:** Any integer that has exactly two factors (1 and itself) is considered a prime number, as discussed in the next section.

Factoring in Prime Time: Prime and Composite Numbers

A grasp of number basics helps you build your strategy for the GRE math questions. All whole positive numbers are either prime or composite. A *prime number* is a positive integer (whole number) that has exactly two positive factors: 1 and itself. Examples include 2, 3, 5, 7, and 11.

These little rules about prime numbers can help you better identify them:

- ✔ Zero isn't a prime number, because it's divisible by more than two factors. Zero divided by anything is still zero.

- ✔ One isn't a prime number, because it has only one factor: itself.

- ✔ Two is the *only* even prime, because it's the only even number with exactly two factors: 1 and itself.

Meanwhile, *composite numbers* have more than two factors and can be divided by more than just 1 and themselves. Examples include 4, 6, 8, and 9.

Any composite number can be broken down to its prime factors. For example, 12 can be broken down to $2 \times 2 \times 3$; 84 can be broken down to $2 \times 2 \times 3 \times 7$; and 125 can be broken down to $5 \times 5 \times 5$.

Here's a GRE question example that challenges your grasp of prime numbers:

Quantity A	**Quantity B**
The number of prime numbers from 0 to 10 inclusive	The number of prime numbers from 11 to 20 inclusive

Ⓐ Quantity A is greater.

Ⓑ Quantity B is greater.

Ⓒ The two quantities are equal.

Ⓓ The relationship cannot be determined from the information given.

In Quantity A, the prime numbers from 0 to 10 inclusive are 2, 3, 5, and 7. In Quantity B, the prime numbers from 11 to 20 inclusive are 11, 13, 17, and 19. Both quantities have four prime numbers, but counting 0 and 1 as prime would lead you to choose Choice (A), which is incorrect. The correct answer is Choice **(C)**.

Reading between the Lines: Absolute Value

The *absolute value,* indicated by two vertical parallel lines, is the positive form of a number. Technically, absolute value refers to the expression's distance from 0 on the number line. Because –7 is 7 units away from 0, the absolute value of –7, written as $|-7|$, is 7.

The GRE likes to play with absolute values and trick you with double negatives. For example, $-|-3|$ is the same thing as $-+3$, which equals -3. The trick is taking the calculations step by step. The absolute value of -3 is 3, which you make negative to get -3.

Here's a trickier example:

$$-|-|-5||=$$

Take it step by step, from the inside out. Say to yourself, "The absolute value of -5 is 5. Then the negative of that is -5. Then the absolute value of that is 5. And finally, the negative of that is **-5.**"

Remembering the Order of Things: Putting PEMDAS to Use

When you encounter a problem on the GRE that includes several different operations, such as addition, subtraction, multiplication, division, squaring, and so on, you must perform those operations in the following order to arrive at the correct answer:

1. **Parentheses:** Start with what's inside parentheses. If they're nested (meaning parentheses inside other parentheses), work them from the inside out.

2. **Exponents:** Any exponents are next.

3. **Multiplication or division:** Work multiplication and division next.

4. **Addition or subtraction:** Finally, add or subtract.

The best way to remember the order of operations is to use the phrase "Please Excuse My Dear Aunt Sally" (PEMDAS), which stands for Parentheses, Exponents, Multiplication, Division, Addition, and Subtraction. Use PEMDAS for the following problem.

$$10(3-5)^2$$

Start with what's inside the parentheses: $3-5=-2$. Then move on to the exponents: -2 squared equals 4. Finally, do the multiplication: $4 \times 10 = 40$. The correct answer is **40.**

The GRE tests your ability to approach these questions *analytically,* which means thinking outside the established methods. PEMDAS is a good rule, but blindly following any rule, including PEMDAS, can lead you into a trap. Instead, take a high-level look at any math question before trying to solve it.

Say you have the following problem:

$$\left(\frac{600}{5}\right)^0 =$$

You could begin with dividing 600 by 5 before raising it to the 0 power. But wait a second — anything to the 0 power equals **1.** By taking a high-level look at the question before trying to solve it, you save yourself the effort of working the parentheses first. (For more on exponents, flip to Chapter 9.)

Taking Advantage of the Distributive, Associative, and Commutative Properties

Adhering to PEMDAS (the order of operations) and working equations from left to right is a foolproof approach to solving equations, but it's not always the most efficient. You can often solve equations faster and without the use of a calculator by taking advantage of the three properties that let you reorder or regroup things: the distributive, associative, and commutative properties of multiplication and addition.

Distributive property

According to the *distributive property*, multiplication distributes over addition. So according to the distributive property, $3(20+22) = (3\times20)+(3\times22) = 60+66 = 126$. That's a little easier than adding $20+22$ first and then multiplying 3×42.

10
not
20

The distributive property also allows you to *factor* numbers; that is, to break them down into more manageable units. For example, you can factor $5\times1{,}232$ as $5(1{,}000+200+30+2) = 5{,}000+1{,}000+150+20 = 6{,}170$. Distributing also comes in handy when you encounter equations that contain variables, such as x and y. Given $4(x+y)$, you know it equals $4x+4y$, which may simplify the process of identifying the value of x or y or both.

Associative property

The *associative property* enables you to regroup values in an equation that involve multiplication or addition in accordance with the following two rules:

$$a+(b+c) = (a+b)+c$$

$$a(bc) = (ab)c$$

This property comes in handy especially when you're tackling an equation that includes multiplication. For example, instead of $(2\times9)\times6 = 18\times6$, which is a little challenging to calculate, you can regroup to get $2\times(9\times6) = 2\times54 = 108$.

Commutative property

The *commutative property* allows you to move values around when performing addition or multiplication. For example, you can rearrange an addition problem to pair up numbers whose ones digits add up to 10. Given $48+245+2$, you can add $48+2 = 50$ before adding 245, giving you $50+245 = 295$. That's easier than adding $48+245$ first.

The distributive, associative, and commutative properties specifically apply to addition and multiplication, but you can extend them to problems that include subtraction and division by

✔ **Treating subtraction as the addition of a negative number:** For example, in $48+756-47$, you can think of -47 as $+(-47)$ and then use the commutative property to rearrange:

$$48+(-47)+756=1+756=757$$

Why bother trying to add $48+756$ first and then subtract out 47 when, with some clever rearranging, the task becomes *that* simple?

✔ **Treating division as multiplication by the reciprocal:** For example, given the expression $35\times15\div7$, you can think of $\div7$ as $\times\frac{1}{7}$ (multiplying by the reciprocal of 7). You can then use the commutative property to rewrite the equation as

$$35\times\frac{1}{7}\times15=\frac{35}{7}\times15=5\times15=75$$

Measuring Up: Units of Measurement

In conversion questions, the GRE gives you the relationship between two units of measurement (*except* for units of time; for example, you won't be told that 60 seconds = 1 minute). If you're asked how many ounces are in 5 pounds, the GRE includes the relationship 1 pound = 16 ounces. To solve the problem, take the following steps:

1. **Set up the conversion equations as fractions to avoid mixing up the multiplying and dividing.**

$$\left(\frac{5\text{ lb}}{1}\right)\left(\frac{16\text{ oz}}{1\text{ lb}}\right)$$

2. **Cancel the common terms.**

   In this example, the *lb* units appear in the numerator and the denominator, so they cancel:

$$\left(\frac{5\text{ \sout{lb}}}{1}\right)\left(\frac{16\text{ oz}}{1\text{ \sout{lb}}}\right)$$

3. **Multiply the fractions.**

$$\left(\frac{80\text{ oz}}{1}\right)=80\text{ oz}$$

When dealing with area and volume, convert values to the unit that the answer needs to be in before performing your calculations. For example, if the question gives you the dimensions of a rectangle as 2 yards by 2 yards and asks for the answer in square feet, convert yards to feet *before* calculating the area. This way, you get the correct answer of 36 square feet (from 6 feet by 6 feet). If you calculate the area in square yards first, you end up with 4 square yards, and then have to convert that to square feet. You may be tempted to do so by multiplying 4 square yards by 3 feet/yard and end up with an incorrect answer of 12 square feet. (There are actually 9 square feet in a square yard.)

If 12 inches are in a foot, then how many square inches are in a square foot? If you say 12, you've fallen for the trap. Why? Because $12\times12=144$, which is the actual number of square inches in a square foot.

Here's how you may fall for that trap in an otherwise easy problem:

Quantity A	**_Quantity B_**
Number of square inches in 3 square feet	36

Ⓐ Quantity A is greater.

Ⓑ Quantity B is greater.

Ⓒ The two quantities are equal.

Ⓓ The relationship cannot be determined from the information given.

You may be tempted to think that the quantities are equal because there are 12 inches to a foot and $12 \times 3 = 36$. However, because a square foot has 144 square inches, and 144×3 is definitely greater than 36 (don't waste any time doing the math), the answer is Choice **(A)**.

Bonus: How many cubic inches are in a cubic foot? Twelve inches per side cubed is $12^3 = 12 \times 12 \times 12$, which equals 1,728 cubic inches. (For more on 3-D geometric shapes, turn to Chapter 10.)

Discovering the Point with Decimals

Working with decimals isn't overly difficult. All you have to do is remember a few key points:

- ✔ Line up the decimal points when adding or subtracting.
- ✔ Count the decimal places when multiplying.
- ✔ Move the decimal points of both numbers when dividing.

Though the GRE features an on-screen calculator, you really don't need it, even with decimal-based math problems. Figuring out how decimals work is easy. The following sections walk you through adding, subtracting, multiplying, and dividing decimals.

Reducing your reliance on the calculator is a sure way to boost your score. Not only can you work problems on scratch paper faster than with the calculator, but you also can make a typo on the calculator, which can lead to a wrong answer that you may not catch.

Adding and subtracting decimals

To add or subtract decimals accurately, first line up the decimal points. Then add or subtract as usual, placing the decimal point in the answer right below where it falls in the original numbers.

```
  4.16
+0.12
  4.28
```

Multiplying decimals

When multiplying decimals, you want to ensure that the number of decimal places in the answer is the same as the *total* number of decimal places in all the numbers you're multiplying. Multiply the numbers first, and then count the decimal places.

$$0.06 \times 0.03 = 0.0018$$

You know that 6×3 is 18. But the 0.06 and the 0.03 each has two decimal places, for a total of four. Therefore, the final answer also has four decimal places.

Don't forget to include the zeros at the end when counting the decimal places. After you have your answer, you can drop the end zeros.

$$0.04 \times 0.05 = 0.0020$$

You know that 4×5 is 20, so be sure to include the entire 20 (two and zero) when counting the decimal places. After you have the decimal set correctly, you can drop the right-side zero, giving you 0.002.

Dividing decimals

Before dividing decimals, turn the decimals into integers by moving the decimal points of both numbers to the right the same number of spaces, until the divisor is a whole number.

A tricky $0.032 \div 0.008$ becomes an easy $32 \div 8$ for a final answer of 4.

Facing Off with Fractions

You probably mastered fractions back in middle school. With some refreshing, you can master them again. The following sections point out how to add, subtract, multiply, and divide fractions and how to handle mixed numbers.

Adding or subtracting fractions

You can add and subtract fractions only if they have a *common denominator* (the same bottom part of the fraction). If your fractions don't have a common denominator, you can give them one and then add or subtract the *numerator* (the top part of the fraction).

$$\frac{2}{5} + \frac{3}{7} =$$

Here, 5 and 7 are different denominators, so you can't add these two fractions. However, make the denominators the same, and then you *can* add the fractions.

To change a denominator without changing the fraction's value, multiply the fraction's numerator and the denominator by the same number; you're not changing the fraction's value because you're essentially multiplying the fraction by 1. When the denominators are the same, you can add the fractions. The common denominator carries over to the answer, but the numerators add together (or subtract) to give you the final answer:

$$\frac{2}{5}+\frac{3}{7}=\frac{2(7)}{5(7)}+\frac{3(5)}{7(5)}=\frac{14}{35}+\frac{15}{35}=\frac{14+15}{35}=\frac{29}{35}$$

To find a common denominator, you can multiply all the denominators. Doing so, however, may not give you the lowest common denominator. Check out this example:

$$\frac{1}{6}-\frac{1}{15}=$$

To find a common denominator for the two fractions, you can multiply 15×6, but that's not the *lowest* common denominator, and that would create a lot of extra work. Instead, count by 15s, because 15 is the larger of the two numbers.

Check each multiple of 15 for divisibility by 6. Does 15 work? No, 6 doesn't go into 15. How about 30? Yes, both 15 and 6 go into 30. There you have it: The lowest common denominator is 30. Then you have to multiply numerator and denominator of each fraction by the number that makes the fraction's bottom number equal to the lowest common denominator; multiply the first fraction by 5 over 5 and the second fraction by 2 over 2; then subtract and simplify to arrive at the answer:

$$\frac{1}{6}-\frac{1}{15}=\frac{1(5)}{6(5)}-\frac{1(2)}{15(2)}=\frac{5}{30}-\frac{2}{30}=\frac{3}{30}=\frac{1}{10}$$

Multiplying fractions

To multiply fractions, just go straight across, multiplying the numerators together and the denominators together:

$$\frac{2}{5}\times\frac{3}{7}=\frac{2\times3}{5\times7}=\frac{6}{35}$$

Always check whether you can cancel out common factors between a numerator and a denominator before you begin multiplying. This way, you avoid dealing with big, awkward numbers and having to reduce fractions at the end. Canceling before multiplying makes the numbers smaller and easier to work with.

For example, in the following fractions, the 6 and the 9 are each divisible by 3. You can cancel those 3s from the numerator and denominator before multiplying the fractions.

$$\frac{2\cancel{6}}{5}\times\frac{4}{\cancel{9}_3}=\frac{2}{5}\times\frac{4}{3}=\frac{8}{15}$$

In this next example, the 4 and the 8 reduce (each is divisible by 4), and the 15 and the 5 reduce (both are divisible by 5), simplifying the problem:

$$\frac{^1\cancel{4}}{\cancel{15}_3}\times\frac{^1\cancel{5}}{\cancel{8}_2}=\frac{1}{3}\times\frac{1}{2}=\frac{1}{6}$$

Dividing fractions

To divide two fractions, you *invert* the second fraction (turn it upside down) and then multiply the two fractions:

$$\frac{1}{3} \div \frac{2}{5} = \frac{1}{3} \times \frac{5}{2} = \frac{5}{6}$$

Mixed numbers

A *mixed number* is a whole number with a fraction, such as $2\frac{1}{3}$, $4\frac{2}{5}$, or $9\frac{1}{2}$. Before you can work with a mixed number (and then add, subtract, multiply, or divide by it), you first have to get it into fraction form. To do so, multiply the denominator (bottom number) by the whole number and add that to the numerator (top number). Then put the sum over the denominator.

$$2\frac{1}{3} = \frac{(3 \times 2) + 1}{3} = \frac{7}{3}$$

$$4\frac{2}{5} = \frac{(5 \times 4) + 2}{5} = \frac{22}{5}$$

$$9\frac{1}{2} = \frac{(2 \times 9) + 1}{2} = \frac{19}{2}$$

This results in an *improper fraction,* where the numerator is larger than the denominator. Converting back an improper fraction to a mixed number is less common, but to do so, divide the numerator by the denominator, write down the whole number, and then place the remainder over the denominator.

For example, to convert the improper fraction $\frac{22}{7}$ to a mixed number, divide the 7 into 22, and you get 3 with a remainder of 1. The 7 stays as the denominator, and the resulting mixed number is $3\frac{1}{7}$.

Manipulating Percentages

The GRE test-writers will probably throw a couple percentage-related questions at you. They're pretty easy if you know how to work them. This section shows you how to convert the percentages into easier forms to work with and how to use formulas to find the answers to the GRE questions.

Converting between percentages and decimals or fractions

When the GRE gives you a percentage-based math question, you don't have to work it as such. Converting the percentage to a decimal or fraction can make the question much easier to answer. You may need to convert back to a percentage to put the answer in the right form. Just do the following:

✔ **To convert a percentage to a decimal:** Move the decimal point two places to the left and drop the % sign.

$$35\% = 0.35 \qquad 6\% = 0.06 \qquad 50\% = 0.5 \qquad 3.33\% = 0.0333$$

✔ **To convert a decimal to a percentage:** Move the decimal point two places to the right and add the % sign.

$$0.32 = 32\% \qquad 0.185 = 18.5\% \qquad 0.05 = 5\%$$

✔ **To convert a percentage to a fraction:** Place the number over 100, drop the % sign, and reduce if possible.

$$50\% = \frac{50}{100} = \frac{1}{2} \qquad 125\% = \frac{125}{100} = \frac{5}{4} \qquad 4\% = \frac{4}{100} = \frac{1}{25}$$

✔ **To convert a fraction to a percentage:** Set the fraction equal to x over 100 and cross-multiply to find x. The x is your percentage. For example, set $\frac{27}{50}$ up as

$$\frac{27}{50} = \frac{x}{100}$$

Cross-multiply to solve for x. To *cross-multiply,* multiply the numerator of the first fraction by the denominator of the second, and set that equal to the product of the denominator of the second fraction and the numerator of the first:

$$\frac{27}{50} = \frac{x}{100}$$
$$50x = 2{,}700$$
$$5x = 270$$
$$x = 54$$

Finding the percent of change

A question may ask for a percent of change from an original amount. To find this, use the following formula:

$$\text{Percent of change} = \frac{\text{Amount of change}}{\text{Original amount}}$$

Finding the percent of change requires a few simple steps:

1. **Find the amount (number) that the item increased or decreased — that is, the amount of change.**

   For example, if a baseball team won 25 games last year and 30 games this year, the amount of change is 5, because the baseball team won five more games this year than last. If a salesperson earned $10,000 last year and $8,000 this year, the amount of change is $2,000.

   Keep in mind that the focus here is on the *amount* of change, not whether the value has increased or decreased. The amount of change is still $2,000 (not –$2,000), regardless of whether the salesperson earned more or less than last year.

2. **Place the amount of change over the original amount.**

   If the team won 25 games last year and 30 games this year, the original amount is 25. If the salesperson earned $10,000 last year and $8,000 this year, the original amount is $10,000.

3. Divide and write the answer as a percentage.

For the baseball team, $\frac{5}{25} = \frac{1}{5} = 20\%$. You divide 1 by 5 to get 0.20 and move the decimal point two places to the right and add the % sign to make it a percentage.

For the **hapless** (meaning unfortunate — think the opposite of *happy*) salesman, $\frac{2,000}{10,000} = \frac{20}{100} = 20\%$. Again, you divide 20 by 100 to get 0.20 and move the decimal point two places to the right and add the % sign to make it a percentage.

Last season, Coach Jamieson's baseball team won 50 games. This season, the team won 30 games. What was the percent decrease?

Ⓐ 10

Ⓑ 20

Ⓒ 30

Ⓓ 40

Ⓔ 50

The number of games that Coach Jamieson's team won decreased by 20 (from 50 to 30). Place the 20 over the original amount of 50 for a decrease of 40%. The correct answer is Choice **(D)**.

Carissa has three quarters. Her father gives her three more. Carissa's wealth has increased by what percent?

Ⓐ 50

Ⓑ 100

Ⓒ 200

Ⓓ 300

Ⓔ 500

Did you fall for the trap answer, Choice (C)? Carissa's wealth has doubled, to be sure, but the percent increase is only 100%. You can prove that with the percent of change formula. The number increase is 0.75 (she has three more quarters, or 75 cents), and her original whole was 0.75. So if you follow the formula, you get $\frac{75}{75} = 100\%$. The right answer is Choice **(B)**.

When you double something, you increase it by 100%. When you triple something, you increase it by 200%. You're looking for the percent of *change,* not the *result.* For example, if you turned $3 into $9, the result is 300%, but the increase — the change — is 200%.

Making Ratios More Rational

A *ratio* is a relationship between two similar numbers or quantities. A ratio is written as either dogs:cats or $\frac{dogs}{cats}$. For example,

The ratio *of* yachts *to* sailboats = yachts:sailboats

The ratio *of* umbrellas *to* people = $\frac{umbrellas}{people}$

After you know the tricks, ratios are some of the easiest problems to answer quickly. The following sections look at two ways to solve simple ratios and the best way to handle combined ratios.

Considering the total number of items

Because ratios compare two amounts, the *total* number of items is a multiple of the sum of the numbers in the ratio. In other words, if the ratio is 3 dogs for every 2 cats, then the total number of animals can't be 7 — it has to be 5, 10, 15, or any multiple of 5, which comes from 3 dogs to 2 cats. The number of dogs can't be 4; it has to be a multiple of 3. Similarly, the number of cats has to be a multiple of 2.

You may encounter a problem like this on the GRE:

At a game, the ratio of your team's fans to the other team's fans is 4:5. Which of the following can be the total number of fans at the game?

Ⓐ 8

Ⓑ 12

Ⓒ 16

Ⓓ 25

Ⓔ 54

To solve this ratio problem, you first add the numbers in the ratio: 4 + 5 = 9. The total number of fans must be a multiple of 9 (9, 18, 27, 36, and so on). Can the total, for example, be 54? Yes, because 9 goes evenly into 54. Can it be 12? No, because 9 doesn't go evenly into 12. The correct answer is Choice **(E)**.

While creating his special dish, Thomas uses 7 teaspoons of sriracha for every 5 teaspoons of soy sauce. Which of the following could be the total number of teaspoons of sriracha and soy sauce in his special dish?

Ⓐ 75

Ⓑ 57

Ⓒ 48

Ⓓ 35

Ⓔ 30

Add the numbers in the ratio: 7 + 5 = 12. The total must be a multiple of 12 (meaning it must be evenly divisible by 12). Only Choice (C), 48, is evenly divisible by 12. Choices (A), 75, and (B), 57, try to trick you by using the numbers 7 and 5 from the ratio. Choice (D) is a trap with the product of 7 and 5. The correct answer is Choice **(C)**.

Notice how the questions ask which answers *could be* the possible totals (any multiple of the sums). They're not asking "which of the following *is* the total," in which case you'd need more information to answer the question.

Quantity A	**Quantity B**
Ratio of CDs to tapes = 2:9	
Total of CDs and tapes	11

Ⓐ Quantity A is greater.

Ⓑ Quantity B is greater.

Ⓒ The two quantities are equal.

Ⓓ The relationship cannot be determined from the information given.

You know the total must be a multiple of 11, but it could be many things: 11, 22, 33, 44, 55, and so on. This type of trap has destroyed many an overly confident test-taker through the years. Quantity A may be equal to or greater than Quantity B; you don't have enough information to make that determination. The correct answer is Choice **(D)**.

Finding the amount of a specific term

When you're given a ratio and a total and are asked to find the amount of a specific term, one way to solve the ratio is to do the following:

1. **Add the numbers in the ratio.**

   The total number of items is a multiple of this sum.

2. **Divide the total number of items by that sum.**

3. **Multiply the result from Step 2 by each term in the ratio.**

4. **Add the answers to double-check that they add up to the total.**

   Be sure to do this step to check your work.

Explaining these steps takes longer than working them. With a little practice, the technique becomes second nature. Consider this example:

To congratulate his team, which had just won the last game for an undefeated season, the ecstatic coach took his team to the local pizza joint, where each player ordered either a deep dish pizza or a calzone. If there were 3 deep dishes for every 4 calzones, and if every member of the 28-man squad ordered either one or the other, how many deep dishes were there?

There are 3 deep dishes for every 4 calzones, so add the numbers in the ratio: $3 + 4 = 7$. Then divide the total number of players by that sum: $\frac{28}{7} = 4$. Now multiply that number by each term in the ratio: $3 \times 4 = 12$ deep dishes; $4 \times 4 = 16$ calzones. The question asks for the number of deep dishes, so the correct answer is **12**. Finally, add the answers to make sure they add up to 28: $12 + 16 = 28$.

Maintaining the ratio

If the GRE math problem features an existing ratio and you have to change the number of items while maintaining the ratio, you can easily calculate the number of items you need by setting the two ratios equal to each other. Make the existing ratio (as a fraction) equal the new items (also as a fraction), and cross-multiply to find the missing value.

Your college has to maintain its current ratio of 3 graduate assistants for every 40 students. If 240 new students are expected this fall, how many new graduate assistants does the school need to hire to maintain the ratio?

1. **Set up the existing ratio as a fraction.**

   $$\frac{\text{Assistants}}{\text{Students}} = \frac{3}{40}$$

2. **Set up the new additions as a fraction, with x as the unknown value.**

   $$\frac{\text{Needed Assistants}}{\text{New Students}} = \frac{x}{240}$$

3. **Set the fractions equal to each other.**

   $$\frac{3}{40} = \frac{x}{240}$$

4. **Solve for x.**

Cross-multiply, multiplying the numerator of each fraction by the denominator of the other:

$$40x = 720$$
$$4x = 72$$
$$x = 18$$

Thus, **18** new graduate assistants are needed to maintain the ratio.

Combining two or more ratios

Sometimes the GRE provides two different ratios, with one common term in each ratio. You can use the common item to combine the ratios for a single three-part ratio.

Combining ratios is a little like adding fractions. When adding fractions, you find the lowest common denominator. Ratios don't have numerators or denominators, but they always have something in common. The following example shows you how to combine ratios.

Sam's jazz shop has 6 saxophones for every 5 drum kits and 2 drum kits for every 3 trombones. What's the ratio of saxophones to trombones?

1. **Set up the ratios as A:B.**

   Place the item that the ratios have in common (drum kits) in a column.

Saxes	Drums	Trombones
6 :	5	
	2 :	3

2. **Find a common multiple for the item that these ratios have in common.**

   In this instance, both ratios include drum kits. The least common multiple of 5 and 2 (the numbers of drum kits) is 10.

3. **Multiply each term in the ratios so the quantity of the item in common equals the common multiple (from Step 2).**

   Now, if you were adding these as fractions, you'd write the drums as the denominators, and your work would start out like this:

   $$\frac{6}{5} + \frac{3}{2} = \frac{6(2)}{5(2)} + \frac{3(5)}{2(5)} = \frac{12}{10} + \frac{15}{10}$$

   Of course, you aren't adding fractions, but you treat the ratios the same way: Multiply both terms of each ratio by the same number, as though you're getting a common denominator. Here, you want the number of drum kits to equal 10. Multiply both terms in the first ratio by 2, and multiply both terms in the second ratio by 5:

Saxes	Drums	Trombones
6(2) :	5(2)	
	2(5) :	3(5)

Saxes	Drums	Trombones
12 :	10	
	10 :	15

4. Write out a combined ratio.

Saxes		Drums		Trombones
12	:	10		
		10	:	15
12	:	10	:	15

The combined ratio of saxophones to drum kits to trombones is 12:10:15. To answer the question, give only the ratio of saxophones to trombones, which is 12:15, or **4:5**.

Working the Numbers: Arithmetic Practice Problems

Now it's your turn. Each of these practice questions is based on at least one concept discussed in this chapter. If you get stuck, flip back a few pages to review the relevant instructions. These concepts are central to GRE math, so being able to solve and understand these practice problems is important for mastering the other five math chapters.

1. After a rough hockey game, Bernie checks his uniform and finds 3 smudges for every 5 tears. Which of the following can be the total number of smudges and tears on Bernie's uniform?

    (A) 53

    (B) 45

    (C) 35

    (D) 33

    (E) 32

    Add the numbers in the ratio: $3+5=8$. The total must be a multiple of 8 (or, looking at it another way, the total must be evenly divisible by 8). Only Choice (E) is a multiple of 8 ($8 \times 4 = 32$). The correct answer is Choice **(E).**

2. Banker's Credit Union has 7 call-center reps on hand for every 200 customers. With an aggressive marketing campaign, the bank just signed up an additional 1,400 customers. How many new reps should the bank hire in order to maintain this ratio?

    (A) 14

    (B) 20

    (C) 35

    (D) 49

    (E) 50

    Set up the equation:

    $$\frac{\text{Reps}}{\text{Customers}} = \frac{7}{200} = \frac{x}{1,400}$$

    Cross-multiply, and you find that $x = 49$. The correct answer is Choice **(D).**

3. A sports shop has 3 jerseys for every 2 helmets and 6 kneepads for every 5 jerseys. What's the ratio of helmets to kneepads?

    Ⓐ 1:3

    Ⓑ 4:9

    Ⓒ 5:9

    Ⓓ 2:3

    Ⓔ 7:9

Set up the ratios:

Jerseys	Helmets	Kneepads
3	2	
5	:	6

Find a common multiple of jerseys. A common multiple of 3 and 5 is 15, so multiply each term of the first ratio by 5 and each term of the second by 3:

Jerseys	Helmets	Kneepads
15 :	10	
15	:	18

Write these out as a combined ratio:

Jerseys	Helmets	Kneepads
15 :	10	
15	:	18
15 :	10 :	18

The ratio of helmets to kneepads is 10:18, or 5:9, so the correct answer is Choice **(C)**.

Chapter 9

Algebra: Finding What *X* Really Means

- -

In This Chapter

▶ Working with bases and exponents

▶ Dealing with *x*, *y*, and other variables

▶ Solving for *x* and algebraic expressions

▶ Digging deep into roots and radicals

▶ Plotting points, lines, and slopes with coordinate geometry

▶ Manipulating functions and sequences

- -

Algebra is a branch of mathematics that uses numbers, letters, and operations to represent the concepts and rules of mathematics. Through an understanding of these concepts and rules, you're often able to use what you know (the information a question provides) to determine what you don't know, such as the value of *x*. You've probably already solved lots of algebra questions in junior high and high school and perhaps even in your college courses. You just need a refresher to get your head back in the game.

This chapter reveals everything you need to know about algebra to be fully prepared for the test. It starts slowly with bases, exponents, and variables such as *x* and *y* and gradually moves on to complicated algebraic concepts. Although you're free to skip around, you may want to start at the very beginning if you're rusty with these concepts.

Tapping the Powers of Bases and Exponents

Many GRE math questions require you to know how to work with bases and exponents. When you multiply a number repeatedly by itself, you raise that number to a certain power; for example, 3 to the power of 4, or 3^4, is $3 \times 3 \times 3 \times 3 = 81$. In this example, 3 is the base, and 4 is the exponent. The *exponent* simply tells you how many times to multiply the *base* (number) by itself. Here are a few more examples:

$$10^2 = 10 \times 10 = 100$$

$$5^3 = 5 \times 5 \times 5 = 125$$

$$x^4 = x \cdot x \cdot x \cdot x$$

Remember the following rules when working with bases and exponents:

▶ **Any number to the zero power always equals 1.**

$$x^0 = 1 \qquad 5^0 = 1 \qquad 129^0 = 1$$

✔ Any number to a negative exponent is the reciprocal of that number to its positive exponent.

$$y^{-4} = \frac{1}{y^4} \qquad 6^{-3} = \frac{1}{6^3} \qquad 325^{-1} = \frac{1}{325}$$

A *number* with a negative exponent isn't negative. When you flip it, you get the reciprocal, and the negative goes away. For example,

$$5^{-3} = \frac{1}{5^3} = \frac{1}{125}$$

✔ When you raise 10 to a power, you get 1 followed by the number of zeros equal to that power.

$$10^2 = 100 \qquad \text{(two zeros)}$$

$$10^3 = 1,000 \qquad \text{(three zeros)}$$

$$10^4 = 10,000 \qquad \text{(four zeros)}$$

Because $10^4 = 10,000$, 5×10^4 is $5 \times 10,000$, which equals 50,000.

✔ To multiply like bases, add their exponents.

$$\left(x^3\right)\left(x^2\right) = x^{(3+2)} = x^5$$

$$5^3 \times 5^4 = 5^{(3+4)} = 5^7$$

$$150^5 \times 150^7 = 150^{(5+7)} = 150^{12}$$

You can't multiply *different* bases. For example, $x^2 \cdot y^3$ stays $x^2 \cdot y^3$, and $14^3 \times 15^5$ stays $14^3 \times 15^5$.

✔ To divide like bases, subtract the exponents.

$$x^5 \div x^3 = x^{(5-3)} = x^2$$

$$5^8 \div 5^4 = 5^{(8-4)} = 5^4$$

$$150^4 \div 150^0 = 150^{(4-0)} = 150^4$$

Did you look at the second example, $5^8 \div 5^4$, and think the answer is 5^2? Falling into the trap of dividing rather than subtracting can happen, especially when you see numbers that just beg to be divided, such as 8 and 4. A common mistake, but don't let it get you.

✔ Multiply the exponents of a base inside and outside of parentheses.

$$\left(x^2\right)^3 = x^{(2 \times 3)} = x^6$$

$$\left(5^3\right)^3 = 5^{(3 \times 3)} = 5^9$$

$$\left(175^0\right)^3 = 175^{(0 \times 3)} = 175^0 = 1$$

✔ **To add or subtract like bases with like powers, add or subtract the numerical coefficients of the bases.** The *numerical coefficient* is the number to the left of the base; for example, in $31x^3$, 31 is the numerical coefficient.

$$37x^3 + 10x^3 = (37+10)x^3 = 47x^3$$

$$15y^2 - 10y^2 = (15-10)y^2 = 5y^2$$

You can't add or subtract the numerical coefficients when the bases are different. For example, $16x^2 - 4y^2$ stays the same and does *not* become $12x^2$, $12y^2$, or $12(xy)^2$. Furthermore, you can't add or subtract like bases with *different* exponents. For example, $14x^3 - 9x^2$ isn't equal to $5x^3$, $5x^2$, or $5x$. It stays $14x^3 - 9x^2$. The bases *and* exponents must be the same for you to add or subtract the terms.

To make sure you're comfortable with the variations, try these Quantitative Comparison (QC) questions with bases and exponents. (In QC questions, you compare the contents in two columns. I explain all about QC questions in Chapter 13.)

For all QC questions on the GRE, you choose from the following answer choices:

Ⓐ Quantity A is greater.

Ⓑ Quantity B is greater.

Ⓒ The two quantities are equal.

Ⓓ The relationship cannot be determined from the information given.

Quantity A	*Quantity B*
x^3	$\dfrac{x^7}{x^4}$

Remember that when you divide, you subtract the exponents, so $x^{(7-4)} = x^3$, no matter what the value of *x* is. *Correct answer:* Choice **(C)**.

Quantity A	*Quantity B*
$(x^3)^4$	x^{12}

Because you multiply exponents together when you take an exponent to a higher power, the two quantities are the same, no matter what *x* is: $(x^3)^4 = x^{(3\times4)} = x^{12}$. *Correct answer:* Choice **(C)**.

Quantity A	*Quantity B*
$(x^3)^4$	12

Because you don't know the value of *x*, you can't tell which quantity is greater. You may think that anything to the 12th power is a large number, making Choice (A) the correct answer, but you need to know more about *x*. If *x* equals 2, then you'd be right. If *x* equals $\frac{1}{2}$, you'd be wrong. This trap is really easy to fall for. See Chapter 13 for info on picking values for *x* to try different possibilities. *Correct answer:* Choice **(D)**.

Quantity A	**Quantity B**
$16x^4 - 4x^3$	$12x$

Because you don't know what x is, as in the preceding question, try different values for x to see which quantity is greater. If you selected Choice (C), you fell for the trap. *Correct answer:* Choice **(D)**.

Quantity A	**Quantity B**
$10x^3 - 2y^3$	$8xy$

Because you don't know what x or y is, you can't tell which quantity is greater. *Correct answer:* Choice **(D)**.

Working with Math Operators and Functions

You may encounter questions based on math operators and functions on the GRE. The approach is simple: substitute for the variable. The math itself is always easy. The trick is knowing how to set up the equation. This section explains how to set up the equations to do the math and arrive at the answer.

Substituting for the variable in the math operator

You see a problem with a strange symbol. It may be a triangle, a star, or a circle with a dot, as in the following example. You've never seen it before, and you're not sure what it means. It's probably a math operator, such as +, −, ×, or ÷, but it's a new one that the GRE uses just for this one math question. Don't worry — the GRE always tells you what the symbol means.

The symbol is included in a short explanation that looks something like this:

$$a \odot b \odot c = \frac{(a+b)}{(b+c)}$$

A question always follows the explanation, like this:

$$3 \odot 4 \odot 5 =$$

Solve this problem by using the preceding explanation and following these steps:

1. **Replace the variables in the explanation with the numbers provided in the question.**

   For this problem, substitute 3, 4, and 5 for a, b, and c, respectively.

   $$3 \odot 4 \odot 5 = \frac{(3+4)}{(4+5)}$$

2. **Simplify the fraction to get the answer.**

   $$\frac{3+4}{4+5} = \frac{7}{9}$$

The GRE keeps things interesting with variations like this:

If $[[x]] = \dfrac{2x}{x+2}$, then $[[-4]] =$

To solve, substitute –4 for *x*:

$$[[-4]] = \frac{2(-4)}{-4+2}$$

Then simplify the fraction for your answer:

$$\frac{2(-4)}{-4+2} = \frac{-8}{-2} = 4$$

Substituting for the variable in the function

You can spot a function question by the distinctive $f(x)$. The letters aren't always f and x (for example, $g(h)$ is common), but the setup is always the same. You may see a problem like this:

$f(x) = (2x)^3$. Solve for $f(2)$.

To solve, substitute the number for the *x* (or whichever letter is in the parentheses). In other words, just plug in the 2 where you see an *x* in the explanation:

$$f(2) = (2 \times 2)^3 = 4^3 = 64$$

Try another one:

$f(x) = x + x^2 + x^3$. Solve for $f(10)$.

Just plug the 10 in for the *x*:

$$f(10) = 10 + 10^2 + 10^3 = 10 + 100 + 1{,}000 = 1{,}110$$

Mastering the Fundamentals of Algebra

To correctly answer algebra questions on the GRE, you must be able to

- ✔ Solve for *x* in an equation.
- ✔ Use the FOIL method to multiply binomials. (Refer to the later section "Multiplying with the FOIL method" for details.)
- ✔ Factor a quadratic equation to its original form of two sets of parentheses and use that factored form to solve for *x*.

The following sections review the basics of algebra that you need for the GRE.

Solving for x

To solve for *x*, follow these steps:

1. Isolate the variable terms.

In other words, get all the *x*'s on one side and all the numbers on the other side.

2. **Add or subtract all the *x* terms on one side; add or subtract all the non-*x* terms on the other side.**

3. **Divide both sides of the equation by the number in front of the *x*.**

Now try it with this equation:

$$3x + 7 = 9x - 5$$

1. **Isolate the variable terms.**

    Move the $3x$ to the right side of the equation, changing the sign to make it $-3x$. Move the -5 to the left, changing the sign to make it $+5$. You now have

    $$7 + 5 = 9x - 3x$$

Forgetting to change the sign is one of the most common, simple mistakes that people make. The test-makers realize this and like to include trap answers. To avoid this common mistake, think of subtracting the same amount from both sides of the equation.

2. **Add or subtract the *x*'s on one side; add or subtract the non-*x*'s on the other side.**

    $$7 + 5 = 9x - 3x$$
    $$12 = 6x$$

3. **Divide both sides by the number next to the *x*.**

    $$\frac{12}{6} = \frac{6x}{6}$$
    $$x = 2$$

To check your answer, plug the 2 back into the original equation to make sure it works:

$$3(2) + 7 = 9(2) - 5$$
$$6 + 7 = 18 - 5$$
$$13 = 13$$

You could also plug in the answer choices until one works. Though usually more time-consuming, this method serves as a last-resort plan if you can't solve for *x* using algebra. Try each answer choice until you find the one that works. Sticking with the example of $3x + 7 = 9x - 5$, suppose these are your answer choices:

Ⓐ 5

Ⓑ $3\frac{1}{2}$

Ⓒ 2

Ⓓ 0

Ⓔ –2

Keep life simple by starting with answer choices that are easy to figure in your head. In this case, the easiest answer choice is 0, because that would make $3x = 0$ and $9x = 0$, making $7 = -5$; scratch that one off the list of options. The choices 2, –2, and 5 are also easy to plug in. If none of the easy answers works, then you can go back and try $3\frac{1}{2}$. *Correct answer:* Choice **(C)**.

Multiplying with the FOIL method

When multiplying any number by a *binomial* (a value expressed as the sum or difference of two numbers), you use the *distributive property,* which tells you to multiply all the values inside the parentheses by the multiplier to the left of the parentheses. For example:

$$9(3x + 2y) = 9(3x) + 9(2y) = 27x + 18y$$

When multiplying two binomials, such as $(a + b)(a - b)$, you also use the distributive property (see Chapter 8). Basically, you multiply everything in one set of parentheses by everything in the other set of parentheses and then add up all the results. This is also known as the FOIL method, which stands for *First, Outer, Inner, Last.* With the equation $(a + b)(a - b)$, you do the following:

1. **Multiply the *First* variables:** $a \times a = a^2$.

2. **Multiply the *Outer* variables:** $a \times (-b) = -ab$.

3. **Multiply the *Inner* variables:** $b \times a = ba$ (which is the same as ab).

4. **Multiply the *Last* variables:** $b \times (-b) = -b^2$.

5. **Combine like terms:** $a^2 - ab + ab - b^2 = a^2 - b^2$. (Here, the $-ab$ and $+ab$ cancel each other out.)

Like terms are two or more terms with the same variable(s) and exponent. For example, $3x^3$ and $2x^3$ are like terms, and you may combine them as follows: $3x^3 + 2x^3 = 5x^3$. You can't, however, combine $3x^3$ and $3y^3$ or $3x^3$ and $3x^5$, because in the first case, the variables differ, and in the second case, the exponents differ.

When multiplying, the order doesn't matter. This means that $5 \times 3 = 3 \times 5$ and $ab = ba$.

Try another one: $(3a + b)(a - 2b)$

1. **Multiply the *First* terms:** $3a \times a = 3a^2$.

2. **Multiply the *Outer* terms:** $3a \times (-2b) = -6ab$.

3. **Multiply the *Inner* terms:** $b \times a = ba$ (which is the same as ab).

4. **Multiply the *Last* terms:** $b \times (-2b) = -2b^2$.

5. **Combine like terms for the final answer:** $-6ab + ab = -5ab$, so $3a^2 - 5ab - 2b^2$.

Memorize the following three FOIL equations so you don't have to bother working them out every time. Knowing these equations can save you time and help you avoid careless mistakes on the actual exam.

✔ $(a + b)^2 = a^2 + 2ab + b^2$

You can prove this equation using FOIL: $(a + b)(a + b)$.

a. **Multiply the *First* terms:** $a \times a = a^2$.

b. **Multiply the *Outer* terms:** $a \times b = ab$.

c. **Multiply the *Inner* terms:** $b \times a = ba$ (which is the same as ab).

d. **Multiply the *Last* terms:** $b \times b = b^2$.

e. **Combine like terms for the final answer:** $ab + ab = 2ab$, so $a^2 + 2ab + b^2$.

✔ $(a-b)^2 = a^2 - 2ab + b^2$

You can also prove this equation using FOIL: $(a-b)(a-b)$.

   a. **Multiply the *First* terms:** $a \times a = a^2$.

   b. **Multiply the *Outer* terms:** $a \times (-b) = -ab$.

   c. **Multiply the *Inner* terms:** $(-b) \times a = -ba$ (which is the same as $-ab$).

   d. **Multiply the *Last* terms:** $(-b) \times (-b) = b^2$.

   e. **Combine like terms for the final answer:** $-ab + -ab = -2ab$, so $a^2 - 2ab + b^2$.

Be careful to note that the b^2 at the end is *positive,* not negative, because multiplying a negative times a negative produces a positive.

✔ $(a-b)(a+b) = a^2 - b^2$

You can also prove this equation with FOIL: $(a-b)(a+b)$.

   a. **Multiply the *First* terms:** $a \times a = a^2$.

   b. **Multiply the *Outer* terms:** $a \times b = ab$.

   c. **Multiply the *Inner* terms:** $(-b) \times a = -ba$ (which is the same as $-ab$).

   d. **Multiply the *Last* terms:** $(-b) \times b = -b^2$.

   e. **Combine like terms for the final answer:** $ab - ab = 0$, so $a^2 - b^2$.

Factoring and the "X Method"

As often as you FOIL terms on the GRE, you also *factor* them, which is the opposite of FOILing. Factoring takes an algebraic expression from its final form back to its original form of two binomials. You perform this operation when an equation contains x^2 to find the two possible values of x.

Given $x^2 - 4x - 12 = 0$, what are the two possible values of x? Work this question one step at a time:

   1. **Draw two sets of parentheses.**

      $(\quad)(\quad) = 0$

   2. **Fill in the *First* terms.**

      To get x^2, the *first* terms have to be x and x.

      $(x\quad)(x\quad) = 0$

   3. **Fill in the *Last* terms.**

      You need two numbers that equal -12 when multiplied together. To get $+12$, the possibilities are 3×4, 2×6, and 1×12. Of course, one of these terms is negative, because the 12 is negative. This means that there are six possibilities: $(-3) \times 4$, $3 \times (-4)$, $(-2) \times 6$, $2 \times (-6)$, $(-1) \times 12$, and $1 \times (-12)$. Because you aren't sure which one to choose yet, go on to the next step.

   4. **Look at the *Inner* terms.**

      You have to add two numbers to get -4. What two numbers add up to -4 and multiply to -12? You can answer this question through trial-and-error in the equation, which on the GRE is effective, because on the exam these equations are simple.

      You can also use the "X method," which is sort of a guided trial-and-error process. Start by placing the -12 and -4 on the top and bottom of the X, respectively.

Now, use the sides of the X for your trial and error.

–3 times 4 equals –12, but –3 *plus* 4 does not equal –4. Try different numbers:

–6 times 2 equals –12, and –6 plus 2 equals –4. Looks like you found the numbers! Now you can complete the equation:

$$(x-6)(x+2)=0$$

Whether you place –6 first or 2 first doesn't matter. These expressions are multiplied, so they can be in either order.

You still need to solve for *x*. Anything times 0 equals 0, so $(x-6)(0)=0$. For this to be true, $(x+2)$ would have to equal 0, meaning $x=-2$. That's one possibility. On the other hand, $(0)(x+2)=0$ could be true, meaning $(x-6)=0$; thus, $x=6$. In other words, given $(x-6)(x+2)=0$, *x* equals either 6 or –2. Note that *x* doesn't equal *both* 6 and –2; it equals one *or* the other, and you don't know which one. That's why the question is phrased, "What are the two *possible* values for *x*?"

The "X method" becomes more complicated when a number is in front of the x^2, as in $6x^2-x-2=0$, but that almost never happens on the GRE, so there's no need to cover it here.

Dealing with Square Roots and Radicals

You're likely to see math problems on the GRE that include square roots or radicals. A *square root* is a number that's multiplied by itself for a result; for example, 3 is the square root of 9 ($3\times3=9$). A *radical* is another way of expressing a square root; for example, the square root of 9 may be represented as $\sqrt{9}$. Though higher-level roots exist in math, the *square* root is the only root you see on the GRE.

If you multiply a negative number by itself, you always get a positive answer. Therefore, you won't see a square root of a negative number on the GRE.

The following sections point out the math problems you may encounter on the exam related to roots and radicals. But first, you need to know how to simplify roots and radicals.

Simplifying square roots and radicals

When possible, simplify radicals to get rid of them. *Simplifying* basically means reducing the radical to its most manageable form, ideally getting rid of the radical altogether. To simplify a radical, you generally factor what's inside the radical and then pull out any squared factors. Here are a few examples where simplification removes the radical completely:

$$\sqrt{4} = \sqrt{2 \times 2} = 2$$

$$\sqrt{9} = \sqrt{3 \times 3} = 3$$

$$\sqrt{16} = \sqrt{4 \times 4} = 4$$

$$\sqrt{25} = \sqrt{5 \times 5} = 5$$

In some cases, removing the radical doesn't happen quite so neatly, but you can still reduce it to make the number easier to work with. In problems where you can't reduce the radical to a whole number, the GRE doesn't expect you to, and the correct answer choice will typically include a radical. Here's an example of a radical that you can't reduce to an integer but you can simplify:

$$\sqrt{300} = \sqrt{100 \times 3}$$
$$= \sqrt{100} \times \sqrt{3}$$
$$= \sqrt{10 \times 10} \times \sqrt{3}$$
$$= 10 \times \sqrt{3}$$
$$= 10\sqrt{3}$$

In this example, the square root of 100 is 10, so the 10 comes out of the radical. The 3, however, stays inside the radical, and the two numbers (10 and $\sqrt{3}$) are multiplied for a result of $10\sqrt{3}$.

If you work a problem and end up with a radical such as $3\sqrt{5}$, look at the answer choices. Usually, $3\sqrt{5}$ will be waiting in the list, and you can leave your answer at that.

However, the question may ask what the number is "approximately equal to" or "closest to," and in that case, you have to estimate the radical, as explained next.

Estimating the radical

When asked to estimate $\sqrt{11}$, consider that it falls between $\sqrt{9}$ and $\sqrt{16}$. Because $\sqrt{9} = 3$ and $\sqrt{16} = 4$, $\sqrt{11}$ is between these and roughly 3.5. Knowing that the answer is between 3 and 4 is good enough to answer the GRE question. You never have to estimate the value more precisely than that.

Memorize $\sqrt{2} \approx 1.41$. Don't worry about memorizing any of the other radicals, but knowing this one can get you out of a pinch.

Adding and subtracting radicals

To add and subtract radicals, adhere to the following two rules:

- **To add or subtract *like* radicals, add or subtract the number in front of the radical (your old friend, the numerical coefficient).**

$$2\sqrt{7}+5\sqrt{7}=(2+5)\sqrt{7}=7\sqrt{7}$$
$$9\sqrt{13}-4\sqrt{13}=(9-4)\sqrt{13}=5\sqrt{13}$$

The absence of a coefficient in front of a radical means the coefficient is 1, so $\sqrt{3}+\sqrt{3}+\sqrt{3}=3\sqrt{3}$.

- **You *can't* add or subtract unlike radicals (just as you can't add or subtract unlike variables).** For example, $6\sqrt{5}+4\sqrt{3}$ can't be simplified.

Don't glance at a problem, see that the radicals aren't the same, and immediately assume that you can't add the two terms. You may be able to simplify one radical to make it match the radical in the other term:

$$\sqrt{52}+\sqrt{13}=\sqrt{4\times13}+\sqrt{13}$$
$$=2\sqrt{13}+\sqrt{13}$$
$$=3\sqrt{13}$$

You can't add or subtract using the numbers contained under the radical. For example,

$\sqrt{64}+\sqrt{16}$ is not $\sqrt{80}$. You have to calculate the root of the radical and then apply the operation:

$$\sqrt{64}+\sqrt{16}=8+4$$
$$=12$$

Multiplying and dividing radicals

To multiply and divide radicals, follow these two rules:

- **Put all the numbers inside one radical and then multiply or divide the numbers.**

$$\sqrt{5}\times\sqrt{6}=\sqrt{5\times6}=\sqrt{30}$$

$$\frac{\sqrt{15}}{\sqrt{5}}=\sqrt{\frac{15}{5}}=\sqrt{3}$$

- **If numbers are in front of the radicals, multiply or divide them as well.** Because the order doesn't matter when multiplying, move the pieces around to make them easier to multiply.

$$6\sqrt{3}\times4\sqrt{2}=6\times4\times\sqrt{3}\times\sqrt{2}$$
$$=24\times\sqrt{6}$$
$$=24\sqrt{6}$$

Dividing works nearly the same way:

$$6\sqrt{16} \div 2\sqrt{4} = (6 \div 2)\left(\sqrt{16 \div 4}\right)$$

$$= (3)\left(\sqrt{4}\right)$$

$$= (3)(2)$$

$$= 6$$

$37\sqrt{5} \times 3\sqrt{6}$

Ⓐ $40\sqrt{11}$

Ⓑ $40\sqrt{30}$

Ⓒ $111\sqrt{11}$

Ⓓ $111\sqrt{30}$

Ⓔ $1,221$

You know that $37 \times 3 = 111$ and that $\sqrt{5} \times \sqrt{6} = \sqrt{30}$, so the answer is $111\sqrt{30}$. This one is straight multiplication. *Correct answer:* Choice **(D)**.

Working radicals from the inside out

When you see an operation under the radical, work it first, and then take the square root of the answer.

$$\sqrt{\frac{1}{3} + \frac{1}{9}}$$

First, simplify $\frac{1}{3} + \frac{1}{9}$. The common denominator is 9, making the numerators 1 and 3, resulting in $\frac{4}{9}$. *Now* take the square roots of the top and bottom, separately:

$$\frac{\sqrt{4}}{\sqrt{9}} = \frac{2}{3}$$

And the answer is $\frac{2}{3}$.

Traversing the X- and Y-Axes with Coordinate Geometry

Coordinate geometry is where algebra and geometry meet — a method of describing points, lines, and shapes by using algebraic expressions. To begin to understand coordinate geometry, you first need to get your bearings on the coordinate plane.

The *coordinate plane,* also known as the *x-y rectangular grid,* is a two-dimensional area defined by a horizontal *x-axis* and a vertical *y-axis* that intersect at a *point of origin* labeled (0, 0). Each point is labeled using an *ordered pair* (*x, y*) with the first number in the parentheses indicating how far to the right or left of (0, 0) the point is and the second number indicating how far above or below (0, 0) the point is. For example, this point has an *x*-value of 2 and a *y*-value of 1, for the coordinates (2, 1):

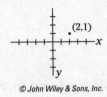

The following sections provide need-to-know information for solving the coordinate geometry questions you may encounter on the GRE.

Using formulas to solve problems

To answer questions related to coordinate geometry, you need to know a few key formulas and how to use them.

Distance formula

If you're asked to find the distance between two points, you can use the *distance formula*, which is based on the Pythagorean theorem (see Chapter 10). In a right triangle, using the lengths of the two shorter sides, the formula lets you determine the length of the longest side (the *hypotenuse*); in equation form, $a^2 + b^2 = c^2$, where a and b are the lengths of the shorter sides and c is the length of the longest side.

In coordinate geometry, you use this formula along with the coordinates of two points to specify the lengths of the sides. Given two points, one with coordinates (x_1, y_1) and the other with coordinates (x_2, y_2), the length of one of the shorter sides is $x_2 - x_1$, and the length of the other shorter side is $y_2 - y_1$. Suppose you're asked to calculate the distance between two points with coordinates (1, 2) and (7, 10). On the coordinate system, the right triangle would look like the following drawing; the length of one short side would be $x_2 - x_1 = 7 - 1 = 6$, and the length of the other short side would be $y_2 - y_1 = 10 - 2 = 8$.

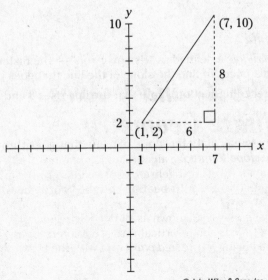

Plug these lengths into the distance formula for a distance of 10:

$$a^2 + b^2 = c^2$$
$$6^2 + 8^2 = c^2$$
$$36 + 64 = c^2$$
$$100 = c^2$$
$$10 = c$$

The distance formula provides another approach for answering questions such as these. With the coordinates of the two points, you can use the following formula to calculate the distance between the two points:

$$\text{distance} = \sqrt{(x_2 - x_1)^2 + (y_2 - y_1)^2}$$
$$= \sqrt{(7-1)^2 + (10-2)^2}$$
$$= \sqrt{6^2 + 8^2}$$
$$= \sqrt{36 + 64}$$
$$= \sqrt{100}$$
$$= 10$$

You can use the distance formula or draw the grid and triangle; both approaches use the Pythagorean theorem to find the length of the hypotenuse in a right triangle when given the lengths of the two shorter sides.

Find the distance from (9, 4) to (8, 6).

$$\text{distance} = \sqrt{(x_2 - x_1)^2 + (y_2 - y_1)^2}$$
$$= \sqrt{(8-9)^2 + (6-4)^2}$$
$$= \sqrt{-1^2 + 2^2}$$
$$= \sqrt{1 + 4}$$
$$= \sqrt{5}$$

Slope formula

The *slope of a line* is defined as "rise over run" — the distance the line rises compared to its horizontal distance. To find the slope of the line that goes through the points (1, 2) and (7, 10) (from the preceding section), note that the line rises 8 and runs 6. The slope is $\frac{8}{6}$, which you can reduce to $\frac{4}{3}$.

Another way to calculate the slope of a line that goes through the points (x_1, y_1) and (x_2, y_2) is to use the *slope formula*:

$$\text{slope} = \frac{y_2 - y_1}{x_2 - x_1}$$

What is the slope of the line connecting the points (–1, –2) and (4, 6)?

$$\text{slope} = \frac{y_2 - y_1}{x_2 - x_1}$$
$$= \frac{6 - (-2)}{4 - (-1)}$$
$$= \frac{6 + 2}{4 + 1}$$
$$= \frac{8}{5}$$

Equation of a line

The general *equation of a line* (also known as the *slope-intercept form*) is $y = mx + b$, where x and y are coordinates of any point on the line, m is the slope, and b is the *y*-intercept (the point at which the line representing the equation intersects the *y*-axis).

Questions on the GRE that involve the slope-intercept form often provide you with the coordinates of a point through which the line passes and require that you calculate the *y*-intercept. For example, the line $y = 7x + b$ passes through point (4, 15). At what point does the line cross the *y*-axis? To get the answer, you plug in 4 for *x* and 15 for *y* and then solve the equation:

$$15 = 7(4) + b$$
$$15 = 28 + b$$
$$15 - 28 = b$$
$$b = -13$$

So the line crosses the *y*-axis at the point (–13, 0).

You can also use the slope-intercept form to find the slope of a line when given its *y*-intercept and the coordinates of any point on the line. Suppose a line crosses the *y*-axis at $x = 5$ and goes through the point (4, 13), and you need to determine its slope. Simply plug the given values into the slope-intercept form:

$$y = mx + b$$
$$13 = m(4) + 5$$
$$13 - 5 = m(4)$$
$$8 = m(4)$$
$$m = 2$$

Midpoint formula

If you're asked to find the midpoint of a line segment defined by the coordinates of two points on the graph, you can draw the triangle again or use the *midpoint formula*:

$$\text{midpoint} = \left(\frac{x_1 + x_2}{2}, \frac{y_1 + y_2}{2} \right)$$

In this formula, (x_1, y_1) are the coordinates of one of the line segment's endpoints, and (x_2, y_2) are the coordinates of the other endpoint.

Performing linear algebraic equations

Linear algebraic equations can be in the form $Ax + By = C$, where neither A nor B is zero. Your task is to find an ordered pair (the *x-y* coordinates of a point) that makes the equation true. To test an ordered pair, plug in values for x and y, and make sure the equation is true. For example, in the equation $2x + 3y = 24$, the ordered pairs (0, 8), (6, 4), and (–3, 10) make the equation true.

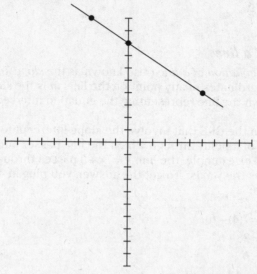

© John Wiley & Sons, Inc.

You may also encounter linear equations in a slightly different format; for example, instead of $2x + 3y = 24$, you may see $3y = 24 - 2x$ or $2x = 24 - 3y$. Regardless of how the equation is presented, you can usually find two points on the line by setting x equal to 0 and solving for y and then setting y equal to 0 and solving for x. Use this method to find two ordered pairs for the equation $2x + 3y = 24$. Here's y if $x = 0$:

$$2x + 3y = 24$$
$$2(0) + 3y = 24$$
$$3y = 24$$
$$y = 8$$

So one point is (0, 8). And here's x if $y = 0$:

$$2x + 3(0) = 24$$
$$2x = 24$$
$$x = 12$$

And the other point is (12, 0).

Identify all of the following that make the expression $5x + 3y = 27$ true.

Select all correct answers.

A (0, 9)

B (6, 1)

C (9, –6)

D (5, 2)

E (6, –1)

F (3, –2)

To solve this problem, substitute the coordinates of each answer into the equation, and make sure the equation is true. You're looking for the *x* and *y* values that make the equation equal to 27:

$$5(0) + 3(9) = 0 + 27 = 27$$
$$5(6) + 3(1) = 30 + 3 = 33$$
$$5(9) + 3(-6) = 45 - 18 = 27$$
$$5(5) + 3(2) = 25 + 6 = 31$$
$$5(6) + 3(-1) = 30 - 3 = 27$$
$$5(3) + 3(-2) = 15 - 6 = 9$$

Correct answers: Choices **(A)**, **(C)**, and **(E)**.

Solving simultaneous equations

Linear equations have an infinite number of solutions, because for every value of *x*, there's a corresponding value of *y*. *Simultaneous equations* refer to two linear equations depicting lines that cross, and they have single values for *x* and *y* that make both equations correct. These *x* and *y* values represent the coordinates of the point where the two lines cross. To solve simultaneous equations, use the method of addition or substitution.

Method of addition

If the two equations contain numbers that are equal but opposite, such as $3y$ and $-3y$, then add the equations to cancel one unknown and solve for the other unknown.

$$5x - 2y = 4$$
$$x + 2y = 8$$

Because the equations include a pair of coefficients that are equal but opposite ($-2y$ and $2y$), first use the method of addition to solve for *x*:

$$
\begin{array}{r}
5x - 2y = 4 \\
+ \quad x + 2y = 8 \\
\hline
6x + 0 = 12 \\
x = 2
\end{array}
$$

Now that you have the value of x, plug it into either equation to find the value of y. You should get the same value of y from either equation.

$$5(2) - 2y = 4$$
$$10 - 2y = 4$$
$$-2y = 4 - 10$$
$$-2y = -6$$
$$y = 3$$

If you were to graph the equations, you would see that the ordered pair (2, 3) is the point where the two lines intersect.

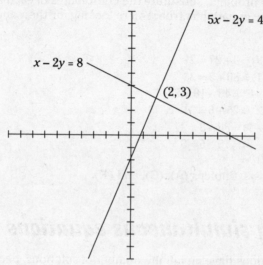

© John Wiley & Sons, Inc.

Method of substitution

One surefire way to solve simultaneous linear equations is with the method of substitution. Just follow these steps:

1. **Solve one of the equations for one unknown (variable) in terms of the other unknown.**

2. **Substitute the result from Step 1 into the other equation and solve for the unknown.**

3. **Plug the value for the first unknown into either equation and solve for the other unknown.**

$$5x - 2y = 4$$
$$x + 2y = 8$$

In this example, the second equation is the easier of the two to start with. Solve for x in terms of y:

$$x = 8 - 2y$$

Now substitute $8 - 2y$ for x in the first equation and solve for y:

$$5(8 - 2y) - 2y = 4$$
$$40 - 10y - 2y = 4$$
$$-12y = 4 - 40$$
$$-12y = -36$$
$$y = 3$$

Finally, plug the value for y into one of the original equations to find the value of x:

$$x + 2y = 8$$
$$x + 2(3) = 8$$
$$x + 6 = 8$$
$$x = 8 - 6$$
$$x = 2$$

The answer is (2, 3).

Recognizing Patterns in Sequential Terms

GRE sequential terms problems challenge you to interpret a numeric pattern from an equation. The term is indicated with a letter, such as a, and counted with a subscript number, such as: $a_1, a_2, a_3, a_4, a_5, ..., a_n$.

You're typically given one value for a, such as $a_1 = 10$. The 1 in a_1 means "the *first a*," and the statement tells you that the first a has a value of 10. Be sure not to confuse the subscript number with the value of that particular a.

Next, you're given an equation that describes the relationship between the sequential terms — in other words, the value of the next a — such as

$$a_{n+1} = a_n + 3$$

Though the value of n (the subscript of a) changes, it has only one value at a time in the equation. For example, if $n = 1$, then $n + 1 = 2$, or the *next n* = 2. The equation can thus be rewritten as this:

$$a_2 = a_1 + 3$$

Though the equation looks menacing, what it tells you is very simple. Each a is 3 more than the previous a. The second a, which is a_2, is 3 more than the first a, a_1.

The next iteration of the equation, with 1 added to n again, looks like this:

$$a_3 = a_2 + 3$$

It tells you that the third a, a_3, is 3 more than the second a, a_2. In other words, if $a_1 = 10$, then $a_2 = 13$, $a_3 = 16$, and so forth. That's the pattern from the equation. The question is then based on this pattern. For example, "What is the value of a_6?" Just keep adding 3 until you reach the sixth a:

$$a_1 = 10$$
$$a_2 = 13$$
$$a_3 = 16$$
$$a_4 = 19$$
$$a_5 = 22$$
$$a_6 = 25$$

Chapter 10

Shaping Up Your Geometry Skills

In This Chapter

▶ Getting straight with lines and angles

▶ Working with polygons

▶ Tackling triangle and quadrilateral questions

▶ Conquering common circle questions

▶ Calculating the volume and surface area of solids

Geometry is all about shapes: lines, angles, triangles, rectangles, squares, circles, cubes, and more. This chapter introduces you to the many shapes you're likely to encounter on the GRE along with the strategies and equations that you'll need to answer the questions. You also get hands-on practice answering a few sample questions at the end.

Exploring Lines and Angles

The fundamental components of many geometric shapes are lines and angles, so before tackling shapes, start with these.

Don't put blind trust in the drawings that go with the questions. For example, an image may appear to contain a right angle, but if the right-angle box is missing and the question doesn't tell you that it's a right angle, you can't assume it is. Images may not be drawn to scale, so when a question presents an image, look for numbers in the question or on the figure that specify dimensions. Two sides of a triangle, for example, may appear to be equal when one is actually slightly longer than the other. **Remember:** If the drawing actually has a label that says, "**Note:** Figure not drawn to scale," then it's *way* off.

Lines

You've probably heard the term *straight line,* but in geometry, that phrase is redundant. By definition, a *line* is straight. If it curves, it's not a line — it's a curve. Also, unless a line is specifically referred to as a *line segment,* assume it goes on forever. If the line has one *endpoint* (point where the line starts) and an arrow at the other end indicates that the line goes on forever, you're looking at a *ray.*

Parallel lines don't cross and are represented by the symbol ‖. *Perpendicular lines* cross at right angles and are represented by the symbol ⊥. A *perpendicular bisector* is a line that both passes through the midpoint of a line segment and is perpendicular to it.

Angles

Angles are a common part of GRE geometry problems. An *angle* is the space between two lines or segments that cross or share an endpoint. Fortunately, understanding angles is easy when you know the different types of angles and a few key concepts.

Finding an angle is usually a matter of simple addition or subtraction. In addition to the rules in the following sections, these three rules apply to the angles on the GRE:

- ✔ Angles can't be negative.

- ✔ Angles can't be 0 degrees or 180 degrees.

- ✔ Fractional angles, such as $44\frac{1}{2}$ degrees or 179.5 degrees, are very rare on the GRE. Angles are typically whole numbers. If you're plugging in a number for an angle, plug in a whole number, such as 30, 45, or 90.

Right angle

Right angles equal 90 degrees and are represented by perpendicular lines with a small box where the two lines meet.

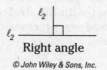

Right angle

© John Wiley & Sons, Inc.

Watch out for lines that appear to be perpendicular but really aren't. An angle is a right angle *only* if the description says, "This is a right angle," you see the perpendicular symbol (⊥), or you see the box in the angle (which is the most common). Otherwise, you can't assume the angle is 90 degrees.

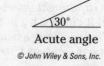

Not necessarily a right angle

© John Wiley & Sons, Inc.

Acute angle

An *acute angle* is any angle greater than 0 degrees but less than 90 degrees.

Acute angle

© John Wiley & Sons, Inc.

Acute means sharp or perceptive, so an acute angle is sharp.

Obtuse angle

An *obtuse angle* is any angle greater than 90 degrees but less than 180 degrees.

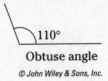

110°

Obtuse angle

© John Wiley & Sons, Inc.

Angles around a point total 360 degrees, just as in a circle.

360°

© John Wiley & Sons, Inc.

Complementary angles

Together, *complementary angles* form a right angle: 90 degrees.

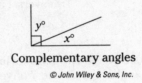

$y°$ $x°$

Complementary angles

© John Wiley & Sons, Inc.

Supplementary angles

Together, *supplementary angles* form a straight line: 180 degrees.

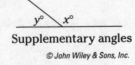

$y°$ $x°$

Supplementary angles

© John Wiley & Sons, Inc.

To avoid mixing the terms *supplementary* and *complementary,* just remember that *c* stands for both *corner* (the lines form a 90-degree corner angle) and *complementary; s* stands for both *straight* and *supplementary.*

Vertical angles

Vertical angles are the opposite angles where two lines cross. Vertical angles have equal measures.

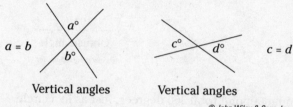

© John Wiley & Sons, Inc.

Just remember that vertical angles are across the *vertex* (the point where intersecting lines cross) from each other, whether one is above the other (vertical) or they're side by side (horizontal).

Transversal angles

A *transversal* is a line that cuts through two other lines. *Transversal angles* are those that are formed where the transversal intersects with the other two lines.

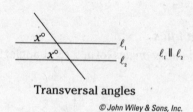

Transversal angles

© John Wiley & Sons, Inc.

When a transversal cuts through two parallel lines, it forms two sets of four equal angles. In the following drawing, angles 1, 3, 5, and 7 have the same measure, and angles 2, 4, 6, and 8 have the same measure.

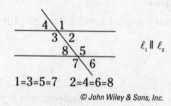

© John Wiley & Sons, Inc.

Never assume that the lines are parallel unless the question states that they are or the image indicates parallel lines; here, $\ell_1 \parallel \ell_2$ indicates that the two lines are parallel. Conversely, if a question states or an image shows that the certain transversal angles (for example, angles 1 and 5 or 4 and 6) are equal, you know that the two lines crossed by the transversal are parallel. If any of the angles 1, 3, 5, and 7 are not equal (or 2, 4, 6, 8 are not equal), then the two lines crossed by the transversal are not parallel.

Recognizing the Many Sides of Polygons

A *polygon* is any closed shape consisting of line segments, which qualifies everything from a *triangle* (three sides) to a *dodecagon* (a dozen sides) and beyond as a polygon. The polygons you're most likely going to encounter on the GRE are triangles and *quadrilaterals* (with four sides). Table 10-1 lists the names of polygons you may bump into.

Table 10-1	Polygons
Number of Sides	*Name*
3	Triangle
4	Quadrilateral
5	Pentagon
6	Hexagon (think of *x* in *six* and *x* in *hex*)
7	Heptagon
8	Octagon
9	Nonagon
10	Decagon

Polygons having all sides equal and all angles equal are called *regular polygons*. For example, an equilateral triangle is a regular triangle, and a square is a regular quadrilateral. *Equilateral* refers to equal side lengths, as in a diamond (rhombus), and *equiangular* refers to equal angles, as in a rectangle. With the equilateral triangle, the equal sides make it have equal angles, but this isn't the case with other shapes.

The GRE usually doesn't ask for the areas of any polygons with more than four sides. It may, however, ask you to find the *perimeter,* which is the sum of the lengths of the sides.

If two polygons are *congruent,* they're identical copies. If they're *similar,* they're identical except that one may be larger. The following explains what you need to know about polygons for the GRE.

Determining total interior angle measure

Because you may be asked to find the total interior angle measure of a particular polygon, keep this formula in mind (where *n* stands for the number of sides):

Angle total $= (n-2)180°$

For example, here are the sums of interior angles of the following polygons:

- **Triangle:** $(3-2)180° = 1 \times 180° = 180°$
- **Quadrilateral:** $(4-2)180° = 2 \times 180° = 360°$
- **Pentagon:** $(5-2)180° = 3 \times 180° = 540°$
- **Hexagon:** $(6-2)180° = 4 \times 180° = 720°$
- **Heptagon:** $(7-2)180° = 5 \times 180° = 900°$
- **Octagon:** $(8-2)180° = 6 \times 180° = 1,080°$
- **Nonagon:** $(9-2)180° = 7 \times 180° = 1,260°$
- **Decagon:** $(10-2)180° = 8 \times 180° = 1,440°$

Finding one interior angle

If you're asked to find the average measure of one angle in a polygon, use the following formula:

$$\frac{(n-2)180°}{n}$$

Here, n stands for the number of sides (which is the same as the number of angles). For example, here's how to find the average angle measure of a pentagon:

$$\frac{(5-2)180°}{5} = \frac{(3)180°}{5} = \frac{540°}{5} = 108°$$

You can't solve for just one angle of a polygon by using this formula, unless you know that the polygon is *regular* or *equiangular*. If the question doesn't specifically state that, don't assume that all sides or all angles of the polygon are equal.

Understanding Triangles from Top to Bottom

Comprised of three sides, the *triangle* is a key figure in geometry, especially on the GRE. Understanding how triangles work leads to mastering other polygons. The following sections introduce you to the types of triangles and explain how to do the related math.

Recognizing triangle types

You need to know three types of triangles for the GRE: equilateral, isosceles, and right, as described in the following sections.

Equilateral triangle

An *equilateral triangle* has three equal sides and three equal angles. Though technically also a *regular* or *equiangular triangle,* it's referred to as *equilateral* on the GRE.

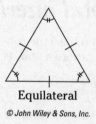

Equilateral

© John Wiley & Sons, Inc.

In this figure, the curved lines with the double lines through them inside the triangle indicate that the angles are equal. The short lines through the sides of the triangle indicate that the sides are equal.

Isosceles triangle

An *isosceles triangle* has two equal sides and two equal angles.

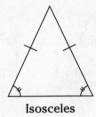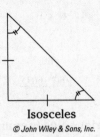

Isosceles   Isosceles

Right triangle

A *right* triangle has one 90-degree angle.

Right triangle

The little box in the lower-left corner of the triangle indicates that the angle is 90 degrees. If the box isn't shown and the question doesn't state that you're looking at a right triangle, then don't assume you are.

Noting key characteristics

Triangles have some notable characteristics that help you field some of the geometry questions on the exam. The following points bring you up to speed:

- ✔ **The largest angle is opposite the longest side.** Conversely, the smallest angle is opposite the shortest side.

- ✔ **The sum of any two sides must be greater than the length of the remaining side.** This idea can be written as $a + b > c$, where a, b, and c are the sides of the triangle.

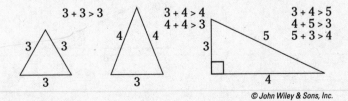

✔ **The sum of the interior angles is always 180 degrees.** Just because one triangle is bigger than another doesn't make the sum of its interior angles any larger. Every triangle has an angle total of 180 degrees.

  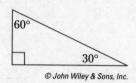

© John Wiley & Sons, Inc.

✔ **Any exterior angle is equal to the sum of the two remote interior angles.** Follow the logic. The sum of supplementary angles is 180 degrees, and x (inside the triangle) and a (outside) are supplementary, so $x + a = 180°$. The sum of the angles inside a triangle is 180 degrees, and x, y, and z are inside the triangle, so $x + y + z = 180°$. If both $x + a$ and $x + y + z$ equal 180 degrees, then $x + a = x + y + z$. Subtract the x's from both sides to get $a = y + z$.

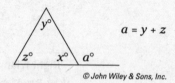

© John Wiley & Sons, Inc.

Calculating a triangle's perimeter and area

You may encounter at least one question on the exam that asks for the *perimeter* or *area* of a triangle. The following sections can help you clear that hurdle.

Calculating perimeter

Perimeter is the distance around a triangle, so add up the lengths of the sides.

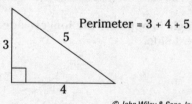

© John Wiley & Sons, Inc.

Calculating area

The area of a triangle is $\frac{1}{2}$ base × height. The height is a line perpendicular to the base. It may be a side of the triangle, as in a right triangle.

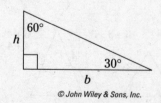

© John Wiley & Sons, Inc.

The height may be inside the triangle, represented by a dashed line and a small 90-degree box.

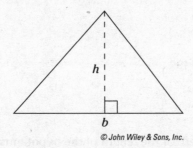

© John Wiley & Sons, Inc.

The height may be outside the triangle. This fact is sometimes used to create trick questions. Regardless, use the same formula to find the area: $\frac{1}{2}$ base × height.

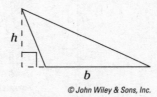

© John Wiley & Sons, Inc.

Understanding the Pythagorean theorem

The *Pythagorean theorem* states that the sum of the squares of the two sides of a right triangle is equal to the square of the hypotenuse. In a right triangle (and only a right triangle), if you know the lengths of two sides, you can find the length of the third side with this formula:

$$a^2 + b^2 = c^2$$

Here, a and b are the legs of the triangle, and c is the hypotenuse. The *hypotenuse* is always opposite the 90-degree angle and is always the longest side of the triangle.

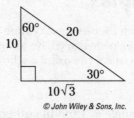

© John Wiley & Sons, Inc.

For example, say you're asked for the length of base of this right triangle:

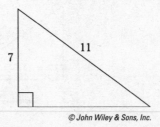

© John Wiley & Sons, Inc.

To find the unknown length of the third side, here's what you do:

$$a^2 + b^2 = c^2$$
$$7^2 + b^2 = 11^2$$
$$49 + b^2 = 121$$
$$b^2 = 121 - 49$$
$$b^2 = 72$$
$$b = 6\sqrt{2}$$

Or, say you're asked for the length of the hypotenuse of this triangle:

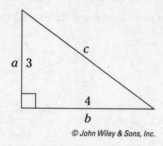

© John Wiley & Sons, Inc.

Here are the calculations:

$$a^2 + b^2 = c^2$$
$$3^2 + 4^2 = c^2$$
$$9 + 16 = c^2$$
$$25 = c^2$$
$$5 = c$$

Identifying common Pythagorean ratios in right triangles

Working the Pythagorean theorem every time you want to find the third side length of a right triangle isn't always necessary. The following sections clue you in to four common Pythagorean ratios that make the exam a whole lot easier.

3:4:5

If one side of a right triangle is 3 and the other is 4, then the hypotenuse must be 5. Likewise, if the hypotenuse is 5 and the length of one side is 4, the other side must be 3. We prove this relationship with the Pythagorean theorem in the preceding section.

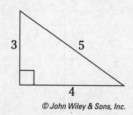

© John Wiley & Sons, Inc.

Because these side lengths are a ratio, the sides of a right triangle can be in any multiple of these numbers, such as 6:8:10 (2×(3:4:5)), 9:12:15 (3×(3:4:5)), or 15:20:25 (5×(3:4:5)).

5:12:13

If one side of a right triangle is 5 and another side is 12, then the hypotenuse must be 13. Likewise, if you know the hypotenuse is 13 and one of the sides is 5, then the other side must be 12. You don't need the Pythagorean theorem.

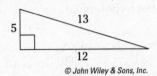

© John Wiley & Sons, Inc.

Because you're dealing with a ratio, the sides can be in any multiple of these numbers, such as 10:24:26 (2×(5:12:13)) or 15:36:39 (3×(5:12:13)).

$s:s:s\sqrt{2}$

This ratio is for an *isosceles right triangle* (containing 45-45-90 degree angles), and *s* stands for *side*. If one side is 2 and a second side is also 2, then the hypotenuse is $2\sqrt{2}$.

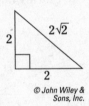

© John Wiley & Sons, Inc.

This formula helps when working with squares. If you know that the side of a square is 5 and you need the diagonal of the square, you know immediately that the diagonal is $5\sqrt{2}$. Why? A square's diagonal cuts the square into two isosceles right triangles (*isosceles* because all sides of the square are equal; *right* because all angles in a square are right angles). This ratio is true regardless of the size of the square; if a side is 64, you know right away that the hypotenuse is $64\sqrt{2}$. If the side length is $\frac{1}{2}$, you know right away that the hypotenuse is $\frac{1}{2}\sqrt{2}$.

If you're given the length of the *hypotenuse* of an isosceles right triangle and need to find the length of the other two sides, use this formula, where *h* is the hypotenuse:

$$\frac{h}{\sqrt{2}}:\frac{h}{\sqrt{2}}:h$$

The diagonal of a square is 5. What is the area of the square?

To determine the area, first you need to know the length of a side, so plug in the numbers:

$$\frac{5}{\sqrt{2}}:\frac{5}{\sqrt{2}}:5$$

The hypotenuse is 5, and the length of any side of the square is $\frac{5}{\sqrt{2}}$. The area of the square is then $\frac{5}{\sqrt{2}} \times \frac{5}{\sqrt{2}} = \frac{25}{2} = 12.5$ square units.

$s:s\sqrt{3}:2s$

This is a special ratio for the sides of a 30:60:90 triangle, which has angles measuring 30, 60, and 90 degrees. S is the length of the short side (opposite the 30-degree angle), $s\sqrt{3}$ is the longer side, and $2s$ is the hypotenuse.

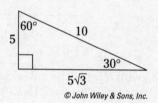

© John Wiley & Sons, Inc.

This type of triangle is a favorite of the test-makers. The important fact to keep in mind here is that the hypotenuse is twice the length of the short side (opposite the 30-degree angle). If you encounter a word problem that says, "Given a 30:60:90 triangle with a hypotenuse of 20, find the area," or "Given a 30:60:90 triangle with a hypotenuse of 100, find the perimeter," you can do so because you can quickly find the lengths of the other sides.

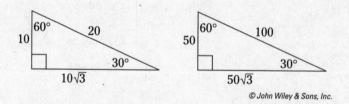

© John Wiley & Sons, Inc.

Knowing Quadrilaterals Inside and Out

After triangles, quadrilaterals are easy. Any four-sided shape is a *quadrilateral*. The interior angles of any quadrilateral total 360 degrees, and you can cut any quadrilateral into two triangles, each of which has total interior angles of 180 degrees. The following sections present everything you need to know about quadrilaterals, including the names of common quadrilaterals.

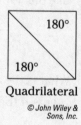

Quadrilateral

© John Wiley & Sons, Inc.

Recognizing a quadrilateral when you see one

Specific quadrilaterals include squares, parallelograms, trapezoids, and other shapes, as described in the following sections.

Square

The simplest quadrilateral is the *square* — a quadrilateral with four equal sides and four right angles. The area of a square is side^2 (that is, base$\times$height), or $\frac{1}{2}$(diagonal)^2.

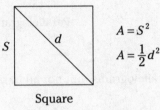

$$A = S^2$$
$$A = \frac{1}{2}d^2$$

Square

Rhombus

A *rhombus* is a quadrilateral with four equal sides and angles that aren't right angles. A rhombus looks like a diamond, except that it can be sideways. The area of a rhombus is $\frac{1}{2}d_1 d_2$, or $\left(\frac{1}{2}\text{diagonal}_1 \times \text{diagonal}_2\right)$.

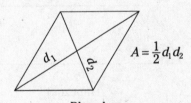

$$A = \frac{1}{2}d_1 d_2$$

Rhombus

Rectangle

A *rectangle* is a quadrilateral that has four right angles and whose opposite sides are equal. (*Rectangle* means "right angle.") The area of a rectangle is length$\times$width (which is the same as base$\times$height).

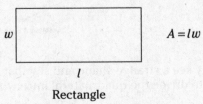

$$A = lw$$

Rectangle

Parallelogram

A *parallelogram* is a quadrilateral where the opposite sides are equal but the angles aren't necessarily right angles. The area of a parallelogram is base×height, and the height is the distance between the two bases. The height is represented by a perpendicular dashed line from the tallest point of the figure down to the base.

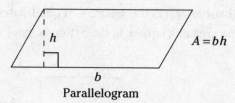

Parallelogram

All rectangles are parallelograms, but not all parallelograms are rectangles.

Trapezoid

A *trapezoid* is a quadrilateral that has only two parallel sides. The other two opposite sides are not parallel. The area of a trapezoid is $\frac{1}{2}$ (base$_1$ + base$_2$) × height. It doesn't matter which base is base$_1$ or base$_2$, because you're adding them together anyway. Just be sure to add them *before* you multiply by $\frac{1}{2}$.

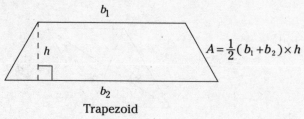

Trapezoid

Other quadrilaterals

Some quadrilaterals don't have nice, neat shapes or special names.

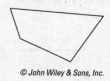

Don't immediately see a strange shape and say that you have no way to find its area. You may be able to divide the quadrilateral into two triangles and find the area of each triangle.

Working with Circles

Determining a circle's *circumference* (distance around the circle) or area using its *radius* (the distance from the center of the circle to its edge) is easy if you know the formulas and the characteristics of the circle. The following sections cover the characteristics and the formulas you need to solve problems related to circles.

Recognizing a circle's characteristics

Circles have several unique characteristics. You need to know what these characteristics are to decipher the terminology used on the test.

- **Center:** The *center* is smack dab in the middle of the circle. If a question refers to the circle by a capital letter, that's both the circle's center and its name.

Circle *M*

Center
© John Wiley & Sons, Inc.

- **Diameter:** The *diameter* is the length of a line segment that passes through the center of the circle and touches the opposite sides. The diameter is equal to two times the radius.

Diameter
© John Wiley &
Sons, Inc.

- **Circumference:** The *circumference* is the distance around a circle, its perimeter.

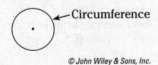

© John Wiley & Sons, Inc.

- **π:** Pronounced *pi,* π is the ratio of the circumference of a circle to the diameter of a circle. It equals approximately 3.14, but more often than not, circle-based questions have answer choices in terms of π, such as 2π, rather than 6.28.

- **Radius:** The *radius* is the distance from the center of the circle to the edge of the circle. The radius of a circle is half the diameter.

Radius
© John Wiley
& Sons, Inc.

✔ **Tangent:** A *tangent* is a line outside a circle that touches the circle at one point.

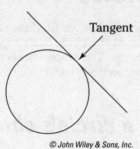

Tangent

© John Wiley & Sons, Inc.

✔ **Chord:** A *chord* is a line segment that crosses through the circle and connects it on two points. The longest chord in a circle is the diameter.

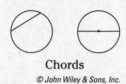

Chords

© John Wiley & Sons, Inc.

Choose from these answer choices for the two example questions that follow:

Ⓐ Quantity A is greater.

Ⓑ Quantity B is greater.

Ⓒ The two quantities are equal.

Ⓓ The relationship cannot be determined from the information given.

Quantity A	_Quantity B_
Area of a circle of radius 6	Area of a circle with a longest chord of 12

The *longest chord* of a circle is the diameter. Because the diameter is twice the radius, a circle with diameter 12 has a radius of 6. In other words, the circles are the same size and have the same area. (Don't worry about solving for that area; you know the two circles are the same.) *Correct answer:* Choice **(C)**.

Quantity A	_Quantity B_
Area of a circle of radius 10	Area of a circle of chord 20

A chord connects any two points on a circle, but you don't know whether this particular chord is the diameter. Quantity B doesn't specify the *longest* chord. If it did, the quantities would be equal, but it doesn't, so you don't know the size of the circle in Quantity B. *Correct answer:* Choice **(D)**.

Mastering essential formulas

Solving circle problems is all about knowing formulas and how to use them. The following sections reveal the formulas and provide guidance on solving problems, complete with sample questions.

Circumference: $C = 2\pi r$

Circumference is a fancy word for perimeter — the distance around a circle. The formula is $C = 2\pi r$ (where C is the circumference and r is radius). Because diameter is twice the radius, you may also use the equation $C = \pi d$ (where d is the diameter).

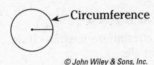

Circumference

© John Wiley & Sons, Inc.

For example, the circumference of a circle with a radius of 3 is

$$2 \times \pi \times 3 = 6\pi$$

Though the answer choices to circle questions are almost always in terms of π, once in a while the answer choices are in regular numbers. You have to calculate the answer by replacing π with 3.14.

A child's wagon has a wheel of radius 6 inches. If the wagon wheel travels 100 revolutions, approximately how many feet has the wagon rolled?

Ⓐ 325

Ⓑ 314

Ⓒ 255

Ⓓ 201

Ⓔ It cannot be determined from the information given.

The question gives the radius in inches, but the answer choices are all in feet, so the first order of business is to convert inches into feet: $6 \div 12 = 0.5$ feet. One revolution of the wheel carries the wagon a distance of one circumference of the wheel, so start by finding the circumference of the circle in feet:

$$C = 2\pi r$$
$$C = 2\pi \times 0.5$$
$$C = \pi$$

Then multiply by the number of revolutions:

$$\pi \times 100 = 100\pi \text{ feet}$$

Because π is approximately 3.14, multiply:

$$100 \times 3.14 = 314 \text{ feet}$$

Choice (E) is definitely not the answer. If you have a radius, you can solve for nearly anything having to do with circles. *Correct answer:* Choice **(B)**.

Area: $A = \pi r^2$

Area is the space inside the circle. The formula is $A = \pi r^2$, so if a circle has a radius of 4, you can find the area as follows:

$$\pi \times 4^2 = 16\pi$$

Arcs and angles inside a circle

An *arc* is a part of the circumference of a circle. This is typically formed by either a central angle or an inscribed angle:

- **Central angle:** A central angle has its vertex at the center of a circle and its endpoints on the circumference. The degree measure of a central angle is the same as the degree measure of its *intercepted arc* (the part of the circle's circumference that falls between the two points where the angle's lines touch the circle).

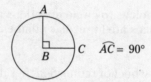

Central angle

- **Inscribed angle:** An inscribed angle has both its vertex and endpoints on the circumference. The degree measure of an inscribed angle is half the degree measure of its intercepted arc, as shown in the following figure. The intercepted arc is 80 degrees, and the inscribed angle is half of that, at 40 degrees.

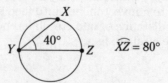

Inscribed angle

Even a drawing that looks like a dream-catcher, with lines running every which way, can be easy if you know how the vertices, arcs, and angles work.

In this figure, find the sum of the degree measures of angles $a+b+c+d+e$.

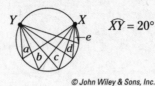

© John Wiley & Sons, Inc.

Note: Figure not drawn to scale.

Ⓐ 65

Ⓑ 60

Ⓒ 55

Ⓓ 50

Ⓔ 45

The angles *a, b, c, d,* and *e* are *inscribed angles,* meaning each angle has half the degree measure of its intercepted arc. You know from the drawing that the endpoints of each angle are *X* and *Y,* and the label tells you that arc *XY* measures 20 degrees. This means that each angle is 10 degrees, for a total of 50. *Correct answer:* Choice **(D).**

The angles certainly don't *look* like 10 degrees, but don't let that shake your confidence in your math. You can never trust the drawing, and when a note indicates that it's not to scale, you know that it's way off.

When a central angle and an inscribed angle have the same endpoints, the degree measure of the central angle is twice that of the inscribed angle.

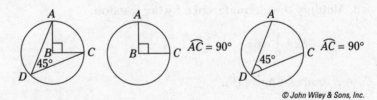

© John Wiley & Sons, Inc.

To find the length of an arc when you have its degree measure, follow these steps:

1. **Find the circumference of the entire circle.**

2. **Put the degree measure of the arc over 360 and then reduce the fraction.**

3. **Multiply the circumference by the fraction.**

Find the length of Arc *AC*.

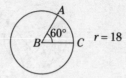

Ⓐ 36π

Ⓑ 27π

Ⓒ 18π

Ⓓ 12π

Ⓔ 6π

Take the steps one at a time:

1. Find the circumference of the entire circle:

$$C = 2\pi r = 2\pi 18 = 36\pi$$

Don't multiply π out; these answer choices are in terms of π.

2. Put the degree measure of the arc over 360.

The degree measure of the arc is the same as its central angle, 60 degrees:

$$\frac{60}{360} = \frac{6}{36} = \frac{1}{6}$$

3. Multiply the circumference by the fraction:

$$36\pi \times \frac{1}{6} = 6\pi$$

Correct answer: Choice **(E)**.

Try another one. Make it intuitive.

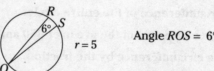

Angle *ROS* = 6°

Find the length of Arc *RS* in this figure.

Ⓐ $\frac{1}{3}\pi$

Ⓑ π

Ⓒ 3π

Ⓓ 4π

Ⓔ 12

1. **Find the circumference of the entire circle:**

$$C = 2\pi r = 2\pi(5) = 10\pi$$

2. **Put the degree measure of the arc over 360.**

    Here, the inscribed angle is 6 degrees. Because the intercepted arc has twice the degree measure of the inscribed angle, the arc is 12 degrees:

$$\frac{12}{360} = \frac{1}{30}$$

3. **Multiply the circumference by the fraction:**

$$10\pi \times \frac{1}{30} = \frac{10}{30}\pi = \frac{1}{3}\pi$$

Correct answer: Choice **(A)**.

Be careful not to confuse the *degree measure* of the arc with the *length* of the arc. The length is always a portion of the circumference and usually has a π in it. If you picked Choice (E), 12, you found the degree measure of the arc rather than its length.

Sectors

A *sector* is a portion of the area of a circle that comes from a central angle. The degree measure of a sector is the same as the degree measure of the central angle. You won't see a sector from an inscribed angle.

To find the area of a sector, do the following:

1. **Find the area of the entire circle.**

2. **Put the degree measure of the sector over 360 and then reduce the fraction.**

3. **Multiply the area by the fraction.**

Finding the area of a sector is similar to finding the length of an arc. The only difference is in the first step: You find the circle's *area,* not *circumference.* With this in mind, try your hand at a few sample sector problems:

Find the area of Sector *ABC.*

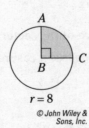

$r = 8$

Ⓐ 64π

Ⓑ 36π

Ⓒ 16π

Ⓓ 12π

Ⓔ 6π

Use the three steps listed previously:

1. **Find the area of the entire circle.**

   $$A = \pi r^2 = \pi(8)^2 = 64\pi$$

2. **Put the degree measure of the sector over 360 and then reduce the fraction.**

   The sector is 90 degrees, the same as its central angle:

   $$\frac{90}{360} = \frac{1}{4}$$

3. **Multiply the area by the fraction.**

   $$64\pi \times \frac{1}{4} = 16\pi$$

Correct answer: Choice **(C).**

Find the area of Sector *XYZ* in this figure.

X 36° Z

Circle *Y*

Y

$r = 9$

© John Wiley & Sons, Inc.

Ⓐ 9.7π

Ⓑ 8.1π

Ⓒ 7.2π

Ⓓ 6.3π

Ⓔ 6π

1. **Find the area of the entire circle.**

   $$A = \pi r^2 = \pi(9)^2 = 81\pi$$

2. **Put the degree measure of the sector over 360 and then reduce the fraction.**

   A sector has the same degree measure as its intercepted arc:

   $$\frac{36}{360} = \frac{1}{10}$$

3. **Multiply the area by the fraction.**

   $$81\pi \times \frac{1}{10} = 8.1\pi$$

Correct answer: Choice **(B).**

Tackling shaded-area problems

A shaded-area problem presents two shapes with one overlapping the other but not completely covering it. The visible part of the shape underneath is the shaded area. Your job is to calculate the total shaded area. Fortunately, you don't always have to find an exact number.

A circle of radius 4 inches is centered over an 8-inch square. Calculate the total shaded area.

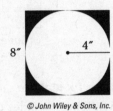

© John Wiley & Sons, Inc.

The shaded part may look funny, but it's just a basic shape that's partly covered up. Here's how to calculate the area of the shaded part:

1. **Calculate the total area of the figure, which is the area of the square.**

   All sides of the square are 8 inches, so

   $$\text{Area}_{\text{Square}} = 8 \times 8 = 64$$

2. **Calculate the area of the circle:**

   $$\text{Area}_{\text{Circle}} = \pi r^2 = \pi(4)^2 = 16\pi$$

3. **Subtract the area of the circle from the area of the square to determine the area of the shaded portion:**

   $$\text{Area}_{\text{Shaded}} = 64 - 16\pi$$

Going 3-D with Volume and Surface Area

You can calculate volume and total surface area for any three-dimensional shape that you encounter on the GRE. Fortunately, the GRE features only two such shapes: the rectangular solid (which includes the cube) and the cylinder. In the following sections, I provide all you need to answer any GRE question based on these shapes.

Calculating volume

Volume is the space inside a three-dimensional object and is always expressed in cubic units. The following sections explain how to calculate the volumes of the 3-D shapes you encounter on the GRE — a cube, a rectangular solid, and a cylinder.

These 3-D volume formulas have one thing in common: Volume = (area of base) × (height). Keep that in mind to help you remember the formulas for cubes, rectangular solids, and cylinders. You simply calculate area as you normally do and then multiply by the object's height.

Cube volume $= e^3$

A *cube* is a three-dimensional square. Think of a six-sided die (one of a pair of dice). The cube's dimensions, *length, width,* and *height,* are the same, so they're called *edges* and are all represented by the letter *e.* The volume of a cube is thus edge $\times$ edge $\times$ edge $= e^3$.

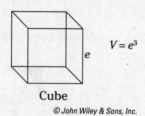

Cube

Rectangular solid volume $= l \times w \times h$

A rectangular solid on the GRE has six sides that are rectangles. It's basically a shoe box. The base is a rectangle, which has an area of length $\times$ width. Multiply that by the box's height to find its volume: $V = l \times w \times h$.

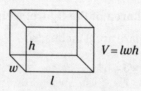

Rectangular solid

Volume of a cylinder $= \pi r^2 h$

A cylinder on the GRE is a *right circular cylinder,* meaning that the top and bottom circles are the same and that the sides go straight up and down. A cylinder is basically a can of soup. The base of the cylinder, being a circle, has an area of πr^2. Multiply that by the cylinder's height to get its volume: $\pi r^2 h$.

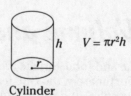

Cylinder

Calculating surface area

Surface area is the outside of an object — basically its skin. The following sections provide formulas for calculating the surface area of these same 3-D shapes — a cube, a rectangular solid, and a cylinder.

Cube surface area $= 6e^2$

A cube has six identical faces, and each face is a square. The area of a square is side^2. On the cube, because you call each side an *edge*, the area of a face is edge^2. Because the cube has six faces, the surface area is $6 \times$ edge^2, or $6e^2$.

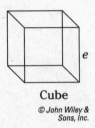

Cube

© John Wiley & Sons, Inc.

Rectangular solid surface area $= 2(lw) + 2(wh) + 2(hl)$

A rectangular solid, like a shoe box, has six rectangular faces. To find the surface area, you need to find the area of each one and add them together. The bottom and top each have the area of $l \times w$. The left and right sides each have an area of $w \times h$. The front and back each have the area of $h \times l$. Together, they total $2(lw) + 2(wh) + 2(hl)$, or $2(lw + wh + hl)$.

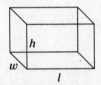

Rectangular solid

© John Wiley & Sons, Inc.

Cylinder surface area $=$ Circumference $\times$ height $+ 2\left(\pi r^2\right)$

To find the surface area of a cylinder, think of pulling the label off a can, flattening it out, finding its area, and then adding that to the areas of the top and bottom lids.

The label is a rectangle whose length equals the circumference of the circle and whose height is the height of the cylinder. The area of a rectangle is $l \times w$, so use the circumference for the length and use the height for the width.

To find the areas of the top and bottom of the cylinder, use the formula for the area of a circle. Together, their areas are $2\left(\pi r^2\right)$. Finally, add everything together for the surface area of the cylinder: Circumference $\times$ height $+ 2\left(\pi r^2\right)$.

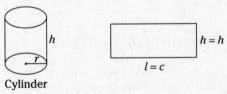

Cylinder

© John Wiley & Sons, Inc.

Chapter 11

Translating Word Problems into Math and Solving Them

● ●

In This Chapter
▶ Making sense of word problems
▶ Calculating distance, rate, time, averages, interest, probability, and more
▶ Grasping set theory with Venn diagrams
▶ Counting the orders of items with permutations and combinations

● ●

*N*umber-crunching alone isn't enough to score well on the GRE. You also need to be able to translate a word problem into math so you can solve it. Fortunately, the GRE uses common types of word problems, each of which you solve using one or more standard strategies. If you can recognize the type of problem and choose the right strategy, you'll do just fine. This chapter introduces you to these common types of word problems along with the strategies for solving them quickly and correctly.

Working a Word Problem Step by Step

When you're up against a word problem, knowing where to start is often the most daunting challenge. The key is to begin with what you know and work toward what you don't know. You can solve almost all word problems by taking the following step-by-step approach:

1. **Read the entire problem carefully.**

   A question may provide three values and then ask for the total or the average. You may not know until the very end of the question what it's asking you to determine, so read the entire question.

2. **Write down all the values and units that you know.**

   When you see all the pieces, the solution to the problem often reveals itself. Values are the clues you need to solve the mystery.

3. **Identify what the question is asking you to find.**

   Look for words such as *what is, how much, how many, how fast, at what price,* and so on. Whatever the question asks you to find is the unknown; you can call it *x*.

4. **Construct the mathematical equation, plugging in all known values and the *x*.**

   In most cases, the word problem is a specific type requiring a special equation. With this equation, known values, and *x* in hand, you have what you need to solve the problem.

5. **Solve the equation.**

   When you have everything in place, do the math.

6. Make sure your answer fits with common sense.

The advantage of most word problems is that they're set in the context of a story, so you can use your common sense to gauge whether the answer is reasonable. Suppose you solve a distance-rate-time problem and find that Grandma was driving 600 miles per hour. Your common sense tells you that this isn't right, so you can check your work instead of moving on. This strategy is especially useful when you're asked to type the answer rather than select it from a list.

Are We There Yet? Calculating Distance, Rate, and Time

You're probably going to encounter at least one question on the GRE that deals with distance, rate, and time. The question typically provides two of the three values and asks for the third value. For example, the question may specify the distance and rate and ask for the time. To solve these types of questions, create a DRT (distance, rate, time) chart and fill in the values.

Chapter 9 discusses how to balance algebraic equations, but another way to solve distance, rate, and time problems is to use the following mnemonic:

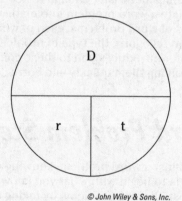

© John Wiley & Sons, Inc.

Cover up the letter for the value that you don't have, and this little tool reveals the equation for determining that value:

- Cover the *D*, and you see that you multiply *r* by *t*.
- Cover the *t*, and you see that you divide *D* by r.
- Cover the *r*, and you see that you divide *D* by *t*.

Jennifer drives 40 miles an hour for two and a half hours. Her friend Ashley goes the same distance but drives at one and a half times Jennifer's speed. How many minutes longer does Jennifer drive than Ashley?

Don't start making crazy formulas with *x*'s and *y*'s. Make a DRT chart instead. This chart sorts what you know from what you need to answer the question:

Distance	=	Rate	×	Time

Start by writing down the values you know, including the units of measurement. When you fill in the 40 miles per hour and 2.5 hours for Jennifer, you can calculate that she went 100 miles. Think of it this way: If she goes 40 miles per hour for one hour, that's 40 miles. For a second hour, she goes another 40 miles. In a half-hour, she goes $\frac{1}{2}$ of 40, or 20 miles: $40 + 40 + 20 = 100$ miles.

Distance	=	Rate	×	Time
100 (Jennifer)		40 mph		2.5 hours

Because Ashley drives the same distance, fill in 100 under *distance* for her. She goes one and a half times as fast, so she's going $40 + \frac{1}{2}(40) = 60$ miles per hour. You know Ashley's distance and rate, and you need to find the time.

Now it gets easier. If Ashley drives 60 miles per hour, she drives $\frac{60 \text{ mi/} \cancel{h}}{60 \text{ mins/} \cancel{h}} = 1$ mile per minute. Therefore, going 100 miles takes her 100 minutes. Because the question asks for your answer in minutes, you're done; no need to convert to hours.

Distance	=	Rate	×	Time
100 (Ashley)		60 mph		100 minutes

Now convert Jennifer's 2.5-hour drive into minutes and subtract. One hour is 60 minutes. A second hour is another 60 minutes. A half-hour is 30 minutes. Add them together: $60 + 60 + 30 = 150$ minutes. If Jennifer drives for 150 minutes and Ashley drives for 100 minutes, Jennifer drives 50 minutes more than Ashley.

Distance	=	Rate	×	Time
100 (Jennifer)		40 mph		150 minutes
100 (Ashley)		60 mph		100 minutes

For distance problems, be careful to note whether the people are traveling in the same direction or opposite directions. Suppose you're asked how far apart drivers are at the end of their trips. If Jordan travels east at 40 miles per hour for 2 hours and Connor travels west at 60 miles per hour for 3 hours, they're going in opposite directions. If they start from the same point at the same time, Jordan has gone 80 miles one way, and Connor has gone 180 miles in the opposite direction. They're actually 260 miles apart. The trap answer is that they're 100 miles apart, because careless people (not you!) simply subtract 80 from 180.

Figuring Averages

When it comes to averages, you can always do them the way your teacher taught you in the third grade: Add the terms together and then divide by the number of terms. First, add up all the terms:

$$5 + 11 + 17 + 23 + 29 = 85$$

Next, divide the total by the number of terms, which is 5:

$$\frac{85}{5} = 17$$

That's the surefire method. It works in every case, regardless of what the numbers look like.

The following sections reveal shortcuts for calculating averages and show you how to tackle problems that are variations on this theme: missing-term average problems and weighted averages.

Taking shortcuts: Finding averages of evenly spaced or consecutive integers

You can quickly find the average if the integers are consecutive or evenly spaced. *Consecutive* means that the numbers come with one right after another, as in the set {2, 3, 4, 5}. *Evenly spaced* means that terms are the same distance apart, as in the set {5, 10, 15, 20}, which are all five apart. Whether the terms are consecutive or evenly spaced, use one of these methods to find the average:

- If the number of terms is odd, the average is equal to the middle term. For example, {3, 4, 5, 6, 7} has an average of 5.

- If the number of terms is even, the average is equal to the average of the two middle terms. For example, {10, 12, 14, 16) has an average of 13, because $\frac{12+14}{2} = \frac{26}{2} = 13$.

- Regardless of the number of terms, when the terms are evenly spaced, the average is always the average of the first and the last terms. For example, {22, 26, 30, 34, 38} has an average of 32, because $\frac{22+38}{2} = \frac{60}{2} = 30$ (and the middle number is 30).

Find the average of these numbers:

{41, 50, 59, 68, 77, 86, 95}

Don't reach for your pencil. Instead, note that the terms are all nine units apart. Because the set is evenly spaced and contains an odd number of terms, go for the middle number: the average is 68.

Find the average of these numbers:

{10, 12, 14, 16, 18, 20, 22, 24, 26, 28, 30, 32, 34, 36, 38, 40}

You see that that they're evenly spaced by twos. Next, look for the middle number. Is it there? The two middle terms are 24 and 26, so you can find the middle between them, but did you count the terms correctly? Or is 26 the middle number? Counting incorrectly is a common mistake.

Instead, use the third method: Add the first and the last terms, which you see at a glance, and divide them by 2. In this case, $10+40=50$, and $\frac{50}{2}=25$.

Solving missing-term average problems

A missing-term average problem is one that gives you the average and all but one of the values and asks for that missing value.

A student takes seven exams. Her scores on the first six are 91, 89, 85, 92, 90, and 88. If her average on all *seven* exams is 90, what did she get on the seventh exam?

To solve a missing-term average problem, use algebra to find the unknown, as explained in Chapter 9. Start with the average equation, plug in a variable for the unknown value, and then solve for that variable:

$$\text{Average} = \frac{\text{Sum of the terms}}{\text{Number of terms}}$$
$$90 = \frac{\text{Sum}}{7}$$

But you don't know the sum of the terms. You have the sum of six terms and one unknown. Call the unknown term x. Add the first six terms and x to get $535 + x$; then solve for x:

$$90 = \frac{535 + x}{7}$$
$$630 = 535 + x$$
$$630 - 535 = x$$
$$95 = x$$

The seventh exam score was 95.

Try solving these missing-term average problems:

A student takes seven exams for an average exam score of 88. Six of the scores are 89, 98, 90, 82, 88, and 87. What is the seventh score?

$$88 = \frac{89 + 98 + 90 + 82 + 88 + 87 + x}{7}$$
$$616 = \frac{534 + x}{7}$$
$$616 = 534 + x$$
$$616 - 534 = x$$
$$82 = x$$

The seventh exam score is 82.

A student takes seven exams for an average score of 85. If five of the scores are 86, 79, 82, 85, and 84, what's the average of the other two exam scores?

$$85 = \frac{(86 + 79 + 82 + 85 + 84) + x + x}{7}$$
$$85(7) = 416 + 2x$$
$$595 = 416 + 2x$$
$$179 = 2x$$
$$x = 89.5$$

The average of the two missing exam scores is 89.5. When you're given a set of scores and asked to find the average of two missing scores, take the same approach as when you have one missing number but divide the missing quantity by 2, because you have two missing numbers.

Working with weighted averages

A *weighted average* is the average of groups, where you have the average value for each group. For example, five juniors have an average score of 120, and ten seniors have an average score of 90. The larger the group, the more it affects — weights — the total average. The ten seniors affect the total average more than the five juniors do.

To calculate a weighted average, multiply each value (such as a specific score) by the number in the group (such as the number of students who got that score). Do this for each group, add the products together, and divide this sum by the total number in all the groups (such as the total number of students).

Find the weighted average score for 15 students with the following scores:

Number of Students	Score
5	120
10	90

Because 5 students got a 120, multiply $5 \times 120 = 600$. Do the same with the other score: $10 \times 90 = 900$. Now, add them up:

$$600 + 900 = 1,500$$

You now have the total number of points that all the students earned. To figure out the average score, divide by the total number of students, which is $5 + 10 = 15$:

$$\frac{1,500}{15} = 100$$

The average score is 100.

Calculating Simple Interest: I = Prt

Interest problems challenge you to calculate gains or losses on investments and the amount of interest paid on loans. To solve these problems, use this formula:

$$I = Prt$$

I is interest, *P* is principal (the amount of money you start with), *r* is the interest rate, and *t* is time (always in years). An interest problem usually asks you how much interest someone earned on his or her investment, but the problem may ask how much interest someone paid on a loan.

Janet invested $1,000 at 5% annual interest for one year. How much interest did she earn?

This is the simplest type of problem. Plug in the numbers and do the math:

$$I = Prt$$
$$I = 1,000 \times 0.05 \times 1$$
$$I = \$50$$

The answer choices may try to trap you with variations on a decimal place, making the choices 5, 50, 500, and so on. You know that $5\% = \dfrac{5}{100} = 0.05$. Just be careful when multiplying and moving the decimal.

The GRE doesn't throw curves on interest problems. You won't see something as technical as "calculate 5% annual interest compounded quarterly for 3 months."

Working Out with Work Problems

Work problems typically tell you how long individuals take to complete a task working alone and then ask you how long they'd take to complete the task working together.

To solve work problems, use this formula:

$$\frac{1}{\text{Time}_A} + \frac{1}{\text{Time}_B} = \frac{1}{\text{Time}_{\text{Total}}}$$

where Time_A is the time it takes the first person (A), Time_B is the time it takes the second person (B), and so on, and $\text{Time}_{\text{Total}}$ is the total time it takes them working together. If you have more than two people working, add people to the left side of the equation as needed.

If Jonathan can paint a house in six days and David can paint a house in eight days, how many days does it take them to paint the house together?

To solve this problem, plug in the numbers and do the math:

$$\frac{1}{6} + \frac{1}{8} = \frac{1}{\text{Time}_{\text{Total}}}$$

$$\frac{8}{48} + \frac{6}{48} = \frac{1}{\text{Time}_{\text{Total}}}$$

$$\frac{14}{48} = \frac{1}{\text{Time}_{\text{Total}}}$$

$$\frac{48}{14} = \text{Time}_{\text{Total}}$$

$$3\frac{6}{14} = \text{Time}_{\text{Total}}$$

$$3\frac{3}{7} \text{ days} = \text{Time}_{\text{Total}}$$

Working together, Jonathan and David would take $3\frac{3}{7}$ days to paint the house.

Double-check your answer by using your common sense. If you get an answer of 10 days, for example, you know you made a mistake somewhere because the two of them working together should be able to do the job in less time than would either one working alone.

Mixing It Up with Mixture Problems

A mixture problem looks much more confusing than it really is. The key to solving it is to set up a table that accounts for both the total mix and the component parts, as in the following example.

Carolyn wants to mix 40 pounds of almonds selling for 30 cents a pound with a quantity of dark chocolate selling for 80 cents a pound. She wants to pay 40 cents per pound for the final mix. How many pounds of dark chocolate should she use?

The hardest part for most test-takers is knowing where to begin. Begin with these steps:

1. **Make a table and start with the labels for all the data you have.**

	Pounds	Price	Total
Almonds			
Dark chocolate			
Mixture			

2. **Fill in the values that the test question gives you.**

   Almonds are 40 pounds at 30 cents a pound, and dark chocolate is 80 cents per pound. Carolyn wants the mixture to cost 40 cents a pound.

	Pounds	Price	Total
Almonds	40	$0.30	
Dark chocolate		$0.80	
Mixture		$0.40	

3. **Use a variable to stand in for your unknown value.**

   You don't know how many pounds of dark chocolate she needs, so that's your variable, x. If Carolyn starts with 40 pounds of almonds and adds x pounds of dark chocolate, she has $40+x$ pounds of mixture.

	Pounds	Price	Total
Almonds	40	$0.30	
Dark chocolate	x	$0.80	
Mixture	$40+x$	$0.40	

4. **Multiply across the rows to fill in the Total column.**

	Pounds	Price	Total
Almonds	40	$0.30	$12.00
Dark chocolate	x	$0.80	$0.80x$
Mixture	$40+x$	$0.40	$0.40(40+x)$

5. **Solve for x.**

   In the Total column, the total cost of almonds plus dark chocolate equals the total cost of the mixture, so the equation looks like this:

   $$\$12.00 + \$0.80x = \$0.40(40+x)$$

   Now do the math:

   $$\$12.00 + \$0.80x = \$0.40(40+x)$$
   $$\$12.00 + \$0.80x = \$16.00 + \$0.40x$$
   $$\$0.40x = \$4.00$$
   $$x = 10$$

   Keep in mind what x stands for: the number of pounds of dark chocolate, which is what the question asks for.

Go back and double-check the answer by plugging this value into the equation. You already know that Carolyn spent $12 on almonds. If she buys 10 pounds of dark chocolate for 80 cents per pound, she spends $8, for a total of $20. She spends that $20 on 50 pounds: $20.00 ÷ 50 = $0.40. Just like that.

Try another one:

A chemistry student has one solution that's 25% saline and another that's 15% saline. Approximately how many liters of the 25% solution must be added to the 15% solution to make 10 liters of a solution that's 20% saline?

Ⓐ 2.5

Ⓑ 3.3

Ⓒ 5.0

Ⓓ 6.7

Ⓔ 7.5

To answer this question, first create your table with the data you have:

	Amount of Solution	% Saline	Amount of Saline
25% solution	x	0.25	$0.25x$
15% solution	$10 - x$	0.15	$0.15(10 - x)$
20% solution	10	0.20	2

Now create your equation and do the math to solve for x. The total 15% saline solution plus the total 25% saline solution equals the total 20% saline solution, so your equation looks like this:

$$0.25x + 0.15(10 - x) = 2$$

Now do the math:

$$0.25x + 0.15(10 - x) = 2$$
$$0.25x + 1.5 - 0.15x = 2$$
$$0.10x = 0.5$$
$$x = 5$$

The student needs to add 5 liters of 25% saline.

Sorting Out Sets and Groups

Set theory is a branch of mathematics that groups numbers, objects, or any items whatsoever into sets and describes the relationships between and among members of those sets. For example, you may group students by male and female and have members of each group form a subset for athletes. Of course, the math gets a little more involved than that, as the following sections reveal.

A *set* is a collection of numbers, values, or objects that are related in some way, like this: {1, 3, 5, 7, 9}. An *empty set,* also referred to as a *null set,* is a set with nothing in it, and it's noted as such by the symbol Ø or the empty brackets { }.

Using the Venn diagram

Sometimes sets overlap. Some or all of the members of one set belong to another set, and vice versa. To describe specifically how the sets overlap, set theory uses a *u*-shaped symbol: ∪. The orientation of the symbol indicates a union or intersection relationship:

- ✔ **Union:** The union of the sets *A* and *B*, written as $A \cup B$, contains all the members of both sets. If Set $A = \{2, 3, 5\}$ and Set $B = \{3, 5, 7\}$, then $A \cup B = \{2, 3, 5, 7\}$.

- ✔ **Intersection:** The intersection of the sets *A* and *B*, written as $A \cap B$, contains only members belonging to both sets. If Set $A = \{2, 3, 5\}$ and Set $B = \{3, 5, 7\}$, then $A \cap B = \{3, 5\}$.

A *Venn diagram* shows the relationship between sets, including the union and intersection. It may consist of a rectangle representing an abstract universal set, but it always has two to three circles representing sets within the universal set. The circles overlap in different ways to show the relationships between members of the sets. If you encounter a set question on the test and have trouble visualizing how the members of two sets relate to one another, draw a Venn diagram on your scratch paper.

In the following figure, the shaded region depicts $A \cap B$.

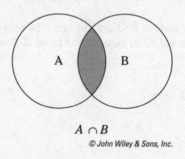

$A \cap B$

This next shaded region depicts $A \cup B$.

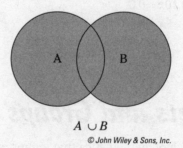

$A \cup B$

What are the elements of Set *C*?

A = {cars, trucks, boats, vans}

B = {boats, vans, ATVs, motorcycles}

$C = A \cap B$

Ⓐ {cars, trucks}

Ⓑ { }

Ⓒ {cars, trucks, boats, vans, ATVs, motorcycles}

Ⓓ {boats, vans}

Ⓔ {A, B}

Set *C* is the *intersection* of *A* and *B*, or the members only in both sets *A* and *B*. Only boats and vans are in both groups. *Correct answer:* Choice **(D).** If you chose Choice (C), you mistook the intersection symbol for the union symbol.

Using the group equation

A Venn diagram may not be the easiest way to solve certain set or group problems. When a question asks you to determine the number of members of both groups, of neither group, or anything along those lines, use the following equation:

$$\text{Group 1} + \text{Group 2} + \text{Neither group} - \text{Both groups} = \text{Total}$$

Of 200 employees, 60 took advantage of educational benefits, 145 participated in the company retirement program, and 40 participated in both programs. How many employees took advantage of neither program?

This group problem is about as straightforward as they get. Jot down the known values and the unknown variable so you know what you have to work with:

Group 1: 60

Group 2: 145

Both groups: 40

Neither group: x

Total: 200

Plug the numbers into the group formula and do the math:

$$60 + 145 + x - 40 = 200$$
$$165 + x = 200$$
$$x = 35$$

Solving Simple Probability Problems

Probability problems may seem daunting at first. For example, a probability problem may ask your chances of drawing an ace, a king, and a queen from a deck of cards. Fortunately, three simple rules can help you solve nearly every probability problem tossed your way. In this section, I tell you how to find probability in general and how to find probabilities when multiple events occur. I also show you how to handle a probability problem involving sets and groups.

A probability is always a number between 0 and 1. A probability of 0 means that an event *won't* happen, and a probability of 1 (or 100%, which equals 1) means it *will* happen. Anything in between 0 and 1 tells you how *likely* it is to happen. You can't have a negative probability, and you can't have a probability greater than 1.

Rule #1: Create a fraction

To find a probability, use this formula, which creates a fraction you can use to solve the problem:

$$\text{Probability} = \frac{\text{Number of possible desired outcomes}}{\text{Number of total possible outcomes}}$$

The denominator (the bottom part of the fraction), containing the total possible number of outcomes, is usually the easier of the two parts to begin with. For example, when you're flipping a coin, two possible outcomes exist: heads or tails, which gives you a denominator of 2. When you're rolling a die, six possible outcomes exist, giving you a denominator of 6. When you're pulling a card out of a deck, 52 possible outcomes exist (because a full deck has 52 cards), giving you a denominator of 52.

The numerator shows the total possible number of the things you want. If you want to get heads when you flip a coin, exactly one side is heads, giving you a numerator of 1. The probability of tossing heads, therefore, is $\frac{1}{2}$ — one desired outcome over two possible outcomes. Suppose you want to get a 5 when you roll a die. A die has exactly one 5 on it, giving you a numerator of 1 and a denominator of 6. The probability of rolling a 5 is $\frac{1}{6}$. What is the probability of drawing a jack out of a deck of playing cards? The deck has 52 cards (the denominator) and 4 jacks (the numerator), so the probability is $\frac{4}{52}$, which reduces to $\frac{1}{13}$. The probability of drawing the jack of hearts, however, is only $\frac{1}{52}$, because the deck contains only one jack of hearts in all the 52 cards.

A jar of marbles has 8 yellow marbles, 6 black marbles, and 12 white marbles. What is the probability of drawing out a black marble?

You have 6 black marbles and 26 marbles total. The number of black marbles goes in the numerator, and the total number of marbles goes in the denominator, for a probability of $\frac{6}{26}$, or $\frac{3}{13}$.

Rule #2: Multiply consecutive probabilities

A *consecutive probability* is the odds that a certain event will occur a specific number of times in a row (for example, if I flip a coin twice, the probability that it comes up heads both times). To solve a consecutive probability problem, find the probability of each event separately and then multiply them.

What's the probability that you'll get heads twice when you toss a coin twice? Find each probability separately and then multiply the two. The chance of tossing a coin the first time and getting heads is $\frac{1}{2}$. The chance of tossing a coin the second time and getting heads is still $\frac{1}{2}$. Multiply these together:

$$\frac{1}{2} \times \frac{1}{2} = \frac{1}{4}$$

The probability of getting heads twice in a row is 1 out of 4. Note that the probability would be the same whether you tossed one coin twice or two coins at the same time.

What's the probability of tossing a die twice and getting a 5 on the first toss and a 6 on the second toss? Treat each toss separately.

The probability of getting a 5 on the first toss is $\frac{1}{6}$. The probability of getting a 6 is $\frac{1}{6}$. Multiply the fractions for your answer:

$$\frac{1}{6} \times \frac{1}{6} = \frac{1}{36}$$

Again, the probability is the same whether you toss one die twice or two dice at the same time.

Rule #3: Add either/or probabilities on a single event

An *either/or probability* on a single event is one in which either of two outcomes may occur. For example, if you reach into a bag containing 10 blue, 10 red, and 10 green marbles, what's the probability that you pull out either a blue or a red marble? To solve this, find the probability of each event separately and then add them together. Drawing a red marble has a 1 in 10 chance of occurring, and drawing a blue marble has the same probability:

$$\frac{1}{10} \text{ and } \frac{1}{10}$$

The probability of pulling either a blue or a red marble is

$$\frac{1}{10} + \frac{1}{10} = \frac{2}{10} = \frac{1}{5}$$

Calculating probability in sets and groups

Sets and groups and probability (discussed in the previous sections) can be packaged together in a single GRE question. Fortunately, your mastery of these concepts is sufficient to answer these questions.

Of the 12 applicants for a job, 6 have master's degrees, 5 have tenure, and 4 have neither the degree nor the tenure. If one applicant is called at random, what is the probability that he or she has both a master's degree and the tenure?

Ⓐ $\frac{1}{12}$

Ⓑ $\frac{1}{4}$

Ⓒ $\frac{1}{3}$

Ⓓ $\frac{5}{12}$

Ⓔ $\frac{1}{2}$

Start with the probability fraction:

$$\text{Probability} = \frac{\text{Number of possible desired outcomes}}{\text{Number of total possible outcomes}}$$

The number of total possible outcomes is easy: 12. The challenge is finding the number of possible desired outcomes. Because this example has members who are in neither group (having master's degrees or having tenure), use the sets-and-groups equation:

$$\text{Group 1} + \text{Group 2} + \text{Neither} - \text{Both} = \text{Total}$$
$$\text{Master's} + \text{Tenure} + \text{Neither} - \text{Both} = \text{Total}$$
$$6 + 5 + 4 - x = 12$$
$$15 - x = 12$$
$$x = 3$$

Three applicants have both a master's degree and tenure. Place the 3 over the total number of applicants, 12:

$$\frac{3}{12} = \frac{1}{4}$$

Answer: Choice **(B)**.

Surveying Different Counting Methods

Counting certainly sounds easy enough, but when you're counting the number of ways that several objects or events can be arranged, selected, or combined, counting becomes much more complex. The following sections explain some tricks to help you count these objects or events quickly and easily.

Putting the counting principle to work

According to the *counting principle,* if an event has m possible outcomes and another independent event has n possible outcomes, then the total possible outcomes of both events occurring together is mn.

Suppose you have five shirts, two pairs of pants, and two jackets. How many different outfits can you put together? To answer this question, apply the counting principle:

1. **Make a space for each item that can change.**

   In this case, you have three spaces: one for shirts, one for pants, and one for jackets.

2. **In each space, jot down the number of options.**

   You now have something like this:

Shirts	Pants	Jackets
5	2	2

3. **Multiply the numbers.**

   $5 \times 2 \times 2 = 20$ different outfits

Use the same technique to calculate the possible combinations you have when rolling two six-sided dice. Each die has 6 possible outcomes, so the total number of different ways the numbers on the dice can be combined is $6 \times 6 = 36$.

When order matters: Permutations

A *permutation* is a change in the arrangement of a given number of items or events. If the order in which items are arranged or in which events occur matters, you're looking at a permutation problem. One of the simplest examples looks at the possible number of ways the three letters A, B, and C can be arranged (the possible number of permutations). The answer is six:

ABC	BAC	CAB
ACB	BCA	CBA

Based on the counting principle discussed in the preceding section, you can figure this out without having to write out all the possible combinations. The first event (or letter in this case) has three possible outcomes (A, B, or C), the second event has two possible outcomes (the remaining two letters), and the third event has only one possible outcome (the last remaining letter):

1st Letter	2nd Letter	3rd Letter
3	2	1

Multiplying gives you

   $3 \times 2 \times 1 = 6$

Whenever a question asks for the possible number of ways a certain number of objects may be arranged or events may occur, you may use the factorial. The *factorial* represents the product of integers up to and including a specific integer, so 3!, which stands for "three factorial," is $3 \times 2 \times 1 = 6$.

0! is an exception: 0! = 1.

You can solve simple permutation problems using $n!$, where n represents the number of objects to arrange or the order of events.

Toby, Jill, Ashley, and Mark are racing their bicycles. In how many different orders can they finish the race?

Because four people are in the race, the different orders in which the four may finish is $4! = 4 \times 3 \times 2 \times 1 = 24$.

Permutation problems become more involved when you're working with a subset of the entire number of objects or events, such as determining the possible number of ways three people out of 20 can finish a race first, second, and third or the total number of 4-digit sequences on a keypad that has 8 digits. To solve this type of permutation problem, use the following formula:

   $$P_r^n = \frac{n!}{(n-r)!}$$

where P is the number of permutations you're trying to determine, n is the total number of objects or events, and r is the subset of objects or events you're working with at one time.

Ten high school soccer teams are competing for a berth in the upcoming tournament. How many possible ways can the top three teams be ranked from first to third?

Because order matters, this is a permutation problem. In this example, you have ten total teams, but you're working with a subset of only three of those teams, so $n = 10$ and $r = 3$. Plug in the numbers and do the math:

$$P_3^{10} = \frac{10!}{(10-3)!} = \frac{10!}{7!}$$

The numbers will always be simple enough to multiply easily. You can make the calculations easier by reducing the fraction to its simplest terms first and then multiplying the remaining factors in the factorial:

$$P_3^{10} = \frac{10 \times 9 \times 8 \times 7!}{7!} = 720$$

Be careful when reducing the fraction. The fraction $\frac{10!}{7!}$ doesn't equal $1\frac{3!}{7!}$, although that may be one of the trap answer choices. However, it does reduce to give you the answer 720:

$$\frac{10!}{7!} = \frac{10 \times 9 \times 8 \times 7!}{7!} = 10 \times 9 \times 8 = 720$$

When order doesn't matter: Combinations

A *combination* is a subset of objects or events in which order doesn't matter (for example, choosing four different business cards from a bowl containing 20 different cards). If a question asks about choosing a number of items and the order in which items are arranged or events occur doesn't matter, you're looking at a combination problem.

To solve a combination problem, use the following formula:

$$C_r^n = \frac{n!}{r!(n-r)!}$$

where C is the number of combinations you're trying to determine, n is the number of objects or events, and r is the number of objects or events you're choosing.

From a group of ten colleagues, Sally must choose three to serve on a committee. How many possible combinations does she have to choose from?

Because the order doesn't matter, this is a combination problem, so proceed as follows:

$$C_{10}^3 = \frac{10!}{3!(10-3)!}$$

$$= \frac{(10)\,(^3\!9)\,(^4\!8)\,(7!)}{(^1\!3)\,(^1\!2)\,(1)(7!)} = 120$$

Joe buys a lottery ticket, picking two numbers out of 200. If the same number cannot be used twice and the order doesn't matter, what are the odds that his two numbers will match the two winning lottery numbers?

Here, Joe is choosing 2 out of 200, and the order doesn't matter, so first use the combinations formula to determine the total possible two-number combinations:

$$C_{200}^2 = \frac{200!}{2!(200-2)!}$$
$$= \frac{200!}{2!(198)!}$$
$$= \frac{(200)(199)\cancel{(198)}}{2!\cancel{(198)}}$$
$$= \frac{(200)(199)}{2}$$
$$= \frac{(100)(199)}{1}$$
$$= 19{,}900$$

Joe has only one ticket, so his chances of winning are 1 out of 19,900, or $\frac{1}{19{,}900}$.

Chapter 12

Interpreting Data and Graphs

- -

In This Chapter
▶ Crunching numbers with basic statistics
▶ Picking details out of tables
▶ Making sense of graphs

- -

Regardless of your area of study or your choice in grad school, you need a general understanding of certain concepts in statistics and the ability to make sense of data presented in tables and graphs. The folks who developed the GRE are well aware of this fact, so they include several questions in the math sections of the exam to test your skills in data analysis.

This chapter gets you up to speed on the basics of understanding graphs and different kinds of data. In this chapter, you wrap your brain around the concepts of median, mode, range, mean, and standard deviation; figure out how to read tables and answer questions about the data they contain; and sharpen your ability to extract and analyze data from graphs.

Brushing Up on Basic Stats

The mere mention of statistics makes some people's brains spin, but most statistics questions on the GRE are fairly basic. If you can master a few concepts, you can solve any statistics problem on the GRE. In this section, I cover the concepts of median, mode, range, mean, and standard deviation.

The only trap you're likely to see in the statistics questions is in the wording of the answer choices. The questions themselves are straightforward, but the answer choices may trick you if you mix up the terms. For example, one answer choice to a *median* question may in fact be the *mean* (the average). One answer choice to a *range* question may be the *mode*. To keep from falling for this trap, be sure to note the word in the question that tells you what you're looking for — median, mode, range, mean, or standard deviation.

Defining the median

The *median* is the middle number when all the terms are arranged in order. The median is the middle, so think of the median strip in the middle of a road. Before you find the median, be sure to arrange the numbers in order (increasing or decreasing, it makes no difference).

Find the median of -3, 18, -4, $\frac{1}{2}$, 11.

Ⓐ -3

Ⓑ 18

Ⓒ -4

Ⓓ $\frac{1}{2}$

Ⓔ 11

Put the numbers in order: -4, -3, $\frac{1}{2}$, 11, 18. The one in the middle, $\frac{1}{2}$, is the median. Finding the median is as simple as that. *Correct answer:* Choice **(D)**.

If the list has an even number of terms, put them in order and find the middle two. Then find the average of those two terms.

Find the median of 5, 0, -3, -5, 1, 2, 8, 6.

Ⓐ 0

Ⓑ 1

Ⓒ 1.5

Ⓓ 2

Ⓔ 5

Put the numbers in order: -5, -3, 0, 1, 2, 5, 6, 8. The middle two terms are 1 and 2, and their average is 1.5. That's it. *Correct answer:* Choice **(C)**.

Don't confuse median (middle) with mean. A *mean* is simply the average, as I explain later in the section "Finding the mean."

Understanding mode

The *mode* is the most frequent number. Think *mode = more = most*. Put the numbers in order so you can more easily spot the number that shows up the most often — that number is the mode.

Find the mode of 11, 18, 29, 17, 18, -4, 0, 19, 0, 11, 18.

Ⓐ 11

Ⓑ 17

Ⓒ 18

Ⓓ 19

Ⓔ 29

The list of terms contains three 18s but no more than two of any other number. *Correct answer:* Choice **(C)**.

A group of numbers can have more than one mode.

Find the modes of 6, 7, 8, 8, 8, 9, 10, 10, 11, 11, 11, 12, 15. Choose more than one answer if necessary.

A 6

B 8

C 10

D 11

E 12

F 15

The list of terms contains three 8s and three 11s, so it has two modes. *Correct answers:* Choices (B) and (D).

If the list has an even number of values, calculate the median by averaging the two middle numbers. If the list has two modes, count them both.

Establishing the range

The *range* is the distance from the largest value to the smallest one. In other words, you find the range by taking the largest term and subtracting the smallest term.

Find the range of the numbers 11, 18, 29, 17, 18, –4, 0, 19, 0, 11, 18.

Ⓐ 33

Ⓑ 29

Ⓒ 19

Ⓓ 0

Ⓔ –4

To find the range, subtract the smallest number from the largest: $29 - (-4) = 29 + 4 = 33$. *Correct answer:* Choice (A).

Finding the mean

Mean is another word for *average*. To calculate the mean, add up all the values and divide by the number of values.

Suppose you have a data set consisting of the numbers 1, 6, 8, 10, 12, and 17. To calculate the mean, do the following:

1. **Add up all the values.**

   $1 + 6 + 8 + 10 + 12 + 17 = 54$

2. **Divide this sum by the number of values.**

   $\frac{54}{6} = 9$

   The mean is 9.

Using the standard deviation

Standard deviation is the average distance from the mean for a set of numbers. Outside the GRE, standard deviation can be very complicated, but for the purposes of the GRE, a general understanding is sufficient.

Every set of data has a mean, and every value of that data is either on the mean or a certain distance from it. Through a complex calculation (which you don't need to worry about), the distances of these points are mixed together to find the standard deviation. Though you don't need to know how to calculate standard deviation, you do need to know how to use it.

If a set of data has a mean of 100 and a standard deviation of 10, then anything 10 away from the mean, whether above or below, is within that standard deviation. For example, 95, being less than 10 away from the mean of 100, is considered within the standard deviation, and 115, being more than 10 away from the mean, is considered outside the standard deviation.

Members of the June High football team have an average height of 6 feet, 3 inches, with a standard deviation of 2.5 inches. Which of the following players are within the standard deviation? Choose more than one answer if necessary.

[A] Smith: 5 feet, 10 inches

[B] Barnes: 6 feet, 1 inch

[C] Carly: 6 feet, 3 inches

[D] Henry: 6 feet, 2 inches

[E] Hodges: 5 feet, 11 inches

[F] Astor: 6 feet

Within one standard deviation is between 6 feet, 0.5 inches (2.5 inches below the mean) and 6 feet, 5.5 inches (2.5 inches above the mean). Barnes, Carly, and Henry are within these heights. *Correct answers:* Choices **(B)**, **(C)**, and **(D)**.

If the question were to ask for players whose heights are within two standard deviations, you'd look for heights 5 inches above and below the mean, because $2 \times 2.5 = 5$.

Mr. Jones's algebra class recently took a test and got an average score of 91.2 with a standard deviation of 5. Which of the following test scores are within 1.2 standard deviations? Choose more than one answer if necessary.

[A] 95

[B] 96

[C] 97

[D] 98

[E] 99

[F] 102 (extra credit)

If one standard deviation is 5, then 1.2 standard deviations is 6, because $5 \times 1.2 = 6$. You're looking for scores that are 6 above and below the class average of 91.2, for a range from 97.2 to 85.2 (91.2 plus and minus 6, respectively). Of the scores listed in the answer choices, 95 and 96 are within that range. Correct answers: Choices **(A)** and **(B)**.

Estimating the standard deviation

A question may ask you to compare two or more standard deviations. You could eyeball them, or you could estimate them. Calculating the actual standard deviation is more work than you'll ever have to do on a single GRE math question. Instead, you can estimate standard deviation by using the *mean deviation,* which is simpler and works perfectly for comparing standard deviations on the GRE.

Here's how to find the mean deviation of the numbers 1, 6, 8, 10, 12, and 17:

1. **Find the average.**

$$\frac{1+6+8+10+12+17}{6} = \frac{54}{6} = 9$$

2. **Find the distance of each value from the mean.**

   This distance is always positive.

   In this example, the first value, 1, has a distance of 8 from the mean $(9-1=8)$. The second value, 6, has a distance of 3 $(9-6=3)$. The remaining values, 8, 10, 12, and 17, have respective distances of 1, 1, 3, and 8.

3. **Take the average of these distances.**

$$\frac{8+3+1+1+3+8}{6} = \frac{24}{6} = 4$$

And the mean deviation for this set of data is 4.

Actual standard deviation is much more complicated than this and has a slightly different result. However, mean deviation is fine for any question you may encounter on the GRE that asks you to compare two or more standard deviations. The test never asks you to actually calculate a standard deviation, but it may ask you which set of data has a greater or lesser standard deviation. If it does, this method is perfect to use.

Analyzing Data in Tables

Tables display data in rows and columns to make it more accessible. You've probably used tables without even knowing it, such as when you look at the channel guide or a scoreboard. On the GRE, however, tables do more than merely help you find pieces of data; they often contain details for analyzing that data.

A table is different from a graph. A *graph,* which I discuss in greater detail later in this chapter, is a drawing that visually shows the relationship between the data and how the data changes. A *table* presents the data in columns and rows.

To handle the table questions that you're likely to encounter on the test, you need an eye for detail and a knack for drawing information from the data. In other words, the GRE challenges you to determine the significance of the data that's in the table. Take the following approach to answering any question that contains a table:

1. **Cover the question and answer choices.**

2. **Read and understand the table's title, column headings, and units of measurement in order to get the gist of the data presented.**

3. **Carefully read the question and understand *exactly* what it's asking.**

4. **Return to the table and collect only the data necessary to answer the question.**

5. **Determine your answer to the question before looking at the answer choices.**

6. **Compare the answer choices to your answer to find the best match.**

Distribution of DVD Rentals by Category for 2014 and 2015

Category	2014	2015
Action	15.2%	13.7%
Comedy	18.9%	19.1%
Drama	7.4%	10.5%
Family	22.0%	19.2%
Foreign	4.8%	7.2%
Independent	5.6%	9.3%
Romance	8.1%	5.2%
Sci-Fi	5.3%	4.0%
Thriller	12.7%	11.8%
Total	100.0%	100.0%
Total video rentals	3,225	4,189

Based on the information in the table, which of the following statements are true? Select all that are true.

[A] In each of the years 2014 and 2015, DVD rentals in the Action, Drama, and Thriller categories accounted for more than 35% of all DVD rentals.

[B] The total number of Sci-Fi rentals increased from 2014 to 2015.

[C] From 2014 to 2015, the total number of DVD rentals increased by more than 25%.

For Choice (A), add the percentages in the Action, Drama, and Thriller categories for each year: $15.2 + 7.4 + 12.7 = 35.3\%$ and $13.7 + 10.5 + 11.8 = 36\%$, so Choice (A) is true. For Choice (B), multiply the Sci-Fi percentage by the total number of DVD rentals for each year and compare the numbers: $0.053 \times 3,225 = 171$ for 2014 and $0.04 \times 4,189 = 168$ for 2015, so Choice (B) is false — the number of Sci-Fi rentals actually decreased slightly. For Choice (C), subtract 2014's total DVD rentals from 2015's total DVD rentals to determine how many more DVDs were rented in 2015, and then divide by 2014's total DVD rentals $(4,189 - 3,225) \div 3,225 \times 100\% = 29\%$ (using the percent of change method from Chapter 8), so Choice (C) is true. The correct answers are Choices **(A)** and **(C)**.

Analyzing Data in Graphs

You'll see graphs on the GRE followed by one or more questions. You need to figure out what's being asked, extract the essential data from the graph, and crunch some numbers to answer each question. To accomplish this effectively and efficiently, you need to know how to make sense of data presented in different types of graphs.

The following sections reveal the graph types you're likely to encounter, provide you with some practice questions to test your graph-reading ability, and reveal a quicker method for estimating graph totals.

The graphs are always drawn to scale, so you can rely on them as accurate visual representations of the data. If you have doubt, the graphs typically include a note that says, "Graphs drawn to scale."

Reading different graph types

To make sense of data presented in a graph, familiarize yourself with the different graph types, as described in the following sections.

Line graphs

Line graphs consist of two or three axes with data points connected by a line, sort of like a connect-the-dots exercise. How data points are plotted on the graph depends on the graph type:

- ✔ **Two axes:** A typical line graph consists of an *x*- (horizontal) and *y*- (vertical) axis, each of which represents a different unit of measure. For example, the *x*-axis may represent years while the *y*-axis represents profits in millions of dollars. In this example, each data point represents the profit for a specific year, and connecting the dots forms a line (hence the name *line* graph).

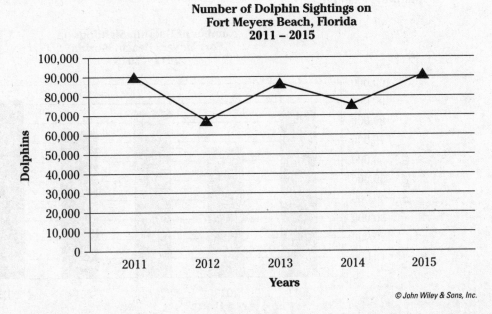

**Number of Dolphin Sightings on
Fort Meyers Beach, Florida
2011 – 2015**

© John Wiley & Sons, Inc.

- ✔ **Three axes:** A graph with three axes contains a second *y*-axis on the right. In this example, the left axis represents the minutes per day spent exercising, whereas the right axis represents the pounds lost per month. You read the points on a three-axis graph the same way you do on a two-axis graph; just make sure you know which axis the data point refers to. Here's an example of a three-axis line graph:

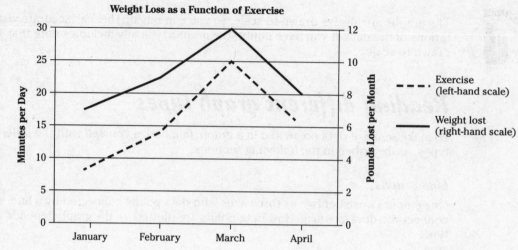

Weight Loss as a Function of Exercise

© John Wiley & Sons, Inc.

Bar graphs

A *bar graph* has vertical or horizontal bars that may represent actual numbers or percentages. Although they look significantly different from line graphs, they're very similar. The only difference is that the data points create bars instead of connecting to form a line. See the following example.

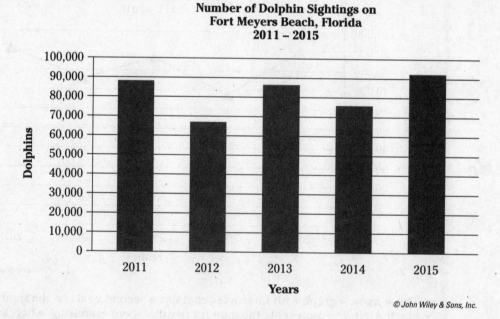

Number of Dolphin Sightings on Fort Meyers Beach, Florida 2011 – 2015

© John Wiley & Sons, Inc.

Pie charts

Each *pie chart* represents 100 percent of the whole, while portions of the graph represent parts of that circle or slices of that pie. To read such a graph, first make a mental note of what the whole circle or pie represents so you know what each portion represents.

For example, below a pie chart, you may be told that 5,000 students graduated with PhDs in the year 2015. A 25% slice of the pie chart is labeled "History," so you know that the number of PhDs in history is 25%, or $\frac{1}{4}$, of 5,000, and $5,000 \times \frac{1}{4} = 1,250$ students. Check out this example of a pie chart.

PhD Graduates per Major

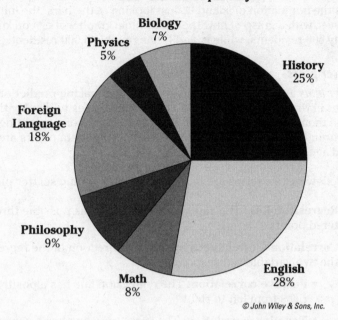

© John Wiley & Sons, Inc.

Logarithmic graphs

A *logarithmic graph* is a graph with an axis scale that changes by multiples of 10. The axis isn't labeled with consecutive numbers (1, 2, 3, 4) or an evenly spaced pattern (5, 10, 15, 20). Instead, each increment is equal to the previous increment multiplied by 10 (1, 10, 100, 1,000, and so on).

Each increment on a logarithmic graph is separated by nine tick marks. Each tick mark indicates the amount of change equal to the increment below it. Between 1 and 10, each tick mark indicates a change of 1. Between 10 and 100, each tick mark indicates a change of 10. Between 10,000 and 100,000, each tick mark indicates a change of 10,000.

The logarithmic graph is useful for tracking small changes with small numbers but ignoring small changes with large numbers. It highlights percents of change. Suppose, for example, you were to measure the populations of a handful of small Pacific islands. If Island A's population of 5 were to increase by 2, this 40% change would clearly show on the logarithmic graph. However, if Island D's population of 2,134 were to increase by the same amount of 2, this 0.00001% change would not show in the logarithmic graph.

Population of Pacific Islands

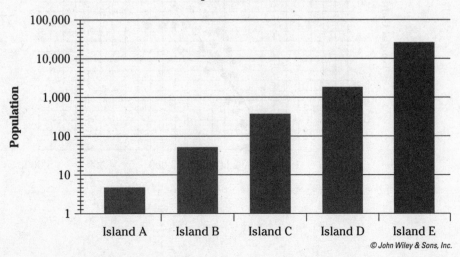

© John Wiley & Sons, Inc.

The type of trick question that the GRE may ask you is whether Island D has more than three times the population of Island C. Just looking at the bars, the initial answer appears to be no. However, with a grasp of how the logarithmic graph works, you know that Island C has approximately 600 residents, while Island D has roughly 3,000 residents, so the answer is yes.

Scatter plots

Scatter plots are useful for spotting trends and making predictions. They're similar to line graphs in that they use horizontal and vertical axes to display the values of the points plotted on them. With a scatter plot, however, instead of connecting the dots, you may draw a line through the data to predict where the future data points are likely to fall. This line is called a *regression* line.

The following two terms are important in interpreting scatter plots:

- **Regression line:** This line passes as closely as possible through the middle of the scattered points.

- **Correlation:** Correlation specifies the direction of the regression line and how closely the two variables correspond:

  - **Positive correlation:** The regression line has a positive slope; that is, the line rises from left to right.

  - **Negative correlation:** The regression line has a negative slope; that is, the line runs downhill from left to right.

  - **No correlation:** If the points are simply scattered all over the graph so that a regression line can't clearly be determined, the variables have no correlation to one another.

  - **Strong or weak correlation:** The closer the points are to the regression line, the stronger the correlation. Conversely, the farther they are from the line, the weaker the correlation.

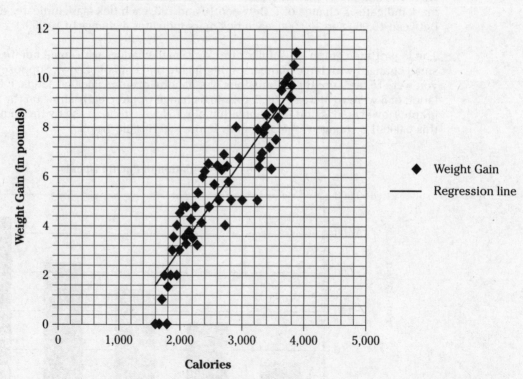

Based on the data in this scatter plot, about how many calories would need to be consumed to result in a 12-pound gain?

Ⓐ 3,000

Ⓑ 3,500

Ⓒ 4,000

Ⓓ 4,500

Ⓔ 5,000

Lay your pencil on top of the regression line to see where it intersects the graph at 12 pounds. Follow the nearest vertical line down, and you have your answer: about 4,500 calories. *Correct answer:* Choice **(D)**.

Answering questions with two graphs

Some graph questions on the GRE contain two graphs, each of which is usually a different type. To answer a question, you may need to extract data from one or both graphs.

Here's an example.

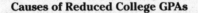

Causes of Reduced College GPAs

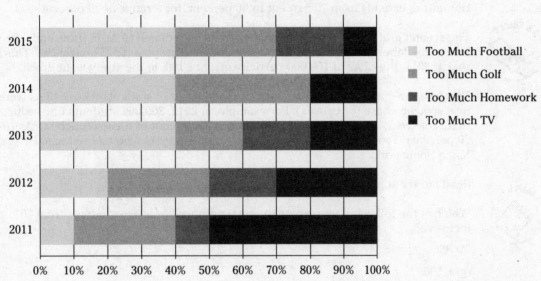

Number of Reduced College GPAs by Year

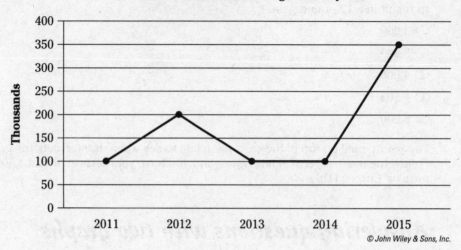

© John Wiley & Sons, Inc.

These two graphs are intended to be used in conjunction. The first graph is a bar graph that ranges from 0 to 100 percent. For this specific graph, calculate the impact of a cause of reduced GPAs by using the length of the bar segment. For example, for 2011, the Too Much Golf category (as a cause of reduced GPAs) begins at 10 percent and extends to 40 percent, for a range of 30 percent. If you say that in 2011, Too Much Golf was 40 percent, you're over-looking the 10-percent segment that is Too Much Football. Also, in 2015, the Too Much Homework extends from 70 percent to 90 percent, for a range of 20 percent.

The second graph gives you the actual number of reduced GPAs in thousands. Be sure to look at the labels of the axes, which for the second graph says "Thousands." This means that in 2011, the GPAs of 100,000 participants, not 100, in the study went down.

Now, use the graphs together to find out the number of students whose GPAs were reduced by a specific cause (or causes). For example, in 2012, 200,000 students had reduced GPAs. In that same year, Too Much Homework caused 20 percent of these reduced GPAs (from 50 to 70 percent). Twenty percent of 200,000 is 40,000 students who had reduced GPAs due to Too Much Homework.

Ready to try some practice questions? Here you go:

Which of the following represents the total number of college students from 2011 to 2015, inclusive?

Ⓐ 850

Ⓑ 8,500

Ⓒ 85,000

Ⓓ 850,000

Ⓔ It cannot be determined from the information given.

Did you fall for the trap and pick Choice (D)? Because the graphs give you only the number of *reduced* GPAs (look at the titles of the graphs), you have no way to determine the total number of college students. *Correct answer:* Choice **(E)**. Note that *inclusive* means that you include 2011 and 2015 (as opposed to "in between 2011 and 2015," which means you *don't* include those years).

The number of GPAs in 2015 that declined due to Too Much Football was what percent greater than the number of GPAs in 2013 that declined due to Too Much TV?

Ⓐ 700%

Ⓑ 600%

Ⓒ 500%

Ⓓ 120%

Ⓔ 7%

In 2015, Too Much Football accounted for 40 percent of reduced college GPAs (from 0 to 40). Because 350,000 GPAs declined in 2015, multiply 0.40 by 350,000 for a total of 140,000 students affected by Too Much Football. In 2013, Too Much TV accounted for 20 percent of reduced college GPAs (80 to 100). That same year, 100,000 GPAs declined. Multiply 0.20 by 100,000 for a total of 20,000 students affected by Too Much TV. Find the percent greater than by reducing the zeros and multiplying by 100%:

$$\text{Percentage Greater Than} = \frac{\text{Football} - \text{TV}}{\text{TV}} \times 100\%$$

$$\text{Percentage Greater Than} = \frac{140{,}000 - 20{,}000}{20{,}000} \times 100\%$$

$$= \frac{12}{2} \times 100\%$$

$$= 600\%$$

Correct answer: Choice **(B)**.

Estimating graph totals quickly

When choosing from answer choices that are far apart, consider rounding as you perform your calculations, especially if you're working with really big numbers and the question says "approximately" or "closest to." Here's an example:

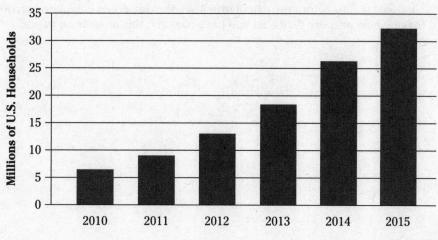

If the average cost of broadband was $43 per month in 2013, which of the following is closest to the gross earnings for U.S. broadband companies in 2013?

Ⓐ $111,000,000

Ⓑ $946,000,000

Ⓒ $11,000,000,000

Ⓓ $94,600,000,000

Ⓔ $946,000,000,000

To estimate the gross earnings for U.S. broadband companies in 2013, you have to multiply the monthly 2013 amount of $43 by the number of 2013 households with broadband, approximately 18 million as shown on the graph, and multiply by 12 to account for the 12 months of the year.

Now you're looking at something like this:

$$(43)(18)\left(10^6\right)(12)$$

Look at the answer choices: They're far apart. To ease the math task, you can round the numbers to the nearest tens place:

$$(40)(20)\left(10^6\right)(10)$$

Because you rounded two numbers down and one number up, you know your answer is slightly shy of the actual answer. Multiply it all out:

$$(40)(20)\left(10^6\right)(10) = 8,000,000,000$$

You don't actually need to multiply $8,000 \times 10^6$, as long as you know that raising 10 to the sixth power gives you 1 with 6 zeros after it (a million); six zeros plus the three zeros after the 8 gives you 8,000,000,000.

Because you rounded more numbers down than up, look for an answer that's *slightly* higher than your result. The 11,000,000,000 answer is the closest answer choice. *Correct answer:* Choice **(C)**.

Because the GRE provides a calculator, you can always just punch in the numbers. However, you're less likely to make a mistake by rounding and multiplying on paper than by entering all these numbers into the calculator. Also, the on-screen calculator errors out at numbers having nine or more digits, so you have to reach this answer on paper.

Chapter 13

Comparing Quantities: Which Is Greater?

....

In This Chapter

▶ Memorizing the rubber-stamped QC answer choices

▶ Knowing how to approach a QC problem

▶ Spotting and avoiding common traps

▶ Putting it all together to work smarter, not harder

....

About one-third of the GRE math questions are Quantitative Comparisons (QC), with plenty of traps to trip you. QCs demand thought and insight to recognize and sidestep common traps; otherwise, you may stumble into some unnecessary, heavy-duty math.

A QC question shows two quantities, intuitively labeled Quantity A and Quantity B. The quantities can be numbers, variables, equations, words, figures, and so on. Your job is to compare the quantities and determine which one is greater or whether they're equal or the relationship can't be determined from the information provided. Fortunately, this chapter gives you the lowdown on QC questions and how to solve them and also points out how to steer clear of common pitfalls.

The Answer Choices Are Always the Same: Memorize Them Now

Due to their number, the QC questions consume a good chunk of your time. To conserve time, memorize the QC answer choices prior to test day. Whatever the information, the answer choices for QCs are always the same:

Ⓐ Quantity A is greater.

Ⓑ Quantity B is greater.

Ⓒ The two quantities are equal.

Ⓓ The relationship cannot be determined from the information given.

As long as you know the choices, you don't need to read and think about them each time.

Consider paraphrasing the answer choices to make them easier to memorize and save even more time:

Ⓐ A is greater.

Ⓑ B is greater.

Ⓒ They're equal.

Ⓓ You need more information.

Easy as π: Approaching QC Questions

The challenge in answering QC questions correctly is knowing where to begin. You can save considerable time and frustration by following this simple, three-step approach:

1. **Simplify Quantity A.**

   Simplify may mean solving an equation, talking through a word problem, or simply taking an estimate of what's there. Sometimes a ballpark estimate is sufficient, as I show you later in this chapter.

2. **Simplify Quantity B.**

   Again, *simplify* can mean solving an equation, talking through a word problem, or estimating the quantity.

3. **Compare the two quantities.**

Here are a few easy quantity-comparisons to get you warmed up:

Quantity A	Quantity B
x^2	x^3

Simplify the two quantities by dividing each side by x^2. You get 1 in Quantity A and x in Quantity B. Because x can be any number, positive or negative, you have no idea whether x is greater than or less than 1, so the correct answer is **(D)**, the relationship cannot be determined from the information given.

Quantity A	Quantity B
40% of 340	340% of 40

Simplify A by taking 10 percent of 340 and multiplying that by 4: 34 times 4 is 68+68, or 136. Simplify Quantity B by taking 300 percent times 40, which equals 120, plus 40 percent of 40, which is 16; then add: 120+16=136. The two quantities are equal. Of course, you could find the answer much more quickly, without actually doing the math, by realizing that each value is 340 times 40 with the decimal point in the answer moved two places to the left (to account for the percentage), so the values are the same.

Quantity A	Quantity B
The number of miles hiked by Ken, who hikes at 3 mph for 6½ hours	18

Simplify A to find that Ken hiked 3 times 6.5 miles, or 18 plus 1.5 miles ($3 \times 6 + 3 \times 0.5$), which equals 19.5; this is 1.5 greater than 18. Quantity A is greater. Again, you can simply eyeball this one, because you instantly know that 3 times 6 is 18, so 3 times anything greater than 6 is more than 18.

These problems certainly seem simple enough, right? But just wait until you see some of the cunning traps the GRE developers build into the QCs.

Gotchas and Other Pitfalls: Tips, Traps, and Tricks

QC questions have so many tricks and traps that I provide a separate section for each one, complete with examples and ways to dodge them.

Keep in mind that the following sections feature tips, not rules. These work most of the time but not always. Never shut off your critical thinking in favor of a tip. The GRE has far too many variations to anticipate them all, so think of these tips as starting points. You still have to use your judgment.

Remembering that equal appearances can be deceiving

If Quantity A and Quantity B appear to be equal at first glance, don't fall for it — a trap is almost always involved. Check out the following examples:

Quantity A	Quantity B
π	3.14

Your gut reaction may be to choose Choice (C) because both quantities are equal. After all, wasn't it drilled into your head in school (and in Chapter 10) that π equals 3.14? You may be very pleased that you remembered the numerical value of π. But hold the phone: The value of π is only *approximately* 3.14. The number π is actually slightly larger than that and continues as a nonrepeating, nonterminating decimal: 3.141592..., making π *greater* than 3.14 and Choice (A) the right choice. *Correct answer:* Choice (**A**).

Quantity A	Quantity B
$0.0062 \times 3,600$	$6,200 \times 0.3600$

You probably checked that the number of digits and decimal places are the same and chose Choice (C). But the answer is Choice (B). Remember the steps I gave you earlier: 1) Simplify Quantity A and 2) Simplify Quantity B. Quantity A equals 22.32, and Quantity B equals 2,232. *Big* difference. The moral of the story? If your first reaction is that the problem is a no-brainer, you may be close to falling for a trap. Look at the problem again, and if you have any doubts whatsoever, do the math. *Correct answer:* Choice (**B**).

Keeping an eye out for scale

If a figure in a QC problem isn't drawn to scale, use other information to try to solve it. Even if the drawing contains the caveat, "***Note:*** Figure not drawn to scale," telling you that it's *way* off, you can still gather information, such as line lengths or angle measurements, that enable you to answer the question. Avoid the temptation to eyeball figures to arrive at your answer.

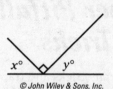

© John Wiley & Sons, Inc.

Note: Figure not drawn to scale.

Quantity A	**Quantity B**
x	y

Sure, x and y each *appear* to be 45 degrees, or roughly 45 degrees, but because you have no other information, you can't make an estimate. You can't deduce that x and y are equal. You do know that x and y add up to 90 degrees, because angles along a straight line add up to 180 degrees, and you already have a right angle (signified by the tiny box): $180 - 90 = 90$. But you *don't* know how much of the 90 is x and how much is y, so go with Choice (D). *Correct answer:* Choice (**D**).

© John Wiley & Sons, Inc.

Note: Figure not drawn to scale.

Quantity A	**Quantity B**
$2x$	y

This QC question is an example of a classic Choice (D) answer. Yes, the figure *appears* to be an isosceles right triangle. The x's *could* each be 45 degrees and the y, 90 degrees. You do know that the two x's are equal and that the angles in a triangle add up to 180 degrees. But the figure doesn't tell you that angle *y* is 90 degrees or equals 2*x* (which would also do the trick), so you can't be sure. ***Remember:*** Nothing is obvious, and anything is possible. *Correct answer:* Choice **(D).**

Remembering that it's not just a pretty picture

The GRE may provide pictures (figures) to assist you in visualizing what the question is asking, but it may also use these pictures as traps. These drawings are almost never to scale. The GRE is challenging your grasp of the concept, not your ability to eyeball the lines and angles.

Two types of drawings are always to scale: the data graph and the coordinate grid (with *x* and *y* axes). (More on these drawings in Chapters 12 and 9, respectively.) Other than that, if the GRE doesn't tell you the shape is a square, you can't assume the angles are 90 degrees or the sides are equal.

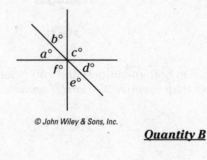

© John Wiley & Sons, Inc.

Quantity A	**Quantity B**
a + *b*	*d* + *e*

Angle *a* is a vertical angle to angle *d*, meaning they're opposite and of equal measure. Angle *b* is a vertical angle to angle *e*, meaning they're opposite and of equal measure. These concepts are true, and you can solve the problem correctly, regardless of whether the drawing is to scale. Because each part of Quantity A is equal to its counterpart in Quantity B, the quantities are equal. *Correct answer:* Choice **(C).**

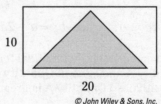

© John Wiley & Sons, Inc.

Quantity A	**Quantity B**
The area of the triangle	100

Don't choose Choice (D) just because you don't have measurements of the triangle. Though the image isn't drawn to scale, you can still estimate what you need in order to answer the question and compare the quantities.

The formula for the area of a triangle is $\frac{1}{2}$ base×height. What's the base? You don't know, but you *do* know that it's less than the base of the rectangle because the sides of the triangle don't extend all the way to the sides of the rectangle. Whether the drawing is to scale or not, you know that the base is less than 20. What's the height? You don't know that either, but you do know that it's less than 10. Multiply less-than-10 by less-than-20 to get less-than-200. Half of less-than-200 is less-than-100. Because less-than-100 is smaller than 100, choose Choice (B). *Correct answer:* Choice **(B)**.

Canceling out identical quantities

Canceling quantities that are identical is like clearing the decks or simplifying the picture so you can more easily compare the two quantities. After all, a QC problem is like a balance: If something is the same on both sides, it doesn't affect the balance, so you can ignore it. Be careful that you cancel only *identical* terms though. For example, you can't cancel –5 from one side and 5 from the other.

Quantity A	**Quantity B**
$x^2 - 21$	$x^2 - 35$

Cancel the x^2 in both quantities, and you're left with –21 and –35. Remember that negative 21 is greater than negative 35. *Correct answer:* Choice **(A)**.

$a < 0$
$b < 0$

Quantity A	**Quantity B**
$(a+b)^2$	$(a-b)^2$

You can't cancel out a and b on both sides and say that the quantities are equal. The expression $(a+b)^2$ is *not* the same as $(a-b)^2$. You should memorize these two expressions (covered in Chapter 9):

$$(a+b)^2 = a^2 + 2ab + b^2 \qquad (a-b)^2 = a^2 - 2ab + b^2$$

After FOILing, you can cancel the identical terms a^2 and b^2 from both quantities. You're left with $+2ab$ in Quantity A and $-2ab$ in Quantity B. You know that because a and b are both negative, ab is positive, so Quantity A is greater. *Correct answer:* Choice **(A)**.

Estimating the quantities

Pretend the QC problem is a balance when comparing each part of Quantity A to its counterpart in Quantity B. If both parts of Quantity A are greater (or heavier) than both parts of Quantity B, Quantity A is greater.

Quantity A	_Quantity B_
$\frac{17}{21} + \frac{47}{80}$	$\frac{19}{81} + \frac{23}{97}$

Don't even *think* about reaching for your pencil to work this problem through. Compare each part of Quantity A to its counterpart in Quantity B. Whereas $\frac{17}{21}$ and $\frac{47}{80}$ are each more than half, $\frac{19}{81}$ and $\frac{23}{97}$ are each roughly a quarter. Two more-than-halves on the left, two quarters on the right: Choice (A) is the answer. No muss, no fuss. *Correct answer:* Choice **(A).**

The point of the question is to recognize and use the test-makers' hidden tricks so you can work smarter, not revert to a basic arithmetic, pull-out-your-pencil-type problem. Working the math may take you into a trap that consumes your time. Once in a while, you have to do the math, but not often.

Plugging in the Sacred Six

Here's the best tip you're likely to get outside a racetrack: Whenever you have variables, plug in the Sacred Six: 1, $\frac{1}{2}$, 2, 0, –1, and –2 . These numbers cover most of the contingencies: positive, negative, zero, odd, even, fraction, and one, which has special properties. Throw these numbers into a problem in place of x (or other variable) whenever possible. *Note:* This tip works even if an equation contains more than one variable.

Quantity A	_Quantity B_
x^2	x^4

The trap answer is Choice (B). Certainly a number to the fourth power is greater than the same number squared, even if it's negative, because a negative number squared or to the fourth number has a positive result. (Two x's in one problem always have the same value at one time, even in Quantities A and B. That is, if x is 5 in Quantity A, it's also 5 in Quantity B. Always. No exceptions.)

Now plug in the Sacred Six to test your answer: If $x = 1$, the two quantities are equal, and Choice (C) prevails. If $x = 2$, Quantity A = 4 and Quantity B = 16, and the answer is Choice (B). You can stop there, because if the toss-up is between Choices (B) and (C), always go with Choice (D). But just to be sure, if $x = \frac{1}{2}$, Quantity A = $\frac{1}{4}$ and Quantity B = $\frac{1}{16}$. There's no doubt that the answer is Choice (D), but only from using the Sacred Six. *Correct answer:* Choice **(D).**

You don't always have to go through all the Sacred Six numbers. As soon as you find two numbers that give you two different answers, you can stop. If plugging in $x = \frac{1}{2}$ and $x = 2$ gives you the same answer, go on to 1, 0, –1, and –2. You'll be pleasantly surprised, however, to find out how often $x = \frac{1}{2}$ and $x = 2$ alone get the job done. Also, if you've figured out that the quantities could be equal *or* one could be greater, go with Choice (D).

When the Sacred Six fail

The Sacred Six method isn't fail-safe. You can plug in all the Sacred Six and still fall for a QC trap, but it's highly unlikely. Here's an example:

Quantity A	Quantity B
$x \neq 0$	
$\frac{1}{x}$	3

Try the Sacred Six, and each time Quantity B is greater. However, x isn't limited to these values; the Six are only a starting point. By now, you have a better grasp of the question and can immediately try a number for x that will make Quantity A greater, such as 0.1. If x were 0.1, then Quantity A would be 10 and greater than Quantity B, making Choice (**D**) the correct answer.

Remember: Shortcuts such as the Sacred Six are helpful, but no rule or method works every time. The Sacred Six is an excellent starting point, but the GRE uses creative ways to challenge your critical-thinking abilities beyond these shortcuts.

Quantity A	Quantity B
	$x \neq 0$
$\frac{1}{x}$	$\frac{x}{1}$

Choice (B) is the trap answer. At first, Quantity A seems to come out as a fraction less than 1. It may or may not. If x were less than 1, then Quantity A would be greater than 1.

Play the what-if game again. What if $x = \frac{1}{2}$? Then Quantity A is greater. What if $x = 2$? Then Quantity B is greater. Because you can make either Quantity A or B greater, choose Choice (D). *Correct answer:* Choice (**D**).

Throwing down a hundred

If a question deals with dollars or percentages, plug in 100 to make it an easier number. Any way to make the question easier is good.

Quantity A	Quantity B
	A book bag costs x dollars.
Cost of the book bag on sale at 60% off	$\$0.6x$

If you make $x = \$100$, you can easily determine that 60% of 100 is 60; subtract 60 from 100, and you get 40. In Quantity B, $0.6(100) = 60$. The answer is Choice (B). This type of problem is easy to miss because of carelessness. Many people choose Choice (C) automatically. When both sides have a percent of x, plug in 100 for x and do the math. *Correct answer:* Choice (**B**).

Quantity A	Quantity B
One year's interest on x dollars at 6% annual interest	$\$12$

If you make $x = \$100$, you know that Quantity A is \$6 while Quantity B is \$12, making the answer Choice (B). But wait — there's no x in Quantity B. Throwing down a hundred (for x) only works when x is on both sides. If $x = \$200$, the quantities would be the same, and anything greater than \$200 makes Quantity A greater. Although plugging in 100 often works, it won't always work (like any shortcut, it's not infallible), which is why you approach these questions critically. *Correct answer:* Choice **(D)**.

Inserting variety when working with multiple variables

Some questions may provide you with multiple variables, such as the following:

$$a > b > c \quad \text{or} \quad x < y < z$$

In questions such as these, plug in consecutive terms first and then nonconsecutive terms. If you need to plug in numbers for two or three variables, first plug in the numbers all in a row: 1, 2, and 3. Then try plugging in numbers that aren't in a row: 1, 5, and 7. Sometimes the spacing between the numbers makes a difference.

Quantity A		Quantity B
	$a < b < c$	
$\dfrac{a+c}{2}$		b

The normal response is to plug in consecutive numbers: 1, 2, and 3. If you do that, Quantity A is $\dfrac{1+3}{2} = 2$ and Quantity B is 2. The quantities are equal — a bright red warning flag. Remember that equal-looking quantities are often a trap, so double-check your work.

Plug in numbers that are farther apart, such as 2, 5, and 200. Now Quantity A is $\dfrac{2+200}{2} = 101$ and Quantity B is 5. Now the answer is Choice (A). If the answer changes based on which values you plug in for the variables, choose Choice (D). *Correct answer:* Choice **(D)**.

Quantity A		Quantity B
$y + z$	$x > y > z$	x

The immediate trap answer is Choice (C), but you know better. Because x, y, and z can be anything, the right answer is Choice (D). If you plug in 3, 2, and 1 for x, y, and z, respectively, Quantity A is $2 + 1$ and Quantity B is 3, making them equal. But when you plug in very different numbers, say 100, 5, and 1, Quantity A is $y + z = 5 + 1 = 6$, and Quantity B, x, is 100, making Quantity B larger. The answer changes depending on what you plug in, making Choice (D) the correct answer. *Correct answer:* Choice **(D)**.

Deciding On Your Own: Quantitative Comparison Practice Questions

Here are some more QC practice questions in case you need a little extra work with these types of problems.

1. $4 < x < 5$

Quantity A	Quantity B
x^3	125

Ⓐ Quantity A is greater.

Ⓑ Quantity B is greater.

Ⓒ The two quantities are equal.

Ⓓ The relationship cannot be determined from the information given.

If x is less than 5, then x^3 must be less than 125, because $5^3 = 125$. *Correct answer:* Choice **(B)**.

2.

Quantity A	Quantity B
5^{-8}	25^{-4}

Ⓐ Quantity A is greater.

Ⓑ Quantity B is greater.

Ⓒ The two quantities are equal.

Ⓓ The relationship cannot be determined from the information given.

Remember that 25^{-4} can also be expressed as $(25)^{-4}$, which becomes $\left(5^2\right)^{-4}$ and then 5^{-8}. *Correct answer:* Choice **(C)**.

3. x and y are integers

Quantity A	Quantity B
The average of x and y	The sum of x and y

Ⓐ Quantity A is greater.

Ⓑ Quantity B is greater.

Ⓒ The two quantities are equal.

Ⓓ The relationship cannot be determined from the information given,

If x and y are positive integers, the correct answer would be Choice (A). If they're negative, then the correct answer would be Choice (B). If they're equal to zero, which is also an integer, the correct answer would be Choice (C). Because you don't know, the relationship can't be determined. *Correct answer:* Choice **(D)**.

4. The lengths of *two* sides of a certain triangle are 12 and 20.

Quantity A	***Quantity B***
The longest possible length of the third side of the triangle	32

Ⓐ Quantity A is greater.

Ⓑ Quantity B is greater.

Ⓒ The two quantities are equal.

Ⓓ The relationship cannot be determined from the information given.

Because the length of the third side of any triangle must be less than the sum of the lengths of the other two sides, the third side of this triangle must be less than 32. *Correct answer:* Choice **(B).**

5. $x > 0$

Quantity A	***Quantity B***
x^2	0.5

Ⓐ Quantity A is greater.

Ⓑ Quantity B is greater.

Ⓒ The two quantities are equal.

Ⓓ The relationship cannot be determined from the information given.

If x is an integer, then any value squared would be more than 0.5. However, x could be a decimal; if x equaled 0.2, x^2 would equal 0.04. Because you can't assume that x is an integer, you can't tell which value is higher. *Correct answer:* Choice **(D).**

6. A circle has a radius of 1.

Quantity A	***Quantity B***
The circumference of the circle	6.28

Ⓐ Quantity A is greater.

Ⓑ Quantity B is greater.

Ⓒ The two quantities are equal.

Ⓓ The relationship cannot be determined from the information given.

The circumference of a circle is $2\pi r$, making the circumference of this circle 2π. If π were equal to 3.14, then the answer would be Choice (C). However, the value of π is slightly higher, closer to 3.14159. You don't have to know the exact value of π, but you do have to know that it's slightly greater than 3.14. *Correct answer:* Choice **(A).**

7. One of the angles of an isosceles triangle is 80°.

<table>
<tr><td align="center">*Quantity A*</td><td align="center">*Quantity B*</td></tr>
<tr><td align="center">The measure of one of the other
two angles of the triangle</td><td align="center">50°</td></tr>
</table>

Ⓐ Quantity A is greater.

Ⓑ Quantity B is greater.

Ⓒ The two quantities are equal.

Ⓓ The relationship cannot be determined from the information given.

If one of the angles is 80 degrees, then the other two angles could each be 50 degrees, for a total angle measure of 180 degrees and a correct answer of Choice (C). However, the other two angles could also be 80 degrees and 20 degrees, bringing the angle total to 180 degrees, for a correct answer of Choice (B). You don't know which one is the case, so you can't tell which quantity is greater. *Correct answer:* Choice **(D).**

8. At a certain factory, machines A and B have a maximum production capacity of p and q parts, respectively, where $p < q < 100$.

<table>
<tr><td align="center">*Quantity A*</td><td align="center">*Quantity B*</td></tr>
<tr><td align="center">The number of days required for
machine A, working at maximum
capacity, to fill an order of 1,000 parts</td><td align="center">The number of days required for
machine B, working at maximum
capacity, to fill an order of 1,000 parts</td></tr>
</table>

Ⓐ Quantity A is greater.

Ⓑ Quantity B is greater.

Ⓒ The two quantities are equal.

Ⓓ The relationship cannot be determined from the information given.

It's easy to get lost in the description, picking numbers and trying math. Actually, after you get past the verbiage, this question is very simple. Pretend machine A produces 1 part per day and machine B produces 99 parts per day. Thus, machine A would take longer to produce 1,000 parts. This is true regardless of the numbers you pick, as long as in one day, machine A produces fewer parts than machine B. *Correct answer:* Choice **(A).**

Part IV
Penning Powerful Analytical Essays

Tackling the GRE Analytical Writing Section

Keep these tips in mind as you work through the Analytical Writing section of the GRE.

When you write the Analyze an Issue essay, remember to

- Jot down some notes that answer the question, provide your own perspective, and include examples that support your position.

- In the introductory paragraph, answer the question specifically, paraphrasing the question and making your opinion known.

- Write two or three paragraphs, discussing your perspective and using the supporting reasons and examples from your notes (and anticipating and addressing counterarguments).

- Compose a final paragraph that summarizes the points of your essay.

As you write the Analyze an Argument essay, remember to

- Write down some notes that identify the assumptions within the argument and comment on how reasonable the assumptions are to the total argument.

- Point out the additional information that's needed to make the argument sound and discuss how this missing information affects the argument.

- Avoid giving your opinion on the topic; instead, discuss logically how well-argued the essay is as written.

Get advice for choosing precise words and constructing strong sentences when writing essays in the free article at www.dummies.com/extras/gre.

In this part . . .

- ✔ Discover the differences between the two essays you have to write and get tips for writing a solid essay in just 30 minutes.

- ✔ Try your hand (or keyboard) at responding to writing prompts and evaluating how your essay might be scored.

Chapter 14

Writing Analytical Essays on Issues and Arguments

In This Chapter

▶ Understanding the two essay-writing tasks on the GRE

▶ Meeting the minimum essay requirements

▶ Knowing how to score well on these essays

▶ Writing sound Issue and Argument Analyses, paragraph by paragraph

The GRE doesn't exactly ease you into the test-taking process. It begins with two challenging essays: Analyze an Issue and Analyze an Argument. You're given 30 minutes to write each essay, for a total of 60 minutes of intense writing before you encounter any of the other test questions. As you prepare for the essay-writing portion, remember the following goals:

✔ Complete each essay in 30 minutes or less.

✔ Write well-organized, insightful essays clearly stating and fully supporting your position.

✔ Avoid grammatical and spelling errors and typos.

✔ Conserve your energy for the rest of the test.

Thirty minutes for each essay should be sufficient — especially if you've practiced. The more essay-writing practice you do, the more comfortable you become with organizing your thoughts and expressing them in words within the time constraints on test day. Take a trial run with the Issue and Argument essays using the topics presented in Chapter 15 and the methods outlined in this chapter. Then you can check your work against the sample essays in Chapter 15.

In this chapter, I explain what evaluators look for and how they ultimately score your essay. I then guide you through the process of writing each essay, paragraph by paragraph.

On the GRE, you write your essays in a text box not unlike the Notepad program on many personal computers. It has cut, copy, and paste features for moving stuff around and an undo feature for reversing changes, but that's it — no spell checker, grammar checker, or automated anything, so the burden of proofreading falls squarely on your shoulders.

Setting Your Sights on the Target: Scoring a Perfect 6

Before you can score well on the essay, you need to have a basic grasp of how the GRE essay section is graded. Your essays are graded one at a time, first by a trained evaluator, and then by a computerized ETS system. Your final score for each essay is the average of the two scores. If the two scores differ by more than a couple points, which is uncommon, then your essay goes to a third, human evaluator, and your score for that essay is the average of the two humans' scores. You get one score for each essay (0 to 6, the higher the better), and your final writing score is the average of the two essay scores.

The following sections break down how the essays are scored and provide some tips for improving your score.

What the essay scores really mean

Knowing what the evaluators look for in your essays enables you to more effectively target your writing for a score of 6. Following are the descriptions evaluators associate with each essay score as they grade your essays:

- ✔ **Outstanding (6):** The essay demonstrates the ability to develop a position on an issue, identify strengths and weaknesses of an argument, support personal views and insights, and write with clarity, focus, and interest — in other words, you don't sound bored. The essay may have a grammar or spelling error but otherwise is well-written with control of the language, good diction (word choice), and variety of sentence structure.

- ✔ **Strong (5):** The essay demonstrates a generally thoughtful analysis of the argument or presentation of the issue. Presentation is logical, and main points are well-supported. The essay may have minor errors in grammar and spelling but demonstrates control of the language, good diction (word choice), and variety of sentence structure.

- ✔ **Adequate (4):** The essay demonstrates overall competence in analyzing the argument or presenting the issue, organizing and supporting thoughts, and expressing them clearly. It may not flow smoothly due to a lack of effective transitions, and it may contain some errors, but it demonstrates sufficient control of the language.

- ✔ **Limited (3):** Competent but flawed, the essay misses the main point or ideas in the argument or presents the issue poorly, lacks order, offers little or no support for the ideas presented, and contains occasional glaring errors or lots of minor errors in grammar, diction, and mechanics.

- ✔ **Seriously flawed (2):** The essay completely misses the point, presents the author's point of view with no support or irrelevant support, is poorly organized, and is riddled with errors in grammar, diction, mechanics, and sentence construction.

- ✔ **Fundamentally deficient (1):** The essay demonstrates little or no evidence of the ability to understand or address the issue or analyze the argument. In addition, the essay contains extensive errors in grammar, diction, mechanics, and sentence structure.

- ✔ **No essay (0):** This one is self-explanatory: If no essay is submitted or only garbage is typed in, the essay score is 0.

The essay section demonstrates your ability to communicate and think critically, which isn't measured anywhere else on the GRE. Whether or not your target school places emphasis on the essay scores, these scores are a reflection of you as an applicant. Furthermore, the essays are *first*, so if you get flustered during this hour of two essays, it will affect your performance on the rest of the test. Essay-writing strategies are easy to learn, and with a little guidance and practice, you'll write excellent essays that reflect well on you and carry you through the test.

Key methods to scoring well

Essay writing (and scoring) is subjective to some degree. There's no right or wrong answer, and every essay is slightly different, based on the test-taker's perspective, knowledge, experience, writing style, and so on. Evaluators, however, have a checklist of specific criteria for grading your essay. To perform well, be sure to do the following:

✔ **Follow the instructions.** The prompt tells you what to do. For example, an Issue Analysis prompt may ask you to consider ways in which the statement may or may not hold true, or it may instruct you to describe circumstances in which taking a certain course of action would or would not be best. To score well, you need to follow those instructions and write about what the prompt asks for.

✔ **Take a clear stand in your essay.** Although arguing both sides of an issue or discussing strengths and weaknesses is fine, you must — *must* — make your opinion or position clear. Don't expect the evaluators to infer your position. (*Infer* means to draw a conclusion based on evidence and reasoning rather than from an explicit statement.) State whether you agree, disagree, or acknowledge the validity of both sides of an issue — just be sure to *declare* that in your introduction and be *consistent* throughout your essay.

✔ **Back up your stance with specific examples.** Anyone can state a position, but you must support your position with specific examples. For example, if you describe why mass-produced goods are both higher quality and less expensive, include a case study, such as how your $40 factory-made Casio wristwatch outperforms your uncle's $7,000 handmade Patek Philippe. You don't have to be right, but you do need to provide solid support for your claim.

Make sure your examples aren't easily refutable. For example, if you're claiming that mass-produced goods are both better and cheaper, don't compare your mass-produced Civic to your grandfather's hand-built Model T. In this case, the improved technology, not the method of production, is obviously the reason for the Civic's superior performance and reliability. This comparison is a poor example because it's too easily refuted.

✔ **Get to the point in each paragraph.** The evaluator will always look for your point in the first two lines of each paragraph, so don't try to be clever and write a paragraph with a surprise ending or twist. State clearly and unequivocally in the first line of each paragraph the point of that paragraph. Then spend the rest of the paragraph supporting that point.

✔ **Stay on topic.** After stating your position in the introductory paragraph, make sure each succeeding paragraph supports that position instead of wandering off topic. If the issue is about low commodity prices versus quality of workmanship, for example, and you're discussing factory output, don't go off topic and start talking about offshore labor — as I once saw a student do on that very subject. Each paragraph should have a sentence (preferably at the end) that ties the paragraph directly to your position statement.

✔ **Avoid fluff.** Though longer essays typically earn higher scores, the higher scores are due to the fact that the essay provides sufficient support, not because it rambles on and on. Your essay won't be judged on word count; it will be judged on how sufficiently you explore the topic.

✔ **Maintain a professional tone.** The essay section isn't for creative writing. It's more like business writing, so avoid off-color language, slang, and inappropriate humor. Creativity, done well, will be appreciated by the evaluators, but be appropriate.

Writing the Issue Essay

In the Analyze an Issue task, the GRE gives you an issue statement and asks you to introduce and then support your position on that issue. The format is like this:

"Today's cheap, mass-produced goods lack the precision and quality of yesterday's hand-built, carefully crafted products."

Directions: Write an essay in response to the preceding statement in which you discuss the extent that you agree or disagree with the statement. Explain your reasoning in a clear, well-organized essay that supports your position. Consider both sides of the issue when developing your response.

Where do you begin? What do they want? Only 29 minutes left! Getting started is the hardest part and staying focused is the most important. By having a game plan and structure in place, you're equipped to do both. The following sections provide details for the plan and structure I recommend.

1. **Read the prompt and understand what it's instructing you to do.**

2. **Identify relevant information you already know about the issue.**

3. **Take a position that's in line with the supporting data you have.**

4. **Write a four- to five-paragraph essay using the following outline as your guide:**

   • **First paragraph:** Introduction stating your position

   • **Second paragraph:** Your best supporting detail

   • **Third and possibly fourth paragraphs:** One or two more supporting details

   • **Final paragraph:** Conclusion reiterating your position statement from your introduction

Your essay doesn't have to be flawless. The evaluators know that you're writing a rough draft under time constraints, so they're ready to forgive the occasional typo and misplaced modifier. Still, they will notice large or repeated errors, so leave yourself a minute at the end of the allotted time to review and edit your essay.

Step 1: Read and understand the prompt

The Issue Analysis essay prompt consists of an issue statement followed by instructions that tell you exactly what to do. Obviously, the issue statements vary, but so too do the accompanying instructions. Here are a few examples that illustrate how the instructions in issue analysis prompts may differ:

✔ Write a response expressing your agreement or disagreement with this statement and the reasoning you followed to arrive at your position. Be sure to consider ways in which the statement may or may not be true and how these considerations influence your position.

✔ Write a response expressing your agreement or disagreement with this statement and addressing the most compelling reasons and/or examples that may challenge your position.

✔ Which do you find more compelling: group A's assertion or group B's response to it? Write a response in which you take a position and explain the reasoning you followed to arrive at your position.

At the time of this writing, ETS has its entire pool of Issue Analysis topics available at `www.ets.org/gre/revised_general/prepare/analytical_writing/issue/pool`. This list contains all the issue statements along with examples of the instructions that accompany those statements so you can develop a better feel for how the prompts may be worded and what they're likely to instruct you to do. You can use this list for extra practice, but don't get bogged down by trying to practice on every topic — there are a *lot* of topics. Just read through some of them so you know what to expect. (My students and I play a game called "topic roulette," where we scroll through the list, randomly pick a topic, and then discuss how we'd write the essay.)

Step 2: Start with your supporting info

Your first inclination may be to state your position on the issue and then try to come up with data to support it. This strategy, though seemingly intuitive, doesn't always work. I've seen students take a stand and then struggle to support it. On the actual GRE, this approach would earn you an essay score of 2. Instead, find your supporting details and then base your position on those details. This way, no matter what, you can support the point that you're making, and the evaluators check off the first thing on their list.

Before taking a position, use your scratch paper to write down five supporting details related to the issue statement. Along with each supporting detail, write down which side of the issue you think it supports. For an essay on handmade versus mass-produced goods, such a list may look something like this:

- ✔ Your mass-produced Casio wristwatch versus your uncle's handmade Patek Philippe — favors cheap manufacturing

- ✔ An off-the-rack suit versus a tailored suit — favors handmade quality

- ✔ Your HP computer versus your friend's custom-built PC from catalog-ordered parts — can go either way

- ✔ The $100 One-Laptop-Per-Child initiative — favors cheap manufacturing as sometimes the only option to distribute laptops to people in poorer areas, but off-topic; the essay is on quality, not availability

- ✔ Your Honda Civic versus your grandpa's Ford Model T — favors cheap manufacturing, but this example can easily be refuted

Don't worry if your examples aren't perfect — you're racing the clock, so just throw some down. You need only two or three examples, so writing down five gives you room to discard a couple.

Your examples can be taken from personal or professional experiences, readings, or other general background knowledge that you possess. What have you seen, done, or heard that formed your opinion on this issue? You may find that your examples support the opposite of your initial response, and you want to discover this before writing the introduction.

Step 3: Take a position that's in line with the supporting data

From your examples, formulate your position. I know, you may feel like you're working backwards, but you want to take the position that you know you're able to support best. This essay isn't a personal statement; it's a test of your ability to compose a clear, coherent essay. In this case, your best examples favor cheap manufacturing over handmade quality. So run with that, even if you personally disagree. If necessary, adjust your personal position for the essay. Your goal isn't self-expression; it's to score a perfect 6.

You're not making a commitment here. You're simply writing a GRE essay. No one is going to bring this essay up in ten years when you're running for office. If your supporting examples don't fit your inherent position, these 30 minutes are not the time for soul-searching on why not (which I have also seen happen). Your task is one thing: Write a level 6 essay. It's okay to declare something that you don't feel. Just look at your examples and write from a position that these examples can support.

The examples you wrote in Step 1 give you a good sense of where your essay will go. Now that your examples are down on paper and you've gathered your thoughts, you're ready to write your introduction.

Step 4: Write your Issue Analysis essay

You've laid the groundwork for writing your Issue Analysis essay. You've read the statement and the instructions, identified supporting details, and shaped your position. The time has come to write your essay. The easiest approach to composing a great essay is to structure it around a very basic four- to five-paragraph outline, as explained in the following sections.

First paragraph: Introduction

Use the first paragraph of your essay (the introduction) to demonstrate your understanding of the issue and clearly state your position. Structure the paragraph as follows:

- ✔ **First sentence:** Introduce the issue and state your position as a response to the prompt.

- ✔ **Second sentence:** Acknowledge the presence of both sides of the issue and that you, in fact, anticipate and address objections to your point of view while alluding to your brilliant logic and reasoning.

- ✔ **Remaining sentences:** Prepare the reader for your supporting details.

Refer to this bulleted list as you read the following example to see how I use this structure.

> The broad assertion that all mass-produced goods are inferior to handcrafted products is clearly overreaching, and I disagree with the statement. Certainly, in some instances handcrafted products are superior, but more often mass production yields more precise, higher-quality products. Considering the type of product and the context of its use is crucial in determining which manufacturing process is best. A few real-world examples, including a wristwatch, car, and personal computer, demonstrate why this is so.

A common pitfall is launching into the examples while still in your introduction. Then, when you get to the paragraph where you describe the example, you have nothing left to say; meanwhile, the supporting detail muddles the introduction. Such an approach demonstrates a lack of organizational skills and will result in a lower score. Instead, allude to your examples by mentioning what you will talk about in just a few words. Look at the last sentence of the sample introduction to see what I mean.

As you write your introductory paragraph, adhere to the following guidelines:

- ✔ **State your position clearly and succinctly.** The evaluators favor a concise writing style. If you can clearly state your point with fewer words, do it. That said, be thorough when making your point.

- ✔ **Convey confidence.** You're stating a position and supporting it with relevant examples. You know you're right, so act like it.

- ✔ **Stay on topic.** Digressing and expanding your scope to support your position is tempting, but keep your discussion within scope of the issue topic. For example, mass production may lower the product cost for increased availability, but the issue is about quality, not distribution. Anything outside what the issue prompt asks you to write about is considered out of scope and will result in a lower score.

- ✔ **Reference key terms.** The topic is about mass production, quality, and precision, so use those terms whenever possible. Doing so signals that you're responding directly to the prompt.

Second paragraph: Your best supporting detail

For the second paragraph, pick your best example and use it to write a single paragraph that supports your position. Structure the paragraph as follows:

✔ **First sentence:** Present your best supporting detail or example and mention that it supports your position as stated in the introduction.

✔ **Next several sentences:** Describe your example in greater detail.

✔ **Next sentence or two:** Show how your example supports your position as stated in the introduction.

✔ **Last sentence:** State unequivocally that the example you just presented clearly supports your position or refutes the counterargument.

Make sure one sentence (preferably the last sentence) of each paragraph connects back to your introduction and the issue topic. This assures the evaluator that you're on track and your thoughts are organized. Check out the following example and compare it to the preceding list to see how I structured this second paragraph.

> The wristwatch is an example of a product that is better when mass-produced. My Casio watch was mass-produced with probably 10,000 other identical units. I purchased this watch five years ago, and it has consistently worked perfectly, with the occasional interruption for a battery replacement. The quality is fine, and the precision couldn't be better. Contrast this with my uncle's Patek Philippe, which was handmade with maybe a dozen others. Due to the motion-generated winding feature, his watch stops working when he doesn't wear it for more than two days! Clearly, this is neither precise timekeeping nor quality of utility. At any given moment, the Casio will always show the correct time, while the Patek's accuracy is a coin toss. The claim that mass-produced products lack the precision and quality of handmade goods, in this commonly occurring context, is clearly wrong.

Your examples don't need to be 100 percent correct. They serve to demonstrate how your powers of observation and insight support your point. The evaluators understand that you can't research anything while writing the essay. However, don't create examples out of thin air, because they're likely to sound phony.

A clever writing style, as in describing the Patek's accuracy as "a coin toss," is encouraged. Again, though, be appropriate.

Third and fourth paragraphs: More supporting detail

The third and fourth paragraphs of your essay are similar to the second paragraph. Each paragraph should present a single supporting example from your notes, show how the example supports your position, and refer back to the introduction. See to the preceding section for info on how to construct a strong paragraph.

> However, some products are better as handmade items than as mass-produced commodities, such as gentlemen's suits. For example, I wore an off-the-rack two-piece suit to my high-school graduation. The jacket was slightly large, but the next size smaller jacket was too small. The workmanship was mediocre, with loose threads and a misplaced stitch. It wasn't cheap, but it was mass-produced, and thus had neither quality nor precision. Contrast this with the handmade, professionally tailored suit that I bought last year. The precise fit is flawless and the quality unparalleled. Though the claim that mass-produced products lack the quality and precision of handmade goods is true in this example, the claim still cannot be applied to all products.

Here's another example paragraph:

> Furthermore, some products can feature high or low quality and precision regardless of whether they are mass-produced or handmade. Computers are a good example of this. My mass-produced HP computer demonstrates both precision and quality, while the eMachines computer I bought in 2001 lacked the quality to last more than 18 months. On the other hand, my friend hand-built a computer from parts ordered in a catalog, and his

computer works with extremely high quality and precision. I have heard stories, however, of hand-built computers that didn't fare as well. Therefore, the general claim that mass-produced products lack the quality and precision of handmade goods is clearly flawed, because in this case, the method of production has no bearing on the outcome.

Final paragraph: The conclusion

Think of the final paragraph, the conclusion, as the closing bracket of your essay, with the introduction being the opening bracket. Your conclusion should mirror your introduction while leaving the evaluator with a sense of closure. Structure your concluding paragraph as follows:

- **First sentence:** Restate your position or once again refute the issue statement presented in the prompt.

- **Middle sentence or two:** Remind the reader of the supporting details and/or examples you presented and the logical conclusion those details and examples support.

- **Final sentence:** Summarize why you agree or disagree with the issue statement presented on the test, leaving the evaluator with a sense of closure. Touch upon but don't re-explore your examples.

As you read the following conclusion, refer to the preceding instructions and see how I followed them.

> To sum up, one cannot correctly claim that all mass-produced products are inferior to handmade goods. The examples describing the wristwatch, the gentlemen's suit, and the personal computer clearly demonstrate that the claim may or may not be true, depending on the context and product. A claim that is sometimes true and sometimes not is an invalid claim, and this claim implies that it is always true. For this reason, I disagree with the statement.

Tying everything together with smooth transitions

As you write, work toward transitioning smoothly from one paragraph to the next. Strong transitions connect the points you're making, especially when your examples take different sides of the issue. Transitions contribute greatly to the organization and coherence of your essay, and they demonstrate control of the language. Here are a few examples of commonly used transitions:

- Closely related to this idea is . . .
- Conversely, . . .
- On the other hand, . . .
- However, . . .
- In contrast, . . .
- Similarly, . . .

Besides transitions, a more subtle technique for tying everything together and staying on point is to repeat key terms throughout the essay. Identify key terms in the issue statement. For example, in the following issue statement, you may identify these as key terms: *cheap, mass-produced, precision, quality,* and *hand-built.*

> "Today's **cheap, mass-produced** goods lack the **precision** and **quality** of yesterday's **hand-built,** carefully crafted products."

Here's the sample second paragraph again, bolding the repetition of key terms drawn directly from the issue statement:

> The wristwatch is an example of a product that is better when **mass-produced.** My Casio watch was **mass-produced** with probably 10,000 other identical units. I purchased this watch five years ago, and it has consistently worked perfectly, with the occasional interruption for a battery replacement. The **quality** is fine, and the **precision** couldn't be better. Contrast this with my uncle's Patek Philippe, which was **handmade** with maybe a dozen others. Due to the motion-generated winding feature, his watch stops working when he doesn't wear it for more than two days! Clearly, this is neither **precise** timekeeping nor **quality** of utility. At any given moment, the Casio will always show the correct time, while the Patek's accuracy is a coin toss. The claim that **mass-produced** products lack the **precision** and **quality** of **handmade** goods, in this commonly occurring context, is clearly wrong.

Writing the Argument Essay

The second essay is called Analyze an Argument. The essay prompt presents a paragraph that states a position and provides several reasons in support of it. Your job is to analyze the argument and its reasoning and evidence and describe why the argument is either faulty or sound. (Usually, though, the argument is faulty.) Check out the following example:

> "Many considerations point to the conclusion that Flint's restaurant should be changed from a youth-oriented, family-style restaurant to a Western-style saloon serving alcoholic beverages and featuring country bands. First, few families live in the area surrounding the restaurant; most have moved farther out into the suburbs. Second, Flint owns and operates two other saloons that have liquor licenses, making him experienced in the field. And finally, alcohol has a higher profit margin than does food."

Directions: Write a response to the preceding argument that analyzes its stated or implied assumptions, reveals how the argument's position depends on the assumptions, and explains the effect of any flawed assumptions on the argument's validity.

The clock's ticking, so you need to work fast, but you also need to analyze the argument before you start writing. By having a plan of attack and a structure in place, you're better equipped to produce an outstanding essay in the allotted time. The following sections provide steps to writing a good argument.

1. **Read the prompt and understand what it's instructing you to do.**

2. **Identify the position stated in the argument.**

3. **List the reasons given to support the stated position.**

4. **Identify any flawed assumptions behind each reason.**

5. **Write a four- or five-paragraph essay using the following outline as your guide:**

   - Introductory paragraph demonstrating your understanding of the position stated in the argument and whether you think the evidence provided supports that position

   - Two or three paragraphs, each of which refutes a faulty assumption/conclusion presented in the argument or, if you agree with the stated position, provides additional evidence to support it

   - Concluding paragraph that recaps your essay and reinforces why the argument is or isn't valid

Unlike the Analyze an Issue essay, which is based on your opinion, the Analyze an Argument essay isn't based on your opinion at all. It's based on your analysis of the argument. For example, in this essay, your personal preference of family restaurants to saloons shouldn't affect what you write.

Step 1: Read and understand the prompt

The Argument Analysis essay prompt contains a brief argument along with instructions that tell you exactly what to do. The instructions vary, so read them carefully and understand what you're being asked to do. Here are a few examples:

- ✔ Write a response that evaluates the stated or unstated assumptions on which this argument is based. Explain how the argument relies on these assumptions and how any of the assumptions, if proven to be untrue, would affect the validity of the argument.

- ✔ Write a response in which you discuss the data that would need to be presented in order to decide whether the recommended course of action would be beneficial or not and whether the argument on which the recommendation is based would be reasonable. Be sure to explain how specific data would help assess the recommendation.

- ✔ Write a response explaining the types of evidence needed to evaluate the argument and how the evidence might weaken or strengthen the argument.

- ✔ Write a response presenting the types of questions that need to be answered in order to determine whether the recommended course of action would be advisable and whether the argument on which the recommended course of action is based is reasonable.

ETS publishes its entire pool of Argument Analysis topics at http://www.ets.org/gre/ revised_general/prepare/analytical_writing/argument/pool. This pool contains all the argument statements along with examples of the accompanying instructions so you can develop a better feel for how the prompts may be worded and what they're likely to instruct you to do. You can use this list for extra practice, but don't get bogged down by trying to practice on every topic — there are a *lot* of topics. Just read through some of them so you know what to expect. (In class, we also play "topic roulette" with the argument topics.)

Step 2: Identify the stated position

The argument on the GRE test is so brief that finding the position statement is a snap. The position statement is almost always in the first sentence. In this example, the position is

> " . . . Flint's restaurant should be changed from a youth-oriented, family-style restaurant to a Western-style saloon serving alcoholic beverages and featuring country bands."

Identifying the position stated in the argument is a crucial first step because you need to show how each reason presented in support of that position succeeds or fails to do so.

Step 3: List the reasons given to support the stated position

Every argument includes a list of facts to support the position. In this Flint's restaurant example, the facts are easy to pick out because they're identified by number:

- ✔ **First:** Few families live in the area surrounding the restaurant; most have moved farther out into the suburbs.

- **Second:** Flint owns and operates two other saloons that have liquor licenses, making him experienced in the field.

- **Third:** Alcohol has a higher profit margin than does food.

Step 4: Analyze the assumption and conclusion based on the facts

As you begin to write your essay, look for the author's flawed assumption(s) — anything the author claims or implies without providing sufficient evidence to back it up. (See Chapter 6 for more about assumptions.) For example, stating that "alcohol has a higher profit margin than does food" doesn't necessarily mean it's more profitable.

You can argue assumptions, but you can't argue facts. In this example, you can argue that selling alcohol in this area may not be more profitable because few residents in the area drink or because the loss of revenue from food sales will more than offset the increased profit from alcohol sales, but you can't argue the fact that alcohol has a higher profit margin than food. The argument analysis consists of providing new evidence that refutes each flawed assumption.

You can either support or refute the argument, but refuting is typically much easier. The arguments presented on the GRE are so brief that they can't possibly provide enough evidence to support a particular position. This enables you to easily poke holes in the argument and the reasons given to support the stated position.

On your scratch paper, jot down about five assumptions and new facts that support or refute those assumptions. Write down only key words — save your prose for the essay. The following list is an example of what someone may come up with to refute the argument presented earlier (you can make your notes less precise):

- **Faulty assumption:** Families won't make the drive from the distant suburbs.

  New fact: Though they don't live nearby, families may drive to the area for other reasons, such as shopping or recreation.

- **Faulty assumption:** Because Flint's other two saloons are successful, this new saloon will also be successful.

  New fact: Several factors may contribute to the success of the two saloons that aren't present in the restaurant's location, such as the proximity of a popular sports arena or theater.

- **Faulty assumption:** Flint's experience with saloons will make this newly converted saloon a success.

  New fact: Other factors affect success, including what else is in the area. There could be five saloons across the street from this restaurant but no other family restaurants within 5 miles.

- **Faulty assumption:** A liquor license that brings success to one locale will bring success to another.

  New fact: Regions are different. What works for a saloon in Dallas may not work for one in Salt Lake City.

- **Faulty Assumption:** Alcohol's higher profit margin will lead to higher overall profits, because the level of sales will be the same.

  New Fact: Though alcohol has a higher profit margin than food, the sales volume could be lower. Selling 200 dinners at a profit margin of 40 percent is more profitable than selling one case of beer at a profit margin of 80 percent.

If you think the argument is valid, list the reasons given in support of the argument followed by new facts that support those reasons. However, even if you believe the argument is fundamentally sound and you support it, you should still be able to show the GRE evaluator that you can recognize claims in the argument and can provide the missing support for those claims.

You don't have to use all five points in your essay. Whittle down your list to the best two or three — while writing the essay, you may discover that a couple points aren't valid. With only 30 minutes, having three well-developed points is very good, and it's far better than having five sketchy ideas.

Never refute a fact; just refute an assumption. You can't refute that alcohol has a higher profit margin, because the prompt presents it as a fact. Instead, accept the fact as true, and think of something else that would affect the outcome, such as sales volume. Refuting facts leads to point reductions on your essay.

Step 5: Write your essay

Essay writing is much easier if you have a structure in place, such as an outline. The structure provides you with a paint-by-numbers format. As you compose your essay, you simply focus on writing one paragraph after another. A good argument essay has four or five paragraphs.

Introductory paragraph

The first paragraph of your Analyze an Argument essay (the introduction) must demonstrate your understanding of the argument and whether you think the argument is valid or invalid. Structure the paragraph as follows:

- ✔ **First sentence:** Briefly state the argument you're analyzing and whether it's sound.

- ✔ **Second sentence:** Acknowledge the reasons in the argument and indicate whether the assumptions are faulty or the reasons provided offer solid evidence in support of the argument's main point.

- ✔ **Remaining sentences:** Touch upon the points you're going to bring up in subsequent paragraphs.

As you read the following example introduction paragraph, refer to the preceding list and see how I apply this structure.

> The author provides a compelling, though flawed, argument for Flint to convert his family restaurant to a saloon. Converting the restaurant may or may not be a wise course of action, and the assumptions used to support the argument lack sufficient evidence, and are, therefore, flawed. A great deal of information is missing that would validate or weaken the assumptions, such as whether how far away the families live makes a difference, whether success in one location promises success in another, and whether profit margin alone determines success. These unknown facts are very important to the validity of the argument, and Flint would be unwise to risk his business without knowing these facts.

Paragraphs two, three, and possibly four

Your example paragraphs each cover one of the argument's reasons or faulty assumptions and present a new fact or reason to support or refute it. Start with your strongest point first, and structure each paragraph as follows:

- ✔ **First sentence or two:** Present one of the argument's reasons/assumptions in your own words.

- ✔ **Next sentence:** Transition into the new fact you have to support or refute this particular reason/assumption.
- ✔ **Remaining sentences:** Provide additional details to support your new fact.
- ✔ **Last sentence:** Summarize how your new fact supports or refutes the argument's reason/assumption.

Read my example second, third, and fourth paragraphs and compare them to this list to see how I use this structure. Following is a sample second paragraph:

> First of all, the author states that most families live too far away. This may be true, but it doesn't mean families won't eat there. The author assumes that because families live so far away, they'll never be in the area. This may not be the case, because families may take a day trip into town and want to stop somewhere to eat. The author doesn't mention whether the restaurant is near a children's museum or a shopping mall that caters to families. The restaurant could be near plenty of family-based traffic, even though the suburbs are far from the restaurant.

Note the transition words at the beginning of each of the following essay paragraphs that help smooth the movement from one paragraph to the next:

> Furthermore, the author attributes the success of Flint's two saloons to the liquor license and asserts that the same will bring success to his restaurant. The author assumes that the conditions are the same at both locations. What works at one location, however, may not necessarily work at another. For example, the saloons could be in Dallas, where saloons can thrive, and the restaurant could be in Salt Lake City, with a much smaller drinking population.

> In addition, the author mentions the higher profit margin of alcohol as key to increased profits. The author assumes, however, that sales will be the same. No information is provided to suggest liquor sales will be comparable to food sales. Although profit margin is key to profits, sales volume is also important. A 20 percent profit from $500,000 in sales is worth more than a 50 percent profit from $100,000 in sales. The level of proposed alcohol sales needs to be known before Flint abandons his existing food sales for a throw-of-the-dice level of alcohol sales, regardless of the profit margin.

As you write your paragraphs, make sure to stick to these fine points:

- ✔ Spell out exactly why each reason is valid or why each assumption is invalid. Don't expect the evaluators to draw conclusions from your description — make it clear.
- ✔ Cover only one reason or assumption per paragraph.
- ✔ Use transition words at the beginning of each subsequent paragraph to move from one paragraph to the next. For more about transitions, see the section "Tying everything together with smooth transitions" earlier in this chapter.

Concluding paragraph

The last step to writing the Analyze an Argument essay is to compose the last paragraph, which is the conclusion. This is the closing bracket of your essay, with the introduction being the opening bracket. Your conclusion should mirror your introduction while leaving the evaluator with a sense of closure. Structure your concluding paragraph as follows:

- ✔ **First sentence:** Acknowledge the argument's main point and generally explain why you think it has or hasn't been adequately proven.
- ✔ **Next sentence or two:** Remind the reader of the reasons or assumptions that you think support or question the main point of the argument.
- ✔ **Closing:** The closing need not be a separate sentence, but it should complete your essay, leaving the evaluator with a sense of closure.

Look at my example conclusion and how I use the preceding list to draft the sentences.

Though the author provides a strong argument for converting Flint's restaurant to a saloon, the argument relies on several assumptions that are based on uncertain facts. These uncertain facts include the importance of how far away the families live, the question of whether success in one location brings success in another, and the dubious assumption that a higher profit margin alone will make the business more profitable. Flint should verify these key facts before making his decision.

The evaluators know that you're writing a rough draft. Your essays don't have to be perfect; they have to be logical, well-organized, and clear.

Chapter 15

Practicing Analytical Writing and Sample Essays

- -

In This Chapter

▶ Creating a realistic setting for writing your sample essays

▶ Composing an Analyze an Issue essay

▶ Composing an Analyze an Argument essay

- -

Knowing how to write the essays and actually writing them on the day of the test are two entirely different things. In this chapter, you get the opportunity to put into practice everything I cover in Chapter 14 so you can write high-scoring essays.

In this chapter, I provide two essay questions — one Analyze an Issue and one Analyze an Argument — complete with the directions similar to those you'll see on the actual GRE. You have 30 minutes to write each essay. Following each essay question, I provide sample essays (one good, one sort of good, and one poor) along with evaluator comments so you can gauge the quality of your essay, comparatively speaking, and have a clearer idea of what evaluators look for.

Practicing the essays is crucial to writing well under pressure, avoiding writer's block, and finishing in the allotted time. Write both essays — the Analyze an Issue and the Analyze an Argument essays — giving yourself 30 minutes each so you have a good feel for what each type of essay entails. After you're done writing, read through the sample essays and evaluator comments so you know what separates an outstanding essay from a mediocre one and a poor one. Writing good essays on the GRE doesn't take much practice, but it does take a little.

Setting the Stage for a Realistic Experience

To make your practice session more like what you'll experience on test day, set the stage by doing the following:

✔ **Write your essay on a computer rather than by hand.** Typing on a computer more effectively simulates the actual test-taking experience. You're more likely to make typos and other careless errors when you type compared to writing by hand.

✔ **Turn off your word processor's spelling and grammar checking features.** The word processor you'll use during the actual test doesn't correct or even check for grammar and spelling errors or typos. You can turn these features back on after writing your essay to identify any errors. (If you have a Windows PC, Notepad is similar to the program the GRE uses.)

> ✔ **Set your timer for 30 minutes per essay, but if time runs out, go ahead and finish the essay anyway.** You still have to practice writing the end of the essay, and the practice will help you write faster next time. Keep track of how much extra time you need so you know how much faster you need to work on test day.

Don't skip ahead and read the essays or evaluations before writing your own essay. Doing so gives you an unfair advantage and an unrealistic experience. Read the directions followed by the issue or argument and then immediately write your essay. If you're not very impressed with your own essay after reading the samples and commentary, go ahead and rewrite your essay. The changes you make in your rewrite will build your skills for the actual essays.

Writing an Analyze an Issue Essay: Some Samples

"Because society is always changing, laws should always change to reflect the times as well. In addition, laws should be open to interpretation based on the facts of each individual circumstance."

Directions: Write an essay in response to the following statement in which you discuss the extent to which you agree or disagree with the statement. Explain your reasoning in a clear, well-organized essay that supports your position. Consider both sides of the issue when developing your response.

Stop reading and write your essay. If you continue reading, you'll gain information and insights that give you an unfair advantage and ruin the practice session. In the following sections, I present sample topics that exemplify various ways to formulate and support a position in response to this Issue Essay prompt. I follow up with three sample essays based on this prompt, presented from best (with a score of 6) to worst (with a score of 2). Following each sample essay are evaluator comments that explain reasons for the score.

Having trouble getting started? Identifying relevant laws: Some examples

If you had trouble getting started, maybe you couldn't think of any laws to write about. This particular essay prompt is on laws that change and those that should be flexible (open to interpretation), so start by jotting down some examples of laws that meet those criteria. Here are a few examples of laws that changed in response to the changing times:

✔ New laws for new situations, such as cyberbullying today, DUI laws 20 years ago, and drivers' licenses 50 years ago

✔ Evolving laws for evolving situations, such as the use of medical marijuana

✔ Laws as a response to an event, such as terrorism or apartheid

Examples of laws that could be flexible or open to interpretation may include the following:

✔ Outdated laws, such as no carrying goldfish in Philadelphia or no singing to your horses

✔ Irrelevant laws, such as no dancing on Sundays

✔ Justified killing, such as self-defense or prevention of a tragedy

✔ Censorship and free speech

And because the prompt specifically instructs you to consider both sides of the issue, you need to consider laws that perhaps should not change over time or be open to interpretation, such as the following:

- First-degree murder
- Assassination
- Assault and battery
- Burglary
- Vandalism
- Hate crimes

Of course, you can't write on all of the examples I present in these three lists. When writing your essay, you need to pick the best few.

Stay away from examples that are out of scope, including the enforcement of laws, punishment, and regional differences. Also, avoid taking a hard line stand on such politically charged topics as gay marriage, abortion, or foreign policy.

Sample essay — score 6 (outstanding)

Though laws should evolve and have some flexibility, I don't agree with the statement that laws should always change and be interpreted by each individual circumstance. Throughout history, laws have existed and evolved with society. Our laws today are based on a balance of rigidity and flexibility. There is always some adjustment and some interpretation, but to take away the foundation of the laws and leave them completely open to popularity and interpretation would lead us either to a libertine or totalitarian society, neither of which would be healthy. In this essay, I will discuss laws that should evolve to keep pace with the new technology of an evolving society, especially regarding computers and cars. I will also discuss laws that should not be interpreted, such as premeditated murder, and finally laws that are no longer relevant and should possibly be scrubbed. Though these are all valid topics for discussion, they do not suggest that all of our laws should be subject to interpretation and flexibility.

There are plenty of examples of laws that evolve with society out of necessity. Cyberbullying wasn't an issue 30 years ago, so there wouldn't be a law regarding this. Today, however, the framework for cyberbullying is in place, so the law exists out of necessity. When cars first came out, there were no laws requiring drivers' licenses or preventing drunk driving. The road was probably a very dangerous place! To keep up with a changing society, laws were introduced to regulate the road. Whether these laws are overreaching is another discussion, but overall the roads are safer with these laws than without. In these cases — cyberbullying and roads — the laws are changing to reflect the times, and this is good.

However, these changes should be careful and deliberate. A law, such as prohibiting premeditated murder, cannot simply be flexible or interpreted based on circumstance. Around 1995, the Israeli prime minister Yitzchak Rabin was assassinated days before signing a peace treaty with Yasser Arafat, the leader of the PLO. The assassin was not a criminal before this, but he felt that the provision of the treaty would have placed the Israeli people in danger, and this was his motive for murder. His rationale was to kill one person to save many. Whether he was right is a topic for debate, but for the purpose of this essay, let's suppose that yes: the treaty would have led to the deaths of many Israelis. Was his act justified? This is the danger of leaving laws to interpretation. If you say that yes, in this case, it was justified, then it basically opens the door to a lawless society. The law against murder becomes null, because there's always a circumstance and interpretation making it OK. Our CEO is leading the company to bankruptcy. Kill her! My neighbor parties all night long and keeps me up, so I may lose my job. Kill him! This is absolutely NOT the direction that things should go. Laws such as this, prohibiting premeditated murder and certain other crimes, should not be open to flexibility and interpretation.

There are also laws that have faded to irrelevancy and are no longer enforced, but this is not the same as interpretation or circumstantial allowance. For example, "It's illegal to walk on the sidewalks of Philadelphia carrying goldfish," or "It is a crime to sing to your horses in the hearing of others" are examples of laws that are no longer relevant. I have always wondered what would happen if one of these obscure laws were suddenly enforced again. Can you imagine walking out of a pet store on a Sunday afternoon with a goldfish and getting busted? Legally, they could do it — it's the law. Fortunately they don't, but it brings up the point that laws may become irrelevant or obsolete, and therefore require some review. However, this is not the same as interpreting or making exceptions. These are laws that are obsolete because society has evolved away from them.

Laws should evolve and have some flexibility, but not too much. New technology, such as cars and computers, require new laws. Some old, obsolete laws probably have no place anymore in our modern society. However, certain laws cannot be flexible, such as killing one person to save many.

Evaluator comments on the score 6 essay

This essay presents an excellent answer to the question. The writer uses powerful, relevant examples to support his point and makes the clear case that though some flexibility and interpretation is warranted, it has to be controlled.

The writer's opinion is clear from the start and is supported by well-reasoned and thoroughly developed examples. The three examples are separated, yet they flow together well via the use of good transitions. The ending sums things up nicely and leaves no doubt as to the author's opinion.

 Your examples are more powerful if they're relevant to real life. Also, the evaluators know that you're not able to do research while taking the GRE, so it's okay if you're not sure of a detail, such as the year something happened or where exactly an event took place. The evaluators are simply interested in whether you can make a point and support it well.

Sample essay — score 4 (adequate)

Laws must change when Society changes. This is true for all types of laws, the major laws and the minor laws. This is true for all types of Societies, the so called First World, and the so-called Third World. This is true for all types of situations, from the serious to the silly to the macabre.

An example of when a law must change is the death penalty. Many years ago, condemned prisoners were executed routinely. Such executions became major events, almost parties, with the public making an excursion to watch the hanging. The irony, of course, is that the huge crowds at the execution attracted additional criminals who then committed more crimes (theft, pickpocketing, assault) and perpetated the cycle. Today, while there are less executions, they have become media events. We don't attend the executions in person, but we live through them vicariously, watching them on tv. When Timothy McVeigh, the Oklahoma City bomber, was given a lethal injection, the tv stations carried a minute-by-minute report. The amount of money and time and energy that was put into this could have been better spent elsewhere.

A second reason laws must be flexible is in time of war or social upheaval. Take, for example, the 1960's. The United States had a sea change during that decade. Many more things were acceptable socially then than had ever been before, and the laws had to change to reflect that fact. The possession of certain drugs became much less serious than it had been before. People weren't sentenced to twenty years for *using* drugs, just for *pushing* them. Today even more liberal attitudes towards drugs enable people to use them legally, as in the case of glaucoma or AIDS patients who smoke pot.

Traffic laws are a less serious, but still good, example of when laws should change. The speed limit in downtown New York must obviously be less than that in the outskirts of Podunk, Idaho (my apologies to the Podunkians!). Many people in Wyoming and other sparsely-populated Western states fought against having a federally-mandated speed limit of 55 on the freeways, argueing that in their areas, 65 or even 75 would be more logical. This is an example of the need for a change to meet the needs of a local community or Society. The same is true for the age at which youngsters can get a license, as they are more mature earlier now than before.

In conclusion, laws are not static because people are not static. We change from decade to decade, and from locale to locale. While it is important to adhere to the Declaration of Independence's statement that "all men are created equal," and thus should have equal rights, not all times are created equal, and thus should not have equal laws.

Evaluator comments on the score 4 essay

This is a generally acceptable response. The writer presents an unequivocal answer to the question and uses some good vocabulary ("macabre," "vicariously"). In addition, the length is good, with three well-organized examples.

However, the examples are out of scope. The money, time, and energy spent watching McVeigh's execution isn't relevant to changing laws. It's not clear why wars and social upheavals mandate a change in laws, or during which times the laws or the enforcement changed. And the speed limit differences in differently populated areas aren't shown to have changed; they are shown to be different.

The essay has additional weaknesses that prevent it from receiving a higher score, such as instances of inappropriate humor ("my apologies to the Podunkians!"). Although minor grammatical flaws are acceptable, "less executions" should be "fewer executions" and therefore isn't acceptable. The essay also contains too many typos and spelling and capitalization errors, including *perpetated* instead of *perpetuated*, *tv* instead of *TV* or *television*, *argueing* instead of *arguing*, and *Society* instead of *society*.

Sample essay — score 2 (seriously flawed)

"Because Society is always changing, laws should always change to reflect the times as well." This is a very true statement. Nothing ever remains exacly the same, and things change all the time. Isn't it logical to think that the laws should change as people and other situations change? My example the American society. We are much more ethnical diverse than we were a generation or two ago, and our laws have guaranteed this diversity. Old laws said that, for example, African-American people were not allowed in certain clubs or given certain jobs and this of course was wrong. Now there are laws to show how Society has changed and accepted this variety of people. Maybe someday there will be laws needed to protect White people who can't get jobs neither.

"In addition, laws should be open to interpretation based on the facts of each individual circumstance." This also is true. What about car accidents? If a person has an honest accident and hits and kills someone because he just lost control, that's a lot different than if he has been drunk and lost control that way and killed someone. It's not fair to send someone to prison for life because he had one horrible minute, but maybe it is fair to send someone to prison for life because he made the choice to drink and drive, the wrong choice.

In conclusion, I agree totally with both parts of the statement above. People need to realize that our Society changes and because laws are meant to protect Society, those laws must also change, too.

Evaluator comments on the score 2 essay

The writer presents a clear response to the question, both at the beginning and the end of the essay. However, the writer simply repeats the issue and makes a general statement of agreement.

Although a few examples are given to support the writer's opinion, the organization of the essay isn't developed well. The writer makes the comment that, "Now there are laws to show how Society has changed. . . . " The quality of the essay would be improved were the writer to add more examples and explain each example more fully. The closing statement in the second paragraph appears to introduce a new topic, which isn't fully covered.

Poor spelling ("exacly") and grammar ("much more ethnical diverse") hurt the response as well. Although the writer's opinion is still understandable, these errors contribute to the low score.

Writing an Analyze an Argument Essay: Some Samples

The following appeared in an in-house memo sent from a marketing director to the editorial department of a television news station.

> "Our research shows that when the news director comes on screen at the end of the newscast to present his perspective on an issue, many viewers switch stations or turn off the television entirely. Besides losing viewers, which lowers our ability to charge top dollar for advertising spots, we are wasting extra time that we could be filling with more ads. In addition, people tell us that they feel editorials are best read in the newspaper, not heard on television. Therefore, we recommend stopping all editorials at the ends of newscasts."

Directions: Write a response to the preceding argument that analyzes its stated or implied assumptions, reveals how the argument's position depends on the assumptions, and explains the effect of any flawed assumptions on the argument's validity.

Stop reading and write your essay. If you continue reading, you'll gain information and insights that give you an unfair advantage and ruin the practice session. In the following sections, I present some of the faulty assumptions included in the argument. I follow up with three sample essays written in response to this Argument, presented from best (with a score of 6) to worst (with a score of 2). Following each sample essay are evaluator comments that explain reasons for the score.

Having trouble getting started? Identifying some faulty assumptions

This particular essay prompt tells you to analyze the argument's stated or implied assumptions. The essay you wrote is a product of whatever you identified as stated or implied assumptions. If you had trouble getting started with your essay, you probably had difficulty identifying the faulty assumptions, which include the following:

- ✔ The author assumes that viewers leave because of the news director or the editorial, but viewers could leave for some other reason, such as another program starting on another channel. You need to know why the viewers leave.

- ✔ The author assumes that the ability to charge top dollar for the concluding ads is lost because viewers leave, but this ad space could be devalued for some other reason, such as that the last ads of any program have reduced value. You need to know why the value of the concluding ads is reduced.

- ✔ The author assumes that additional ads at the end can also be charged top dollar and implies that this will lead to more revenue, but additional ads may dilute the value of the ad spots. You need to know the number of ads that can run at the end of a program and still hold value.

- ✔ The author assumes that because editorials are better in newspapers, they aren't welcome on TV, but plenty of TV viewers may also enjoy the editorials on TV. You need to know whether viewers appreciate or resent the TV editorials.

- ✔ The author assumes that "people tell us" is a reliable source of feedback, but it could be a small, nonrepresentative sample group, such as retirees or high-school students. You need to know what a representative sample of viewers would say.

- ✔ The author assumes that the newscast would conclude smoothly without the wrapping-up editorial, but the newscast may actually appear to end abruptly. You need to know how the proposed changes would be received by the TV audience.

Of course, you can't write on *all* of these. When writing your essay, you'd need to pick the best two or three.

Sample essay — score 6 (outstanding)

The marketing director concludes that the news station should stop all editorials because viewership decreases when the news director presents his perspective on an issue at the end of the newscast. The memo argues that the news director and editorial drive viewers away, and that when people don't watch the end of the newscast, the station loses advertising revenue. This argument is based on a number of questionable assumptions, such as the reason why viewers leave at the end of the program, what the viewers would watch at the end of the newscast, and the reliability of the feedback on the editorial content.

First of all, the director recommends that the station stop the editorials at the end of newscasts because people are turning off what is currently offered. However, it is not known why viewers leave or change the channel. They could be flipping to watch *The Evening Show* on the other channel, so regardless of whether we run an editorial or who runs it, viewership could be lost.

Second, the director claims that the time devoted to the current editorial could be sold to advertisers. He assumes, then, that people who turn off the television or switch stations when the news director comes on will not do so when an advertisement comes on in the editorial's place. If viewers stop watching the station when they know the news is over, they will probably do the same when commercials come on instead of the editorial. When advertisers find out that people are not watching their commercials, they will cancel their contracts.

Finally, the director notes that "people tell" the station's marketing team that editorials are best read in the newspaper, not heard on television. Who are these people? As with any survey, the response is valid only if the sample is representative of the larger population. In other words, the marketing department assumes that these "people" are representative of the station's viewers. The memo is vague about the identity of these people, so they could be anyone. Perhaps they are not viewers at all and, therefore, cannot be used to represent the television viewing audience. Or, they could represent a specific segment of the market that favors newspapers. The director also fails to mention how numerous these people are and does not include any information about how many people may have expressed the opposite opinion to the marketing team. Really, the comments have no value without this information, and the TV station would thus be ill advised to follow their guidance.

Therefore, to improve his argument, the news director needs to address the above issues. He needs evidence that shows that viewers would turn off any kind of editorial at the end of the newscast. He also needs to demonstrate that viewers would watch advertisements after the presentation of news. He should also clarify the source of the comments about editorials in newspapers: are the comments from people who actually watch the news station? Without the answers to these questions, it is not recommended that the TV station take this course of action and change its format.

Evaluator comments on the score 6 essay

This very strong response presents a coherent, well-organized, direct analysis that introduces and fully develops the various points. It identifies three central gaps in knowledge that weaken or even undermine the argument, and it summarizes these in a brief conclusion. The language, grammar, spelling, and general writing skills also contribute to the excellence of this essay.

Sample essay — score 4 (adequate)

The argument presented in this memo is relatively well-reasoned, although flawed in some aspects. The primary weakness, in my opinion, is found at the beginning, where the memo states, "Our research has shown. . . . " without specifying what that research is. Did someone poll viewers who regularly watched the show? Did someone send out a questionaire which was returned only by a small percentage of people, some of whom did not regularly watch the news? How were the questions phrased by the researcher (as we all know, a question can easily beg the answer, be skewed so as to direct the response in the direction the questioner wants it to go). A good argument will state the basis for the conclusions it makes.

The argument has inspecificity. Nowhere does the memo say why the viewers switch stations. Maybe they don't like that particular news director. The station can experiment by having the editorials read by others on the staff, by reporters, or even by the public at large. There are some stations where I live that do that, have local people at the end of the newscasts tell their opinions. Many of my friends, at least, tune in to watch what their peers have to say.

Is the purpose of the last few minutes of a newscast to sell ads? Maybe, if there were no editorial, there would be an extra two minutes of news reporting, not of advertisements. There are already so many ads in a newscast as it is; more would possibly alienate the viewers even more than the editorial does. Also, I believe there is an FCC mandate as to how many minutes per hour or half hour can be commercials, at least in prime time. If the station didn't have the editorial, but ran commercials, they may acceed this limit.

Evaluator comments on the score 4 essay

This response is adequate. The organization is acceptable, although it would be improved by the use of transitional phrases. The writer appears to have a basic understanding of the argument but doesn't fully develop her comments except in a personal vein.

The writer seems to come close to nailing the points but doesn't quite do so. The start of the second paragraph says, "Nowhere does the memo say why the viewers switch stations." That the research, not the memo, indicates viewers switch stations notwithstanding, I was expecting the writer to hit the nail on the head with "We don't know why viewers switch stations, so we can't attribute it to the editorial." Instead, the author speculates as to why viewers switch, proposes an evaluation of the news director and editorial, then follows up with a digression about her own local news stations. While these points might be relevant in an editorial meeting, they neither support nor weaken the argument.

Finally, the lack of a coherent conclusion shifts this paper from a possible 5 to a 4.

Sample essay — score 2 (seriously flawed)

The reasoning in this arguement is not well-reasoned. The writer didn't convince me of their point at all. He doesn't talk about the possibility of moving the editorial, maybe putting the perspective at the beginning of the newscast, when people are probly more interested than at the end when they already heard everything they tuned in for. He doesn't say anything about maybe having the editorials paid for by an advertisement. He doesn't cover the possibility of the fact that the government considers some editorials public service anouncements. He doesn't go into enough detail to make a good case on anything.

If I was the memo-writer, I would also talk about how the editorials maybe appeal to a more educated, higher-class (to use a politically incorrect term) audience, one that maybe spends more money on the products. Like some sitcoms appeals to a different audience (some to older viewers or white viewers, some to younger more hip maybe black viewers) the newscast can appeal to more educated viewers with the editorials.

Evaluator comments on the score 2 essay

This essay is seriously hurt by the lack of organization. Ideas are introduced but not fully developed before new ideas are added. No one argument or theme is developed. There are too many errors in grammar (pronoun agreement, saying "The writer" and "their" and "If I was") and spelling ("arguement," "probly," "anouncements"), and the essay demonstrates a lack of variety in its sentence structure.

The writer shows little ability to analyze the argument and gives no support for the points made. Instead, the writer presents a personal opinion, giving his own views rather than analyzing and evaluating the points made by the author of the memo.

Part V
Taking Full-Length Practice GREs: It's All You

What to Do the Night before the Test

✔ **Gather everything you need.** Make sure you have the directions to the test center, your picture ID, your authorization voucher from ETS, water and a snack, and your lucky socks.

✔ **Get a good night's sleep.** Wait until you get your passing scores to celebrate with your friends.

✔ **Avoid junk food.** Salty and sugary foods are the enemy and will drain your energy. Eat fruits and vegetables for fuel that will carry you through the test.

If you don't score as well as you hope to on the GRE, check out the free article at www.dummies.com/extras/gre to decide whether you should retake the exam.

In this part . . .

✔ Discover your areas of strength and weakness by taking a full-length GRE practice test or two (or three).

✔ Score your test quickly with an answer key.

✔ Determine where you went wrong (or right) by reading through answer explanations for all practice test questions.

Chapter 16

Practice Exam 1

∙ ∙

You're now ready to take a practice GRE. Like the actual, computer-based GRE, the following exam consists of two 30-minute essays, two 30-minute Verbal Reasoning sections (20 questions each), and two 35-minute Quantitative Reasoning sections (20 questions each). The actual GRE may also include an extra Verbal or Quantitative Reasoning section, which doesn't count toward your score, but this practice exam has nothing like that.

Take this practice test under normal exam conditions and approach it as you would the real GRE:

- ✔ **Work when you won't be interrupted.**

- ✔ **Use scratch paper that's free of any prepared notes.** On the actual GRE, you receive blank scratch paper before your test begins.

- ✔ **Answer as many questions as time allows.** Consider answering all the easier questions within each section first and then going back to answer the remaining, harder questions. Because you're not penalized for guessing, go ahead and guess on the remaining questions before time expires.

- ✔ **Set a timer for each section.** If you have time left at the end, you may go back and review answers (within the section), continue and finish your test early, or pause and catch your mental breath before moving on to the next section.

- ✔ **Don't leave your desk while the clock is running on any section.** Though technically you're allowed to do this, it's not conducive to an effective time-management strategy.

- ✔ **Take breaks between sections.** Take a one-minute break after each section and the optional ten-minute break after the first Verbal section.

- ✔ **Type the essays.** Because you type the essays on the actual GRE, typing them now is good practice. Don't use software, such as Microsoft Word, with automatic spell-checker or other formatting features. Instead, use a simple text editor, such as Notepad, with copy and paste but no other features. The GRE essay-writing field features undo, redo, copy, and paste functionality but nothing else.

After completing this entire practice test, go to Chapter 17 to check your answers. Be sure to review the explanations for *all* the questions, not just the ones you miss. The answer explanations provide insight and a review of everything you went over in the previous chapters. This way, too, you review the explanations for questions that you guessed correctly on.

Chances are good that you'll be taking the computerized GRE, which doesn't have answer choices marked with A, B, C, D, E, and F. Instead, you'll see clickable ovals and check boxes, fill-in-the-blank text boxes, and click-a-sentence options (in some Reading Comprehension questions). I formatted the questions and answer choices to make them appear as similar as possible to what you'll see on the computer-based test, but I had to retain the A, B, C, D, E, F choices for marking your answers.

Answer Sheet for Practice Exam 1

Section 1:
Verbal Reasoning

1. Ⓐ Ⓑ Ⓒ Ⓓ Ⓔ
2. Ⓐ Ⓑ Ⓒ Ⓓ Ⓔ
3. Ⓐ Ⓑ Ⓒ Ⓓ Ⓔ Ⓕ
4. Ⓐ Ⓑ Ⓒ Ⓓ Ⓔ Ⓕ
5. Ⓐ Ⓑ Ⓒ Ⓓ Ⓔ Ⓕ Ⓖ Ⓗ Ⓘ
6. Ⓐ Ⓑ Ⓒ Ⓓ Ⓔ Ⓕ Ⓖ Ⓗ Ⓘ
7. Ⓐ Ⓑ Ⓒ Ⓓ Ⓔ
8. Ⓐ Ⓑ Ⓒ Ⓓ Ⓔ
9. Ⓐ Ⓑ Ⓒ
10. Ⓐ Ⓑ Ⓒ
11. Ⓐ Ⓑ Ⓒ Ⓓ Ⓔ
12. Ⓐ Ⓑ Ⓒ
13. Ⓐ Ⓑ Ⓒ Ⓓ Ⓔ
14. Ⓐ Ⓑ Ⓒ Ⓓ Ⓔ
15. Ⓐ Ⓑ Ⓒ Ⓓ Ⓔ
16. Ⓐ Ⓑ Ⓒ Ⓓ Ⓔ
17. Ⓐ Ⓑ Ⓒ Ⓓ Ⓔ Ⓕ
18. Ⓐ Ⓑ Ⓒ Ⓓ Ⓔ Ⓕ
19. Ⓐ Ⓑ Ⓒ Ⓓ Ⓔ Ⓕ
20. Ⓐ Ⓑ Ⓒ Ⓓ Ⓔ Ⓕ

Section 2:
Quantitative Reasoning

1. Ⓐ Ⓑ Ⓒ Ⓓ Ⓔ
2. Ⓐ Ⓑ Ⓒ Ⓓ Ⓔ
3. [＿＿＿＿＿]
4. [＿＿＿＿＿]
5. Ⓐ Ⓑ Ⓒ Ⓓ
6. Ⓐ Ⓑ Ⓒ Ⓓ
7. Ⓐ Ⓑ Ⓒ Ⓓ
8. Ⓐ Ⓑ Ⓒ Ⓓ
9. Ⓐ Ⓑ Ⓒ Ⓓ
10. Ⓐ Ⓑ Ⓒ Ⓓ
11. Ⓐ Ⓑ Ⓒ Ⓓ
12. [＿＿＿＿＿]
13. Ⓐ Ⓑ Ⓒ Ⓓ Ⓔ
14. Ⓐ Ⓑ Ⓒ Ⓓ Ⓔ
15. [＿＿＿＿＿]
16. Ⓐ Ⓑ Ⓒ Ⓓ Ⓔ
17. Ⓐ Ⓑ Ⓒ Ⓓ Ⓔ
18. Ⓐ Ⓑ Ⓒ Ⓓ Ⓔ
19. Ⓐ Ⓑ Ⓒ Ⓓ Ⓔ
20. Ⓐ Ⓑ Ⓒ Ⓓ Ⓔ Ⓕ

Section 3:
Verbal Reasoning

1. Ⓐ Ⓑ Ⓒ Ⓓ Ⓔ
2. Ⓐ Ⓑ Ⓒ Ⓓ Ⓔ
3. Ⓐ Ⓑ Ⓒ Ⓓ Ⓔ Ⓕ
4. Ⓐ Ⓑ Ⓒ Ⓓ Ⓔ Ⓕ
5. Ⓐ Ⓑ Ⓒ Ⓓ Ⓔ Ⓕ
6. Ⓐ Ⓑ Ⓒ Ⓓ Ⓔ Ⓕ Ⓖ Ⓗ Ⓘ
7. Ⓐ Ⓑ Ⓒ Ⓓ Ⓔ Ⓕ Ⓖ Ⓗ Ⓘ
8. Ⓐ Ⓑ Ⓒ Ⓓ Ⓔ
9. Ⓐ Ⓑ Ⓒ
10. Ⓐ Ⓑ Ⓒ Ⓓ Ⓔ
11. Ⓐ Ⓑ Ⓒ Ⓓ Ⓔ
12. Ⓐ Ⓑ Ⓒ Ⓓ Ⓔ
13. Ⓐ Ⓑ Ⓒ
14. Ⓐ Ⓑ Ⓒ Ⓓ Ⓔ
15. Ⓐ Ⓑ Ⓒ Ⓓ Ⓔ
16. Ⓐ Ⓑ Ⓒ Ⓓ Ⓔ
17. Ⓐ Ⓑ Ⓒ Ⓓ Ⓔ Ⓕ
18. Ⓐ Ⓑ Ⓒ Ⓓ Ⓔ Ⓕ
19. Ⓐ Ⓑ Ⓒ Ⓓ Ⓔ Ⓕ
20. Ⓐ Ⓑ Ⓒ Ⓓ Ⓔ

Section 4:
Quantitative Reasoning

1. Ⓐ Ⓑ Ⓒ Ⓓ Ⓔ
2. Ⓐ Ⓑ Ⓒ Ⓓ Ⓔ
3. Ⓐ Ⓑ Ⓒ Ⓓ Ⓔ
4. Ⓐ Ⓑ Ⓒ Ⓓ
5. Ⓐ Ⓑ Ⓒ Ⓓ
6. Ⓐ Ⓑ Ⓒ Ⓓ
7. Ⓐ Ⓑ Ⓒ Ⓓ
8. Ⓐ Ⓑ Ⓒ Ⓓ
9. Ⓐ Ⓑ Ⓒ Ⓓ
10. Ⓐ Ⓑ Ⓒ Ⓓ
11. Ⓐ Ⓑ Ⓒ Ⓓ Ⓔ
12. Ⓐ Ⓑ Ⓒ Ⓓ Ⓔ
13. Ⓐ Ⓑ Ⓒ Ⓓ Ⓔ
14. Ⓐ Ⓑ Ⓒ
15. [＿＿＿＿＿]
16. [＿＿＿＿＿]
17. Ⓐ Ⓑ Ⓒ Ⓓ Ⓔ Ⓕ
18. Ⓐ Ⓑ Ⓒ Ⓓ Ⓔ
19. [＿＿＿＿＿]
20. Ⓐ Ⓑ Ⓒ Ⓓ Ⓔ Ⓕ

Analytical Writing 1: Analyze an Issue

Time: 30 minutes

"Oversight of media and personal expression is an important part of any mature society."

Directions: Write a response in which you express the extent to which you agree or disagree with the preceding statement and explain the reasoning behind your position. In support of your position, think of ways in which the statement may or may not be true and how these considerations influence your position.

Analytical Writing 2: Analyze an Argument

Time: 30 minutes

The following appeared in a letter to the editor of the *Arlington Town Times*.

"To serve the housing needs of our community, the Arlington council should encourage land developers to build many new houses, condominiums, and apartments. Arlington's population is growing and, based on current trends, will double over the next 40 years, thus making the existing housing inadequate. Furthermore, the average home price has risen in recent years, probably due to a shortage of supply. This initiative could further serve to grow the town, as attractive new homes could make prospective residents more likely to move to Arlington."

Directions: Write a response in which you discuss the merits of the preceding argument. Analyze the evidence used as well as the general reasoning. Present points that would strengthen the argument or challenge it.

STOP DO NOT TURN THE PAGE UNTIL TOLD TO DO SO.
DO NOT RETURN TO A PREVIOUS TEST.

Section 1
Verbal Reasoning

Time: 30 minutes for 20 questions

Directions: Choose the best answer to each question. Blacken the corresponding ovals or boxes on the answer sheet.

Directions: For Questions 1–7, choose the one entry best suited for each blank from its corresponding column of choices.

1. Corporate leaders often try to _____ their intentions. After all, disclosing the motives that drive certain business decisions is likely to put their company's strategic advantage at risk.

Ⓐ occlude
Ⓑ stipulate
Ⓒ obfuscate
Ⓓ preclude
Ⓔ abjure

2. Individuals in positions of power often suffer at the hands of their own _____. Refusing to consider criticism, however valid, often leads them to make decisions that ultimately produce catastrophic results.

Ⓐ miscalculations
Ⓑ ambivalence
Ⓒ perfidy
Ⓓ ineptitude
Ⓔ hubris

3. Many observers of the trial believed that the judge's (i) _____ of Reed for prosecutorial misconduct ultimately led to the defendant's (ii) _____. Reed appeared despondent for the remainder of the trial.

Blank (i)	Blank (ii)
Ⓐ adjudication	Ⓓ conviction
Ⓑ excoriation	Ⓔ deposition
Ⓒ exoneration	Ⓕ exoneration

4. The report, (i) _____ from the company's own internal documents, revealed that security was not as (ii) _____ as the IT department had originally reported. Hackers easily bypassed the firewall.

Blank (i)	Blank (ii)
Ⓐ coerced	Ⓓ vulnerable
Ⓑ gleaned	Ⓔ implacable
Ⓒ redacted	Ⓕ impregnable

Go on to next page

5. A (i) _____ democracy must be built on certain (ii) _____ in order to survive. Giving the populace the right to vote without establishing the rule of law makes a young democracy (iii) _____ to evolving into a dictatorship.

Blank (i)	Blank (ii)	Blank (iii)
⒜ well-established	⒟ precepts	⒢ dedicated
⒝ nascent	⒠ criteria	⒣ resolute
⒞ representative	⒡ precedents	⒤ prone

6. A curved mirror produces an optical (i) _____ — a (ii) _____ in the appearance of the object it reflects. While looking in such a mirror may amuse some, others may find it (iii) _____.

Blank (i)	Blank (ii)	Blank (iii)
⒜ vacillation	⒟ distortion	⒢ debilitating
⒝ aberration	⒠ divergence	⒣ humorous
⒞ translucence	⒡ detraction	⒤ discomfiting

Go on to next page

Directions: Each of the following passages is followed by questions pertaining to the passage. Read the passage and answer the questions based on information stated or implied in that passage. For each question, select one answer choice unless instructed otherwise.

The following passage is an excerpt from The Role of the Father in Childhood Development, *5th Edition, by Michael E. Lamb, editor (Wiley).*

Whether and how much time fathers spend with their children are questions at the heart of much research conducted over the past three decades. In the mid-1970s a number of investigators sought to describe — often by detailed observation and sometimes also through detailed maternal and paternal reports — the extent of paternal interactions with children (Pleck & Masciadrelli, this volume; Lamb & Lewis, this volume). Many of these researchers have framed their research around the three types of paternal involvement (engagement, accessibility, responsibility) described by Lamb, Pleck, Charnov, and Levine (1987). As Pleck and Masciadrelli note, researchers have consistently shown that fathers spend much less time with their children than do mothers. In two-parent families in which mothers are unemployed, fathers spend about one-fourth as much time as mothers in direct interaction or engagement with their children, and about a third as much time being accessible to their children. Many fathers assume essentially no responsibility (as defined by participation in key decisions, availability at short notice, involvement in the care of sick children, management and selection of alternative child care, etc.) for their children's care or rearing, however, and the small subgroup of fathers who assume high degrees of responsibility has not been studied extensively. Average levels of paternal responsibility have increased over time, albeit slowly, and there appear to be small but continuing increases over time in average levels of all types of parental involvement.

7. Which sentence most clearly summarizes the research supporting the primary conclusion stated in this article?

Ⓐ Whether and how much time fathers spend with their children are questions at the heart of much research conducted over the past three decades.

Ⓑ Many of these researchers have framed their research around the three types of paternal involvement (engagement, accessibility, responsibility) described by Lamb, Pleck, Charnov, and Levine (1987).

Ⓒ As Pleck and Masciadrelli note, researchers have consistently shown that fathers spend much less time with their children than do mothers.

Ⓓ In two-parent families in which mothers are unemployed, fathers spend about one-fourth as much time as mothers in direct interaction or engagement with their children, and about a third as much time being accessible to their children.

Ⓔ Average levels of paternal responsibility have increased over time, albeit slowly, and there appear to be small but continuing increases over time in average levels of all types of parental involvement.

8. In the context of this paragraph, which of the following would not constitute "paternal responsibility"?

Ⓐ Taking care of a child who is ill

Ⓑ Reading to a child

Ⓒ Choosing a child care provider

Ⓓ Providing food, clothing, and housing for a child

Ⓔ Playing a game with a child

For Questions 9 and 10, consider each answer choice separately and select all answer choices that are correct.

9. Data from which of the following were not included in the research?

Ⓐ Single-parent families

Ⓑ Two-parent families in which the fathers are unemployed

Ⓒ Two-parent families in which the mothers are unemployed

10. Which of the following did researchers use as a measure of paternal involvement or responsibility?

Ⓐ Engagement, accessibility, and the care of sick children

Ⓑ Accessibility, responsibility, and financial support

Ⓒ Engagement and availability at short notice

Go on to next page

The following passage is an excerpt from World Literature in Theory *by David Damrosch, editor (Wiley-Blackwell).*

What are we to make of world literature today? The cultural and political realignments of the past two decades have opened the field of world literature to an unprecedented, even <u>vertiginous</u> variety of authors and countries. At once exhilarating and unsettling, the range and variety of literatures now in view raise serious questions of scale, of translation and comprehension, and of persisting imbalances of economic and cultural power. At the same time, the shifting landscape of world literature offers new opportunities for readers to encounter writers located well beyond the select few western European countries whose works long dominated worldwide attention. Whereas in past eras works usually spread from imperial centers to peripheral regions (from China to Vietnam, from London to Australia and Kenya, from Paris to almost everywhere), an increasingly multipolar literary landscape allows writers from smaller countries to achieve rapid worldwide fame. While still in his fifties, Orhan Pamuk became the second-youngest recipient of the Nobel Prize for Literature and was translated into 56 languages, Vietnamese included; he has many more readers abroad than in his native Turkey. Increasingly complex patterns of travel, emigration, and publication make "national" languages and literatures more and more international in character. The winner of the Nobel Prize in 2000, Gao Xingjian, has long lived in France and has become a French citizen, yet he continues to write in Chinese. Cultural hybridity is also found within the borders of China itself, as in the stories of the Sino-Tibetan writer Tashi Dawa, who has blended elements drawn from Tibetan folklore and international magical realism for his writings in Chinese; in a very real sense, his works were participating in world literature even before they began to be translated and read abroad.

11. In the context in which it appears, "vertiginous" most nearly means

Ⓐ Conceivable

Ⓑ Plausible

Ⓒ Dizzying

Ⓓ Enlightening

Ⓔ Edifying

For Question 12, consider each answer choice separately and select <u>all</u> answer choices that are correct.

12. Which of the following is/are given as example(s) of cross-cultural influence in literature?

[A] Distributing literary works from London to Kenya

[B] A French citizen writing in Chinese

[C] Blending magical realism with Tibetan folklore

The following passage is an excerpt from Sensory Evaluation: A Practical Handbook *by Susan Kemp, Tracey Hollowood, and Joanne Hort (Wiley-Blackwell).*

<u>Volatile</u> molecules are sensed by olfactory receptors on the millions of hair-like cilia that cover the nasal epithelium (located in the roof of the nasal cavity). Consequently, for something to have an odour or aroma, volatile molecules must be transported in air to the nose. Volatile molecules enter the nose orthonasally during breathing/sniffing, or retronasally via the back of the throat during eating. There are around 17,000 different volatile compounds. A particular odour may be made up of several volatile compounds, but sometimes particular volatiles (character-impact compounds) can be associated with a particular smell, e.g. iso-amyl acetate and banana/pear drops. Individuals may perceive and/or describe single compounds differently, e.g. hexenol can be described as grass, green, unripe. Similarly, an odour quality may be perceived and/or described in different compounds, e.g. minty is used to describe both menthol and carvone.

Go on to next page

13. Which of the following is not mentioned as a reason that associating an odor with a specific volatile compound may be difficult?

    Ⓐ Several volatiles may contribute to producing a specific odor.

    Ⓑ People may perceive the odor of compounds differently.

    Ⓒ A character-impact compound can be associated with a particular smell.

    Ⓓ The odors of different compounds may be perceived or described as having the same quality.

    Ⓔ People may describe the odor of compounds differently.

14. In the context in which it appears, "volatile" most nearly means

    Ⓐ Explosive

    Ⓑ Evaporating rapidly

    Ⓒ Fleeting; transient

    Ⓓ Tending to fluctuate rapidly and regularly

    Ⓔ Changeable

Typical silt loam soil is comprised of approximately 50 percent soil particles, 25 percent water, and 25 percent air. **Heavy farm equipment compacts the soil, significantly reducing the amount of air and water it can store and inhibiting the movement of air and water through the soil.** Soil compaction reduces crop yields in several ways. It impedes root penetration, reduces the amount of beneficial bacteria and fungi in the soil, increases the potential for runoff and soil erosion, reduces nutrient uptake, and stunts plant growth. To reduce soil compaction, **farmers are advised to avoid trafficking on wet soil, avoid using oversized equipment, reduce axle loads, limit tilling, and increase the soil's organic matter content.**

15. In this passage, the bolded portions play which of the following roles?

    Ⓐ The first states a conclusion; the second provides evidence to support that conclusion.

    Ⓑ The first states a problem, the effects of which are detailed in the second.

    Ⓒ The first states a conclusion that the second opposes.

    Ⓓ The first serves as an intermediate conclusion that supports a further conclusion stated in the second.

    Ⓔ The first asks a question that the second answers.

State lotteries lower taxes while increasing revenue for education. Since 1985, California's lottery contributed more than $24 billion to public schools. K–12 schools alone received over $19 billion.

16. Which of the following, if true, most seriously undermines the argument?

    Ⓐ In states without lotteries, citizens often cross the state line to play the lottery in a neighboring state.

    Ⓑ The California Lottery is required to provide at least 34 percent of its revenues to public education.

    Ⓒ The South Dakota Lottery has provided more than $1.7 billion to the Property Tax Reduction Fund.

    Ⓓ Lottery revenue represents less than 1 to 5 percent of the total education budget in states that use lottery revenue for education.

    Ⓔ Many states divert lottery dollars from their K–12 education programs to their general funds to make up for shortfalls.

> *Directions: Each of the following sentences has a blank indicating that a word or phrase is omitted. Choose the two answer choices that best complete the sentence and result in two sentences most alike in meaning.*

17. After campaigning to the point of exhaustion, somehow representative Hershel managed to remain _____ during his electrifying though brief victory speech.

    Ⓐ vivacious

    Ⓑ lugubrious

    Ⓒ ebullient

    Ⓓ laconic

    Ⓔ mendacious

    Ⓕ disingenuous

Go on to next page

18. Con artists have been known to actually steal homes right out from under homeowners without their knowledge. Key to these scams is the filing of _____ quit claim deeds, which transfer ownership to the con artist.

   A embezzled

   B photocopied

   C counterfeit

   D duplicate

   E pilfered

   F spurious

19. In the United States, the Federal Communications Commission (FCC) enforces laws that prohibit indecent programming and profane language during certain hours. Unfortunately, the FCC has had no success in eliminating the proliferation of television shows that glorify _____.

   A truculence

   B turpitude

   C asperity

   D infidelity

   E depravity

   F impertinence

20. The keynote speaker was incredibly _____, exceeding her allotted time by more than 45 minutes.

   A eloquent

   B loquacious

   C voluble

   D vivacious

   E voluminous

   F articulate

STOP DO NOT TURN THE PAGE UNTIL TOLD TO DO SO. DO NOT RETURN TO A PREVIOUS TEST.

Section 2

Quantitative Reasoning

Time: 35 minutes for 20 questions

Notes:

- ✔ All numbers used in this exam are real numbers.
- ✔ All figures lie in a plane.
- ✔ Angle measures are positive; points and angles are in the position shown.

1. Simplify $\left(\sqrt{64 \times 25} \right)^0$.

    Ⓐ 1

    Ⓑ 4

    Ⓒ 16

    Ⓓ 24

    Ⓔ 40

2. One bowl contains 5 hard candies, 3 of which are grape flavored. Another bowl contains 3 hard candies, 2 of which are grape flavored. If the candies all look the same and a child takes 1 candy from each bowl, what is the probability that the 2 selected candies are both grape flavored?

    Ⓐ $\dfrac{1}{5}$

    Ⓑ $\dfrac{2}{15}$

    Ⓒ $\dfrac{2}{5}$

    Ⓓ $\dfrac{4}{15}$

    Ⓔ $\dfrac{1}{3}$

3. If n is the units digit of 5^{50}, what is the value of n?

4. $\dfrac{\sqrt{27} \times \sqrt{3}}{\sqrt{9}} =$

Directions: For Questions 5–11, choose from the following answer choices:

Ⓐ *Quantity A is greater.*

Ⓑ *Quantity B is greater.*

Ⓒ *The two quantities are equal.*

Ⓓ *The relationship cannot be determined from the information given.*

5. A cart carries 5 parcels weighing 3 pounds each and 10 parcels weighing 9 pounds each.

Quantity A	**Quantity B**
The average parcel weight	8 pounds

6.

Quantity A	**Quantity B**
$\dfrac{9.99^{-10}}{9.99^{-9}}$	0.1

7.

Quantity A	**Quantity B**
$\dfrac{1{,}000!}{997!}$	999^3

Go on to next page

8.

Quantity A	Quantity B
$\sqrt{27}$	6

9. $(x-1)(x+1)=0$

Quantity A	Quantity B
x	0

10.

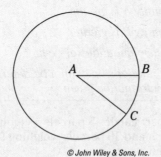

© John Wiley & Sons, Inc.

The circle shown has a radius of 5. Angle *CAB* originates at the center of the circle and measures 36°.

Quantity A	Quantity B
The length of minor arc *BC*.	π

11.

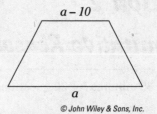

© John Wiley & Sons, Inc.

The trapezoid shown has an area of $(a-5)^2$.

Quantity A	Quantity B
The height of the trapezoid	$a-5$

Go on to next page

Questions 12–14 are based on the following graphs.

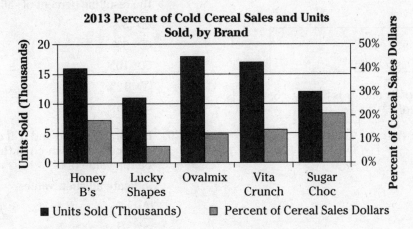

2013 Cold Cereal Sales per County, in Thousands

© John Wiley & Sons, Inc.

12. If the total 2013 cold cereal sales for the seven counties assessed is $150,000, what percent of these sales were purchased by Humboldt County?

 %

13. Which brand of cereal has the highest average selling price per box?

Ⓐ Honey B's

Ⓑ Lucky Shapes

Ⓒ Ovalmix

Ⓓ Vita Crunch

Ⓔ Sugar Choc

14. If residents of Glenn County primarily purchase the Lucky Shapes brand cereal and residents of Trinity County primarily purchase the Sugar Choc brand cereal, what is the approximate ratio of the number of boxes sold in Glenn County to the number of boxes sold in Trinity County?

Ⓐ 5:1

Ⓑ 3:1

Ⓒ 1:1

Ⓓ 1:3

Ⓔ 1:7

Go on to next page

15. $\dfrac{2^{17}}{16^4} =$

16. The sum of $3x$ and $4y$ is 50. If $y = 5$, what is the value of x?

    Ⓐ   5

    Ⓑ   10

    Ⓒ   12

    Ⓓ   15

    Ⓔ   18

17. If n is a positive integer, which of the following represents the product of n and the integer following n?

    Ⓐ $n^2 + 1$

    Ⓑ $n^2 + 2$

    Ⓒ $(n+1)^2$

    Ⓓ $n^2 + n$

    Ⓔ $2n^2$

18. If a boy on a snow sled travels downhill at a constant rate of 25 kilometers per hour, how many meters does he travel in 18 seconds? (1 kilometer = 1,000 meters)

    Ⓐ   5

    Ⓑ   18

    Ⓒ   25

    Ⓓ   75

    Ⓔ   125

19. If 10 liters of a 6% saline solution are mixed with 5 liters of a 9% saline solution, what is the resulting percent of saline concentration?

    Ⓐ   3%

    Ⓑ   5%

    Ⓒ   10%

    Ⓓ   12%

    Ⓔ   15%

20. For all integers a and b, if $a \odot b = (ab)^2$ and $a \odot b < 25$, then which of the following could be the value of b?

Indicate <u>all</u> such values.

    Ａ -7

    Ｂ -3

    Ｃ 0

    Ｄ $\dfrac{1}{2}$

    Ｅ $\sqrt{3}$

    Ｆ 5

STOP   DO NOT TURN THE PAGE UNTIL TOLD TO DO SO. DO NOT RETURN TO A PREVIOUS TEST.

Section 3
Verbal Reasoning

Time: 30 minutes for 20 questions

Directions: Choose the best answer to each question. Blacken the corresponding ovals or boxes on the answer sheet.

Directions: For Questions 1–7, choose the one entry best suited for each blank from its corresponding column of choices.

1. Although product customization has been a popular feature of smartphones and other electronic devices for many years, it has become _____ throughout the retail market. Now consumers can even design their own t-shirts and tennis shoes!

   Ⓐ inaccessible

   Ⓑ indispensable

   Ⓒ ubiquitous

   Ⓓ scarce

   Ⓔ salubrious

2. The _____ Dr. Mandalow was not the best choice to present the group's findings. Following the presentation, he left the room without asking whether anyone in attendance had any questions.

   Ⓐ taciturn

   Ⓑ effusive

   Ⓒ indignant

   Ⓓ despondent

   Ⓔ malevolent

3. To some degree, epigenetics (i) _____ the Darwinian notion that gene mutations and natural selection alone drive evolution. Research in epigenetics has shown that an organism's genes are not (ii) _____ as Darwin claimed. Environmental factors have been shown to alter a gene's expression, and these changes may be passed down to subsequent generations.

Blank (i)	Blank (ii)
Ⓐ obviates	Ⓓ imperturbable
Ⓑ expatiates	Ⓔ immutable
Ⓒ repudiates	Ⓕ inimitable

4. Accountants and other financial experts are often depicted as being (i) _____. When it comes to investing, however, these individuals are often extremely (ii) _____, especially when they are allowed to gamble with other people's money.

Blank (i)	Blank (ii)
Ⓐ dissident	Ⓓ audacious
Ⓑ diffident	Ⓔ pusillanimous
Ⓒ confident	Ⓕ aloof

Go on to next page

5. Given the (i) _____ of livestock and the (ii) _____ of corn, farmers decided to market their corn for use in producing biodiesel fuel instead of using it as feed.

Blank (i)	Blank (ii)
Ⓐ plethora	Ⓓ dearth
Ⓑ paucity	Ⓔ scarcity
Ⓒ overabundance	Ⓕ surfeit

6. The (i) _____ nature of the situation required that the CEO consult her most (ii) _____ advisors. After considering their advice, the CEO was able to make (iii) _____ decisions that greatly improved her company's market share.

Blank (i)	Blank (ii)	Blank (iii)
Ⓐ delicate	Ⓓ conscientious	Ⓖ sagacious
Ⓑ sensitive	Ⓔ confidential	Ⓗ salacious
Ⓒ involute	Ⓕ trenchant	Ⓘ sententious

7. Some teachers (i) _____ charter schools, claiming that the schools have an unfair advantage. (ii) _____ by Department of Education policies and state laws that govern education, charter schools can set very selective admissions standards and (iii) _____ their own policies, while traditional public schools cannot.

Blank (i)	Blank (ii)	Blank (iii)
Ⓐ extoll	Ⓓ unencumbered	Ⓖ disallow
Ⓑ advocate	Ⓔ hampered	Ⓗ forge
Ⓒ deprecate	Ⓕ constrained	Ⓘ correlate

Go on to next page

Directions: Each of the following passages is followed by questions pertaining to the passage. Read the passage and answer the questions based on information stated or implied in that passage. For each question, select one answer choice unless instructed otherwise.

The following passage is an excerpt from Electricity from Wave and Tide: An Introduction, *by Paul A. Lynn (Wiley).*

In his famous book *Small is Beautiful,* first published in 1973, E. F. Schumacher poured scorn on the idea that the problems of production in the industrialised world had been solved. Modern society, he claimed, does not experience itself as part of nature, but as an outside force seeking to dominate and conquer it. And it is the illusion of unlimited powers deriving from the undoubted successes of much of modern technology that is the root cause of our present difficulties, in particular because we are failing to distinguish between capital and income components of the earth's resources. We use up capital, including coal, oil and gas reserves, as if they were steady and sustainable income, but they are actually once-and-only capital. Schumacher's heartfelt plea encouraged us to start basing industrial and energy policy on what we now call sustainability, recognising the distinction between capital and income and the paramount need to respect the planet's finite ability to absorb the polluting products of industrial processes — including electricity production.

Schumacher's message, once ignored or derided by the majority, is now seen as mainstream. For the good of Planet Earth and future generations we have started to distinguish between capital and income and to invest heavily in renewable technologies that produce electricity free of carbon emissions.

8. In the context of this passage, which of the following energy sources would be classified as income?

Ⓐ Heating oil

Ⓑ Hydroelectricity

Ⓒ Natural gas

Ⓓ Uranium

Ⓔ Coal

For Question 9, consider each answer choice separately and select all answer choices that are correct.

9. Which of the following notions are mentioned in this passage as being disparaged?

Ⓐ Shumacher's message

Ⓑ Modern society's attempt to dominate and conquer nature

Ⓒ The assumption that production problems in the industrial world had been solved

10. Which sentence most clearly summarizes the research supporting the primary conclusion stated in this article?

Ⓐ In his famous book *Small is Beautiful,* first published in 1973, E. F. Schumacher poured scorn on the idea that the problems of production in the industrialised world had been solved.

Ⓑ Modern society, he claimed, does not experience itself as part of nature, but as an outside force seeking to dominate and conquer it.

Ⓒ We use up capital, including coal, oil and gas reserves, as if they were steady and sustainable income, but they are actually once-and-only capital.

Ⓓ Schumacher's heartfelt plea encouraged us to start basing industrial and energy policy on what we now call sustainability, recognising the distinction between capital and income and the paramount need to respect the planet's finite ability to absorb the polluting products of industrial processes — including electricity production.

Ⓔ For the good of Planet Earth and future generations we have started to distinguish between capital and income and to invest heavily in renewable technologies that produce electricity free of carbon emissions.

Go on to next page →

> The following passage is an excerpt from
> Leverage: How Cheap Money Will Destroy the
> World, by Karl Denninger (Wiley).

The economic crisis that gripped the nation in 2007 was not an accident, and the people responsible not only saw it coming but also knew the crisis would occur. It was inevitable and created by unsound policies at all levels of government and finance. The latest economic upheaval is nothing more than another in a long series of economic catastrophes that stem from fundamental failures to recognize and act on the mathematical realities of finance and rein in abuses of leverage promulgated by the rich and powerful in our society.

None of these issues has been addressed. Dodd-Frank, the recent financial reform law, does not force price transparency on derivatives and contains enough loopholes to drive a Mack truck through. The 2008 emergency bill, EESA/TARP, passed in no small part due to threats of financial Armageddon by both Ben Bernanke of the Federal Reserve and Hank Paulson of Treasury, in fact contained a Trojan horse provision that removed the legal requirement for all bank reserves, allowing banks to create infinite leverage. We have failed to force recognition of losses by the banking industry and have protected various firms from the consequences of their bad lending decisions. By failing to force banks to lend only in a safe and sound manner and to back up their unsecured lending with actual capital, we continue to perpetuate the myth that we can forevermore say, "Charge it" and never pay off the debt we accumulate.

All of these acts have served to hold systemic debt at unsustainable levels rather than allow it to default. As a consequence, our economy remains <u>moribund</u> and employment anemic, despite claimed improvement.

11. Which of the following statements most accurately summarizes the main point of this passage?

    Ⓐ Accumulated debt must eventually be paid off.

    Ⓑ Establishing and enforcing sound financial policies is essential for a strong economy.

    Ⓒ Economic crises are caused by rich and powerful people who abuse their financial leverage.

    Ⓓ Legislation designed to rein in abuses in the financial markets are full of loopholes.

    Ⓔ Corrupt politicians protect banks from making bad lending decisions.

12. In the context in which it appears, "moribund" most nearly means

    Ⓐ Robust

    Ⓑ Extinct

    Ⓒ Stout

    Ⓓ Stagnant

    Ⓔ Dead

> For Question 13, consider each answer choice
> separately and select all answer choices that
> are correct.

13. Which of the following issues that contributed to the economic crisis of 2007 has/have not been addressed?

    A   Dodd-Frank

    B   Forcing banks to back up unsecured loans with capital

    C   Price transparency on derivatives

> The following passage is an excerpt from The
> Prosperity Agenda: What the World Wants
> from America — and What We Need in Return,
> by Nancy Soderberg (Wiley).

A crucial reason fewer people in the world trust the United States is that countries do not see America helping them with their interests and addressing common threats. In 2007, citizens around the globe cited crime, political corruption, drugs, infectious disease, and pollution as their top national concerns. Terrorism, the poor quality of drinking water, and conflict were also high on the list. Unless America is seen to be helping with these issues, the world will not help America.

American leaders tend to center U.S. foreign policy entirely on "hard power" security issues such as proliferation and terrorism (and, in all honesty, oil). This is an incomplete approach because much good can be done to benefit our own interests while helping other countries with a global campaign against crime, infectious diseases, and dirty water. The world will not follow the United States unless it is seen to be helping the world address its challenges.

In today's dangerous world, the United States must again become the world's great persuader; not only the enforcer. To do so, America must act in a way that regains the world's trust. The good news is that if it does so, America can quickly regain the political support it has lost around the world.

Go on to next page

When America does the right thing, the world notices. For instance, favorable opinions of America in southeast Asia reached record lows during the first year after the United States started the Iraq War. Yet that image began to rebound when America used its military and economic power to help the victims of the 2004 tsunami, which set off tidal waves that wiped out communities across the coastal areas of Indonesia, Thailand, Sri Lanka, India, Malaysia, and parts of Africa. America took the lead in providing military and logistical support, including $350 million in immediate humanitarian relief assistance. (For comparison, the United States spends twice that much money every day in Iraq.)

14. Which of the following statements most accurately summarizes this passage?

    Ⓐ Humanitarian aid is more effective than military might in helping foreign countries.

    Ⓑ The United States must use its military and economic power for good, not evil.

    Ⓒ Foreign countries do not see America helping them address common threats.

    Ⓓ U.S. foreign policy should focus on stopping nuclear proliferation and terrorism.

    Ⓔ The United States can expand its influence in the world by building trust.

15. Assuming each of the following statements is true, which of these statements most effectively challenges the claims made in this passage?

    Ⓐ The President's Malaria Initiative (PMI) works in 19 countries in sub-Saharan Africa and the Greater Mekong Subregion in Asia to fight malaria.

    Ⓑ The U.S. launched the Global Health Initiative in 2009 to address global health challenges that threaten lives at home and abroad.

    Ⓒ In the Iraq War, the U.S. removed from power Saddam Hussein, the President of Iraq who skimmed billions of dollars from the United Nation's oil-for-food program.

    Ⓓ Secret documents prove that the U.S. National Security Agency has spied on its own allies, including Israel, France, and Germany.

    Ⓔ USAid spent more than $270 million on projects in Haiti in 2013, but U.S. companies received more than half of that amount, and American nonprofits, another 37 percent.

What are the costs to society of treating mental illness? Perhaps the better question is what are the costs to society of *not* treating mental illness? Failure to treat mental illness often leads to job loss, homelessness, and sometimes even incarceration. Prisoners with mental illness cost the nation on average nearly $9 billion annually. By diagnosing and treating people with mental illness, state, federal, and local governments can actually save money while helping to preserve the dignity of the person with mental illness.

16. Which of the following sentences from the passage offers evidence to support an answer to a question in the passage?

    Ⓐ What are the costs to society of treating mental illness?

    Ⓑ Perhaps the better question is what are the costs to society of *not* treating mental illness?

    Ⓒ Failure to treat mental illness often leads to job loss, homelessness, and sometimes even incarceration.

    Ⓓ Prisoners with mental illness cost the nation on average nearly $9 billion annually.

    Ⓔ By diagnosing and treating people with mental illness, state, federal, and local governments can actually save money while helping to preserve the dignity of the person with mental illness.

    Directions: Each of the following sentences has a blank indicating that a word or phrase is omitted. Choose the two answer choices that best complete the sentence and result in two sentences most alike in meaning.

17. Members of both parties encouraged their constituents to _____ violence on the grounds that it would be counterproductive.

    Ⓐ embrace

    Ⓑ avoid

    Ⓒ appropriate

    Ⓓ incite

    Ⓔ eschew

    Ⓕ denounce

Go on to next page

18. One of Nikola Tesla's many _____ is that he calculated the cubic volume of each meal before eating it.

    A endowments

    B passions

    C quirks

    D idiosyncrasies

    E assimilations

    F obsessions

19. Choosing a career is _____ in deciding on a course of study. If you choose medicine, your focus will be on science and math. If you choose law, your course load will focus on the humanities.

    A inconsequential

    B paramount

    C trivial

    D marginal

    E pivotal

    F urgent

Read the passage and answer the question based on information stated or implied in the passage.

The following passage is an excerpt from The Human Impact on the Natural Environment: Past, Present, and Future, *by Andrew S. Goudie (Wiley-Blackwell).*

A distinction can be drawn between cultivation and domestication. Whereas cultivation involves deliberate sowing or other management, and entails plants which do not necessarily differ genetically from wild populations of the same species, <u>domestication</u> results in genetic change brought about through conscious or unconscious human selection. This creates plants that differ morphologically from their wild relatives and which may be dependent on humans for their survival. Domesticated plants are thus necessarily cultivated plants, but cultivated plants may or may not be domesticated. For example, the first plantations of *Hevea* rubber and quinine in the Far East were established from seed which had been collected from the wild in South America. Thus at this stage in their history these crops were cultivated but not yet domesticated.

20. Based on the definition of "domestication" given in this passage, which of the following is not an example of domestication?

    Ⓐ Genetically modified corn

    Ⓑ Farm-raised catfish

    Ⓒ Hybrid crops

    Ⓓ Purebred dogs

    Ⓔ Seedless watermelon

STOP DO NOT TURN THE PAGE UNTIL TOLD TO DO SO.
DO NOT RETURN TO A PREVIOUS TEST.

Section 4
Quantitative Reasoning

Time: 35 minutes for 20 questions

Notes:

✔ All numbers used in this exam are real numbers.

✔ All figures lie in a plane.

✔ Angle measures are positive; points and angles are in the position shown.

1. $\dfrac{5\left(2^{12}\right)}{4^5} =$

   (A) 5
   (B) 10
   (C) 15
   (D) 20
   (E) 25

2. If y is an integer and $\sqrt{48y}$ is an integer, which of the following is the lowest possible value of y?

   (A) 1
   (B) 2
   (C) 3
   (D) 4
   (E) 6

3. If n is an integer and $\dfrac{210}{n}$ is an integer, which of the following could be the value of n?

   Indicate <u>all</u> such values.

   [A] 6
   [B] 12
   [C] 14
   [D] 35
   [E] 42

Directions: For Questions 4–10, choose from the following answer choices:

(A) *Quantity A is greater.*

(B) *Quantity B is greater.*

(C) *The two quantities are equal.*

(D) *The relationship cannot be determined from the information given.*

4. Fifteen candies are to be divided up among six children so that each child receives at least two candies.

Quantity A	**Quantity B**
The probability that any child receives six candies	0

5. Davis travels at a constant speed of 40 miles per hour for two hours and then at a constant speed of 60 miles per hour for one hour.

Quantity A	**Quantity B**
Davis's average speed for the entire trip	45 miles per hour

6.

Quantity A	**Quantity B**
900	$\sqrt{(30)(30)(30)(30)}$

Go on to next page

7. $f(x) = x^2 + 2x - 2$

Quantity A	*Quantity B*
The value of x when $f(x) = 13$	3

8.

Quantity A	*Quantity B*
$(0.99)^{99}$	1

9.

Quantity A	*Quantity B*
$5!$	$\dfrac{6!}{3!}$

10.   A right circular cylinder has a volume of 36π.

Quantity A	*Quantity B*
The sum of the radius and height of the cylinder if the radius and height are both integers greater than 1	12

Questions 11–13 are based on the following graphs.

Physics Grades and Enrollments of Middle School Students in the Fraser School District Enrollment

Subdistrict	6th Grade	7th Grade	8th Grade	Totals
Aguilar	83	99	89	271
Bayfield	107	103	96	306
Creede	74	70	67	211
De Beque	40	36	39	115
Eaton	69	64	69	202
Totals	373	372	360	1,105

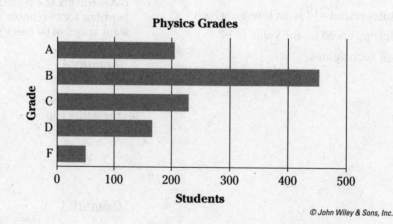

Physics Grades

Go on to next page →

11. What is the approximate ratio of students earning a C to those earning a B?

    Ⓐ 1:2

    Ⓑ 2:1

    Ⓒ 3:2

    Ⓓ 4:3

    Ⓔ 1:1

12. If all the students from Creede, and only those students, are earning A's and the rest of the grades are evenly distributed among students in the other subdistricts, approximately how many students from Bayfield are earning B's?

    Ⓐ 50

    Ⓑ 75

    Ⓒ 150

    Ⓓ 225

    Ⓔ 306

13. If all the grades are evenly distributed throughout all districts and classes, approximately how many students in De Beque are *not* earning a B?

    Ⓐ 20

    Ⓑ 40

    Ⓒ 70

    Ⓓ 100

    Ⓔ 115

14. If the range of set S is 9 and $S = \{2,4,5,7,8,9,x\}$, which of the following *could* be the median of set *S?*

    Indicate <u>all</u> possible answers.

    Ⓐ 5

    Ⓑ 6

    Ⓒ 7

15. $\left(\frac{1}{8}-\frac{3}{10}\right)+\left(\frac{1}{4}-\frac{1}{5}\right)+\left(\frac{5}{8}-\frac{1}{2}\right)=$

16. $\sqrt{9(36)+12(36)+15(36)}=$

17. Given the inequality $x^2 < 25$, which of the following *could* be the value of *x?*

    Indicate <u>all</u> such values.

    Ⓐ −6

    Ⓑ −5

    Ⓒ −3

    Ⓓ 0

    Ⓔ 3

    Ⓕ 5

18.

© John Wiley & Sons, Inc.

The square is inscribed within the circle and has a side length of $\sqrt{2}$. What is the area of the shaded portion of the drawing?

    Ⓐ $2-\pi$

    Ⓑ $\pi-2$

    Ⓒ $\pi-\sqrt{2}$

    Ⓓ $\pi-4$

    Ⓔ $4-\pi$

Go on to next page

19.

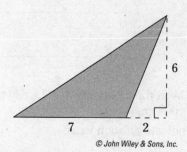

© John Wiley & Sons, Inc.

The area of the shaded triangle is

20. If Clarissa's monthly mortgage payment is less than $\frac{1}{3}$ but more than $\frac{1}{4}$ of her monthly income, and if the monthly mortgage payment is $600, which of the following could not be her annual income?

Indicate <u>all</u> such values.

- [A] $12,200
- [B] $17,400
- [C] $21,600
- [D] $24,200
- [E] $28,800
- [F] $31,300

Chapter 17

Practice Exam 1: Answers and Explanations

∙∙∙

After taking Practice Exam 1 in Chapter 16, use this chapter to check your answers and see how you did. Carefully review the explanations because doing so can help you understand why you missed the questions you did and also give you a better understanding of the thought process that helped you select the correct answers. If you're in a hurry, flip to the end of the chapter for an abbreviated answer key.

Analytical Writing Sections

Give your essays to someone to read and evaluate for you. Refer that helpful person to Chapters 14 and 15 for scoring guidelines.

Section 1: Verbal Reasoning

1. **C.** Corporate leaders would try to *obfuscate* (conceal) their intentions in order to maintain a competitive advantage. *Occlude* makes a good runner-up, but it carries a meaning more along the lines of blocking off access to something. None of the other three choices is close: *Stipulate* means to demand something specific, *preclude* means to prevent or prohibit, and *abjure* means to avoid or reject.

2. **E.** *Hubris* is excessive pride or self-confidence, which is often characterized by a refusal to consider any criticism, as expressed in the second sentence. If it weren't for that second sentence, any of the other answer choices would work: *miscalculations* can undermine a leader's plans, *ambivalence* is uncertainty or indecisiveness, *perfidy* is treachery, and *ineptitude* is incompetence.

3. **B, F.** The judge must have *excoriated* (severely criticized) Reed in order for him to be despondent, and that despondency likely led to the defendant's *exoneration* (acquittal), because the despondent Reed would be less effective in her role as prosecutor. If Reed were not described as despondent, you could make a case for choosing *exoneration* for the first blank and *conviction* for the second. Although *adjudication* (a court order) is a legal term, a judge doesn't adjudicate a person.

4. **B, F.** The report would have been *gleaned* (gathered) from internal documents, not *coerced* (gotten by force) or *redacted* (put into a suitable literary form). If hackers easily bypassed the firewall, the security must not have been as *impregnable* (able to withstand attack) as IT had reported. *Vulnerable* would imply that security was stronger than IT had thought. *Implacable* means unable to be satisfied or appeased.

5. **B, D, I.** The second sentence references a democracy in early development, so it must be a *nascent* (emerging) democracy that would need to be built on certain *precepts* (principles or guidelines) in order to be strong. Otherwise, the government would be *prone* (disposed to) to evolving into a dictatorship.

For the first blank, you can rule out *well-established*, which is the opposite of **nascent,** and *representative*, which is just a type of democracy (direct or representative). For the second blank, both *criteria* and **precedents** would be good second choices, but because the second sentence mentions the right to vote and the rule of law, **precepts** is more accurate. For the third blank, you can rule out *dedicated,* because no democracy dedicates itself to becoming a dictatorship. You can rule out **resolute** (determined) for much the same reason.

6. **B, D, I.** The reflection in a curved mirror would be an **aberration** (an abnormality), not a **vacillation** (wavering) or **translucence** (semi-transparency), so the reflection in the mirror would be a *distortion* (misrepresentation). For the second blank, **divergence** (deviation or departure) would be a good second choice, but **distortion** is more precise. **Detraction** (disparagement or denigration) doesn't work. Some people find such a distorted reflection of themselves **discomfiting** (unsettling). **Debilitating** (incapacitating) is too strong a word, and *humorous* doesn't work, because the last sentence is structured in a way that the missing word must be nearly the opposite of *amusing*.

7. **C.** You may be tempted to select the last sentence because it presents a summary of the data, but the main conclusion in this passage is that fathers spend considerably less time with their children than do mothers.

8. **D.** Evidence to support the claim that fathers spend considerably less time with their children than mothers do involves actual time spent with the child or choosing a child-care provider who will spend considerable time with the child. Supporting the child financially by providing food, clothing, and housing doesn't necessarily involve spending time with the child.

9. **A, B.** The passage focuses on two-parent families in which mothers are unemployed and only mentions "the small subgroup of fathers who assume high degrees of responsibility." It doesn't provide data related to single-parent families or two-parent families in which the father stays home with the children.

10. **A, C.** Researchers did not include mention of financial support as a measure of parental responsibility, so you can rule out answer Choice (B). Engagement, accessibility, availability at short notice, and the care of sick children are all mentioned as measures of parental responsibility.

11. **C. Vertiginous** means spinning, whirling — movement that would cause someone to become dizzy. Because this passage describes the variety of literature as overwhelming, in both positive and negative ways, the variety of authors and countries is considered vertiginous. You can immediately rule out the first two options, which both mean something along the lines of believable. Although literature may be *enlightening* (informative) and **edifying** (intellectually enriching), the *variety* of authors and countries would probably not be considered enlightening or edifying in this context.

12. **B, C.** Gao Xingjian is mentioned as a French citizen who continues to write in Chinese, while Tashi Dawa blends elements drawn from Tibetan folklore and international magical realism for his writings in Chinese. This question is a little tricky, because cultural hybridity isn't mentioned until the second example of it is presented. Choice (A) is wrong because in this passage, *cultural hybridity* refers to the blending of cultures within a literary work, not the exchange of literary works between countries or cultures, although such exchanges no doubt promote cultural hybridity in literature.

13. **C.** The fact that a character-impact compound can be associated with a particular smell would help, not hinder, the ability to associate an odor with a specific volatile compound.

14. **B.** All of the answer choices are definitions of **volatile,** but because the passage discusses molecules being distributed through the air, *evaporating rapidly* is the most accurate meaning.

15. **D.** The first bolded portion states the conclusion that heavy farm equipment compacts the soil, and the second bolded portion concludes that farmers must employ various strategies to reduce soil compaction. You can rule out Choice (A) because although the first states a conclusion, the second doesn't provide supporting evidence. Rule out Choice (B) because although the first states a problem, the second describes a possible solution to

the problem, not the effects of that problem. Rule out Choice (C) because the second bolded portion doesn't contradict the first. And rule out Choice (E) because the first bolded portion doesn't ask a question, nor does the second bolded portion answer a question.

16. **E.** Although none of the answer choices provided completely undermines the argument for having a state lottery, Choice (E) states that at least some of the money collected from state lotteries presumably to be used for education is not being used to fund schools. Choice (A) is irrelevant, (B) and (C) support the argument, and (D) simply states that lottery funding represents a small portion of the total education budget in a state.

17. **A, C.** Knowing that representative Hershel was exhausted, it would have taken some effort for him to remain *vivacious* (energetic) and *ebullient* (enthusiastic) while delivering his speech. You can easily rule out *lugubrious,* which means sad or gloomy, because he won and gave an electrifying speech. *Laconic,* which means terse or concise, would be a reasonable choice, but it has no close match in the answer selections. *Mendacious* and *disingenuous* do match, both meaning dishonest, but neither word is a good fit for the blank, which calls for a word whose meaning implies that Hershel managed to overcome his exhaustion.

18. **C, F.** The deeds described here would be fake — *counterfeit, spurious. Embezzled* and *pilfered* both mean stolen, but filing a stolen deed wouldn't allow the con artist to transfer ownership of a property to himself; he would need to use the pilfered deed to create a counterfeit. Likewise, using a *photocopied* or *duplicate* deed would do little good unless it were modified in some way to create a counterfeit.

19. **B, E.** *Turpitude* and *depravity* both mean immorality. Because the passage focuses on indecent programming, these two choices are best. *Truculence* and *impertinence* would make good second choices, because they both imply disrespectful behavior that the media probably shouldn't promote; however, this sort of behavior doesn't rise to the level of indecency in programming. *Asperity,* which means harshness or sternness, has no choice comparable in meaning. Choice (D), *infidelity,* is tempting, but the answer choices don't contain a word similar in meaning.

20. **B, C.** If the speaker exceeded her allotted time, she must have been *loquacious* or *voluble,* which both imply long-winded. She may have been *eloquent* and *articulate* (well-spoken) as well, but that wouldn't necessarily cause her to exceed her allotted speaking time. *Vivacious* means lively or energetic, and *voluminous* means large, neither of which has a comparable word in the list of answer choices and neither of which would necessarily cause the keynote speaker to run past her allotted time.

Section 2: Quantitative Reasoning

1. **A.** Any value raised to the 0 power equals 1, so $\left(\sqrt{64\times25}\right)^0=1$.

2. **C.** You find the probability of an event (selecting 1 grape candy from the first bowl) by putting the number of possibilities (3 grape candies) over the total number of outcomes (5 candies total). Thus, the probability of selecting a grape candy from the first bowl is $\frac{3}{5}$. Similarly, the probability of selecting a grape candy from the second bowl is $\frac{2}{3}$.

The probability of two independent events occurring together (selecting a grape candy each from the first and second bowls) is the product of the first probability and the second probability:

$$\frac{3}{5}\times\frac{2}{3}=\frac{6}{15}=\frac{2}{5}$$

3. **5.** The *units digit* is the digit in the ones place, just before where the decimal point would be. For example, in the number 123, the units digit is 3. When you're multiplying two whole numbers, the units digits of the multipliers produce the units digit of the product. So when you multiply 12×13, for example, the 2 in 12 times the 3 in 13 produces the 6 in the product, 156.

For this question, 5 times itself any number of times results in a product with a units digit of 5:

$$5\times5=25$$
$$5\times5\times5=125$$

and so on.

4. **3.** First, determine the value at the top of the fraction (the numerator): Multiply the $\sqrt{27}$ by $\sqrt{3}$ for $\sqrt{81}$, which equals 9. Determining the value at the bottom of the fraction (the denominator) is easy, because the square root of 9 is 3. Divide the numerator by the denominator for the correct answer:

$$\frac{9}{\sqrt{9}}=\frac{9}{3}=3$$

5. **B.** To determine Quantity A, calculate the average parcel weight by totaling the weight of the parcels and then dividing the total weight by the number of parcels. You can use the following equation for weighted average:

$$\text{Weighted average}=\frac{(5\times3)+(10\times9)}{5+10}$$
$$=\frac{15+90}{15}$$
$$=\frac{105}{15}$$
$$=7$$

Quantity A is 7 pounds, which is 1 pound less than Quantity B's 8 pounds, so Quantity B is greater.

6. **A.** To determine Quantity A, simplify the exponents and the fraction. To simplify each negative exponent, place a 1 on top:

$$\frac{\frac{1}{9.99^{10}}}{\frac{1}{9.99^{9}}}$$

To divide the fractions, flip the bottom fraction and multiply it by the top fraction:

$$\frac{1}{9.99^{10}}\times\frac{9.99^{9}}{1}$$
$$=\frac{9.99^{9}}{9.99^{10}}$$
$$=\frac{9.99^{9}}{9.99^{9}\times9.99}$$
$$=\frac{1}{9.99}$$
$$=0.1001001$$

You simplify the resulting fraction with the on-screen calculator; $0.1\overline{001}$ is slightly greater than 0.1, so Quantity A is greater.

7. **B.** Simplify the quantities so that A reads

$$1,000\times999\times998$$

and B reads

$$999 \times 999 \times 999$$

These products are still too big for the on-screen calculator. To resolve this, eliminate one 999 from each quantity so that A reads

$$1{,}000 \times 998$$

and B reads

$$999 \times 999$$

Using the on-screen calculator, find the resulting values as 998,000 and 998,001. You see that Quantity B is greater.

8. **B.** $\sqrt{36}$ equals 6, so $\sqrt{27}$ is less than 6.

9. **D.** Given $(x-1)(x+1)=0$, x equals either 1 or -1. You don't know which one, so you can't determine which quantity is greater based on the information given.

10. **C.** If the angle CAB measures 36°, minor arc BC also measures 36°, making it one tenth of the circle:

$$\frac{36°}{360°} = \frac{1}{10}$$

A circle with a radius of 5 has a circumference of $2\pi r = 2 \times \pi \times 5 = 10\pi$. Multiply this circumference by the fraction of the circle, giving you a minor arc length of $10\pi \times \frac{1}{10} = \pi$. Therefore, the two values are equal.

11. **C.** You can find the area of a trapezoid with the formula

$$\left(\frac{b_1 + b_2}{2} \right) h$$

where b_1 represents one base, b_2 represents the other base, and h represents the height. To find the height, set the formula equal to the area and simplify it:

$$\text{Area} = \left(\frac{b_1 + b_2}{2} \right) h$$
$$(a-5)^2 = \left(\frac{a-10+a}{2} \right) h$$
$$(a-5)^2 = \left(\frac{2a-10}{2} \right) h$$
$$(a-5)^2 = (a-5)h$$
$$a-5 = h$$

12. **24.** If total sales are $150,000 and Humboldt County spent $36,000, you can find the percent by placing the Humboldt County sales over the total sales:

$$\frac{36{,}000}{150{,}000} = \frac{24}{100} = 24\%$$

You can't type the percent symbol into the answer box. Because the percent symbol is already in place and the question asks for the percent, the correct answer is 24, not 0.24.

13. **E.** You can compare the box prices of each brand by estimating the ratio of sales dollars to units sold. The higher the ratio, the higher the brand's average selling price. Sugar Choc has the highest ratio of dollar sales to units sold, making it the highest-priced brand of cereal.

14. **C.** Though actual numbers aren't provided, you can use the bar graph to approximate the ratios. Because the question asks for an "approximate" answer and the answer choices are far apart, you can eyeball your numbers from the graphs.

Lucky Shapes and Sugar Choc show similar numbers of units sold, but the Sugar Choc sales dollars is about three times that of Lucky Shapes. This means, box for box, Sugar Choc costs approximately three times as much as Lucky Shapes.

If the Trinity County spending (at $27,000) is three times that of the Glenn County spending (at $9,000), and if the Trinity cereal box costs three times as much as the Glenn cereal box, then the two counties are purchasing approximately the same number of cereal boxes.

15. **2.** Reduce the exponents by converting 16^4 to 2^{16}:

$$16^4 = (16)^4 = \left(2^4\right)^4 = 2^{16}$$

Now reduce the fraction by subtracting the exponents:

$$\frac{2^{17}}{2^{16}} = 2$$

16. **B.** Set up the equation and substitute 5 for y:

$$3x + 4y = 50$$
$$3x + 4(5) = 50$$
$$3x + 20 = 50$$
$$3x = 30$$
$$x = 10$$

17. **D.** Suppose $n = 9$. You're looking for 9×10, which is the same as $(9 \times 9) + (9 \times 1)$, or $(9 \times 9) + 9$. Substitute n for 9, and you have $(n \times n) + n$, or $n^2 + n$.

18. **E.** You're given the number of kilometers per hour, and you need to determine the number of meters per second, so focus on the units of measurement: 25 kilometers is 25,000 meters, and 1 hour is 60 minutes times 60 seconds, or 3,600 seconds. You know that the sled is travelling 25,000 kilometers per 3,600 seconds for 18 seconds. Now do the math:

$$\frac{25,000}{3,600} \times 18 = \frac{250}{36} \times 18 = \frac{250}{2} = 125$$

19. **E.** First, identify the unknown. You know that you end up with 15 liters of a solution, but you don't know what its saline concentration is, so you have 15 liters of x.

Ten liters of 6% solution plus 5 liters of 9% solution gives you 15 liters of x, so set up the equation and simplify:

$$(10)(0.06) + (5)(0.09) = (15)(x)$$
$$0.6 + 0.45 = 15x$$
$$1.05 = 15x$$
$$0.15 = x$$
$$15\% = x$$

20. **A, B, C, F.** Don't let the circle with the dot inside confound you. The question indicates that its value is $(ab)^2$. If a equals 0, b could be any number and $a \odot b$ would be less than 25.

However, the question states that b is an integer, so it can't be $\frac{1}{2}$ or $\sqrt{3}$.

Section 3: Verbal Reasoning

1. **C.** *Ubiquitous* means existing everywhere, which is what product customization is if it can be found in such a wide variety of products. *Inaccessible* and *scarce* convey nearly the opposite meaning. Product customization can't really be considered *indispensable,* because consumers lived without it for so long. *Salubrious* doesn't fit, because it means conducive to good health.

2. **A.** *Taciturn* means aloof or uncommunicative, which is what Dr. Mandalow would be if he left the room without asking whether anyone had questions. *Effusive* means outwardly enthusiastic, so you can immediately rule out (B). *Indignant* means outraged or annoyed, but there's no evidence that the doctor was indignant; he didn't lash out at anyone in the audience. *Despondent* means depressed or dejected, which could lead the doctor to exit prematurely, but the passage contains nothing to indicate that the doctor was depressed. And *malevolent* would indicate that the good doctor was evil, and nothing in the passage supports that description.

3. **C, E.** Epigenetics is the study of changes in gene activity that can be passed down to future generations. To some degree, it *repudiates* (rejects) Darwin's theory of evolution because a gene's expression can change; genes are not *immutable* (unchangeable). For the first blank, *obviates* (takes steps to render something unnecessary) doesn't work, nor does *expatiates,* which would imply that epigenetics elaborates on Darwin's theory of evolution. For the second blank, *imperturbable* would be a good second choice, but it means something more along the lines of being calm, cool, and collected. *Inimitable* (incomparable) just doesn't fit.

4. **B, D.** Financial experts are often depicted as being *diffident* (shy or insecure), but when it comes to investing other people's money, they become the opposite — *audacious* (bold, daring). You can rule out *dissident* (rebellious) and *confident* based on the meaning of the second sentence — the word *however* indicates that whatever quality was mentioned in the first sentence will have an opposing quality in the second sentence. The word *gamble* clues you in to the fact that these individuals are going to be *audacious* (aggressive) when investing other people's money, not *pusillanimous* (timid) or *aloof* (standoffish).

5. **B, F.** With a *paucity* (too little) of livestock and a *surfeit* (too much) of corn, farmers would be more likely to market their corn for use in producing biodiesel fuel instead of using it as feed. For the first blank, both of the other choices — *plethora* and *overabundance* — mean the opposite of *paucity.* For the second blank, both of the other choices — *dearth* and *scarcity* — are the opposite of *surfeit.*

6. **C, F, G.** The nature of the situation must have been *involute* (complex) to require input from *trenchant* (clever) advisors so that the CEO could make *sagacious* (shrewd) decisions. By starting at the end of the passage, you know that the decisions needed to be wise and not *salacious* (obscene) or *sententious* (self-righteous). *Conscientious* or *confidential* advisors wouldn't be the best qualified to advise the CEO on making wise decisions; they'd be better in situations that were delicate or sensitive in nature and that probably wouldn't lead to greatly improving the company's market share.

7. **C, D, H.** If teachers are claiming that charter schools have an unfair advantage, they must be critical of charter schools, so they would *deprecate* (express disapproval of) them, not *extoll* (praise) or *advocate* (speak or write in favor of) them. For the second blank, if charter schools have the power to set very selective admissions standards, they must be *unencumbered* (free of) Department of Education policies, not *hampered* or *constrained,* which both mean constricted or limited by. And given that they're unencumbered by Department of Education policies, they must be free to *forge* their own policies. *Disallow* means prohibited, which is opposite of the meaning this blank calls for, and *correlate* means to arrange in some orderly fashion, which doesn't quite fit.

8. **B.** The passage classifies energy sources in two categories: capital, which is available in limited quantities, and income, which is clean and renewable. *Hydroelectricity* is the only answer choice that represents a renewable energy source. All the other energy sources (heating oil, natural gas, uranium, and coal) are nonrenewable.

9. **A, C.** In the first sentence of the passage, Shumacher pours scorn on the idea that problems in the industrialized world had been solved. Near the end of the passage, the author mentions that Shumacher's message was derided by the majority of people. *Derided* and *scorned* are synonymous.

10. **C.** The only specific human activity that's pointed out as unsustainable is the use of limited energy resources as though they were unlimited. You may be tempted to choose the sentence that mentions "the polluting products of industrial processes — including electricity production," but that phrase is more about the planet's ability to absorb pollution than about the unsustainable use of nonrenewable resources.

11. **B.** This passage is primarily about the need to establish and enforce sound financial policies. You can rule out Choice (A) because the passage doesn't mention the need to pay off debt; in fact, it mentions the possibility of defaulting on debt. Choices (C), (D), and (E) are all specific problems that occur when sound financial policies are not in place or not enforced; they serve as evidence to support the author's main point in the passage.

12. **D.** *Moribund* means declining or not progressing, *stagnant*. **Robust** and **stout** carry the opposite meaning and would be used to describe a healthy economy. The economy described in the passage is still a working economy, so it can't be *extinct* (nonexistent) or *dead* (kaput).

13. **B, C.** Dodd-Frank isn't an issue, so you can rule out Choice (A); Dodd-Frank is described in the passage as a financial reform law. The passage states that the 2008 EESA/TARP bill failed to cure bad lending decisions by banks, Choice (B), and that Dodd-Frank failed to force transparency on derivatives, Choice (C).

14. **E.** The main point of this passage is that the United States can expand its influence in the world by building trust. The passage does imply that humanitarian aid is more effective than military might in improving how the world views the United States, but this is only one example of how to build trust — it's supporting evidence, not the main point. You can rule out Choice (B) because the passage doesn't mention the United States using its military and economic power for anything evil. You can also quickly rule out Choice (D) because it's not mentioned in the passage. Choice (C) represents an assumption on which the main point of the article is based, but it's not the main point.

15. **C.** This passage uses the Iraq War as an example of action that harmed the reputation of the United States, while Choice (C) points out that this action removed the corrupt Iraqi president from power; political corruption is second on the list of concerns from citizens around the world, as stated in the first paragraph. Choices (A) and (B) are examples of United States' initiatives developed to help other countries pursue their interests. The passage doesn't state that the United States doesn't have such programs in place, so these choices don't challenge a claim made in the passage. Choice (D) is irrelevant. Choice (E) suggests that the United States serves its own internal interests while reaching out to help other countries.

16. **D.** One of the costs of the failure to treat mental illness is the $9 billion annually to house those with mental illness in the prison system. If you chose the sentence immediately after the question, you fell for a common trap. Although that sentence answers the question, it doesn't offer evidence — specific data or an example — to support the question.

17. **B, E.** If the violence were counterproductive, then politicians from both parties would encourage their constituents to *avoid* or **eschew** violence, which carry nearly the same meaning. *Embrace, appropriate,* and *incite* would actually promote violence, which isn't something politicians would encourage if it were counterproductive. *Denounce* means to condemn, which sort of works in the sentence, but none of the other answer choices conveys a similar meaning.

18. **C, D.** Calculating the cubic volume of a meal before partaking in it would be a *quirk* or *idiosyncrasy*. *Passions* and *obsessions* make a fairly good pairing, but the behavior being described isn't ordinary, so these two choices aren't the best. Likewise, calculating the cubic volume of a meal may be considered an *endowment* (talent), but *idiosyncrasies* and *quirks* are more fitting choices; besides, none of the other answer choices is similar in meaning to *endowment*. *Assimilation* means the acquisition of something, such as a cultural trait; again, this isn't the best choice, and it has no synonym in the answer choices.

19. **B, E.** The second and third sentences express the *pivotal* nature of the career choice — you can envision an arrow turning around a pivot point depending on which career choice is made. The closest match to *pivotal* is *paramount,* which means "of great importance." Choices (A), (C), and (D) would make good pairings but mean the opposite of *pivotal* and *paramount.* The meaning of *urgent* is more in line with *pivotal* and *paramount* but conveys more of a sense of requiring immediate action.

20. **B.** The definition of *domestication* in this passage is activity that "results in genetic change brought about through conscious or unconscious human selection." Farm-raised catfish is an example of cultivation — taking catfish from the wild and breeding and growing them in managed ponds or tanks. All the other answer choices indicate situations in which human selection resulted in genetic change in a plant or animal.

Section 4: Quantitative Reasoning

1. **D.** First convert the 4^5 into 2^{10}. Then simplify the fraction by subtracting the exponents:

$$\frac{5\left(2^{12}\right)}{4^5}=\frac{5\left(2^{12}\right)}{2^{10}}=5\left(2^2\right)=5(4)=20$$

2. **C.** Factor the $\sqrt{48y}$ into $\sqrt{4\times4\times3\times y}$. The lowest possible value of y is 3, because in order for the square root of 48y to be an integer, the factors inside the square root symbol must form numbers squared — you have one 4×3, and you need to multiply it by another 4×3 to square it.

    You could also plug in the answer choices, starting with the lowest value and working your way up: $\sqrt{48\times1}=\sqrt{48}$, which isn't an integer. $\sqrt{48\times2}=\sqrt{96}$, which isn't an integer. $\sqrt{48\times3}=\sqrt{144}=12$, which is an integer. Factoring is faster, however.

3. **A, C, D.** $210=2\times3\times5\times7$, so *n* could be any product of 2, 3, 5, and 7, as long as any factor is used only once. 12 and 42 are wrong, because 12 uses the factor 2 twice and 42 uses the factor 3 twice.

    You could also solve this one by plugging in answer choices, but that's a lot of math.

4. **C.** Regardless of the distribution, no child will receive six candies. After giving each child two candies, three candies are left over. If these are given to one child, he will have a total of five.

5. **A.** You can find the average speed by placing the entire distance over the entire time. If Davis travels at 40 miles per hour for two hours, he travels 80 miles during that time. Combine this with 60 miles for one hour for a total of 140 miles in three hours:

$$\frac{140 \text{ miles}}{3 \text{ hours}}=\frac{47 \text{ miles}}{1 \text{ hour}}$$

6. **C.** Simplify the radical:

$$\sqrt{(30)(30)(30)(30)}=(30)(30)=900$$

7. **D.** Given that $f(x) = x^2 + 2x - 2$ and $f(x) = 13$, set up and simplify the equation without the $f(x)$:

$$f(x) = x^2 + 2x - 2$$
$$13 = x^2 + 2x - 2$$
$$0 = x^2 + 2x - 15$$
$$0 = (x - 3)(x + 5)$$

Therefore, $x = 3$ or -5, but you don't know which one, so Quantity A could be either equal to or less than Quantity B. Because you don't know, go with Choice (D).

8. **B.** Any number between zero and one becomes smaller when multiplied by itself. For example,

$$\left(\frac{1}{2}\right)^2 = \frac{1}{4}$$

Each time you multiply 0.99 by itself, the quantity becomes smaller and remains less than 1.

9. **C.** Simplify the factorial expressions:

$$5! = 5 \times 4 \times 3 \times 2 = 120$$

$$\frac{6!}{3!} = \frac{6 \times 5 \times 4 \times 3 \times 2}{3 \times 2} = 120$$

10. **B.** You can find the volume of a right circular cylinder with $\pi r^2 h$, where r is the radius and h is the height. If r and h are integers, the only way the volume can be 36π is if r is 3 and h is 4, with a sum of 7, or r is 2 and h is 9, with a sum of 11. Either way, the sum is less than 12.

11. **A.** The question asks for an "approximate" ratio, so eyeball the graph and compare the bars. The C bar is half the B bar, making the ratio 1:2.

12. **C.** If the 211 Creede students are earning A's, the remaining 894 students are earning all the other grades. Looking at the bar chart, the B bar is the length of the C, D, and F bars put together. This means that about half the remaining students are earning B's. Bayfield has 306 students, so approximately half that is 150.

13. **C.** From the bar chart, about $\frac{2}{5}$ of the grades are B grades, so about $\frac{3}{5}$ are the other grades.

De Beque has 115 students, and the only answer choice that's about $\frac{3}{5}$ of that is 70.

An approximate estimate is usually good enough for these questions. The answer 70 isn't really close to the other answers, so if you eyeball the graph differently, you'll still get the right answer.

14. **A, C.** The range is the difference between the lowest and highest numbers. If the range of set S is 9 and none of the given numbers are 9 apart, x has to be either 0 or 11.

The median is the middle number of the set. If x is 0, the median is 5; if x is 11, the median is 7.

15. **0.** The correct answer is 0.

The trap here is doing a lot of extra math work. Drop the parentheses to avoid this trap:

$$\frac{1}{8} - \frac{3}{10} + \frac{1}{4} - \frac{1}{5} + \frac{5}{8} - \frac{1}{2}$$

Now give the fractions common denominators of either 8 or 10:

$$\frac{1}{8} - \frac{3}{10} + \frac{2}{8} - \frac{2}{10} + \frac{5}{8} - \frac{5}{10}$$

The $\frac{1}{8}$, $\frac{2}{8}$, and $\frac{5}{8}$ add up to 1, and the $-\frac{3}{10}$, $-\frac{2}{10}$, and $-\frac{5}{10}$ add up to –1. The sum, therefore, equals 0.

Note that there are other ways to simplify the fractions. On the GRE, especially with fractions, you're looking for ways to cancel and simplify.

16. **36.** The correct answer is 36.

Combine $\sqrt{9(36) + 12(36) + 15(36)} = $ into $\sqrt{36(36)}$, which equals 36.

17. **C, D, E.** If $x^2 < 25$, x is either less than 5 or greater than –5, which you can write as

$$-5 < x < 5$$

The value x cannot be equal to 5 or –5. It's greater than –5 and less than 5, so from the list of answer choices, x could be equal to –3, 0, or 3.

18. **B.** First find the area of the square:

$$s^2 = \left(\sqrt{2}\right)^2 = 2$$

For the area of the circle, you need its radius. Cut the square in half, corner to corner, to form two 45-45-90 triangles, where each hypotenuse is the diameter of the circle. If the side of this triangle is $\sqrt{2}$, the hypotenuse is 2, because in a right triangle, the square of the hypotenuse is the sum of the squares of the other two sides:

$$c^2 = a^2 + b^2$$
$$= \sqrt{2}^2 + \sqrt{2}^2$$
$$= 2 + 2$$
$$= 4$$

$c^2 = 4$, so $c = \sqrt{4} = 2$ is the circumference of the circle, and the radius of the circle is half the diameter, or 1. Now for the area of the circle:

$$\pi r^2 = \pi(1)^2 = \pi$$

Subtract the area of the square from the area of the circle for your answer:

$$\pi - 2$$

19. **21.** For the area of a triangle, multiply the base by the height and divide by 2. The base of this triangle is 7 and the height is 6, for an area of 21. The 2 in the drawing has no bearing.

20. **A, B, C, E, F.** $600 is $\frac{1}{3}$ of $1,800 and $\frac{1}{4}$ of $2,400. This means that Clarissa's monthly income is greater than $1,800 and less than $2,400. Multiply these values by 12 for an annual income greater than $21,600 and less than $28,800. Note that her income can't equal these amounts — her income is greater than the lower number and less than the higher number.

Answer Key for Practice Exam 1

Section 1: Verbal Reasoning	Section 2: Quantitative Reasoning	Section 3: Verbal Reasoning	Section 4: Quantitative Reasoning
1. C	1. A	1. C	1. D
2. E	2. C	2. A	2. C
3. B, F	3. 5	3. C, E	3. A, C, D
4. B, F	4. 3	4. B, D	4. C
5. B, D, I	5. B	5. B, F	5. A
6. B, D, I	6. A	6. C, F, G	6. C
7. C	7. B	7. C, D, H	7. D
8. D	8. B	8. B	8. B
9. A, B	9. D	9. A, C	9. C
10. A, C	10. C	10. C	10. B
11. C	11. C	11. B	11. A
12. B, C	12. 24	12. D	12. C
13. C	13. E	13. B, C	13. C
14. B	14. C	14. E	14. A, C
15. D	15. 2	15. C	15. 0
16. E	16. B	16. D	16. 36
17. A, C	17. D	17. B, E	17. C, D, E
18. C, F	18. E	18. C, D	18. B
19. B, E	19. E	19. B, E	19. 21
20. B, C	20. A, B, C, F	20. B	20. A, B, C, E, F

Chapter 18

Practice Exam 2

• •

*L*ike the actual, computer-based GRE, the following exam consists of two 30-minute essays, two 30-minute Verbal Reasoning sections (20 questions each), and two 35-minute Quantitative Reasoning sections (20 questions each). The actual GRE may also include an extra Verbal or Quantitative Reasoning section (which doesn't count toward your score), but this practice exam does not.

Take this practice test under normal exam conditions and approach it as you would the real GRE:

- ✓ **Work when you won't be interrupted.**

- ✓ **Use scratch paper that's free of any prepared notes.** On the actual GRE, you receive blank scratch paper before your test begins.

- ✓ **Answer as many questions as time allows.** Consider answering all the easier questions within each section first and then going back to answer the remaining, harder questions. Because you're not penalized for guessing, go ahead and guess on the remaining questions before time expires.

- ✓ **Set a timer for each section.** If you have time left at the end, you may go back and review answers (within the section), continue and finish your test early, or pause and catch your mental breath before moving on to the next section.

- ✓ **Don't leave your desk while the clock is running on any section.** Though technically you're allowed to do this, it's not conducive to an effective time-management strategy.

- ✓ **Take breaks between sections.** Take a one-minute break after each section and the optional ten-minute break after the first Verbal section.

- ✓ **Type the essays.** Because you type the essays on the actual GRE, typing them now is good practice. Don't use software that has an automatic spell-checker, like Microsoft Word. Instead, use a simple text editor, such as Notepad, with copy and paste but no other features. The GRE essay-writing field features undo, redo, copy, and paste functionality but nothing else.

After completing this entire practice test, go to Chapter 19 to check your answers. Be sure to review the explanations for *all* the questions, not just the ones you miss. The answer explanations provide insight and a review of everything you went over in the previous chapters. This way, too, you review the explanations for questions that you guessed correctly on.

I formatted the questions and answer choices to make them appear as similar as possible to what you'll see on the computer-based test, but I had to retain the letters (A, B, C, D, E, F) to label the answer choices. The actual exam doesn't use letters to mark the answer choices — it simply has ovals, boxes, or selectable text.

Answer Sheet for Practice Exam 2

Section 1:
Verbal Reasoning

1. Ⓐ Ⓑ Ⓒ Ⓓ Ⓔ
2. Ⓐ Ⓑ Ⓒ Ⓓ Ⓔ
3. Ⓐ Ⓑ Ⓒ Ⓓ Ⓔ Ⓕ
4. Ⓐ Ⓑ Ⓒ Ⓓ Ⓔ Ⓕ
5. Ⓐ Ⓑ Ⓒ Ⓓ Ⓔ Ⓕ
6. Ⓐ Ⓑ Ⓒ Ⓓ Ⓔ Ⓕ Ⓖ Ⓗ Ⓘ
7. Ⓐ Ⓑ Ⓒ Ⓓ Ⓔ Ⓕ Ⓖ Ⓗ Ⓘ
8. Ⓐ Ⓑ Ⓒ Ⓓ Ⓔ
9. Ⓐ Ⓑ Ⓒ Ⓓ Ⓔ
10. [A] [B] [C]
11. Ⓐ Ⓑ Ⓒ Ⓓ Ⓔ
12. Ⓐ Ⓑ Ⓒ Ⓓ Ⓔ
13. Ⓐ Ⓑ Ⓒ Ⓓ Ⓔ
14. Ⓐ Ⓑ Ⓒ Ⓓ Ⓔ
15. [A] [B] [C] [D] [E] [F]
16. [A] [B] [C] [D] [E] [F]
17. [A] [B] [C] [D] [E] [F]
18. [A] [B] [C] [D] [E] [F]
19. [A] [B] [C] [D] [E] [F]
20. Ⓐ Ⓑ Ⓒ Ⓓ Ⓔ

Section 2:
Quantitative Reasoning

1. Ⓐ Ⓑ Ⓒ Ⓓ
2. Ⓐ Ⓑ Ⓒ Ⓓ
3. Ⓐ Ⓑ Ⓒ Ⓓ
4. Ⓐ Ⓑ Ⓒ Ⓓ
5. Ⓐ Ⓑ Ⓒ Ⓓ
6. Ⓐ Ⓑ Ⓒ Ⓓ
7. Ⓐ Ⓑ Ⓒ Ⓓ
8. Ⓐ Ⓑ Ⓒ Ⓓ
9. Ⓐ Ⓑ Ⓒ Ⓓ Ⓔ
10. Ⓐ Ⓑ Ⓒ Ⓓ Ⓔ
11. [A] [B] [C] [D] [E] [F]
12. [   ]
13. [   ]
14. Ⓐ Ⓑ Ⓒ Ⓓ Ⓔ
15. Ⓐ Ⓑ Ⓒ Ⓓ Ⓔ
16. Ⓐ Ⓑ Ⓒ Ⓓ Ⓔ
17. Ⓐ Ⓑ Ⓒ Ⓓ Ⓔ
18. Ⓐ Ⓑ Ⓒ Ⓓ Ⓔ
19. Ⓐ Ⓑ Ⓒ Ⓓ Ⓔ
20. [   ]

Section 3:
Verbal Reasoning

1. Ⓐ Ⓑ Ⓒ Ⓓ Ⓔ
2. Ⓐ Ⓑ Ⓒ Ⓓ Ⓔ
3. Ⓐ Ⓑ Ⓒ Ⓓ Ⓔ Ⓕ
4. Ⓐ Ⓑ Ⓒ Ⓓ Ⓔ Ⓕ
5. Ⓐ Ⓑ Ⓒ Ⓓ Ⓔ Ⓕ
6. Ⓐ Ⓑ Ⓒ Ⓓ Ⓔ Ⓕ Ⓖ Ⓗ Ⓘ
7. Ⓐ Ⓑ Ⓒ Ⓓ Ⓔ Ⓕ Ⓖ Ⓗ Ⓘ
8. [A] [B] [C]
9. Ⓐ Ⓑ Ⓒ Ⓓ Ⓔ
10. Ⓐ Ⓑ Ⓒ Ⓓ Ⓔ
11. Ⓐ Ⓑ Ⓒ Ⓓ Ⓔ
12. Ⓐ Ⓑ Ⓒ Ⓓ Ⓔ
13. Ⓐ Ⓑ Ⓒ Ⓓ Ⓔ
14. [A] [B] [C]
15. [A] [B] [C] [D] [E] [F]
16. [A] [B] [C] [D] [E] [F]
17. [A] [B] [C] [D] [E] [F]
18. [A] [B] [C] [D] [E] [F]
19. [A] [B] [C] [D] [E] [F]
20. Ⓐ Ⓑ Ⓒ Ⓓ Ⓔ

Section 4:
Quantitative Reasoning

1. Ⓐ Ⓑ Ⓒ Ⓓ
2. Ⓐ Ⓑ Ⓒ Ⓓ
3. Ⓐ Ⓑ Ⓒ Ⓓ
4. Ⓐ Ⓑ Ⓒ Ⓓ
5. Ⓐ Ⓑ Ⓒ Ⓓ
6. Ⓐ Ⓑ Ⓒ Ⓓ
7. Ⓐ Ⓑ Ⓒ Ⓓ
8. Ⓐ Ⓑ Ⓒ Ⓓ Ⓔ
9. [A] [B] [C] [D] [E] [F]
10. Ⓐ Ⓑ Ⓒ Ⓓ Ⓔ
11. [   ]
12. [   ]
13. Ⓐ Ⓑ Ⓒ Ⓓ Ⓔ
14. Ⓐ Ⓑ Ⓒ Ⓓ Ⓔ
15. Ⓐ Ⓑ Ⓒ Ⓓ Ⓔ
16. Ⓐ Ⓑ Ⓒ Ⓓ Ⓔ
17. Ⓐ Ⓑ Ⓒ Ⓓ Ⓔ
18. [A] [B] [C] [D] [E] [F]
19. Ⓐ Ⓑ Ⓒ Ⓓ Ⓔ
20. Ⓐ Ⓑ Ⓒ Ⓓ Ⓔ

Analytical Writing 1: Analyze an Issue

Time: 30 minutes

Directions: Present and explain your view on the following issue. Although there is no one right or wrong response, be sure to consider various points of view as you explain the reasons behind your own perspective. Support your position with reasons and examples from your own reading, personal or professional experience, and observations.

"Equal opportunity means parity in pay. Everyone should not earn the same amount of money, but it's ridiculous to see an athlete earning tens of millions of dollars in a single year while the average household income is slightly above $50,000."

Express the extent to which you agree or disagree with the preceding statement and explain the reasoning behind your position. In support of your position, think of ways in which the statement may or may not be true and how these considerations influence your position.

STOP DO NOT TURN THE PAGE UNTIL TOLD TO DO SO.
DO NOT RETURN TO A PREVIOUS TEST.

Analytical Writing 2: Analyze an Argument

Time: 30 minutes

Directions: Critique the following argument. Identify evidence that strengthens or weakens the argument, point out assumptions underlying the argument, and offer counterexamples to the argument.

"More and more cities and towns are installing speed limit enforcement cameras on freeways to catch speeders in the act. In one year alone, speeding accounted for 7,620 fatal crashes in the United States and 137,000 injuries. A study conducted by the Federal Highway Administration noted a 25 percent reduction in speed-related accidents at sections of freeways having these cameras. Because people fail to voluntarily honor the law, these speed limit enforcement cameras are essential to enforcing the law and ensuring public safety."

Discuss the merits of the preceding argument. Analyze the evidence used as well as the general reasoning. Present points that would strengthen the argument or challenge it.

STOP DO NOT TURN THE PAGE UNTIL TOLD TO DO SO.
DO NOT RETURN TO A PREVIOUS TEST.

Section 1:

Verbal Reasoning

Time: 30 minutes for 20 questions

Directions: Choose the best answer to each question. Blacken the corresponding ovals or boxes on the answer sheet.

Directions: For Questions 1–7, choose the one entry best suited for each blank from its corresponding column of choices.

1. The Republic of India currently ranks ninth in military _____ among nations, leading it to have the third-largest standing army in the world.

Ⓐ prowess
Ⓑ innovation
Ⓒ legacy
Ⓓ expenditure
Ⓔ allegiance

2. The creators of *Sesame Street* were the first to use _____ to shape a TV show's content and achieve educational goals.

Ⓐ innovation
Ⓑ a curriculum
Ⓒ adroitness
Ⓓ a timetable
Ⓔ a character lineup

3. Although the (i) _____ system typically can detect only five different tastes, individuals with a more (ii) _____ palate are capable of distinguishing subtle differences in even the most similar foods.

Blank (i)	Blank (ii)
Ⓐ gustatory	Ⓓ discrete
Ⓑ lymphatic	Ⓔ discerning
Ⓒ digestive	Ⓕ distended

4. The latest tsunami (i) _____ the small seaside resort. Fortunately, no lives were lost, and the loss of property served as a (ii) _____ for a much-needed renovation.

Blank (i)	Blank (ii)
Ⓐ inundated	Ⓓ symbol
Ⓑ dissembled	Ⓔ mendicant
Ⓒ drowned	Ⓕ catalyst

5. The castle walls were (i) _____ to attack. After several unsuccessful assaults, the enemy's enthusiasm began to (ii) _____, and the troops dispersed.

Blank (i)	Blank (ii)
Ⓐ amenable	Ⓓ flag
Ⓑ impeccable	Ⓔ rally
Ⓒ impervious	Ⓕ flee

Go on to next page

6. Aware of the (i) _____ national debt, Congress passed legislation to impose a strict (ii) _____ program to (iii) _____ spending.

Blank (i)	Blank (ii)	Blank (iii)
Ⓐ pervasive	Ⓓ austerity	Ⓖ curtail
Ⓑ shrinking	Ⓔ spending	Ⓗ attenuate
Ⓒ burgeoning	Ⓕ defense	Ⓘ desiccate

7. The (i) _____ between the man's demeanor and his account of what he was doing at the time of the crime made police officers suspicious, but with so much of the evidence (ii) _____, their case against him was (iii) _____ at best.

Blank (i)	Blank (ii)	Blank (iii)
Ⓐ correlation	Ⓓ corroborated	Ⓖ compelling
Ⓑ discrepancy	Ⓔ vetted	Ⓗ tenuous
Ⓒ relationship	Ⓕ unsubstantiated	Ⓘ conclusive

Go on to next page

Directions: Each of the following passages is followed by questions pertaining to the passage. Read the passage and answer the questions based on information stated or implied in that passage. For each question, select one answer choice unless instructed otherwise.

In a poll conducted by Washington Post-ABC News, 70 percent of Americans support the use of passenger profiling to determine which passengers are most closely scrutinized at airports. They believe that the cost savings and added convenience for a large majority of passengers is worth the questionable practice of singling out specific passengers for closer scrutiny. In addition, passengers feel that pat-downs and full body scans are highly invasive.

When most Americans discuss profiling, they are referring to profiling based on race, nationality, religion, and gender, which many people consider a civil rights violation. Most experts agree that profiling in this way is inefficient and ineffective. They recommend profiling by behavior and intelligence, using no-fly and watch lists, personal data, travel histories, and so forth to identify potential threats.

Civil liberty organizations claim that this solution is no better and perhaps worse in terms of violating civil liberties, because it gives government agencies license to collect sensitive information on any and all citizens. They believe that the only fair solution is to inspect all or randomly selected passengers and luggage.

When it comes to airport security, ultimately we face a choice. Either we protect civil liberties and accept the cost and inconvenience of inspecting all passengers and luggage, or we relinquish our civil liberties or the civil liberties of certain groups or individuals to increase effectiveness, reduce costs, and streamline baggage and checkpoint inspections.

8. According to experts, which of the following is most effective in ensuring airline security?

   Ⓐ Profiling passengers based on race, nationality, religion, and gender

   Ⓑ Inspecting all passengers and their luggage

   Ⓒ Profiling by behavior and intelligence

   Ⓓ Interviewing all passengers before boarding

   Ⓔ Streamlining baggage and checkpoint inspections

9. Which of the following, if true, most effectively undermines the argument that the only choice we have is between security and civil liberties?

   Ⓐ Bomb-sniffing dogs are more effective and less intrusive at detecting explosives than human inspectors or electronic security devices.

   Ⓑ A combination of profiling and targeted interviews has proven most effective and efficient.

   Ⓒ Precertification as a safe flyer significantly improves efficiency at checkpoints.

   Ⓓ Checked baggage is more likely than carry-on luggage to contain explosives.

   Ⓔ No security measures are 100 percent effective.

The following passage is an excerpt from Causes of War *by Jack S. Levy and William R. Thompson (Wiley-Blackwell).*

It is hard to imagine what life would have been like in the late twentieth century in the absence of World War I and World War II, which had such profound effects on the global system and on domestic societies. The same can be said for the Cold War. For nearly a half century it shaped both international and domestic politics and cultures, not only in the United States and the Soviet Union but also in Western Europe and the Third World (Weart, 1989). The development of new states in the contemporary era continues to be influenced by warfare and preparations for war. With the proliferation of nuclear weapons, and with the threat of the acquisition of nuclear weapons by terrorist groups and "rogue states," new threats to the security of even the most powerful states in the system have emerged. The proliferation of civil wars and conflicts involving "non-state" actors has changed life throughout the developing world. A better understanding of the causes of war is a necessary first step if we are to have any hope of reducing the occurrence of war and perhaps mitigating its severity and consequences.

Go on to next page ⟩

For the Question 10, consider each answer choice separately and select all answer choices that are correct.

10. According to the passage, which of the following are effects of war and preparations for war?

   A Reshaping of international and domestic politics and cultures

   B The proliferation of civil wars and conflicts

   C Development of new states

11. One could reasonably infer from this passage that the greatest security threat is which of the following?

   Ⓐ Proliferation of civil wars

   Ⓑ Terrorists

   Ⓒ Rogue states

   Ⓓ The Cold War

   Ⓔ Proliferation of nuclear weapons

The following passage is an excerpt from UnMarketing: Stop Marketing. Start Engaging. *by Scott Stratten (Wiley).*

To successfully UnMarket your business, your goal should be to get to the point where you are a recognized expert in your field. You can choose to be recognized for a certain discipline, whether it is time management or sales or marketing in general. You can also aim to be recognized as an expert to a specific industry. What you have to realize is that there is an important difference between somebody who is selling something and somebody who is an expert. This is one of the problems when you use advertising or direct mail for your marketing — if your potential customer does not have an immediate need for your product or service, then you are potentially turning them off and losing them for

the future. When you position yourself as an expert with useful information for people, your marketplace will always have a need for that information. You have successfully pulled people into your funnel, you have their attention, and now you need to do something great for them.

12. Which of the following sentences most clearly describes the goal of UnMarketing?

   Ⓐ Sentence 2: "You can choose . . . in general."

   Ⓑ Sentence 4: "What you have to . . . an expert."

   Ⓒ Sentence 5: "This is . . . the future."

   Ⓓ Sentence 6: "When you position . . . that information."

   Ⓔ Sentence 7: "You have successfully . . . for them."

13. Which of the following is the most important difference between marketing and UnMarketing as explained in the passage?

   Ⓐ Advertising versus direct mail

   Ⓑ Salesperson versus expert

   Ⓒ Time management versus marketing

   Ⓓ Expert in a field versus expert in a discipline

   Ⓔ Salesperson versus marketing maven

With the passage of a universal healthcare bill, the government not only has the right but also the responsibility to regulate what people eat. Face it, the fact that the United States spends 50 percent more per capita for healthcare than most European countries is because people in the United States consume far more junk food. If taxpayers are footing the bill for healthcare, then the government is responsible for controlling healthcare costs, and the most effective way to do that is to crack down on the junk food industry.

Go on to next page

14. Which of the following, if true, most effectively challenges the argument that poor dietary habits, such as junk food, lead to higher healthcare costs?

    Ⓐ Countries in Europe do not impose such regulations on their food producers.

    Ⓑ Labeling foods enables people to regulate their own consumption.

    Ⓒ Prices of health services are on average more than 50 percent higher in the United States than in most European countries.

    Ⓓ The healthcare bill does not mandate dietary restrictions.

    Ⓔ Some food items considered junk food actually contain healthy ingredients.

Directions: Each of the following sentences has a blank indicating that a word or phrase is omitted. Choose the two answer choices that best complete the sentence and result in two sentences most alike in meaning.

---

15. With nothing to lose and the coach's _____ approval, the teammates decided to abandon the game plan and just have some fun.

    A ambiguous
    B tacit
    C cautious
    D implicit
    E enthusiastic
    F salubrious

16. Few could believe that Thomas was a champion competitive eater, because he was generally so _____ while dining socially.

    A hedonistic
    B self-indulgent
    C epicurean
    D courteous
    E abstemious
    F ascetic

17. The actual incident had been nothing out of the ordinary, but when Mark told it with his penchant for _____, the audience was captivated.

    A sarcasm
    B allegory
    C embellishment
    D hyperbole
    E ennui
    F overemphasis

18. Nobody understood why the puppy was so _____; others in the same litter seemed to have a much gentler disposition.

    A pugnacious
    B lackadaisical
    C quiescent
    D truculent
    E irascible
    F soporific

19. Mary's offer to help plan the party struck everyone as _____, because in her characteristic fashion, she seemed to be up to something.

    A sincere
    B disingenuous
    C duplicitous
    D unpretentious
    E hypocritical
    F authentic

Go on to next page

Directions: The following passage is followed by a question pertaining to the passage. Read the passage and answer the question based on information stated or implied in the passage. Select only one answer.

To reduce the number of factory accidents, mangers at Smith Inc. are implementing a workplace training program for all of the company's factory workers. The program places emphasis on preventing, recognizing, and avoiding safety and health hazards while providing information on workers' rights, employer responsibilities, and filing complaints.

20. Which of the following, if true, suggests that the managers' plan to reduce factory accidents through training will not succeed?

    Ⓐ Many workers are from the Wilson factory, where such training programs are in place and workers attend regularly.

    Ⓑ Both factory accidents this year and the two accidents last year were from delivery drivers unable to navigate the sharp turn to the loading dock.

    Ⓒ The Smith factory has already implemented advanced safety measures and has fewer factory accidents than the industry standard.

    Ⓓ While potentially damaging to equipment and products, most factory accidents are not actually dangerous to workers.

    Ⓔ The same workplace training program did not reduce the number of accidents at the Olson factory, which, like the Smith factory, produces machine shop supplies.

STOP DO NOT TURN THE PAGE UNTIL TOLD TO DO SO. DO NOT RETURN TO A PREVIOUS TEST.

Section 2

Quantitative Reasoning

Time: 35 minutes for 20 questions

Notes:

- All numbers used in this exam are real numbers.
- All figures lie in a plane.
- Angle measures are positive; points and angles are in the position shown.

Directions: For Questions 1–8, choose from the following answer choices:

Ⓐ *Quantity A is greater.*

Ⓑ *Quantity B is greater.*

Ⓒ *The two quantities are equal.*

Ⓓ *The relationship cannot be determined from the information given.*

1.

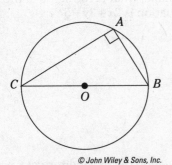

© John Wiley & Sons, Inc.

O is the center of the circle, *BC* passes through the center of the circle, the radius of the circle is 1, and $AB = 1$.

Quantity A	**Quantity B**
The area of triangle *ABC*	$\dfrac{\sqrt{3}}{2}$

2. The average (arithmetic mean) of ten test scores is 120, and the average of 20 additional test scores is 90.

Quantity A	**Quantity B**
The weighted average of these scores	105

3. $10 < n < 15$ and $d = 20$

Quantity A	**Quantity B**
$\dfrac{n}{d}$	0.72

4. A certain recipe requires $\dfrac{4}{3}$ cups of lentils and makes six servings.

Quantity A	**Quantity B**
The amount of lentils required for the same recipe to make 15 servings	3 cups

Go on to next page

5.

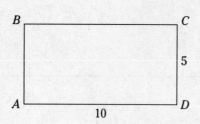

© John Wiley & Sons, Inc.

Quantity A

The area of rectangle
ABCD

Quantity B

The area of trapezoid
EFGH

6.

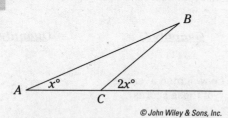

© John Wiley & Sons, Inc.

Quantity A

Line segment AC

Quantity B

Line segment BC

7. $x^2 - x - 6 = 0$

Quantity A

The sum of the
roots of the
equation

Quantity B

-1

8. Set S contains the numbers 3, 4, 5, 6, 7,
and 8.

Quantity A

The range
of set S

Quantity B

The median
of set S

9. What is the units digit of $219,473 \times 162,597$?

Ⓐ 1

Ⓑ 2

Ⓒ 3

Ⓓ 4

Ⓔ 5

10. In the xy plane, what is the slope of the line
whose equation is $2x + 3y = 5$?

Ⓐ 1

Ⓑ $\dfrac{3}{2}$

Ⓒ $-\dfrac{3}{2}$

Ⓓ $\dfrac{2}{3}$

Ⓔ $-\dfrac{2}{3}$

11. Bill is budgeting the expenditure of a new
car based on his gross income from last
year. If his gross income from last year was
$50,000 and Bill wants to spend between
15% and 30% on a new car, which of the following could be the cost of the new car?

Indicate <u>all</u> possible costs of the new car.

Ⓐ $8,000

Ⓑ $10,000

Ⓒ $12,000

Ⓓ $14,000

Ⓔ $16,000

Ⓕ $18,000

Go on to next page

12. If the sporting center has 2 baseballs for every 9 baseball gloves and 3 baseball bats for every 5 baseballs, what is the lowest number of sporting items that could be in the sporting center?

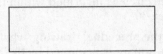

13. If the average of x, y, and z is 5, what is the average of $4x+y$, $2y-x$, and $3z+27$?

14.

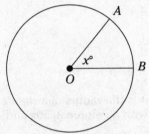

© John Wiley & Sons, Inc.

The circle shown has the center O and a radius of 8. If $x=45$, what is the length of minor arc AB?

Ⓐ $\dfrac{\pi}{2}$

Ⓑ π

Ⓒ $\dfrac{3\pi}{2}$

Ⓓ 2π

Ⓔ $\dfrac{5\pi}{2}$

Questions 15–17 are based on the following data.

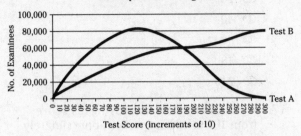

Score Distribution of 1,412,393 Examinees from Sept. 2007 to Aug. 2010

Test Score (increments of 10)

Note: *Chart is drawn to scale.*

Percentile Ranking Based on Score

Score	Test A Percentile	Test B Percentile
0	0	0
10	0	1
20	1	1
30	2	2
40	4	3
50	7	4
60	12	6
70	17	7
80	22	9
90	27	11
100	33	13
110	38	16
120	44	18
130	50	21
140	55	24
150	61	28
160	66	32
170	71	35
180	77	40
190	81	44
200	85	48
210	89	53
220	91	58
230	94	63
240	96	67
250	97	72
260	98	76
270	99	81
280	99	86
290	99	90
300	99	94

© John Wiley & Sons, Inc.

15. Approximately what ratio of examinees taking Test B scored a perfect 300?

Ⓐ 1 out of 100

Ⓑ 1 out of 90

Ⓒ 1 out of 50

Ⓓ 1 out of 20

Ⓔ 1 out of 10

Go on to next page

16. If a Test A examinee is among a group of 40,000 examinees with the same score, what could be the examinee's score?

    Ⓐ 20

    Ⓑ 40

    Ⓒ 90

    Ⓓ 180

    Ⓔ 210

17. A Test A examinee improving his score from 100 to 120 surpasses approximately how many other examinees?

    Ⓐ 40,000

    Ⓑ 80,000

    Ⓒ 150,000

    Ⓓ 240,000

    Ⓔ 300,000

18. If the radius r of a circle increases by 50%, what is the area of the new circle in terms of r?

    Ⓐ $\dfrac{3\pi r^2}{2}$

    Ⓑ $2\pi r^2$

    Ⓒ $\dfrac{4\pi r^2}{3}$

    Ⓓ $3\pi r^2$

    Ⓔ $\dfrac{9\pi r^2}{4}$

19.

© John Wiley & Sons, Inc.

The circle is inscribed within the square of area 36.

In the preceding drawing, what fraction of the square is occupied by the circle?

Ⓐ $\dfrac{\pi}{2}$

Ⓑ $\dfrac{\pi}{3}$

Ⓒ $\dfrac{\pi}{4}$

Ⓓ $\dfrac{1}{3}$

Ⓔ $\dfrac{1}{6}$

20. What is the radius of a right circular cylinder with a volume of 50π and a height of 2?

STOP DO NOT TURN THE PAGE UNTIL TOLD TO DO SO.
DO NOT RETURN TO A PREVIOUS TEST.

Section 3

Verbal Reasoning

Time: 30 minutes for 20 questions

Directions: Choose the best answer to each question. Blacken the corresponding ovals or boxes on the answer sheet.

Directions: For Questions 1–7, choose the one entry best suited for each blank from its corresponding column of choices.

1. Linguists and etymologists use a technique known as the *comparative method* to compare related languages and make inferences about the shared language structure and _____.

Ⓐ culture
Ⓑ grammar
Ⓒ vocabulary
Ⓓ politics
Ⓔ decorum

2. Driven by the rotation of the Earth, the wind flow around an atmospheric high-pressure area can go in a clockwise or counterclockwise direction, depending on the _____.

Ⓐ hemisphere
Ⓑ stratosphere
Ⓒ moon's orbit
Ⓓ solar winds
Ⓔ wind circulation

3. More than 50 percent of online shoppers abandon their shopping carts simply because they've changed their minds, proving just how (i) _____ they can be. Many online merchants have observed shoppers' (ii) _____ for failing to complete their transactions.

Blank (i)	Blank (ii)
Ⓐ capricious	Ⓓ inkling
Ⓑ predictable	Ⓔ penchant
Ⓒ fatuous	Ⓕ passion

4. Because his salary and benefits were (i) _____ with the time and effort he expected to invest in the project, Jerry decided not to (ii) _____ over the deadlines.

Blank (i)	Blank (ii)
Ⓐ discordant	Ⓓ quibble
Ⓑ pursuant	Ⓔ acquiesce
Ⓒ commensurate	Ⓕ concede

Go on to next page

5. By the time the speaker approached the microphone, the impatient audience was (i) _____. Everything he said in an attempt to silence the rabble only seemed to (ii) _____ the situation.

Blank (i)	Blank (ii)
Ⓐ intractable	Ⓓ precipitate
Ⓑ imperturbable	Ⓔ exonerate
Ⓒ indolent	Ⓕ exacerbate

6. With the accidental addition of the (i) _____, the mixture became very (ii) _____. Knowing that student safety (iii) _____ all other concerns, the teacher ushered her students out of the lab.

Blank (i)	Blank (ii)	Blank (iii)
Ⓐ neutralizer	Ⓓ volatile	Ⓖ superseded
Ⓑ chemical	Ⓔ acidic	Ⓗ preceded
Ⓒ catalyst	Ⓕ piquant	Ⓘ negated

7. When asked whether the antique vase was in (i) _____ condition, its owner (ii) _____ that it certainly was. When the buyer received it, however, she discovered that she had been (iii) _____.

Blank (i)	Blank (ii)	Blank (iii)
Ⓐ pristine	Ⓓ corroborated	Ⓖ sidetracked
Ⓑ primordial	Ⓔ proved	Ⓗ duped
Ⓒ rudimentary	Ⓕ averred	Ⓘ ostracized

Go on to next page

Directions: Each of the following passages is followed by questions pertaining to the passage. Read the passage and answer the questions based on information stated or implied in that passage. For each question, select one answer choice unless instructed otherwise.

The following passage is an excerpt from Carnegie *by Peter Krass (Wiley).*

Great Britain had taken an early lead in the Industrial Revolution. The isles, with rich coal-fields to provide fuel for steam engines, many natural waterways for cheap transportation, and a booming international trade with its colonies, was ideally suited for a transformation from an agricultural-based economy to a manufacturing-based economy, from a handicraft system to a factory system. As country folk, in search for steady jobs, migrated to the cities in increasing numbers, the transition proved painful because already poor living conditions in urban centers were exacerbated by a population explosion. Contributing to this unprecedented growth were the Irish, who, seeking work, arrived in waves. Thus, employers had such a large labor pool to select from that they were able to dictate low wages and long hours, further suppressing the working poor. Disillusioned and embittered, the working class formed both trade and political unions to exert pressure, and activism increased dramatically.

For Question 8, consider each answer choice separately and select all answer choices that are correct.

8. Which of the following is specifically cited as contributing to Great Britain's ability to take an early lead in the Industrial Revolution?

   A Trade unions

   B International trade

   C Abundance of coal

9. Which one of the following sentences most clearly explains why wages were so low?

   Ⓐ Sentence 2: "The isles . . . factory system."

   Ⓑ Sentence 3: "As country folk . . . population explosion."

   Ⓒ Sentence 4: "Contributing . . . arrived in waves."

   Ⓓ Sentence 5: "Thus, employers . . . working poor."

   Ⓔ Sentence 6: "Disillusioned and embittered . . . increased dramatically."

10. Which of the following would make the most accurate title for this passage?

   Ⓐ Great Britain's Industrial Revolution: From Boom to Bust

   Ⓑ Exploitation of the Poor during Great Britain's Industrial Revolution

   Ⓒ The Birth of Unions in the Industrial Revolution

   Ⓓ Britain's Industrial Revolution from the Eyes of the Poor

   Ⓔ Great Britain's Industrial Revolution: Natural Resources, Migration, and Unions

Go on to next page

The current trend to hold teachers accountable for the failures of our school systems and students is nothing more than a blame game that makes teachers the scapegoats. Even with the passage of No Child Left Behind, which was intended to make our schools and teachers more accountable, students in the U.S. continue to underperform students in other countries in math and science. If we are to get serious about education in the United States, we need to hold everyone accountable, not only schools and teachers but also students, parents, and society at large. As long as sports, celebrity worship, television, video games, and consumerism are higher on our list of priorities than education, academic performance will continue to decline.

11. Which of the following, if true, most effectively undermines the argument that holding teachers accountable is not a solution to improving student academic performance?

Ⓐ A study conducted at one school found that students of some of the teachers showed significant improvement year after year while students of other teachers at the same school did not.

Ⓑ Socioeconomic differences among students contribute significantly to student performance.

Ⓒ Studies show a direct link between school funding and student performance.

Ⓓ With the passage of No Child Left Behind, students of teachers who teach to the test perform significantly better on standardized tests.

Ⓔ The decline in SAT scores from 1975 to 1990 can be attributed to the fact that more lower-ranking students now take the test.

Many argue that at the root of the most serious threats to human existence is overpopulation. Putting the blame solely on overpopulation, however, is an oversimplification. You also need to account for consumption. For example, Americans constitute 5 percent of the world's population but consume 24 percent of its energy. While more than half of the world's population lives on 25 gallons of water per day, the average American uses 159 gallons daily. In addition, 56 percent of the available farmland is used for beef production. That overconsumption is a far bigger problem than overpopulation is obvious.

12. Which of the following is most effective in countering the argument that overconsumption is a bigger problem than overpopulation?

Ⓐ The world population doubles every 40 years.

Ⓑ Consumption rates are on the rise in developing countries.

Ⓒ Population growth offsets any savings in resources from improved efficiency as well as gains in per-capita consumption reduction.

Ⓓ As average incomes rise, per capita consumption also increases.

Ⓔ One-third of the population living in South Asia and sub-Saharan Africa account for only 3.2 percent of consumer spending.

Go on to next page

This passage is an excerpt from Film Theory: An Introduction *by Robert Stam (Wiley-Blackwell).*

There are many possible ways to describe the history of film theory. It can be a triumphant parade of "great men and women": Munsterberg, Eisenstein, Arnheim, Dulac, Bazin, Mulvey. It can be a history of orienting metaphors: "cine-eye," "film language," "window on the world," camera-pen," "film language," "film mirror," "film dream." It can be a story of the impact of philosophy on theory: Kant and Munsterberg, Mounier and Bazin, Bergson and Deleuze. It can be a history of cinema's *rapprochement* with (or rejection of) other arts: film as painting, film as music, film as theater (or anti-theater). It can be a sequence of paradigmatic shifts in theoretical/interpretive grids and discursive styles — formalism, semiology, psychoanalysis, feminism, cognitivism, queer theory, postcolonial theory — each with its talismanic keywords, tacit assumptions, and characteristic jargon.

13. In the context of this passage, which of the following is the best synonym for the word *rapprochement*?

    Ⓐ relationship

    Ⓑ reconciliation

    Ⓒ disapproval

    Ⓓ agreement

    Ⓔ harmony

For Question 14, consider each answer choice separately and select all answer choices that are correct.

14. Which of the following does the author list as possible ways to describe the history of film theory?

    Ⓐ History of psychoanalysis

    Ⓑ History of film language

    Ⓒ Triumphant parade of great men and women

Directions: Each of the following sentences has a blank indicating that a word or phrase is omitted. Choose the two answer choices that best complete the sentence and result in two sentences most alike in meaning.

15. Among her peers, Amanda was known as the life of the party, but during the graduation ceremony, her antics made her appear _____.

    Ⓐ courteous

    Ⓑ loutish

    Ⓒ decorous

    Ⓓ capricious

    Ⓔ boorish

    Ⓕ contentious

16. The plans were so _____ that nobody on staff could figure out exactly what was supposed to be done.

    Ⓐ straightforward

    Ⓑ desultory

    Ⓒ methodical

    Ⓓ convoluted

    Ⓔ proscribed

    Ⓕ tortuous

17. While citizens were demanding strong leadership, the _____ candidates continued to pander to the polls.

    Ⓐ pusillanimous

    Ⓑ impudent

    Ⓒ audacious

    Ⓓ sanctimonious

    Ⓔ craven

    Ⓕ intransigent

Go on to next page

18. Although parents are often reluctant to _____ their children, they know it is their duty to do so.

    A sanction

    B admonish

    C vilify

    D disparage

    E castigate

    F congratulate

19. The department of transportation offered the _____ couple double the market value of their home, but they continued to refuse to move out.

    A obdurate

    B recalcitrant

    C obstinate

    D assiduous

    E subversive

    F fundamentalist

Directions: The following passage is followed by a question pertaining to the passage. Read the passage and answer the question based on information stated or implied in the passage. Select only one answer.

This passage is an excerpt from Art in Theory: 1900–2000: An Anthology of Changing Ideas *edited by Charles Harrison and Dr. Paul J. Wood (Wiley-Blackwell).*

In Naturalist theories the effect of the work of art was supposed to be traceable back into the world. That it had its origin in that world — or some direct experience of it — was the guarantee of the work's authenticity. In forms of theory subject to the gravitational pull of Symbolism, on the other hand, the effects of art were signs of the authenticity of an inner life; they were understood, that is to say, as originating in the mind or soul of the artist. There were some clear implications of this position. With the abandonment of naturalistic correspondence as a criterion, a premium was placed on the strength and authenticity of individual responses and feelings. A requirement of vividness of expression tended to supplant the traditional requirement of accuracy of description.

20. Which of the following comparisons is the main focus of this passage?

    Ⓐ Art versus nature

    Ⓑ Description versus expression

    Ⓒ Mind versus soul

    Ⓓ Theory versus reality

    Ⓔ Authenticity versus vividness

STOP DO NOT TURN THE PAGE UNTIL TOLD TO DO SO. DO NOT RETURN TO A PREVIOUS TEST.

Section 4
Quantitative Reasoning

Time: 35 minutes for 20 questions

Notes:

- ✔ All numbers used in this exam are real numbers.
- ✔ All figures lie in a plane.
- ✔ Angle measures are positive; points and angles are in the position shown.

Directions: For Questions 1–7, choose from the following answer choices:

- Ⓐ *Quantity A is greater.*
- Ⓑ *Quantity B is greater.*
- Ⓒ *The two quantities are equal.*
- Ⓓ *The relationship cannot be determined from the information given.*

1. A furniture dealer sold two sofas for $400 each, for a 25% profit on one and a 20% loss on the other.

Quantity A	**Quantity B**
The dealer's net gain	The dealer's net loss

2. n is a positive integer between 200 and 500.

Quantity A	**Quantity B**
The number of possible values of n with a units digit of 5	31

3. $ab < 0$

Quantity A	**Quantity B**
$|a+b|$	$|a|+|b|$

4. $\dfrac{x}{y} = \dfrac{2}{3}$

Quantity A	**Quantity B**
x	y

Questions 5 and 6 are based on the following information:

Square $ABCD$ is in the xy-coordinate plane, and each side of the square is parallel to either the x-axis or the y-axis. Points A and C have coordinates $(-2, -1)$ and $(3, 4)$, respectively.

5.

Quantity A	**Quantity B**
The area of square $ABCD$	24

Go on to next page

6.

Quantity A	Quantity B
The distance between points A and C	$5\sqrt{2}$

7. $n > 0$

Quantity A	Quantity B
n	$\dfrac{1}{n}$

8. A car travels at a constant rate of 20 meters per second. How many kilometers does it travel in 10 minutes? (1 kilometer = 1,000 meters)

Ⓐ 5

Ⓑ 12

Ⓒ 15

Ⓓ 20

Ⓔ 25

9. If $(x-5)^2 = 900$, what are the two possible values of x?

Indicate <u>two</u> such numbers.

A 10

B −10

C −25

D 30

E 35

F 40

10. A circular pool of radius r feet is surrounded by a circular sidewalk of width $\dfrac{r}{2}$ feet. In terms of r, what is the area of the sidewalk?

Ⓐ $2\pi r^2$

Ⓑ $\dfrac{5\pi r^2}{4}$

Ⓒ $\dfrac{9\pi r^2}{4}$

Ⓓ πr^2

Ⓔ $\dfrac{\pi r^2}{2}$

11.

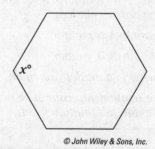

© John Wiley & Sons, Inc.

The preceding figure shows a regular hexagon. What is the value of x?

12. If n divided by 35 has a remainder of 3, what is the remainder when n is divided by 7?

13. If the length of a rectangle were increased by 20% and the width were decreased by 20%, what is the ratio of the original area to the new area?

Ⓐ 4:3

Ⓑ 5:4

Ⓒ 10:9

Ⓓ 15:13

Ⓔ 25:24

Go on to next page

Questions 14–16 are based on the following data.

Education pays

Unemployment rate in 2008

2.0	Doctoral degree
1.7	Professional degree
2.4	Master's degree
2.8	Bachelor's degree
3.7	Associate degree
5.1	Some college, no degree
5.7	High school graduate
9.0	Less than a high school diploma

Median weekly earnings in 2008

Doctoral degree	$1,561
Professional degree	1,531
Master's degree	1,233
Bachelor's degree	1,012
Associate degree	757
Some college, no degree	699
High school graduate	618
Less than a high school diploma	453

Source: Bureau of Labor Statistics. Current Population Survey

© John Wiley & Sons, Inc.

14. Approximately what were the median monthly earnings of someone with a bachelor's degree in 2008?

    Ⓐ $1,012

    Ⓑ $1,233

    Ⓒ $4,050

    Ⓓ $4,400

    Ⓔ $4,750

15. In 2008, if there were 10,000 doctoral-degree holders and 200,000 master's-degree holders, what was the ratio of unemployed doctoral-degree holders to unemployed master's-degree holders?

    Ⓐ 1:20

    Ⓑ 1:24

    Ⓒ 1:48

    Ⓓ 1:50

    Ⓔ 1:200

16. If an associate-degree holder earning 20% less than the median for that degree went on to get a bachelor's degree and earn 25% more than the median for that degree, which of the following is closest to the change in the degree holder's annual income?

    Ⓐ $28,200

    Ⓑ $30,500

    Ⓒ $31,500

    Ⓓ $34,300

    Ⓔ $49,500

17. What is the area of an equilateral triangle with a base of 6?

    Ⓐ $6\sqrt{3}$

    Ⓑ $9\sqrt{3}$

    Ⓒ $12\sqrt{3}$

    Ⓓ $15\sqrt{3}$

    Ⓔ $18\sqrt{3}$

Go on to next page

Part V: Taking Full-Length Practice GREs: It's All You

18.

House Values of a Neighborhood in Town *X*

Value Range (In Thousands of Dollars)	Number of Houses
Under $100	6
$100–$149	14
$150–$199	12
$200–$250	10
Over $250	7

For the 49 houses from the neighborhood in Town *X*, which of the following could be the median value, in thousands of dollars?

Indicate all such values.

- [A] $148
- [B] $162
- [C] $170
- [D] $195
- [E] $210
- [F] $225

19. Two lines represented by the equations $y = x + 1$ and $y = 2x + 3$ intersect at point *P*. What are the coordinates of *P*?

- Ⓐ (–2, –1)
- Ⓑ (–1, 2)
- Ⓒ (1, –2)
- Ⓓ (2, –1)
- Ⓔ (1, 2)

20. $\dfrac{5^{10} - 5^8}{5^9 - 5^7} =$

- Ⓐ 0
- Ⓑ 1
- Ⓒ 5
- Ⓓ 25
- Ⓔ 125

STOP DO NOT TURN THE PAGE UNTIL TOLD TO DO SO. DO NOT RETURN TO A PREVIOUS TEST.

Chapter 19

Practice Exam 2: Answers and Explanations

• •

After taking Practice Exam 2 in Chapter 18, use this chapter to check your answers and see how you did. Carefully review the explanations because doing so can help you understand why you missed the questions you did and also give you a better understanding of the thought process that helped you select the correct answers. If you're in a hurry, flip to the end of the chapter for an abbreviated answer key.

Analytical Writing Sections

Give your essays to someone to read and evaluate for you. Refer that helpful person to Chapters 14 and 15 for scoring guidelines.

Section 1: Verbal Reasoning

1. **D.** Military *expenditure,* which is the money spent on the military, leads to the military's size. Even though the other qualities may be true, the size of the military often hinges on the money spent on it

2. **B.** A *curriculum* leads to educational goals, though the other qualities may be true. *Adroitness* is the quality of being clever and appropriate, but it isn't specific enough to reach educational goals.

3. **A, E.** The *gustatory* system is responsible for the sense of taste, and a more *discerning* (perceptive) palate is able to distinguish subtle differences. The *lymphatic* system fights infection, while the *digestive* system breaks down food. For the second blank, *discrete* (distinct) doesn't work, and *distended* (swollen) isn't even in the ballpark.

4. **A, F.** A *tsunami* is a wave that would *inundate* (flood) the resort, causing a loss of property that would act as a *catalyst* (stimulus) for any renovation. Choice (C), *drowned,* fits the meaning but isn't the proper word. Because the resort isn't a living thing, it can't drown. *Dissembled* (concealed) isn't even close. Although a loss of property could be a *symbol* for something, it's not a very good symbol for much-needed renovation. A loss of property could result in many *mendicants* (vagrants), but the word doesn't make sense in context.

5. **C, D.** Castle walls that are *impervious* to attack cannot be penetrated, and after several attempts to break through the walls, an enemy's energy and enthusiasm would begin to *flag* (weaken). Walls cannot be *amenable* (agreeable). The walls may be *impeccable* (flawless), but because they frustrated the enemy's attempts to get inside, *impervious* is a better choice. As for the other choices for the second blank, the enemy's enthusiasm wouldn't *rally* (become stronger) as a result of failure, nor would it *flee* (run away), although the enemy certainly would.

6. **C, D, G.** Aware of the ***burgeoning*** (growing) debt, Congress would impose an ***austerity*** (disciplined) program to ***curtail*** (reduce) spending. For the first blank, *pervasive* (widespread) would be a good second choice, but *shrinking* is the opposite of what's needed here. For the second blank, *spending* would be a decent second choice, but it's not quite strong enough and it's a little redundant because it appears at the end of the sentence. *Defense* definitely doesn't fit. For the third blank, ***attenuate*** may be okay, but it means something more like to decrease in strength. ***Desiccate*** (dehydrate) doesn't make the cut, either.

7. **B, F, H.** A ***discrepancy*** (difference) between a person's demeanor and statement would make officers suspicious; a ***correlation*** or ***relationship,*** both meaning connection, would not. The word *but* provides a clue that although the officers were suspicious, they couldn't do much, so you know that their evidence would be ***unsubstantiated*** (without support), not ***corroborated*** (confirmed) or ***vetted*** (examined closely). This means their case would be ***tenuous*** (shaky) at best, not ***compelling*** (convincing) or ***conclusive*** (certain).

8. **C.** The second paragraph, third sentence states that experts recommend profiling by behavior and intelligence.

9. **A.** If true, Choice (A) describes a solution that improves security without compromising civil liberties. Choice (B) may be true, but the passage cites profiling as a violation of civil liberties. Choice (C) also may be true, but precertification requires a background check, which some people may consider a violation of civil liberties. Choices (D) and (E) fail to address the question.

10. **A, C.** The third sentence states that the Cold War shaped international and domestic politics and cultures, and the fourth sentence states that war has influenced the development of new states. Choice (B) is wrong, because the next-to-last sentence presents civil wars and conflicts as causes of change, not effects of war.

11. **E.** Terrorists and rogue states are mentioned only in respect to the possibility that they'll acquire nuclear weapons, while nuclear proliferation — which includes the acquisition of nuclear weapons by rogue states — is singled out as a threat in itself. According to the passage, the Cold War has ended and the proliferation of civil wars is mentioned not as a threat but only as an agent of change in the developing world.

12. **D.** The sixth sentence describes the goal stated in the first sentence — to position yourself as an expert with useful information so the marketplace will always need what you have to offer.

13. **B.** The fourth sentence answers this question in saying that "there is an important difference between somebody who is selling something and somebody who is an expert." Most of the choices are differences mentioned in the passage but are not *the* difference between marketing and UnMarketing.

14. **C.** If the prices of health services are more than 50 percent higher in the United States, then this accounts for the fact that the United States spends more than 50 percent as much per capita on healthcare than most European countries, undermining the argument that poor diet is responsible for the difference.

15. **B, D.** ***Tacit*** and ***implicit*** both indicate that the coach approved without having to say so. Perhaps during practice the coach had expressed a desire that the team play with more heart and throw caution to the wind. Choices (C), *cautious,* and (E), *enthusiastic,* both are fitting words to describe approval, but neither has a suitable match in the list. ***Ambiguous*** (unclear) and ***salubrious*** (healthy) obviously don't fit.

16. **E, F.** As a champion competitive eater, Thomas would need a hearty appetite, so people may be surprised to see him so ***abstemious*** (moderate) or ***ascetic*** (prone to self-denial) while dining socially. Choice (D), *courteous,* doesn't fit, and the other three choices all mean the opposite of moderate.

17. **C, D.** ***Embellishment*** is an addition or ornament, such as details added to a story, and ***hyperbole*** is an exaggeration; both words carry the positive connotation of improving something or making it more interesting. Choice (F), *overemphasis* is an overstated importance placed on something, which doesn't change the nature of what's being overstated. None of the remaining choices come close: ***sarcasm*** (irony), ***allegory*** (parable), and ***ennui*** (boredom).

18. **A, D.** *Pugnacious* means aggressive and *truculent* means defiantly aggressive. *Irascible* (irritable) is nearly a match, but the two correct choices are better. Choices (B) and (C), *lackadaisical* (easygoing) and *quiescent* (calm) are nearly identical in meaning, but they don't fit the sentence; because the other puppies in the litter were gentle, this one would stand out as being the opposite. If the puppy were *soporific* (sleep-inducing), it would tend to calm those around it.

19. **B, C.** If Mary seemed to be up to something (in a bad way), then her offer to help would come across as *disingenuous* (think *genuine* with a *dis-* in front of it) or *duplicitous* (think of *dupli* as two or two-faced). Choices (A), *sincere,* and (F), *authentic,* are nearly the opposite of what's needed here, both meaning genuine or real. *Hypocritical* is close but has more to do with pretending to hold a certain belief.

20. **B.** If accidents are caused by delivery drivers, then training factory workers won't change anything. There are trap answers, however. In Choice (A), if some workers are already trained, then others (who cause accidents) may still need training. In Choice (C), though the Smith factory already has a good safety record, it could still improve. In Choice (D), the result of the accident isn't part of prevention. And finally, in Choice (E), the program could be effective, but the Olson factory could be accident-prone for other reasons, such as a poor setup.

Section 2: Quantitative Reasoning

1. **C.** To get the area of triangle *ABC,* you need the base and the height. Because the radius of the circle is 1, side *CB* is 2. You already know $AB = 1$, making the right triangle a 30-60-90 triangle. Because the side ratio of this triangle is $1:2:\sqrt{3}$, the base is 1 and the height is $\sqrt{3}$. The area of the triangle is $\frac{1}{2}$base $\times$ height $= \frac{\text{base} \times \text{height}}{2}$, making Quantity A equal to Quantity B.

2. **B.** To get the weighted average, add the product of 10 and 120 to the product of 20 and 90: $1,200 + 1,800 = 3,000$. Divide by the total number of test scores (30), and the weighted average is 100.

3. **D.** If you assumed the highest possible value of *n* is 14, making $\frac{n}{d} = \frac{14}{20} = 0.7$, then you fell for the trap and chose Choice (B). However, because *n* isn't necessarily an integer, it could be equal to 14.999, which is greater than 0.72 when placed over 20. Because *n* could also be 11, $\frac{n}{d}$ could be either less than or greater than 0.72.

4. **A.** If you need $\frac{4}{3}$ cups of lentils to make six servings and $(2)(6) + \frac{1}{2}(6) = 15$ servings, the amount of lentils required to make 15 servings is

$$(2)\left(\frac{4}{3}\right) + \frac{1}{1\slash 2}\left(\frac{^2\slash4}{3}\right) = \frac{8}{3} + \frac{2}{3} = \frac{10}{3}$$

Because $\frac{10}{3}$ is more than 3, Choice **(A)** is the correct answer.

5. **C.** Remember how to find the area of a trapezoid? Average the two bases and multiply by the height. Because the bases are 9 and 11, the average is 10. Multiplying by the height gives you 50, which is the same as the area of the rectangle.

6. **C.** Call the interior angles of the triangle *A, B,* and *C,* according to the labels on the drawing. Because the angle supplementary to angle *C* is $2x$, angle C equals $180 - 2x$. The three angles of any triangle total 180, making angle *B* equal to 180 minus the other two angles, or $180 - x - (180 - 2x)$, which you can rewrite as $180 - x - 180 + 2x$. The 180s cancel, and $-x + 2x$ becomes *x.* Now you know two of the angles are equal, making the triangle isosceles and segments *AC* and *BC* equal.

7. **A.** The equation $x^2 - x - 6 = 0$ becomes $(x-3)(x+2) = 0$, making the roots of the equation 3 and –2. (The roots are the two values for x, either of which makes the statement true.) The sum of these two numbers is 1, making Quantity A greater than Quantity B. If you thought the roots are –3 and 2 and chose Choice (C), then you fell for the trap by thinking that –3 and +2 in the factored equation are the roots.

8. **B.** The *median* is the middle number, but if you have two middle numbers, you average them. The two middle numbers are 5 and 6, which averages to 5.5. The *range* is the distance between the lowest and highest values. The range of this set is $8 - 3 = 5$.

9. **A.** The units digit of any product depends on the units digits of the two numbers being multiplied. To find the units digit of $219,473 \times 162,597$, just use the units digits of the two numbers: 3 and 7. Then $3 \times 7 = 21$, so the units digit of $219,473 \times 162,597$ is 1.

10. **E.** To find the slope of the line, convert the equation to slope-intercept form, which is $y = mx + b$. Solve for y, and m is the slope.

$$2x + 3y = 5$$
$$3y = -2x + 5$$
$$y = \frac{-2}{3}x + \frac{5}{3}$$

11. **A, B, C, and D.** These four answer choices are correct because 15 to 30 percent of $50,000 is $7,500 to $15,000. In this type of question, you select *all* correct answer choices.

12. **61.** Set the ratios up as baseballs : gloves = 2 : 9 and baseballs : bats = 5 : 3. Because baseballs are in both ratios, once as 2 and once as 5, the actual number of baseballs has to be a multiple of both 2 and 5. The question asks for the *lowest* number, and the lowest common multiple of 2 and 5 is 10. If the ratio of baseballs to gloves is 2 : 9 and there are 10 baseballs, there must be 45 gloves (multiply both sides of the ratio by 5). Also, if the ratio of baseballs to bats is 5 : 3 and there are 10 baseballs, there must be 6 bats (multiply both sides of the ratio by 2). Add these up for the number of sporting items: 10 baseballs + 45 gloves + 6 bats = 61 items.

13. **24.** If the average of x, y, and z is 5, then $x + y + z = 15$. To find the average of the expressions $4x + y$, $2y - x$, and $3z + 27$, add them up and divide by 3. The equations $4x + y$, $2y - x$, and $3z + 27$ simplify to $3x + 3y + 3z + 27$. Because $x + y + z = 15$, $3x + 3y + 3z = 3(15)$, or 45. Add the 27 for a total of 72. Finally, $72 \div 3$ is 24.

14. **D.** If the central angle is 45 degrees, then the resulting arc is also 45 degrees, which is $\frac{1}{8}$ of the circle. If the radius of the circle is 8, then the circumference is 16π. And $\frac{1}{8}$ of 16π is 2π.

15. **D.** The table shows that on Test B, a score of 300 placed the examinee in the 94th percentile ranking. This means that the examinee scored higher than 94 percent of the other examinees. Therefore, 5 percent of the examinees, or 1 out of every 20 examinees, scored 300.

16. **E.** In the first graph, the line for Test A examinees crosses the 40,000 line at two points: 30 and 210. However, 30 isn't an answer choice, so if you chose Choice (A) or (B), you fell for the trap of not looking far enough on the chart. This examinee could also have a score of 210, which *is* an answer choice and the correct answer. Choice (C), 90, is the group of 40,000 like scorers on Test B, another trap. Choice (D), 180, is the score at which the two testing trend lines cross.

17. **C.** Using the line chart, you see that approximately 70,000 examinees scored 100 and 80,000 scored 110. By jumping from 100 to 120, the examinee surpasses about $70,000 + 80,000 = 150,000$ examinees. Note that the graph label says that the test scores are in "increments of 10," so you know that no one scored, say, 105 or 109. You only need to account for students with scores of 100 and 110.

18. **E.** The area of any circle is πr^2. Because the radius of the original circle increased by 50 percent, the new radius is $\frac{3r}{2}$. Plug the new radius into the area formula, or square it and multiply by π for $\frac{9\pi r^2}{4}$.

19. **C.** If the circle is inscribed within the square, then the diameter of the circle is equal to one side of the square, which is 6. This makes the radius of the circle 3 and the area $\pi(3)^2 = 9\pi$. The circle occupies $\frac{9\pi}{36}$ of the square, which reduces to $\frac{\pi}{4}$.

20. **5.** You can find the volume of a cylinder with $\pi r^2 h$ (the base area times the height). You're given the volume and height, so back-solve to find the radius. Begin with $50\pi = \pi r^2 2$ (because the height is 2). Eliminate the π and 2 from both sides for $25 = r^2$, making the radius 5.

Section 3: Verbal Reasoning

1. **C.** A language is comprised of structure and **vocabulary,** and an **etymologist** studies the history of language. Though *grammar* is also relevant, it's redundant to structure, which is already in the sentence. The other choices, *culture, politics,* and **decorum** (proper behavior), are not directly related to languages or language structure.

2. **A.** The wind flow is driven by the rotation of the Earth, so look for an answer choice related to that — especially one with a clockwise or counterclockwise orientation. Only *hemisphere* is related to the rotation of the Earth, which would appear to go clockwise in one hemisphere and counterclockwise in the other. You don't need geographical knowledge to answer this question — just eliminate answer choices that aren't related to the rotation of the Earth.

3. **A, E.** People who are **capricious** tend to change their minds easily, so they have a **penchant** for or tendency to abandon their shopping carts before checking out. For the first blank, *predictable* doesn't work because it's the opposite of capricious, and **fatuous** means silly or inane. For the second blank, neither **inkling** (hunch) nor **passion** (desire) makes sense in this context.

4. **C, D.** Because the compensation was **commensurate** (proportional), Jerry wouldn't **quibble** (argue) over the deadlines. For the first blank, **discordant** (conflicting) means nearly the opposite of *commensurate,* and **pursuant** means in agreement with (as in the terms of a contract). **Acquiesce** and **concede** both mean to go along with, neither of which fits the connotation of this sentence.

5. **A, F.** Because the audience was impatient, it was more likely **intractable** (difficult to control) than **imperturbable** (calm and cool) or **indolent** (lazy). If everything the speaker said to silence the rabble didn't work, his efforts must have **exacerbated** the situation (made it worse), not **precipitated** (triggered) or **exonerated** (forgave) it.

6. **C, D, G.** Reading the sentence from the end, you know that the teacher was concerned about student safety, so safety issues would have **superseded** (taken precedence over) all other concerns and not **preceded** (come earlier) or **negated** (canceled) them. If safety became a concern, the mixture must have become **volatile** (changing rapidly, which could be dangerous), definitely not **piquant** (spicy) but perhaps **acidic,** although that wouldn't necessarily require an evacuation. Something helped change the nature of the mixture, so that would be a **catalyst** (an agent of change), not just any old *chemical,* and certainly not a *neutralizer,* which would have made the mixture less volatile.

7. **A, F, H.** **Pristine** means perfect. **Primordial** is more along the lines of prehistoric, and **rudimentary** means basic. If the owner said that the vase *certainly was,* he **averred** (confirmed) that the vase was in pristine condition. **Corroborated** would have required

someone else saying it before he did, and if he *proved* it, the vase really would have been in pristine condition. For the last blank, *however* is the key word; knowing that the owner claimed the vase was in pristine condition, *however* clues you in that it really wasn't, in which case the buyer was *duped* (fooled), not *sidetracked* (diverted) or *ostracized* (excluded).

8. **B, C.** The second sentence names three factors that contributed to Great Britain's ability to take an early lead in the Industrial Revolution: coal, waterways, and international trade. Choice (A), trade unions, is mentioned near the end but only as a reaction by the working class to the low pay and poor working conditions.

9. **D.** "Thus, employers had such a large labor pool to select from that they were able to dictate low wages and long hours, further suppressing the working poor." The sentence clearly states that the wages were so low because "employers had such a large labor pool to select from."

10. **E.** "Great Britain's Industrial Revolution: Natural Resources, Migration, and Unions." The passage covers these three topics but isn't entirely based on any one. Choice (A) is wrong because the passage never says Great Britain went bust. Choice (B) is wrong because it describes only half of the passage. Choice (C) is wrong because unions are mentioned only in the final sentence and the passage doesn't say that unions originated in Great Britain. Choice (D) is wrong because the perspective in the passage is one of historian, not one of the exploited poor.

11. **A.** If some teachers have a better track record than others in educating students at the same school, the difference in teacher expertise is probably the reason why. Choices (B), (C), and (E) would help point toward some other cause, while Choice (D) is off topic.

12. **C.** If population growth offsets any savings in resources from reducing consumption, then regardless how much consumption is reduced, the population will eventually be too large for the planet to sustain it. Choice (A) is wrong because the fact that the population doubles every 40 years is not necessarily a problem in and of itself. Choice (B) is wrong because it doesn't counter the argument. Choice (D) is off topic, and Choice (E) is more in support of the argument.

13. **B.** Even if you don't know the meaning of *rapprochement,* the following parenthetical *rejection of* provides a clue that it means the opposite of rejection of, so it means something like acceptance of. *Reconciliation* is the closest in meaning to acceptance of.

14. **C.** The second sentence mentions the only answer choice that's correct: "It can be a triumphant parade of 'great men and women.'" Choice (A) is wrong because although the passage mentions psychoanalysis, it does so only as one of a sequence of paradigmatic shifts. Choice (B) is wrong because although the passage mentions film language, it does so only as an example of an orienting metaphor.

15. **B, E.** If Amanda was known as the life of the party and acted that way during a ceremony of any sort, her behavior would appear *loutish* or *boorish,* both of which mean rude. At a ceremony, people are expected to be *courteous* or *decorous,* both of which mean polite. *Capricious* means fickle, and *contentious* means quarrelsome, neither of which fits in this context.

16. **D, F.** *Convoluted* and *tortuous* both mean complex, full of twists and turns, which would make the plans difficult to follow and execute. *Desultory* means aimless or unfocused, making it a good word to describe the plans, but it doesn't have a match in the answer choices. If the plans were *methodical* (systematic), they'd be easy to follow, and if they were *proscribed* (prohibited), nobody on staff would be allowed to carry them out.

17. **A, E.** If the candidates weren't strong and were pandering, they must have been *pusillanimous* or *craven* (cowardly). They certainly would not be *impudent* (bold, in a disrespectful way), *audacious* (daring), *sanctimonious* (self-righteous), or *intransigent* (stubborn).

18. **B, E.** When children misbehave, parents are expected to *admonish* (scold) or *castigate* (punish) them but not *vilify* (slander) or *disparage* (ridicule) them. Of course, parents should never *sanction* (approve of) such behavior or congratulate the child for it.

19. **A, C.** *Obdurate* and *obstinate* both convey a sense of stubbornness. *Recalcitrant* and *subversive* are a little too strong, conveying a sense of rebellion. *Assiduous* means hard-working, which the couple may have been, but that wouldn't necessarily make them reluctant to move. *Fundamentalist* (die-hard, or one who is unyielding) isn't even in the ballpark.

20. **B.** The answer is most clearly provided in the final sentence. Naturalism relied on accuracy of description, whereas symbolism requires vividness of expression. Choice (E) is tempting, but *authenticity* is used to describe both naturalism and symbolism. Choice (A) is also a little tempting, but the passage mentions two types of art — that which is rooted in the real world (such as nature) and that which originates in the artist's soul (symbolism) — so it's not exactly art versus nature. Neither of the remaining two choices comes close.

Section 4: Quantitative Reasoning

1. **B.** The percents profit and loss are based on the dealer's purchase price, not the dealer's selling price. If he sold a sofa for $400 at a 25 percent profit, then he sold it for 125 percent, or $\frac{5}{4}$, of what he paid for it, which is x, so

$$\frac{5}{4}x = \$400$$
$$x = \$^{80}\cancel{400} \cdot \frac{4}{1\cancel{5}}$$
$$x = \$320$$

The net gain was $400 - $320 = $80.

The dealer sold the other sofa for $400 at a 20 percent loss, or for $100\% - 20\% = 80\%$, or $\frac{8}{10} = \frac{4}{5}$ of what he paid for it (call it y). Therefore, the dealer purchased it for

$$\frac{4}{5}y = \$400$$
$$y = \$^{100}\cancel{400} \cdot \frac{5}{1\cancel{4}}$$
$$y = \$500$$

The net loss was $500 - $400 = $100, so Quantity B is larger. If you chose Choice (A), then you calculated the profit and loss on the dealer's *sale* prices of $400, not the dealer's *purchase* prices.

2. **B.** The number of integers between 200 and 500 with a units digit of 5 is 30.

3. **B.** If $ab < 0$, then either a or b is negative but not both. Making them both positive, as in Quantity B, and then adding them produces a higher number than adding them first (with one as a negative) and then making the result positive.

4. **D.** If you chose Choice (B), then you fell for the trap. Just because $\frac{x}{y} = \frac{2}{3}$ doesn't mean that $x = 2$ or $y = 3$. They could be 20 and 30, for example. Or x and y could also be negative, such as –2 and –3.

5. **A.** Draw the xy-coordinate plane and place the points A and C as directed. These are two points of the square, and you know they're the opposite corners because the question tells you the sides of the square are parallel to the axes. Measure the width and height and multiply for an area of 25. (Or to save time, you can measure the width *or* the height and then square that value to find the answer, because the width and height of a square are equal.)

6. **C.** Drawing a line from point A to point C splits the square into two 45-45-90 triangles. The side ratio of this triangle is $x{:}x{:}x\sqrt{2}$, so if two of the sides are 5, then the hypotenuse is $5\sqrt{2}$.

7. **D.** If n equals 2, then Quantity A is greater; if n equals $\frac{1}{2}$, then Quantity B is greater. All you know is that n is positive, not whether it's an integer or a fraction that's less than 1.

8. **B.** Set up the conversions as fractions and do the math:

$$\left(\frac{20\ \text{meters}}{1\ \text{sec}}\right)\left(\frac{1\ \text{km}}{1,000\ \text{meters}}\right)\left(\frac{60\ \text{sec}}{1\ \text{min}}\right)\left(\frac{10\ \text{min}}{1}\right)=12\ \text{km}$$

Note that the three zeros in the numerators cancel the three zeros in the denominator of the second fraction.

9. **C, E.** If $(x-5)^2=900$, then take the square root of both sides to get $x-5=30$ and $x-5=-30$. Add 5s all around, and x equals either 35 or –25.

10. **B.** If the radius of the pool is r, then the radius from the center of the pool to the outer circumference of the sidewalk is $r+\frac{r}{2}$. First, calculate the area of the pool and sidewalk by substituting $\left(r+\frac{r}{2}\right)$ for r in the equation for the area of a circle:

$$A=\pi\left(r+\frac{r}{2}\right)^2$$
$$A=\pi\left(\frac{2r}{2}+\frac{r}{2}\right)^2$$
$$A=\pi\left(\frac{3r}{2}\right)^2$$
$$A=\frac{9\pi r^2}{4}$$

Next, calculate the area of the pool alone, which is easy: $A=\pi r^2$. Finally, subtract the area of the pool from the total area of the pool plus the sidewalk, remembering that you need a common denominator to subtract:

$$\frac{9\pi r^2}{4}-\pi r^2=\frac{9\pi r^2}{4}-\frac{4\pi r^2}{4}=\frac{5\pi r^2}{4}$$

11. **120.** The sum of angles for any shape (other than a circle) can be found with the formula $(n-2)\left(180°\right)$, making the sum of the hexagon's angles 720 degrees. The hexagon is a regular hexagon, meaning all sides and angles are the same, so each angle is 120 degrees.

12. **3.** Pick a number that has a remainder of 3 when divided by 35, such as 38 or 73. Divide the number by 7, and it has the same remainder.

13. **E.** Pick simple numbers for the length and width of the rectangle, such as 5 and 5, for an area of 25. Increase one by 20 percent and decrease the other by 20 percent, for new sides of 6 and 4 and a new area of 24. Regardless of the numbers you pick, the ratio of the area of the original rectangle to the area of the new rectangle is the same.

14. **D.** If you multiplied the bachelor's-degree holder's median weekly earnings of $1,012 by 4 and chose Choice (C), you fell for the trap. An average month is $4\frac{1}{3}$ weeks long:

$$\frac{52\ \text{weeks}}{12\ \text{months}}=4\frac{4}{12}=4\frac{1}{3}\text{weeks/month}$$

Now multiply the median weekly earnings of $1,012 by the number of weeks per month:

$1,012\times4\frac{1}{3}=\$4,385.33$, which is closest to Choice (D), \$4,400.

15. **B.** To count the unemployed doctoral-degree holders, take 2 percent of 10,000, which is 200. To count the unemployed master's-degree holders, take 2.4 percent of 200,000, which is 4,800. Reduce the ratio of 200:4,800 to 1:24.

16. **D.** Good thing you're allowed to use a calculator. To find the annual earnings of the associate-degree holder earning 20 percent less than the median, multiply the median amount of $757 by 0.8 and by 52, for an annual salary of $31,491. To find the annual earnings of the bachelor's-degree holder earning 25 percent above the median, multiply the median amount of $1,012 by 1.25 and by 52, for an annual salary of $65,780. The difference is $34,290, making the closest answer choice $34,300.

17. **B.** You can find the area of an equilateral triangle by using the formula $\frac{s^2\sqrt{3}}{4}$, where s is any of the sides, including the base. You can also consider the equilateral triangle to be two 30-60-90 triangles, giving the triangle a height of $3\sqrt{3}$, and use the $A = \frac{1}{2}\text{base}\times\text{height}$ formula.

18. **B, C, D.** Of the 49 houses, the median value will be of house number 25, in order of value. This places the median house in the third group, valued in thousands from $150 to $199. The median value can be any value in that range.

19. **A.** With the two equations, solve for x by eliminating y. Because $y = x + 1$ and $y = 2x + 3$, replace the y in one equation with its value from the other equation: $x + 1 = 2x + 3$. Solve for x as –2; then substitute x in either original equation to get the value of y as –1.

20. **C.** The idea is to simplify this fraction as quickly and easily as possible. Factor the $\frac{5^{10} - 5^8}{5^9 - 5^7}$ into $\frac{5^8\left(5^2 - 1\right)}{5^7\left(5^2 - 1\right)}$. Cancel the $\left(5^2 - 1\right)$ from the top and bottom, and reduce the $\frac{5^8}{5^7}$ to 5.

Answer Key for Practice Exam 2

Section 1: Verbal Reasoning	Section 2: Quantitative Reasoning	Section 3: Verbal Reasoning	Section 4: Quantitative Reasoning
1. D	1. C	1. C	1. B
2. B	2. B	2. A	2. B
3. A, E	3. D	3. A, E	3. B
4. A, F	4. A	4. C, D	4. D
5. C, D	5. C	5. A, F	5. A
6. C, D, G	6. C	6. C, D, G	6. C
7. B, F, H	7. A	7. A, F, H	7. D
8. C	8. B	8. B, C	8. B
9. A	9. A	9. D	9. C, E
10. A, C	10. E	10. E	10. B
11. E	11. A, B, C, D	11. A	11. **120**
12. D	12. **61**	12. C	12. **3**
13. B	13. **24**	13. B	13. E
14. C	14. D	14. C	14. D
15. B, D	15. D	15. B, E	15. B
16. E, F	16. E	16. D, F	16. D
17. C, D	17. C	17. A, E	17. B
18. A, D	18. E	18. B, E	18. B, C, D
19. B, C	19. C	19. A, C	19. A
20. B	20. **5**	20. B	20. C

Chapter 20

Practice Exam 3

• •

*Y*ou're now ready to take another practice GRE. Like the actual, computer-based GRE, the following exam consists of two 30-minute essays, two 30-minute Verbal Reasoning sections (20 questions each), and two 35-minute Quantitative Reasoning sections (20 questions each). The actual GRE may also include an extra Verbal or Quantitative Reasoning section, which doesn't count toward your score, but this practice exam has nothing like that.

Take this practice test under normal exam conditions and approach it as you would the real GRE:

- ✔ **Work when you won't be interrupted.**

- ✔ **Use scratch paper that's free of any prepared notes.** On the actual GRE, you receive blank scratch paper before your test begins.

- ✔ **Answer as many questions as time allows.** Consider answering all the easier questions within each section first and then going back to answer the remaining, harder questions. Because you're not penalized for guessing, go ahead and guess on the remaining questions before time expires.

- ✔ **Set a timer for each section.** If you have time left at the end, you may go back and review answers (within the section), continue and finish your test early, or pause and catch your mental breath before moving on to the next section.

- ✔ **Don't leave your desk while the clock is running on any section.** Though technically you're allowed to do this, it's not conducive to an effective time-management strategy.

- ✔ **Take a one-minute break after each section and the optional ten-minute break after the first Verbal section.**

- ✔ **Type the essays.** Because you type the essays on the actual GRE, typing them now is good practice. Don't use software with an automatic spell-checker, such as Microsoft Word. Instead, use a simple text editor, such as Notepad, with copy and paste but no other features. The GRE essay-writing field features undo, redo, copy, and paste functionality but nothing else.

After completing this entire practice test, go to Chapter 21 to check your answers. Be sure to review the explanations for *all* the questions, not just the ones you miss. The answer explanations provide insight and a review of everything you went over in the previous chapters. This way, too, you review the explanations to questions that you guessed correctly on.

I formatted the questions and answer choices to make them appear as similar as possible to what you'll see on the computer-based test, but I had to retain the letters (A, B, C, D, E, F) to label the answer choices. The actual exam doesn't use letters to mark the answer choices — it simply has ovals, boxes, or selectable text.

Answer Sheet for Practice Exam 3

Section 1:
Verbal Reasoning

1. Ⓐ Ⓑ Ⓒ Ⓓ Ⓔ
2. Ⓐ Ⓑ Ⓒ Ⓓ Ⓔ
3. Ⓐ Ⓑ Ⓒ Ⓓ Ⓔ Ⓕ
4. Ⓐ Ⓑ Ⓒ Ⓓ Ⓔ Ⓕ
5. Ⓐ Ⓑ Ⓒ Ⓓ Ⓔ Ⓕ
6. Ⓐ Ⓑ Ⓒ Ⓓ Ⓔ Ⓕ Ⓖ Ⓗ Ⓘ
7. Ⓐ Ⓑ Ⓒ Ⓓ Ⓔ Ⓕ Ⓖ Ⓗ Ⓘ
8. [A] [B] [C]
9. Ⓐ Ⓑ Ⓒ Ⓓ Ⓔ
10. Ⓐ Ⓑ Ⓒ Ⓓ Ⓔ
11. [A] [B] [C]
12. Ⓐ Ⓑ Ⓒ Ⓓ Ⓔ
13. Ⓐ Ⓑ Ⓒ Ⓓ Ⓔ
14. Ⓐ Ⓑ Ⓒ Ⓓ Ⓔ
15. [A] [B] [C] [D] [E] [F]
16. [A] [B] [C] [D] [E] [F]
17. [A] [B] [C] [D] [E] [F]
18. [A] [B] [C] [D] [E] [F]
19. [A] [B] [C] [D] [E] [F]
20. Ⓐ Ⓑ Ⓒ Ⓓ Ⓔ

Section 2:
Quantitative Reasoning

1. Ⓐ Ⓑ Ⓒ Ⓓ
2. Ⓐ Ⓑ Ⓒ Ⓓ
3. Ⓐ Ⓑ Ⓒ Ⓓ
4. Ⓐ Ⓑ Ⓒ Ⓓ
5. Ⓐ Ⓑ Ⓒ Ⓓ
6. Ⓐ Ⓑ Ⓒ Ⓓ
7. Ⓐ Ⓑ Ⓒ Ⓓ
8. Ⓐ Ⓑ Ⓒ Ⓓ
9. Ⓐ Ⓑ Ⓒ Ⓓ
10. Ⓐ Ⓑ Ⓒ Ⓓ
11. Ⓐ Ⓑ Ⓒ Ⓓ
12. Ⓐ Ⓑ Ⓒ Ⓓ
13. Ⓐ Ⓑ Ⓒ Ⓓ
14. [A] [B] [C]
15. [＿＿＿＿＿]
16. [＿＿＿＿＿]
17. [＿＿＿＿＿]
18. [A] [B] [C] [D] [E] [F]
19. [A] [B] [C] [D] [E] [F]
20. [A] [B] [C]

Section 3:
Verbal Reasoning

1. Ⓐ Ⓑ Ⓒ Ⓓ Ⓔ
2. Ⓐ Ⓑ Ⓒ Ⓓ Ⓔ
3. Ⓐ Ⓑ Ⓒ Ⓓ Ⓔ Ⓕ
4. Ⓐ Ⓑ Ⓒ Ⓓ Ⓔ Ⓕ
5. Ⓐ Ⓑ Ⓒ Ⓓ Ⓔ Ⓕ
6. Ⓐ Ⓑ Ⓒ Ⓓ Ⓔ Ⓕ Ⓖ Ⓗ Ⓘ
7. Ⓐ Ⓑ Ⓒ Ⓓ Ⓔ Ⓕ Ⓖ Ⓗ Ⓘ
8. Ⓐ Ⓑ Ⓒ Ⓓ Ⓔ
9. Ⓐ Ⓑ Ⓒ Ⓓ Ⓔ
10. [A] [B] [C]
11. [A] [B] [C]
12. Ⓐ Ⓑ Ⓒ Ⓓ Ⓔ
13. Ⓐ Ⓑ Ⓒ Ⓓ Ⓔ
14. Ⓐ Ⓑ Ⓒ Ⓓ Ⓔ
15. Ⓐ Ⓑ Ⓒ Ⓓ Ⓔ
16. [A] [B] [C] [D] [E] [F]
17. [A] [B] [C] [D] [E] [F]
18. [A] [B] [C] [D] [E] [F]
19. [A] [B] [C] [D] [E] [F]
20. [A] [B] [C] [D] [E] [F]

Section 4:
Quantitative Reasoning

1. Ⓐ Ⓑ Ⓒ Ⓓ
2. Ⓐ Ⓑ Ⓒ Ⓓ
3. Ⓐ Ⓑ Ⓒ Ⓓ
4. Ⓐ Ⓑ Ⓒ Ⓓ
5. Ⓐ Ⓑ Ⓒ Ⓓ
6. Ⓐ Ⓑ Ⓒ Ⓓ
7. Ⓐ Ⓑ Ⓒ Ⓓ
8. Ⓐ Ⓑ Ⓒ Ⓓ
9. Ⓐ Ⓑ Ⓒ Ⓓ Ⓔ
10. Ⓐ Ⓑ Ⓒ Ⓓ Ⓔ
11. Ⓐ Ⓑ Ⓒ Ⓓ Ⓔ
12. Ⓐ Ⓑ Ⓒ Ⓓ Ⓔ
13. Ⓐ Ⓑ Ⓒ Ⓓ Ⓔ
14. [A] [B] [C]
15. [＿＿＿＿＿]
16. [＿＿＿＿＿]
17. [＿＿＿＿＿]
18. [A] [B] [C] [D] [E] [F]
19. [A] [B] [C]
20. [A] [B] [C]

Analytical Writing 1: Analyze an Issue

Time: 30 minutes

Directions: Present and explain your view on the following issue. Although there is no one right or wrong response, be sure to consider various points of view as you explain the reasons behind your own perspective. Support your position with reasons and examples from your own reading, personal or professional experience, and observations.

"Consumerism has contributed significantly to alleviating human suffering."

Express the extent to which you agree or disagree with the preceding statement and explain the reasoning behind your position. In support of your position, think of ways in which the statement may or may not be true and how these considerations influence your position.

STOP DO NOT TURN THE PAGE UNTIL TOLD TO DO SO. DO NOT RETURN TO A PREVIOUS TEST.

Analytical Writing 2: Analyze an Argument

Time: 30 minutes

Directions: Critique the following argument. Identify evidence that will strengthen or weaken the argument, point out assumptions underlying the argument, and offer counterexamples to the argument.

"Though touted as the key to building a strong economy, microlending (making small loans to entrepreneurs in impoverished countries) can actually do more harm than good. In the small country of Bogata, for instance, microlending was introduced in key regions, and the gross domestic product (total value of all goods and services produced) declined by 40%. During the same time, the neighboring country of Byrn did not introduce microlending practices, and its gross domestic product increased 25%. The practice of microlending, therefore, should be discouraged from any economy."

Discuss the merits of the preceding argument. Analyze the evidence used as well as the general reasoning. Present points that would strengthen the argument or make it more compelling.

STOP DO NOT TURN THE PAGE UNTIL TOLD TO DO SO. DO NOT RETURN TO A PREVIOUS TEST.

Section 1
Verbal Reasoning

Time: 30 minutes for 20 questions

Directions: Choose the best answer to each question. Blacken the corresponding ovals or boxes on the answer sheet.

Directions: For Questions 1–7, choose the one entry best suited for each blank from its corresponding column of choices.

1. In Shakespeare's *Julius Caesar,* Act II, scene I, lines 193 to 194, Brutus and Cassius make reference to a clock that struck three o'clock. Given the fact that at the time of Julius Caesar, the mechanical clock had not yet been invented, this reference is quite _____.

Ⓐ archaic
Ⓑ a relic
Ⓒ a tropism
Ⓓ an anachronism
Ⓔ a euphemism

2. The journalism student must study not only the craft of writing but also the ethics of accuracy. The journalist is responsible to the public and his profession for the _____ of his story.

Ⓐ veracity
Ⓑ plausibility
Ⓒ tenacity
Ⓓ originality
Ⓔ righteousness

3. Galileo was not the first astronomer to question the (i) _____ view of the Earth as being at the center of the universe, but he was certainly the most vocal. Ultimately, he was labeled a heretic for publicly supporting Copernicanism, and his ideas were (ii) _____ by the Catholic Church.

Blank (i)	Blank (ii)
Ⓐ heliocentric	Ⓓ authorized
Ⓑ Eurocentric	Ⓔ proscribed
Ⓒ geocentric	Ⓕ legitimized

4. The question of whether the common (i) _____ used in dental fillings poses a significant health risk plagues dental professionals. Although it contains mercury (among other metals), most dentists advocate its use, because it is inexpensive, easy to use, and durable. Experts question the (ii) _____ that because mercury is toxic, its use in fillings must be unhealthy. They believe that the level of mercury exposure is too low to pose a serious threat.

Blank (i)	Blank (ii)
Ⓐ element	Ⓓ supposition
Ⓑ metal	Ⓔ accusation
Ⓒ amalgam	Ⓕ allegation

Go on to next page

5. Law students often have (i) _____ to study the letter of the law at the expense of grasping the spirit of the law. As a result, many of these students become so consumed in (ii) _____ legal language and technicalities that they completely miss the point.

Blank (i)	Blank (ii)
Ⓐ an aptitude	Ⓓ sophisticated
Ⓑ the propensity	Ⓔ recondite
Ⓒ a desire	Ⓕ erudite

6. Teachers with a temperament that is more (i) _____ typically perform better and last longer than those who are choleric. In junior high especially, classroom management can become quite (ii) _____. Over time, an irritable temperament only deepens one's (iii) _____ to the students and the profession.

Blank (i)	Blank (ii)	Blank (iii)
Ⓐ phlegmatic	Ⓓ truculent	Ⓖ antipathy
Ⓑ sanguine	Ⓔ elementary	Ⓗ opposition
Ⓒ melancholic	Ⓕ onerous	Ⓘ hostility

7. Arguments for increasing domestic oil production instead of investing in renewable energy resources are (i) _____ at best. When one considers that the entire world is at or about to reach *peak oil* (maximum world oil production), it is (ii) _____ obvious that regardless of how much oil we produce domestically, it will eventually be insufficient to meet the (iii) _____ demand.

Blank (i)	Blank (ii)	Blank (iii)
Ⓐ specious	Ⓓ deliberately	Ⓖ nascent
Ⓑ standard	Ⓔ consummately	Ⓗ escalating
Ⓒ surreptitious	Ⓕ manifestly	Ⓘ proliferating

Go on to next page ⟹

Directions: Each of the following passages is followed by questions pertaining to the passage. Read the passage and answer the questions based on information stated or implied in that passage. For each question, select one answer choice unless instructed otherwise.

This passage is an excerpt from Psychology *by Robin M. Kowalski, PhD, and Drew Westen (Wiley).*

Since its origins in the nineteenth century, one of the major issues in behavioral neuroscience has been **localization of function.** In 1836, a physician named Marc Dax presented a paper suggesting that lesions on the left side of the brain were associated with *aphasia,* or language disorders. The notion that language was localized to the left side of the brain (the left hemisphere) developed momentum with new discoveries linking specific language functions to specific regions of the left hemisphere. Paul Broca (1824–1880) discovered that brain-injured people with lesions in the front section of the left hemisphere were often unable to speak fluently but could comprehend language. Carl Wernicke (1848–1904) showed that damage to an area a few centimeters behind the section Broca had discovered could lead to another kind of aphasia: These individuals can speak fluently and follow rules of grammar, but they cannot understand language, and their words make little sense to others (e.g., "I saw the bats and cuticles as the dog lifted the hoof, the pauser").

For the following question, consider each of the choices separately and choose all that apply.

8. Which of the following, if true, supports the notion of localization of function?

    A A person suffering from a lesion in part of the frontal lobe of the left hemisphere of the brain can no longer recall certain words.

    B The region of the brain known as the *fusiform gyrus* is more active than other regions of the brain when the subject is engaged in facial recognition.

    C Unconsciousness occurs when almost the entire cortex has been destroyed or invaded by convulsive activity.

9. Which of the following statements, if true, would most effectively challenge the notion that complex thoughts or emotions happen exclusively in a single localized part of the brain?

    Ⓐ While nearly 95 percent of right-handed people are left-hemisphere dominated for language, only 18 percent of left-handed people are right-hemisphere dominated for language.

    Ⓑ While the back edge of the frontal lobes control voluntary motor movement, the occipital lobe controls one's visual ability.

    Ⓒ A woman with lesions in the top part of the temporal lobe suffers hearing loss, but her vision improves.

    Ⓓ Due to a lesion in one area of his brain, a man cannot consciously recognize his wife's face, but his heart rate increases upon seeing her face.

    Ⓔ Convulsions may be accompanied by a loss of consciousness.

10. The discoveries of Broca and Wernicke contribute to Dax's findings by showing that

    Ⓐ Language functions are not as localized as Dax had suspected.

    Ⓑ Language comprehension is not localized to the left hemisphere of the brain.

    Ⓒ Language functions are even more localized than Dax had suspected.

    Ⓓ Language acquisition and grammar are localized in different areas of the brain.

    Ⓔ Aphasia encompasses more than simply language disorders.

Go on to next page

This passage is taken from The Egyptians (Peoples of Africa) *by Barbara Watterson (Wiley-Blackwell).*

The Egyptian section of the Nile — the 1,250 kilometers from the First Cataract to the Mediterranean — was, in its formative stage, much wider than it is today, and bordered by marshland and swamps. Gradually, the river bed cut deeper and the Nile narrowed, flowing through terrain that was rocky and barren. The land sloped very gently to the north, and large quantities of the gravel, sand and silt carried by the river were deposited at its mouth to form the delta, later to become one of the most fertile areas of Egypt. In addition, large amounts of detritus sank to the bottom of the river so that, over the millennia, it aggraded: the different levels of the river are still visible, in the form of cliffs and terraces on the east and west sides of the Nile Valley.

For the following question, consider each of the choices separately and choose all that apply.

11. According to the passage, compared to earlier times, parts of the Nile River are now
    - A Wider
    - B Deeper
    - C More fertile

12. Which of the following is the most accurate definition of the word *terraces* as used in the passage?
    - Ⓐ A strip of land having an abrupt descent
    - Ⓑ A raised platform faced with masonry or turf
    - Ⓒ The platform top of a structure
    - Ⓓ A flat roof
    - Ⓔ An outdoor living area, such as a deck

This passage is taken from The Idea of Culture (Blackwell Manifestos) *by Terry Eagleton (Wiley-Blackwell).*

'Culture' is said to be one of the two or three most complex words in the English language, and the term which is sometimes considered to be its opposite — nature — is commonly awarded the accolade of being the most complex of all. Yet though it is fashionable these days to see nature as a derivative of culture, culture, etymologically speaking, is a concept derived from nature. One of its original meanings is 'husbandry' or the tending of natural growth. The same is true of our words for law and justice, as well as of terms like 'capital', 'stock', 'pecuniary' and 'sterling'. The word 'coulter', which is a cognate of 'culture', means the blade of a ploughshare. We derive our word for the finest of human activities from labour and agriculture, crops and cultivation. Francis Bacon writes of 'the culture and manurance of mines', in a suggestive hesitancy between dung and mental distinction. 'Culture' here means an activity, and it was a long time before the word came to denote an entity. Even then, it was probably not until Matthew Arnold that the word dropped such adjectives as 'moral' and 'intellectual' and came to be just 'culture', an abstraction of itself.

13. Select the sentence in the passage that most accurately expresses the main idea of the passage.
    - Ⓐ First sentence: "'Culture' is said to be . . . the most complex of all."
    - Ⓑ Second sentence: "Yet though it is fashionable . . . a concept derived from nature."
    - Ⓒ Third sentence: "One of its original meanings . . . of natural growth."
    - Ⓓ Fourth sentence: "The same is true of our words . . . 'pecuniary' and 'sterling'."
    - Ⓔ Sixth sentence: "We derive our word for . . . crops and cultivation."

Go on to next page

14. Which of the following words does the author of the passage not cite as being a concept derived from nature?

    Ⓐ Capital

    Ⓑ Culture

    Ⓒ Stock

    Ⓓ Pecuniary

    Ⓔ Manurance

Directions: Each of the following sentences has a blank indicating that a word or phrase is omitted. Choose the two answer choices that best complete the sentence and result in two sentences most alike in meaning.

---

15. To most Western listeners, traditional Japanese music may sound _____, aimless, and even monotonous, but this is only because we lack the foundation for appreciating it.

    A dissonant

    B symphonic

    C disparate

    D raucous

    E cacophonous

    F mellifluous

16. Filmmakers have a tendency to stereotype scientists, choosing to depict them as either _____ humanitarians, like Paul Muni in *The Story of Louis Pasteur,* or passionately mad scientists, like Dr. Strangelove, portrayed by Peter Sellers.

    A sentient

    B stygian

    C impassive

    D zealous

    E profound

    F stolid

17. People with diabetes are more prone to simple yet _____ wounds that require long-term treatment.

    A refractory

    B recalcitrant

    C acute

    D severe

    E perspicacious

    F excruciating

18. Although communities often must deal with it locally, _____ is a global issue requiring a global solution and is not always the result of laziness.

    A malnutrition

    B illiteracy

    C indigence

    D famine

    E penury

    F squalor

19. By focusing almost exclusively on the contentious dialogue between the countries' leaders, the media brings misconceptions that lead to irrational enmity between the people of the two countries; instead, the media should _____ this potential antagonism.

    A mitigate

    B augment

    C assuage

    D incite

    E repress

    F subjugate

Go on to next page ⇨

Directions: *The following passage is followed by a question pertaining to that passage. Read the passage and answer the question based on information stated or implied in the passage. Select only one answer.*

This passage is taken from Healing Gardens: Therapeutic Benefits and Design Recommendations *by Clare Cooper Marcus and Marni Barnes (Wiley).*

The idea of a healing garden is both ancient and modern. Long after humans had begun to erect dwellings, local healing places were nearly always found in nature — a healing spring, a sacred grove, a special rock or cave. The earliest hospitals in the Western world were infirmaries in monastic communities where herbs and prayer were the focus of healing and a cloistered garden was an essential part of the environment.

Over the centuries, the connection between healing and nature was gradually superseded by increasingly technical approaches — surgery, medicines, drugs, X-rays. A separation occurred between attention to body and spirit and increasingly, different parts of the body (eyes, heart, digestive tract, etc.) and different afflictions (cancer, arthritis, etc.) were treated by specialists. The idea that access to nature could assist in healing was all but lost. By the late twentieth century, in many health care settings, "landscaping" came to be seen as merely decoration used to offset the hospital building or perhaps to impress potential customers. Even when a courtyard or roof garden exists, it rarely appears on hospital way-finding maps or signage.

20. One could reasonably infer from this passage that the author believes which of the following?

Ⓐ Natural remedies are superior to modern medicine.

Ⓑ Hospitals should be located in natural settings.

Ⓒ Nature can improve the healing process.

Ⓓ The earliest hospitals are superior to their modern counterparts.

Ⓔ Every hospital should have a courtyard or roof garden.

STOP DO NOT TURN THE PAGE UNTIL TOLD TO DO SO.
DO NOT RETURN TO A PREVIOUS TEST.

Section 2
Quantitative Reasoning

Time: 35 minutes for 20 questions

Notes:

- ✔ All numbers used in this exam are real numbers.
- ✔ All figures lie in a plane.
- ✔ Angle measures are positive; points and angles are in the position shown.

Directions: For Questions 1–8, choose from the following answer choices:

Ⓐ *Quantity A is greater.*

Ⓑ *Quantity B is greater.*

Ⓒ *The two quantities are equal.*

Ⓓ *The relationship cannot be determined from the information given.*

1.

Quantity A	**Quantity B**
$\dfrac{\sqrt{25} \times \sqrt{4}}{\sqrt{10}}$	3.5

2.

Quantity A	**Quantity B**
The sum of all integers from 99 to 198, inclusive	The sum of all integers from 101 to 199, inclusive

3. $9 < x < 10$

Quantity A	**Quantity B**
x^2	99

4. For all integers a and b, $a \triangle b = ab + 2(a + b)$.

Quantity A	**Quantity B**
$\dfrac{1}{1 \triangle 2}$	$(0 \triangle 1)^{-3}$

5. The perimeter of a certain right triangle with the two other angles measuring 30° and 60° is $3 + \sqrt{3}$.

Quantity A	**Quantity B**
The hypotenuse of the right triangle	2

6. From a group of ten students, three are attending a meeting.

Quantity A	**Quantity B**
The number of different groups that could attend from the 10 students	720

7. A standard six-sided die is thrown.

Quantity A	**Quantity B**
The probability that the die will show either an odd number or a 2	$\dfrac{2}{3}$

Go on to next page ➡

8. Tom invested part of $8,000 at 3% and the rest at 5% annual interest for a total return of $340.

Quantity A	_Quantity B_
The amount invested at 3%	The amount invested at 5%

9. If n is a positive even integer, which of the following represents the product of n and the consecutive even integer following n?

Ⓐ $n^2 + 2$

Ⓑ $(n+2)^2$

Ⓒ $n^2 + 2n$

Ⓓ $2n^2$

Ⓔ It cannot be represented.

10. If a circular garden with a radius of three feet is surrounded by a circular sidewalk two feet wide, then the area of the sidewalk is

Ⓐ 4π

Ⓑ 9π

Ⓒ 12π

Ⓓ 15π

Ⓔ 16π

11. Bobby has eight more cars than Jackie. If Bobby gives two of his cars to Jackie, Bobby will have twice the cars that Jackie has. How many cars does Bobby currently have?

Ⓐ 2

Ⓑ 4

Ⓒ 6

Ⓓ 8

Ⓔ 10

Use the following graphs to answer Questions 12–14.

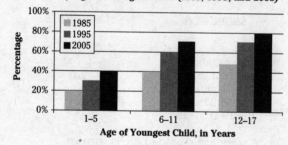

Percentage of Mothers in the Workforce in Country X by Age of Youngest Child (1985, 1995, and 2005)

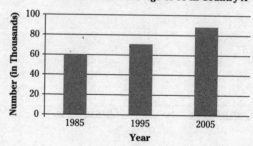

Approximate Number of Mothers with Children under the Age of 18 in Country X

Note: Graphs drawn to scale.

Go on to next page

12. If the number of mothers with children under the age of 18 increased by 10% from 2005 to 2010 and the percentage of mothers in the workforce stayed about the same during that time, what was the approximate number of mothers with youngest children ages 12 to 17 in the workforce in 2010?

    Ⓐ 75,000

    Ⓑ 80,000

    Ⓒ 85,000

    Ⓓ 90,000

    Ⓔ 95,000

13. What is the approximate ratio of the percentage of mothers in the workforce in 1985 with youngest children ages 1 to 5 to the percentage of mothers in the workforce in 1995 with youngest children ages 12 to 17?

    Ⓐ 2 to 7

    Ⓑ 4 to 7

    Ⓒ 1 to 3

    Ⓓ 5 to 9

    Ⓔ 6 to 11

    > *For the following question, choose all answer choices that apply.*

14. Which of the following can be inferred from the data in the graphs?

    A The population of Country X is steadily increasing.

    B The percentage of single mothers is steadily increasing.

    C The demand for day care in Country X is steadily increasing.

15. In the given sequence $a_1, a_2, a_3, a_4, a_5, \ldots$, a_n, where $a_1 = 38$ and $a_{n+1} = \dfrac{a_n + 2}{2}$, what is the lowest value of n for which a_n is not an integer?

16. $\sqrt{(6)(7)(18)(21)} =$

17. What is the smallest prime factor of 120,248?

    > *For the following question, choose all that apply.*

18. A certain manufacturer produces an engine lift with three pulleys and seven levers. If each box contains eight pulleys and the manufacturer is starting with unopened boxes and does not want to have a partial box of pulleys remaining, which of the following could *not* be the number of levers used in the manufacturing job?

    A 56

    B 84

    C 112

    D 168

    E 196

    F 224

Go on to next page ➡

For the following question, choose all that apply.

19. If n is an integer and $\frac{396}{n}$ is an integer, which of the following could be the value of n?

- [A] 11
- [B] 12
- [C] 18
- [D] 24
- [E] 27
- [F] 66

For the following question, choose exactly two answer choices.

20. If n is a positive integer, for which of the following would the units digit always be equal to the units digit of n?

- [A] n^5
- [B] n^{10}
- [C] n^{25}

STOP DO NOT TURN THE PAGE UNTIL TOLD TO DO SO.
DO NOT RETURN TO A PREVIOUS TEST.

Section 3
Verbal Reasoning

Time: 30 minutes for 20 questions

Directions: Choose the best answer to each question. Blacken the corresponding ovals and boxes on the answer sheet.

Directions: For Questions 1–7, choose the one entry best suited for each blank from its corresponding column of choices.

1. Many of Shakespeare's plays contain scenes or discussions that may appear, on their surface, to be _____. On closer inspection, however, most readers discover that these scenes and discussions are central to the theme.

Ⓐ essential
Ⓑ incisive
Ⓒ tangential
Ⓓ concurrent
Ⓔ predominant

2. The speaker presented and supported the case in such a way that he _____ the need for further clarification.

Ⓐ precluded
Ⓑ anticipated
Ⓒ adjourned
Ⓓ prohibited
Ⓔ obviated

3. A(n) (i) _____ existence typically leads to a loss of self-discipline followed by self-loathing. What once seemed a hedonistic paradise becomes a (ii) _____ asylum.

Blank (i)	Blank (ii)
Ⓐ ascetic	Ⓓ stygian
Ⓑ libertine	Ⓔ quixotic
Ⓒ Spartan	Ⓕ utopian

4. In Ayn Rand's *For the New Intellectual*, Galt questions the overriding belief at the time in the (i) _____ of body and soul. According to Galt, proponents of this belief have (ii) _____ the individual into two elements, both symbols of death — a corpse (a body without a soul) and a ghost (a soul without a body).

Blank (i)	Blank (ii)
Ⓐ paradox	Ⓓ dissected
Ⓑ irony	Ⓔ bifurcated
Ⓒ dichotomy	Ⓕ bisected

Go on to next page ⇨

5. In diplomacy, talks often fail or at least fail to move forward for some time. When this occurs, one party almost invariably accuses the other of (i) _____. In worst-case scenarios, negotiations break down completely, which may (ii) _____ conflict.

Blank (i)	Blank (ii)
Ⓐ tractability	Ⓓ expedite
Ⓑ indolence	Ⓔ precipitate
Ⓒ intransigence	Ⓕ motivate

6. Over the years, interrogators have learned a great deal about what works and what doesn't. They have discovered that overly aggressive interrogations often (i) _____ bad information. Rather than engage or give in, suspects often (ii) _____ to "give the interrogator what he or she wants." This calls into question not only the ethics of overly aggressive tactics but also their (iii) _____.

Blank (i)	Blank (ii)	Blank (iii)
Ⓐ dissemble	Ⓓ prevaricate	Ⓖ efficiency
Ⓑ elicit	Ⓔ prognosticate	Ⓗ alacrity
Ⓒ disseminate	Ⓕ adjudicate	Ⓘ efficacy

7. With no land masses to (i) _____ them, high winds and large waves are (i) _____ to the Southern Ocean. Plankton gather in relatively (iii) _____ pools, where they attract additional wildlife.

Blank (i)	Blank (ii)	Blank (iii)
Ⓐ debilitate	Ⓓ endemic	Ⓖ quiescent
Ⓑ impede	Ⓔ pandemic	Ⓗ dormant
Ⓒ disperce	Ⓕ intrinsic	Ⓘ truculent

Go on to next page

Directions: Each of the following passages is followed by questions pertaining to the passage. Read the passage and answer the questions based on information stated or implied in that passage. For each question, select one answer choice unless instructed otherwise.

This passage is taken from Better Living through Reality TV: Television and Post-Welfare Citizenship *by Laurie Ouellette and James Hay (Wiley-Blackwell).*

To understand the political rationality of reality-based charity TV, a brief detour through the conceptual history of welfare will be helpful. We take our bearings partly from political theorist Nikolas Rose, who situates the changing "mentalities" of government leading up to welfare reform within the stages of liberalism. According to Rose's account, the liberal state was called upon to become more directly involved in the care of citizens in the late nineteenth and early twentieth centuries, a period of time that happens to correspond with the development and progression of industrial capitalism. As relations among elites and workers became increasingly antagonistic, rulers were "urged to accept the obligation to tame and govern the undesirable consequences of industrial life, wage labor and urban existence in the name of society." What Rose calls a "state of welfare" emerged to provide basic forms of social insurance, child welfare, health, mental hygiene, universal education, and similar services that both "civilized" the working class and joined citizens to the State and to each other through formalized "solidarities and dependencies." Through this new "social contract" between the State and the population, Rose contends, the autonomous political subject of liberal rule was reconstituted as a "citizen with rights to social protection and social education in return for duties of social obligation and social responsibility."

8. Select the sentence in the passage that explains the purpose of welfare, according to Nikolas Rose, in greatest detail.

Ⓐ First sentence: "To understand the political rationality . . . will be helpful."

Ⓑ Second sentence: "We take our bearings partly from . . . the stages of liberalism."

Ⓒ Third sentence: "According to Rose's account . . . progression of industrial capitalism."

Ⓓ Fourth sentence: "As relations among elites and workers . . . in the name of society.'"

Ⓔ Fifth sentence: "What Rose calls a "state of welfare" . . . through formalized 'solidarities and dependencies.'"

This passage is taken from GMAT For Dummies, *5th Edition by Scott Hatch, JD, and Lisa Hatch, MA (Wiley).*

It is hard for us to imagine today how utterly different the world of night used to be from the daylight world. Of course, we can still re-create something of that lost mystique. When we sit around a campfire and tell ghost stories, our goose bumps (and our children's) remind us of the terrors that night used to hold. But it is all too easy for us to pile in the car at the end of our camping trip and return to the comfort of our incandescent, fluorescent, floodlit modern world. Two thousand, or even two hundred, years ago there was no such escape from the darkness. It was a physical presence that gripped the world from sunset until the cock's crow.

"As different as night and day," we say today. But in centuries past, night and day really were different. In a time when every scrap of light after sunset was desperately appreciated, when travelers would mark the road by piling up light stones or by stripping the bark off of trees to expose the lighter wood underneath, the Moon was the traveler's greatest friend. It was known in folklore as "the parish lantern." It was steady, portable, and—unlike a torch—entailed no risk of fire. It would never blow out, although it could, of course, hide behind a cloud.

Go on to next page

Nowadays we don't need the moon to divide the light from the darkness because electric lights do it for us. Many of us never even see a truly dark sky. According to a recent survey on light pollution, 97 percent of the U.S. population lives under a night sky at least as bright as it was on a half-moon night in ancient times. Many city-dwellers live their entire lives under the equivalent of a full moon.

9. The primary purpose of this passage is to

   Ⓐ Compare and contrast nighttime in the modern world with the dark nights of centuries past.

   Ⓑ Explain why the invention of the electric light was essential to increasing worker productivity.

   Ⓒ Lament the loss of the dark nights and the danger and excitement that moon-less nights would bring.

   Ⓓ Describe the diminishing brightness of the moon and the subsequent need for more electric lights.

   Ⓔ Argue for an end to the excessive light pollution that plagues 97 percent of the U.S. population.

For the following question, consider each of the choices separately and choose all that apply.

10. The passage mentions which of the following as possible ways for travelers to find the path at night?

   Ⓐ Piles of light-colored stones or trees with the bark stripped off

   Ⓑ The moon or a torch

   Ⓒ Railings made of light wood

This passage is taken from Bad Medicine: Misconceptions and Misuses Revealed, from Distance Healing to Vitamin O *by Christopher Wanjek (Wiley).*

How can we be certain that we don't use only 10 percent of the brain? As Beyerstein succinctly says, "The armamentarium of modern neuroscience decisively repudiates this notion." CAT, PET and MRI scans, along with a battery of other tests, show that there are no inactive regions of the brain, even during sleep. Neuroscientists regularly hook up patients to these devices and ask them to do math problems, listen to music, paint, or do whatever they please. Certain regions of the brain fire up with activity depending on what task is performed. The scans catch all this activity; the entire brain has been mapped this way.

Further debunking of the myth is the fact that the brain, like any other body part, must be used to remain healthy. If your leg remains in a cast for a month, it wilts. A 90-percent brain inactivity rate would result in 90 percent of the brain rapidly deteriorating. Unused neurons (brain cells) would shrivel and die. Clearly, this doesn't happen in healthy individuals. In Alzheimer's disease, there is a diffuse 10 percent to 20 percent loss of neurons. This has a devastating effect on memory and consciousness. A person would be comatose if 90 percent of the brain — any 90 percent — were inactive.

For the following question, consider each of the choices separately and choose all that apply.

11. Which of the following does the passage provide as scientific evidence to disprove the myth that humans use only 10 percent of their brains?

   Ⓐ Brain scans show activity in all regions of the brain, even during sleep.

   Ⓑ Brain cells shrivel and die when not in use.

   Ⓒ A loss of 10 to 20 percent of the brain results in Alzheimer's disease.

Go on to next page ➡

This passage is taken from The Daily Show and Philosophy: Moments of Zen in the Art of Fake News *by Jason Holt (Wiley-Blackwell).*

The fact that television provides entertainment isn't, in and of itself, a problem for Postman. He warns, however, that dire consequences can befall a culture in which the most important public discourse, conducted via television, becomes little more than irrational, irrelevant, and incoherent entertainment. Again, we shall see that this is a point often suggested by *The Daily Show*'s biting satire. In a healthy democracy, the open discussion of important issues must be serious, rational, and coherent. But such discussion is often time-consuming and unpleasant, and thus incompatible with television's drive to entertain. So, it's hardly surprising to see television serving up important news analyses in sound bites surrounded by irrelevant graphics and video footage, or substituting half-minute ad spots for substantial political debates. On television, thoughtful conversations about serious issues are reserved for only the lowest-rated niche programs. Just as ventriloquism and mime don't play well on radio, "thinking does not play well on television." Instead, television serves as the sort of "gut"–based discourse celebrated by Stephen Colbert.

12. Which of the following most accurately expresses the main point of this passage?

    Ⓐ Television can entertain, but it cannot inform.

    Ⓑ Television inherently is a poor medium for discussion of important issues.

    Ⓒ Conversations about serious issues play better on radio than on TV.

    Ⓓ Television's drive to entertain is incompatible with serious discussion of complex issues.

    Ⓔ Public discourse presented on TV is irrational, irrelevant, incoherent entertainment.

This passage is taken from GMAT For Dummies, *5th Edition, by Scott Hatch, JD, and Lisa Hatch, MA (Wiley).*

Snakes exist on every continent except for Antarctica, which is inhospitable to all cold-blooded animals. The continent of Australia is home to many of the deadliest snakes in the world. However, the nearby island nation of New Zealand has no snakes at all. Scientists estimate that snakes originated about 100 million years ago when the continents were joined and the snakes stayed on the main land masses of the continents when they split apart. Snakes are absent from New Zealand because they are unable to swim and therefore could not make the journey.

13. Which of the following, if true, would most weaken the premise that certain species of snake are absent from New Zealand because they are unable to swim?

    Ⓐ Snakes are found in South America at latitudes farther south than New Zealand.

    Ⓑ Islands like Hawaii and New Zealand are very aggressive about preventing an accidental introduction of snakes.

    Ⓒ Sea snakes can swim and are present in the warmer oceans of the world.

    Ⓓ The Tasman Sea, separating Australia from New Zealand, is home to sharks that prey on snakes.

    Ⓔ Snakes are found on many other islands of the Pacific Ocean.

Although many people in the United States complain about the tax burden, some of the countries with the highest taxes are ranked happiest in the world. One notable example is Denmark, where some of the happiest people in the world pay some of the highest taxes — between 50 and 70 percent of their total income.

How can that be? The reason is Denmark's healthcare and education services. In exchange for handing over 50 to 70 percent of their income, Danes receive universal healthcare coverage and free, quality education. While in school, students receive a stipend to cover living expenses and free daycare if they have children. The government also spends more per capita on caring for children and the elderly than any country in the world. Without having to worry so much about paying doctor bills and sending their kids to college, no wonder the Danes are so happy.

Go on to next page

14. Which of the following, if true, most effectively challenges the connection between social services and happiness?

Ⓐ The United States pays more per capita on healthcare.

Ⓑ Denmark is a relatively small country with a population of approximately 5.5 million people.

Ⓒ Between 2004 and 2008, Denmark's per capita GDP grew at an average annual rate of 1.5 percent — one of the lowest in the world.

Ⓓ Several countries that provide universal healthcare and free education rank much lower in happiness than Denmark.

Ⓔ Denmark is ranked first in entrepreneurship and opportunity.

15. Which of the following does this passage most strongly imply?

Ⓐ Money can't buy happiness.

Ⓑ Higher taxes are essential to providing for the needs of citizens.

Ⓒ There's more to life than low taxes.

Ⓓ Universal healthcare coverage is essential for happiness.

Ⓔ We should all move to Denmark.

Directions: Each of the following sentences has a blank indicating that a word or phrase is omitted. Choose the two answer choices that best complete the sentence and result in two sentences most alike in meaning.

---

16. Communications experts recommend taking a time-out to remove the emotional component of a heated debate and return to discussions with a more _____ attitude.

Ⓐ complaisant

Ⓑ incendiary

Ⓒ apprehensive

Ⓓ conciliatory

Ⓔ beguiling

Ⓕ complacent

17. When the goal is to foster bipartisanship and encourage cooperation, one should deliver a prepared speech rather than allow extemporaneous discourse to lapse into an impassioned _____.

Ⓐ supplication

Ⓑ vernacular

Ⓒ malapropism

Ⓓ invective

Ⓔ hyperbole

Ⓕ diatribe

18. Although most employers want team players, _____ individuals are more prone to cheer from the sidelines than get into the game.

Ⓐ fawning

Ⓑ assertive

Ⓒ timorous

Ⓓ obsequious

Ⓔ indignant

Ⓕ aggressive

19. Though delivered out of a genuine desire to help the community, the presentation seemed exaggerated and thus came across as _____.

Ⓐ erroneous

Ⓑ duplicitous

Ⓒ mendacious

Ⓓ disingenuous

Ⓔ sagacious

Ⓕ pretentious

20. Two hours playing outdoor sports is more _____ than two hours watching TV.

Ⓐ salacious

Ⓑ specious

Ⓒ salubrious

Ⓓ pernicious

Ⓔ wholesome

Ⓕ propitious

STOP DO NOT TURN THE PAGE UNTIL TOLD TO DO SO. DO NOT RETURN TO A PREVIOUS TEST.

Section 4

Quantitative Reasoning

Time: 35 minutes for 20 questions

Notes:

- ✔ All numbers used in this exam are real numbers.
- ✔ All figures lie in a plane.
- ✔ Angle measures are positive; points and angles are in the position shown.

Directions: For Questions 1–8, choose from the following answer choices:

- Ⓐ *Quantity A is greater.*
- Ⓑ *Quantity B is greater.*
- Ⓒ *The two quantities are equal.*
- Ⓓ *The relationship cannot be determined from the information given.*

1.

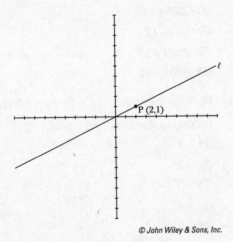

© John Wiley & Sons, Inc.

In the *xy*-coordinate plane shown above, line ℓ passes through the origin, point *P* lies on line ℓ, and the (*x*, *y*) coordinates of point *P* are (2, 1).

Quantity A	*Quantity B*
The slope of the line	1

2.

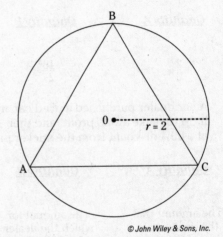

© John Wiley & Sons, Inc.

The equilateral triangle, shown above, is inscribed within the circle of radius 2.

Quantity A	*Quantity B*
The length of minor arc *AC*	π

Go on to next page

3.

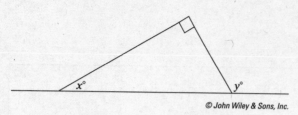

© John Wiley & Sons, Inc.

Quantity A	Quantity B
x	$y - 90$

4.

Quantity A	Quantity B
$\dfrac{2^{20}}{3^{15}}$	$\dfrac{16^5}{27^5}$

5. A car dealer purchased a used car, marked it up to make a 20% profit, and then sold it at a 20% discount from the sticker price.

Quantity A	Quantity B
The amount that the dealer paid for the car, before taxes and fees	The amount for which the dealer sold the car, before taxes and fees

6.

Quantity A	Quantity B
$\dfrac{100!}{98!}$	99^2

7.

Quantity A	Quantity B
The sum of all the integers from 1 to 20	210

8.

Quantity A	Quantity B
$\sqrt{4 \times 9 \times 25 \times 49 \times 121}$	$\sqrt{2{,}310 \times 2{,}310}$

9. If a jogger runs 10 kilometers per hour, how many meters does he run in 30 seconds? (1 kilometer = 1,000 meters)

Ⓐ $\dfrac{5}{54}$

Ⓑ $\dfrac{25}{18}$

Ⓒ $\dfrac{250}{3}$

Ⓓ $\dfrac{250}{9}$

Ⓔ $\dfrac{125}{18}$

10. If a chalkboard eraser measuring 1 inch by 2 inches by 6 inches is placed inside a tennis ball can with a radius of 1.5 inches and a height of 10 inches, what is the volume of the unoccupied space in the tennis ball can?

Ⓐ $3\pi - 12$

Ⓑ $22.5\pi - 12$

Ⓒ $30\pi - 12$

Ⓓ $225\pi - 12$

Ⓔ $300\pi - 12$

11. Given the equation $|x^2 - 2| > 1$, which of the following could *not* be a value of *x?*

Ⓐ -1

Ⓑ -2

Ⓒ -3

Ⓓ -4

Ⓔ -5

Go on to next page

Questions 12–14 refer to the following graphs.

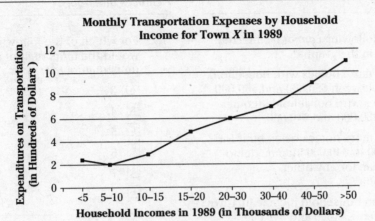

Monthly Transportation Expenses by Household Income for Town *X* in 1989

Expenditures on Transportation (in Hundreds of Dollars)

Household Incomes in 1989 (in Thousands of Dollars)

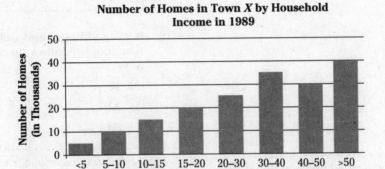

Number of Homes in Town *X* by Household Income in 1989

Number of Homes (in Thousands)

Household Incomes in 1989 (in Thousands of Dollars)

Note: Graphs drawn to scale.

© John Wiley & Sons, Inc.

12. For the homes with household incomes of $20,000 to $30,000, what was the approximate total expenditure for Town *X* on transportation in 1989?

Ⓐ $1,500,000

Ⓑ $15,000,000

Ⓒ $18,000,000

Ⓓ $150,000,000

Ⓔ $180,000,000

13. What is the approximate ratio of homes with household incomes between $5,000 and $10,000 to homes with household incomes between $30,000 and $40,000?

Ⓐ 2 to 7

Ⓑ 4 to 7

Ⓒ 1 to 3

Ⓓ 5 to 9

Ⓔ 6 to 11

Go on to next page

14. Which of the following *cannot* be inferred from the data in the graphs?

    [A] There are more homes with household incomes between $50,000 and $60,000 than homes with household incomes between $30,000 and $40,000.

    [B] There are more homes being built for the $30,000 to $40,000 income demographic than for any other demographic.

    [C] The median household income in Town X is between $30,000 and $40,000.

15.

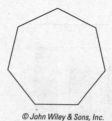

© John Wiley & Sons, Inc.

The drawing above shows a heptagon, which is a seven-sided polygon. What is the sum of its angles?

16. At a certain dinner party, there are three drinking glasses for every four utensils and six utensils for every seven plates. If there are 27 drinking glasses total, how many plates are there?

17. If the average of x, y, and z is 1, what is the average of $8x+2z$, $z-2x+3y$, $y-x+z$, and $4-x$?

18. For which of the following values of n would the units digit of n be equal to the units digit of n^3?

    [A] 3

    [B] 4

    [C] 5

    [D] 6

    [E] 7

    [F] 8

19. If y is an integer and $\sqrt{60y}$ is an integer, which of the following could be the value of y?

    [A] 15

    [B] 30

    [C] 60

20. If $x^2 - 4x = 0$, which could be the value of x?

    [A] 0

    [B] 2

    [C] 4

STOP DO NOT TURN THE PAGE UNTIL TOLD TO DO SO.
DO NOT RETURN TO A PREVIOUS TEST.

Chapter 21

Practice Exam 3: Answers and Explanations

. . . .

After taking the Practice Exam 3 in Chapter 20, use this chapter to check your answers and see how you did. Carefully review the explanations, because doing so can help you understand why you missed the questions you did and also give you a better understanding of the thought processes that helped you select the correct answers. If you're in a hurry, flip to the end of the chapter for an abbreviated answer key.

Analytical Writing Sections

Give your essays to someone to read and evaluate for you. Refer that helpful person to Chapters 14 and 15 for scoring guidelines.

Section 1: Verbal Reasoning

1. **D.** An *anachronism* is a reference to something that couldn't have existed in the time it's referenced, like Brutus and Cassius's discussion of a mechanical clock (a clock that can strike a specific time) when no such clock existed. *Archaic* (outdated) also refers to time, but it doesn't work as well as *anachronism* in this context. *Relic* refers to something really old, which the reference itself may be, but in the context of referring to a mechanical clock, it doesn't fit, either. *Tropism* refers to the orientation of an organism in response to a stimulus, such as a plant growing toward sunlight, so it obviously doesn't work here. And a *euphemism* is a mild form of an expression that may be offensive or not politically correct.

2. **A.** *Veracity* means truth, or accuracy, which is an essential quality of any story a journalist may report. The only other choice that comes close is *plausibility,* but that doesn't necessarily mean the story is true, only believable. None of the remaining choices (*tenacity,* meaning persistence, *originality,* and *righteousness*) work here.

3. **C, E.** *Geocentric* means, as the phrase after it explains, that the Earth is at the center of the universe. If Galileo was labeled as a heretic for questioning a belief, his ideas would be *proscribed* (prohibited).

4. **C, D.** *Amalgam* is a metal alloy (mixture) commonly used in dental fillings. Although amalgam is *metal,* it contains several metals, as explained in the second sentence, so *amalgam* is the better choice. Experts would question the *supposition* (speculation), because people who believe amalgam fillings pose a health risk are not only making the *accusation* or *allegation* but also basing their hypothesis on the reasoning that because the fillings contain mercury, the mercury must leach out in levels high enough to pose a threat.

5. **B, E.** *Propensity* means the inclination. Law students may also have an *aptitude* (skill) and *desire,* but *propensity* conveys a sense that they're more likely than not to do something. As a result, law students would become consumed in *recondite* (obscure) language, not *sophisticated* (refined) or *erudite* (learned) language.

6. **A, F, G.** *Phlegmatic* (unflappable) teachers would be the opposite of *choleric* (irritable) and would perform better and last longer in junior high school, where classroom management can become *onerous* (burdensome), certainly not *elementary* and not necessarily *truculent* (aggressive, hostile), although the students may be. *Sanguine* (confident, optimistic) could work for the first blank, but because the rest of the passage talks about oppositional students, *phlegmatic* is a better choice. *Melancholic* (sad) teachers would certainly not perform as well under such conditions. Over time, a choleric temperament would increase *antipathy* (aversion), not *opposition* (resistance) and usually not *hostility* (aggression), which is too strong of a word.

7. **A, F, H.** *Specious* arguments are unsound, unsupported. In this case, arguments for increasing domestic oil production at the expense of developing renewable energy sources would be *specious,* because it's *manifestly* (clearly) obvious that oil production can't possibly keep pace with *escalating* (growing) demand. For the first blank, *standard* obviously doesn't work. *Surreptitious* (sneaky, underhanded) may make a good second choice, but *specious* is a better fit. For the second blank, *deliberately* obviously doesn't fit, and *consummately* means complete or perfect, which would also be a poor choice. For the third blank, *nascent* means emerging, as in being born, and it doesn't work because the demand already exists. *Proliferating* is sort of like escalating but refers more to growing in number than amount.

8. **A, B.** Choices (A) and (B) are correct because they demonstrate specific regions of the brain that control specific functions. The third choice is wrong, because it describes a case in which a large portion of the brain must be affected for something to occur.

9. **D.** Choice (D) is correct because it shows that facial recognition is not linked solely to the damaged area of the man's brain.

10. **C.** The big clue here is the sentence that transitions from Dax's to Broca's research: "The notion that language was localized to the left side of the brain (the left hemisphere) developed momentum with new discoveries linking specific language functions to specific regions of the left hemisphere."

11. **B, C.** The passage states that the river bed cut deeper and the Nile *narrowed* (the opposite of becoming wider). Also, it states that the delta, which is part of the river, became more fertile over time.

12. **A.** The terraces in this passage are features carved by the Nile River. The four other answer choices refer to features of man-made structures.

13. **B.** The second sentence explains that the word *culture* is derived from nature. The rest of the passage provides details supporting that statement.

14. **E.** *Manurance* (cultivation) appears in the passage but only as part of one of the examples showing that the word *culture* was first used to describe an activity. All the other words in the answer choices are specifically cited as being derived from nature.

15. **A, E.** *Dissonant* (harsh sounding) and *cacophonous* (grating) are the two correct answers. *Symphonic* and *mellifluous* both mean *harmonious,* which is the opposite of what's needed here. *Disparate* means dissimilar, and *raucous* means something more like loud and unruly, which is close but not the best match.

16. **C, F.** *Impassive* and *stolid* both mean unemotional, which would be the opposite of passionately mad. *Sentient* means conscious of or aware, which doesn't fit the meaning of the sentence or have a suitable match among the answer choices. *Stygian* means hellish, which doesn't generally apply to scientists. *Zealous* (passionate, enthusiastic) doesn't work, because it doesn't contrast with the idea of a passionately mad scientist. Finally, although most scientists have *profound* thoughts, you wouldn't describe someone as profound.

17. **A, B.** *Refractory* and *recalcitrant* mean resistant to treatment in this context. An *acute* wound would probably not require long-term treatment, and although the wounds may be *severe* or *excruciating,* neither of those qualities would necessarily make the wounds resistant to treatment. *Perspicacious* means wise, so it definitely doesn't work here.

18. **C, E.** *Indigence* and ***penury*** both mean poverty. They're the only two words in the list that match. *Malnutrition* and *famine* are related but not very close in meaning, and neither is commonly attributed to laziness. *Illiteracy* has no match, and ***squalor*** means something more like filth or uncleanliness, which may accompany poverty but isn't the same as poverty.

19. **A, C.** *Mitigate* and ***assuage*** both mean to lessen or alleviate. ***Augment*** (amplify) and ***incite*** (provoke) obviously don't work, and ***repress*** and ***subjugate,*** both of which mean to put down by force, are too strong.

20. **C.** "Nature can improve the healing process" is the best answer. The answer is in the third sentence of the second paragraph: "The idea that access to nature could assist in healing was all but lost." All the other choices go too far and lack support in the passage.

Section 2: Quantitative Reasoning

1. **B.** Combine the $\sqrt{25} \times \sqrt{4}$ to equal $\sqrt{100}$, and reduce $\dfrac{\sqrt{100}}{\sqrt{10}}$ to $\sqrt{10}$. Because $\sqrt{10}$ is closer to $\sqrt{9}$ than to $\sqrt{16}$, its value is closer to 3 than to 4.

2. **C.** For each quantity, count only the numbers that aren't in the other quantity. Both quantities have the numbers 101 to 198, so those numbers won't affect which is greater. Only Quantity A has 99 and 100 (which total 199), and only Quantity B has 199.

3. **D.** Because x is between 9 and 10, it could be equal to 9.001 or 9.999. Don't square those — square the 9 and the 10 instead for 81 and 100.

4. **C.** To use the equation $a \triangle b = ab + 2(a+b)$, substitute the numbers before and after the triangle for a and b, respectively, in the equation. For Quantity A, $\dfrac{1}{1 \triangle 2}$ becomes $\dfrac{1}{(1 \times 2) + 2(1+2)} = \dfrac{1}{8}$. For Quantity B, $0 \triangle 1$ becomes $(0 \times 1) + 2(0+1) = 2$. To the power of -3, the answer becomes $\dfrac{1}{8}$, the same as Quantity A.

5. **C.** The side ratio of the 30-60-90 triangle is $x : x\sqrt{3} : 2x$, with $2x$ being the hypotenuse. The only way that the perimeter could be $3 + \sqrt{3}$ is if x were 1, making the hypotenuse 2.

6. **B.** The formula for combinations is $C_r^n = \dfrac{n!}{r!(n-r)!}$, with C being the number of possibilities, n being the group of students, and r being the students attending the meeting. And $\dfrac{10!}{3!7!}$ reduces to 120 as follows: $\dfrac{10!}{3!7!} = \dfrac{10 \times \cancel{9}^{3} \times \cancel{8}^{4} \times \cancel{7!}}{\cancel{3} \times \cancel{2} \times 1 \times \cancel{7!}} = 120$.

7. **C.** The formula for probability is $P = \dfrac{\text{Number of possible desired outcomes}}{\text{Number of total possible outcomes}}$. The number of desired possible outcomes is four (three odd numbers plus one even number), and the number of total possible outcomes is six. So $\dfrac{4}{6}$ reduces to $\dfrac{2}{3}$.

8. **B.** Let x represent the amount invested at 3% and set the equation up like this:

    $(x)(0.03) + (8{,}000 - x)(0.05) = 340$

    Solve for x, and Tom invested \$3,000 at 3% and \$5,000 at 5%.

9. **C.** Pick two consecutive even integers, such as 8 and 10, giving you a product of 80. Only one formula will return 80 if you plug in 8 for n.

10. **E.** This is basically a large circle around a small circle, and your task is to find the difference between the two. The large circle has a radius of 5 (the 3-foot-radius garden plus the 2-foot-wide sidewalk), giving it an area of 25π. Subtract from that the area of the small circle (the garden), 9π, for a difference of 16π.

11. **E.** Set this up as two different equations: $b-8=j$ and $b-2=2(j+2)$. Solve for b by substituting $(b-8)$ for j in the second equation: $b-2=2(b-8+2)$. Solve for b, which equals 10.

12. **B.** The number of mothers with children under the age of 18 in 2005 was about 90,000. A 10% increase in 2010 brings the number to about 100,000. The percentage of mothers in the workforce with youngest children ages 12 to 17 in 2005 was 80%. The percentage stays about the same in 2010, and 80% of 100,000 is 80,000.

13. **A.** The first number is 20%, and the second number is 70%. This produces a ratio of 2 to 7.

14. **A, C.** Choice (A) is correct because more mothers are having children, so the population is increasing. Choice (B) is wrong because mothers in the workforce aren't necessarily single. Choice (C) is correct because with more mothers working and more babies, the demand for day care increases.

15. **4.** To solve for a_2, substitute a_1 for a_n and a_2 for a_{n+1} in the equation provided. Because a_1 equals 38, a_2 equals 20. Now use the equation to solve for a_3 by substituting 20 for a_2 and a_3 for a_{n+1}. Thus, a_3 equals 11. Do this again for a_4, which equals 6.5 and is the first non-integer value of a_n, so 4 is the lowest value for n.

16. **126.** Factor the numbers under the radical: $\sqrt{(6)(7)(18)(21)}$ becomes $\sqrt{(2\times3)(7)(2\times3\times3)(7\times3)}$. Find number pairs to remove from the radical: Two 7s means a 7 comes out; two 2s means a 2 comes out; four 3s means two 3s come out. Nothing is left under the radical. Multiply all the numbers that came out: $7\times3\times3\times2=126$.

17. **2.** Because 120,248 is even, one of its factors is 2, which is the smallest prime factor.

18. **B, E.** Each engine lift uses three pulleys, and each box contains eight pulleys. To avoid having any pulleys left over, the number of pulleys used has to be a multiple of 24. The ratio of pulleys to levers is 3:7, so the ratio used in the manufacturing job has to be a multiple of 24:56. Any number of levers that isn't a multiple of 56 can't be the number used in the manufacturing job.

19. **A, B, C, F.** Because $396=2\times2\times3\times3\times11$, any answer choice that cancels completely with those primes produces an integer. The remaining answer choices don't work because 24 has too many 2s and 27 has too many 3s.

20. **A, C.** The units digit of any product depends on the units digit of the numbers multiplied. For example, any number with a units digit of 7 times any number with a units digit of 3 produces a number ending with a units digit of 1, because $7\times3=21$. The units digit of any number to the fifth power is the same as the units digit of the original number. For example, $2^5=32$, $3^5=243$, and $4^5=1,024$, making n^5 one of the answers. And $n^{10}=\left(n^5\right)^2$, so if n is 2, 32 squared has a units digit of 4. However, $n^{25}=\left(n^5\right)^5$, preserving the n^5 rule and making n^{25} the other answer.

The makers of the GRE don't expect you to just *know* all these things. The point isn't the mathematical principles. It's that you're resourceful and can solve problems on the fly. By trying out simple numbers (such as 2^5 and 3^5) to see how the math works, you use your creativity to solve the problem.

Section 3: Verbal Reasoning

1. **C.** *Tangential* conveys a sense of not being essential or central to the play. *Essential* (necessary) is the opposite of what's needed here, and neither *incisive* (perceptive) nor *predominant* (main, principal) fits the context. Scenes could be *concurrent* (happening at the same time), but this wouldn't convey the sense that the scenes are of less importance.

2. **E.** You know that the speaker made the need for further clarification either necessary or unnecessary; the note that he "supported" the case tells you that his speech was sound and that clarification was unnecessary. *Obviated* means something along the lines of "made unnecessary." *Precluded* (prevented) and *prohibited* (banned) are too strong, and although the speaker *anticipated* the questions, that would not anticipate the need for clarification. *Adjourned* doesn't work, because you adjourn a meeting, but you don't adjourn a need.

3. **B, D.** A *libertine* (morally unrestrained) existence could conceivably lead to a loss of self-discipline, but a *Spartan* (simple) or *ascetic* (puritan) lifestyle would tend to make someone more disciplined. For the second blank, you'd expect something opposite to "hedonistic paradise," making *stygian* (hellish) the only choice. *Quixotic* means idealistic, and *utopian* means perfect (in a good way).

4. **C, F.** This passage is all about twos — the body and soul — so filling the first blank is relatively easy: *Dichotomy* is a separation into two. A *paradox* is an apparent contradiction that may be true, and *irony* is the use of words to express the opposite of what the words mean. Finding the right match for the second blank is more challenging because all the words have *two* or *separation* in their meaning. *Bisected* (divided in two) is the best choice. *Bifurcated* is divided but more like a fork in a road, and *dissected* is more along the lines of dividing into several parts.

5. **C, E.** *Intransigence* is inflexibility, and *precipitate* means to bring about. *Tractability* (compliance) is the opposite of what's needed for the first blank, and *indolence* means laziness. For the second blank, *expedite* (hasten) would make a decent second choice, but *precipitate* is more fitting. *Motivate* (provide with a motive) doesn't work, because you may motivate individuals but not actions such as conflict.

6. **B, D, I.** During an interrogation, you want to *elicit* (extract) information, not *dissemble* (mislead) or *disseminate* (spread) it. To stop interrogations without giving in, suspects may *prevaricate* (mislead, lie), not *prognosticate* (predict) or *adjudicate* (mediate). The prevaricating would call into question the *efficacy* (effectiveness) of such methods, not their *efficiency* (ability to accomplish something with minimal effort) or *alacrity* (speed).

7. **B, D, G.** High winds and large waves would occur if nothing was in their way to *impede* (slow) them, not *debilitate* (incapacitate) them. *Disperse* (scatter) would make a good second choice. These high winds and large waves would be *endemic* (characteristic of) rather than *pandemic* (epidemic) or *intrinsic* (fundamental). Plankton would gather in pools, which tend to be more *quiescent* (calm) than a wavy ocean, not *dormant* (sleeping) and definitely not *truculent* (hostile).

8. **E.** Fifth sentence: "What Rose calls a 'state of welfare' emerged to provide basic forms of social insurance, child welfare, health, mental hygiene, universal education, and similar services that both 'civilized' the working class and joined citizens to the State and to each other through formalized 'solidarities and dependencies.'" Several other sentences explain the purpose of welfare, but this sentence does so in the greatest detail.

9. **A.** *Compare and contrast, explain,* and *describe* reflect the author's purpose, but *lament* and *argue* imply more emotion on the part of the author than is displayed in the passage, so eliminate Choices (C) and (E). Worker productivity has nothing to do with showing how our ancestors perceived night differently, so you can eliminate Choice (B). Choice (D) is simply wrong; the author doesn't maintain that the moon is actually getting darker, just that it's become outshone by electric lights.

10. **A, B.** This specific information exception question asks you to refer to the text to eliminate answers that *are* ways in the passage that travelers can find a path at night. The second paragraph specifically mentions Choice (A), light-colored stones or trees with bark stripped off, and Choice (B), the moon or a torch. Railings aren't mentioned anywhere in the passage.

11. **A.** Choice (B) is wrong because although the passage implies that brain cells shrivel and die when not in use, it provides no scientific evidence to support this claim. Choice (C) is wrong because cause and effect are flipped; although a 10 to 20 percent loss of neurons may occur in Alzheimer's, the passage doesn't state that a 10 to 20 percent loss of neurons causes Alzheimer's.

12. **D.** "Television's drive to entertain is incompatible with serious discussion of complex issues." The other choices go too far, saying that TV *cannot* instead of that it *does not*. The passage doesn't criticize television itself but how it's used.

13. **D.** To weaken the argument, find a reason for the absence of snakes other than that they can't swim. Choice (D) suggests that maybe the snakes *can* swim, but they get eaten by sharks before reaching New Zealand.

14. **D.** "Several countries that provide universal healthcare and free education rank much lower in happiness than Denmark." If other countries provide the same social services as Denmark but rank lower in happiness, then something *other* than social services is boosting Denmark to the number one position.

15. **B.** "Higher taxes are essential to providing for the needs of citizens." The passage focuses on taxes and how Denmark uses them to provide for the needs of its citizens. Choice (C) is a reasonable candidate, but the phrase *more to life* extends its reach outside the scope of the passage.

16. **A, D.** *Complaisant* and *conciliatory* mean inclined to please. *Incendiary* (provocative) means the opposite, and *beguiling* means deceiving with trickery. *Apprehensive* means anxious, and *complacent,* which is included to trip you up with its similarity to *complaisant,* means satisfied, content.

17. **D, F.** *Invective* and *diatribe* refer to bitter, abusive language, something you'd want to avoid if your goal was to foster bipartisanship and cooperation. None of the other choices are good matches: *supplication* (plea), *vernacular* (dialect), *malapropism* (confusion of words with similar sounds), and *hyperbole* (exaggeration).

18. **A, D.** *Fawning* and *obsequious* refer to agreeably showing favor, which would incline people to act as cheerleaders instead of players. *Assertive* and *aggressive* mean the opposite of what's required here. *Timorous* means shy, which would make a good second choice, but it has no match. *Indignant* is more along the lines of being annoyed.

19. **B, D.** *Duplicitous* and *disingenuous* mean deceitful. *Erroneous* means false. *Mendacious* is more along the lines of being a compulsive liar. *Sagacious* means wise, and *pretentious* describes someone who's phony.

20. **C, E.** *Salubrious* and *wholesome* are both good for you. *Salacious* (scandalous), *specious* (unsupported), and *pernicious* (malicious) aren't. *Propitious* (favorable) could be good for you but doesn't express the meaning of being healthy, which is what's needed here.

Section 4: Quantitative Reasoning

1. **B.** Because the line passes through both the origin and point (2, 1), calculate the slope of the line as follows: Slope $= \dfrac{\text{rise}}{\text{run}} = \dfrac{(y_2 - y_1)}{(x_2 - x_1)} = \dfrac{(1-0)}{(2-0)} = \dfrac{1}{2} = 0.5$.

2. **A.** Minor arc *AC* originates from the angle of the equilateral triangle and is 60 degrees and one-third of the circle. Because the circle has a radius of 2, its circumference is 4π. One-third of that is $\dfrac{4\pi}{3}$, which is greater than π.

3. **C.** The angle supplementary to *y,* inside the triangle, can be represented as $(180 - y)°$. Because the triangle's angles total 180 degrees, add up the angles and set them equal to 180:

$$x + 90 + 180 - y = 180$$

Solve for *x,* which equals $y - 90$.

4. **C.** The two numerators are equal: $2^{20} = \left(2^4\right)^5 = 16^5$. The two denominators are also equal: $3^{15} = \left(3^3\right)^5 = 27^5$. Therefore, the two quantities are equal.

5. **A.** Because no price is given, pick $100 as the starting point for the value of the car. So $100 marked up 20 percent is $120, and the 20 percent discount from $120 brings the price to $96.

6. **A.** From Quantity A, $\dfrac{100!}{98!}$ becomes $\dfrac{100 \times 99 \times 98!}{98!}$, which reduces to 100×99 and is greater than 99^2.

7. **A.** You can find the sum of all integers from 1 to 20 using the formula $\dfrac{n(n+1)}{2}$, where n represents the 20:

$$\frac{20(21)}{2} = 210$$

8. **C.** Don't fall for the trap of multiplying all these numbers and looking for the square roots. Instead, solve for Quantity A by finding and multiplying the square roots of each of the numbers under the radical: $\sqrt{4 \times 9 \times 25 \times 49 \times 121} = 2 \times 3 \times 5 \times 7 \times 11 = 2{,}310$. To compare this to Quantity B, consider that $2{,}310 = \sqrt{2{,}310 \times 2{,}310}$.

9. **C.** Set up the conversion steps as a series of fractions with "unit" as the 30-second interval, which thus happens twice per minute.

$$\left(\frac{10 \text{ km}}{1 \text{ hour}}\right)\left(\frac{1{,}000 \text{ meters}}{1 \text{ km}}\right)\left(\frac{1 \text{ hour}}{60 \text{ mins}}\right)\left(\frac{1 \text{ min}}{2 \text{ units}}\right)$$

First cancel the labels:

$$\left(\frac{10}{1}\right)\left(\frac{1{,}000 \text{ meters}}{1}\right)\left(\frac{1}{60}\right)\left(\frac{1}{2 \text{ units}}\right)$$

Next, cancel the numbers:

$$\left(\frac{1}{1}\right)\left(\frac{250 \text{ meters}}{1}\right)\left(\frac{1}{3}\right)\left(\frac{1}{1 \text{ unit}}\right) = \frac{250}{3} \text{ meters/unit}$$

The *unit* represents the 30-second interval that the question asks for. Avoid putting *30 secs* as the unit, which will lead to a math mistake.

10. **B.** To find the volume of the remaining space, subtract the volume of the eraser, which is $1 \times 2 \times 6 = 12$, from the volume of the tennis ball can, which is $\pi r^2 h = \pi (1.5)^2 (10) = 22.5\pi$.

11. **A.** Plug in each answer choice for x and see what works. The only number that doesn't work is -1: $\left|(-1)^2 - 2\right| > 1$ becomes $|1 - 2| > 1$ and then $1 > 1$, which isn't true.

12. **E.** Check both graphs at the 20–30 points. The first graph shows $600 per month. The second graph shows 25,000 homes. Multiply these together for a monthly expenditure of $15,000,000. Multiply this by 12 for an annual expenditure of $180,000,000.

13. **A.** The graph shows approximately 10,000 homes with household incomes between $5,000 and $10,000 and approximately 35,000 homes with household incomes between $30,000 and $40,000. The ratio of 10,000 to 35,000 reduces to 2 to 7.

14. **A, B.** This question asks you to choose the answer choices that *cannot* be inferred. For Choice (A), you don't know how many of those homes have incomes between $50,000 and $60,000. For Choice (B), you don't know how many homes are being built and for what demographic. Finally, for Choice (C), 75,000 homes have incomes lower than $30,000 to

$40,000, and 70,000 homes have higher incomes. Because 35,000 homes are within the $30,000 to $40,000 bracket, the median income is also in that bracket.

15. **900.** The formula for calculating the sum of angles of any polygon is $(n-2)180$, where n represents the number of angles. Therefore, $(7-2)180$, or 5×180, is 900.

16. **42.** Combine the ratios so that 3:4 glasses to utensils combined with 6:7 utensils to plates produces a combined ratio of glasses to utensils to plates of 9:12:14. To get 27 drinking glasses total, multiply the entire ratio by 3, for a proportion of 27:36:42.

17. **4.** Because the average of x, y, and z is 1, write out the equation as an averages formula: $\frac{x+y+z}{3} = 1$, which tells you that $x+y+z=3$. From the question, simplify $8x+2z$, $z-2x+3y$, $y-x+3$, and $4-x$ by adding them together, giving you $4x+4y+4z+4$. Divide this sum by 4 for an average of $x+y+z+1$. Because $x+y+z=3$, the answer is 4.

18. **B, C, D.** Try each answer choice: $3^3=27$, $4^3=64$, $5^3=125$, $6^3=216$, $7^3=343$, and $8^3=512$.

19. **A, C.** For any square root to be an integer, each factor under the radical has to be in a pair. For example, $\sqrt{4}$ is an integer because it equals $\sqrt{2 \times 2}$ and the 2s are in a pair. For $\sqrt{60y}$ to be an integer, all the factors of 60 have to be in pairs: $\sqrt{60y} = \sqrt{2 \times 2 \times 3 \times 5 \times y}$. The 2s are in a pair, but the y has to complete the 3 pair and the 5 pair to make an integer. So y has to contain 3 and 5, making 15 one possible value. However, y could also be 15 times any other perfect square, such as 4; $15 \times 4 = 60$, which is the other possible value of y in this list.

20. **A, C.** Factor $x^2 - 4x = 0$ into $x(x-4) = 0$, making both 0 and 4 possible answers for x.

Answer Key for Practice Exam 3

Section 1: Verbal Reasoning	Section 2: Quantitative Reasoning	Section 3: Verbal Reasoning	Section 4: Quantitative Reasoning
1. D	1. B	1. C	1. B
2. A	2. C	2. E	2. A
3. C, E	3. D	3. B, D	3. C
4. C, D	4. C	4. C, F	4. C
5. B, E	5. C	5. C, E	5. A
6. A, F, G	6. B	6. B, D, I	6. A
7. A, F, H	7. C	7. B, D, G	7. A
8. A, B	8. B	8. E	8. C
9. D	9. C	9. A	9. C
10. C	10. E	10. A, B	10. B
11. B, C	11. E	11. A	11. A
12. A	12. B	12. D	12. E
13. B	13. A	13. D	13. A
14. E	14. A, C	14. D	14. A, B
15. A, E	15. 4	15. B	15. **900**
16. C, F	16. **126**	16. A, D	16. **42**
17. A, B	17. **2**	17. D, F	17. **4**
18. C, E	18. B, E	18. A, D	18. B, C, D
19. A, C	19. A, B, C, F	19. B, D	19. A, C
20. C	20. A, C	20. C, E	20. A, C

Part VI
The Part of Tens

web extras

A free article at www.dummies.com/extras/gre outlines ten physical and mental exercises that will prepare you for the exam and carry you through to the final question.

In this part . . .

- ✔ Find out ten important points about the GRE that can make a difference to your score.

- ✔ Know the ten mistakes to avoid while taking the exam.

- ✔ Discover ten ways to make the most of the online practice exams.

Chapter 22

Ten Key Facts about the GRE

You've probably heard stories from your friends about the GRE. Rumors abound, growing wilder with each telling: "You have to know calculus!" (Absolutely not true.) "It's an open-book test this year!" (You wish!) "You can use an on-screen calculator!" (Actually, this one is true.)

As a GRE-prep instructor, I field questions all the time from students trying to get a sense of what to expect on the test. This chapter reveals several key facts that you need to know when prepping for the exam and heading into the testing center.

You May Return to Previous Questions in the Same Section

The GRE allows you to return to previous questions in any given math or verbal section as long as you haven't moved on to the next section, which wasn't true with earlier versions of the GRE. One effective strategy is to flip through the questions, answer all the easy ones first, and then go back through to tackle the challenging questions.

You can flag questions that you want to come back to by clicking the Mark for Review button at the top of the screen. You can also visit a review screen at any time during the section by clicking the Review button (also at the top of the screen). At a glance, the review screen shows you which questions are unanswered and which are marked for review. From there, you can jump directly to any question. Practice navigating the questions and review screen with the Powerprep software provided by ETS at www.ets.org so you're familiar with this feature on test day.

When you skip over a challenging question, either guess and flag the answer for review, or save a couple of minutes at the end of the section to go back and guess on questions that you haven't answered. Because you're not penalized for guessing, you want to make sure that an answer is selected for each question, even if you didn't have time to work the question.

The GRE Doesn't Penalize for Guessing

To discourage examinees from making wild guesses, some standardized tests deduct points for wrong answers. The GRE doesn't do this. Questions answered incorrectly count exactly the same as questions left unanswered, so you're better off guessing than skipping.

By going through the chapters, practice questions, and practice tests included in this book, you dramatically reduce the chances of having to guess on the GRE. Make sure to spend extra time on the areas you need more help with — closing the gaps is the most important thing you can do to prepare for the GRE.

The GRE Uses a Percentile-Based Scoring System

The GRE is a competitive test. Immediately after you complete the test, you receive an estimated percentile ranking based on the test-takers' scores from the previous year.

The number of GRE test-takers worldwide increases each year. More test-takers means more graduate-school applicants, which makes admissions more competitive. This means that scoring as well as you can on the GRE is more important than ever.

Find out what the acceptable GRE score range is for admissions and scholarships at the schools you're applying to and ask whether that range is expected to change. (Flip to Chapter 1 for info on how your score fits into the application process.)

Practice Makes All the Difference

Although you may not be able to dress-rehearse the entire test-taking experience, practicing the test makes the actual test-taking experience feel more familiar and reduces the element of surprise. Take advantage of the practice tests included in this book. Also, the practice software ETS provides has the exact feel of the actual GRE, so make it something you know well. Write the practice essays, too, making the entire experience as familiar as a day at the office (flip to Part IV for more on essay writing).

Reviewing your practice tests also helps you discover a lot of silly mistakes that can lead to wrong answers. Making these mistakes *in practice* is okay. Knowing you're prone to these mistakes decreases your chances of making the same types of mistakes in the actual test.

A good sense of familiarity and knowing what to expect truly boosts your confidence on test day. I require a five-practice-test minimum from my students, and getting them to do this is like pulling teeth. But I also track their progress and always see a marked improvement from one practice test to the next. At what point on the improvement curve do you want to be when you take the actual GRE?

You Must Study for the GRE

Though stories of unprepared folks scoring dramatically high are out there, incidents of unprepared folks bombing and having to retake the GRE are far more common. I'd put my money on an average Joe or Josephine who's well-prepared over a budding Einstein going in cold — every time. So prepare for the exam. This book is your best resource and includes all the study materials you need.

The GRE Is Different from the SAT

You're not the same person you were in high school. You've matured, developed better study habits, and come to the shocking realization that you're in charge of your own destiny. Maybe you didn't study much for the SAT, figuring that you could always get into *some* college, somewhere, regardless of your score. You were probably right. But getting into graduate school isn't as easy, and the GRE is more challenging than the SAT.

As you mature, you tend to become more serious, so approach the GRE with this mature, serious mind-set. Doing so allows you to leverage the power of your improved study habits and concentration to better prepare yourself for the test.

The GRE Also Measures Your Stamina and Performance under Pressure

The GRE measures a number of things besides your math and verbal aptitude. It measures your ability to prepare, your stamina, and your performance under pressure. Many people are quite capable of solving math problems with plenty of time and room for mistakes, but only those who have honed their skills through practice can come up with the right answers when the timer is ticking and the pressure is on. The good news: You can build or strengthen these skills, too!

The General GRE Is Not Program-Specific

The GRE is accepted for entrance into almost any graduate program, from Construction Management to Physician Assistant to Master of Social Work. Even MBA programs are accepting the GRE. Regardless of your field of study, the GRE is probably part of the admissions process.

You Can Practice the GRE on Your Own Computer

The only way to experience the real GRE is to take it. However, you can simulate the test-taking experience on your own computer and get as close to a real-life experience as possible. After you've studied and acquainted yourself with the different question types, practice on your own computer. Visit learn.dummies.com to access the practice questions online and get comfortable with answering questions on the computer.

Try to simulate, as closely as possible, the actual test-taking experience. Set aside several hours to take the equivalent of a practice test (two sets of 20 Verbal Reasoning questions and two sets of 20 Quantitative Reasoning questions and two essays). If you live alone or have a room in your house or apartment insulated from the usual hustle and bustle, that's perfect. Otherwise, consider taking the test in a library or other quiet place.

For additional practice, you can download the practice software provided by ETS. Go to www.ets.org/gre/revised_general/prepare, click the link to download the Powerprep software, install it on your computer, and then take one of the sample tests.

You Can't Bring Anything into the Testing Center

I once saw a photo of a confiscated plastic water bottle with math formulas printed on the inside of the label. Though you may not go to such lengths, the testing center staff wants to ensure zero opportunities of cheating on the GRE. Because of this, you can't take anything in with you — not even a wristwatch. You can store food and water in a locker, but be prepared to empty your pockets and be fingerprinted upon entering the actual testing area.

Don't bring your GRE books, even if you intend to leave them in the locker. If the proctors suspect you of checking the books during your breaks, you may not be allowed to finish the exam.

Chapter 23

Ten Mistakes You Won't Make (But Others Will)

- -

In This Chapter

▶ Avoiding the temptation to cheat

▶ Building endurance and taking advantage of breaks to finish strong

▶ Taking charge of what you can control and letting the rest fall into place

▶ Testing with the clock (or your best bud)

- -

Throughout this book, you discover techniques for doing your best on the GRE. I'm sorry to say, however, that you may encounter just as many pitfalls for messing up big time on the test. The good news is that you can avoid those pitfalls. Take a few minutes to read through these mistakes now to see the mistakes that other people make to tank the exam. By becoming aware of these catastrophes, you may prevent them from happening to you.

Cheating

Cheating on the GRE simply doesn't work, so don't even consider it. When you get to the testing center, and before you begin your test, the proctors separate you from anything that you can possibly use to cheat, including your phone, wristwatch, water bottle, jacket, and hat. On top of that, you're monitored by a camera while taking the test. Any semblance of privacy goes right out the window.

How would you cheat anyway? You can't copy all those vocabulary words or write all the math formulas on anything accessible during the test. Besides, the GRE tests your critical-reasoning and problem-solving skills more than your memorization skills.

Those caught cheating can be banned from taking the test for up to ten years! In the world of careers and education, that's nearly a lifetime.

Running Out of Steam

The GRE tests your stamina as much as anything else. Most people aren't able to maintain these levels of concentration for four straight hours, so they end up petering out. Through preparation and practice, you have a definite edge over the other test-takers.

Like preparing for a marathon, you must slowly build yourself up for the long GRE. Practice for a few hours at a time and stop when you get tired. Repeat this exercise, and eventually you'll be able to go the full distance without fail. Don't push yourself too hard, though, because you'll burn yourself out. As they say in the weight room, "Train, don't strain."

Not Planning for Your Breaks

Some people don't take advantage of the short breaks offered during the GRE. Be sure you don't miss the opportunity to take a breather. You're offered a short break (in one- or ten-minute increments) between sections. If you don't take these breaks, you'll be sitting still for hours. Though your stamina may be good (because you practiced), you still want to stay hydrated, eat a power bar, and walk around every now and then to keep your mind clear. Don't plan on studying during your breaks, though — the review of any GRE-prep materials during breaks is strictly forbidden.

Pack some water bottles and power bars to keep in a locker for your breaks. You won't have time to go grab something. Don't drink too much water, though — you can't pause the test to run to the restroom.

Worrying about Questions in the Previous Sections

When skipping a question or marking it for review, let it go until the end of the section so you can focus on the other questions at hand. When you reach the end of the section (but before moving on to the next section or before the time expires), you may return to the questions you skipped or marked and check or change your answers.

When you move on to the next section, however, that's it: You can't go back to a previous section. You have no choice but to move forward, so don't waste mental energy by focusing on past questions you can do nothing about.

Although you can go back and change answers within each section, it's not always a good idea unless you had serious doubts about your answer. Studies show that the first answer is usually the best. Think twice and rule out all other choices before changing your answer.

Panicking Over the Time Limit

Some test-takers fret over the clock. The key to success is to be aware of the clock while remaining calm. Practice working with a timer, because a timer appears on the GRE exam screen. As you become more accustomed to working with the clock during practice, you'll eventually settle into a comfortable pace and be used to the timer on test day.

The mistakes you make while relaxed are different from the mistakes you make while under pressure from the clock. Practice with a timer to get used to the pressure and become aware of the timer-pressure mistakes — and fix them *before* the test.

Rushing through the Questions

Some test-takers are so worried about finishing the test that they rush through it, taking shortcuts and making careless errors. Although they finish early, they don't have time to check *all* their work.

Because the easy questions are worth exactly as much as the hard questions, it makes sense to knock out the easy ones first. For questions that you're not so sure of, take advantage of the Mark for Review button available for each question. At the end of each section, a review screen shows you which questions are unanswered and which are marked for review. You can jump straight to those questions to work them further.

Choking on the Essays

Choking, by definition (on the GRE), means getting stuck on something and becoming so flustered that you can't focus on anything after that. Choking can happen at any point on the test, but because you can flag the multiple-choice questions and go back to them at the end of the section, you're unlikely to choke on the questions.

Essays, however, are another story. On the GRE, you have to write two essays with 30 minutes to write each one. What's worse, they're at the beginning of the test, so if you choke on one, you're toast for the entire test. Of course, this won't happen to you, because in Chapters 14 and 15, I guide you through writing two perfect essays, step by step. This makes writer's block something of the past.

Practice writing the essays! Like any skill, essay-writing takes practice, and you don't want to be at the start of the learning curve on test day.

Fretting Over the Hard Questions

The GRE contains some incredibly difficult questions, and most test-takers don't get perfect scores. Do the best you can, score in the high percentiles, and get accepted to graduate school! No one expects a perfect score, so you shouldn't, either.

The GRE is only one of many parts of the application process. Your GPA, work experience, essays, and any other relevant character-building experience (such as sports participation, military service, volunteer work, or leadership training) also count toward your chances of admission. Turn to Chapter 1 for more on how your score fits with the application process.

Taking the Test with Your Best Friend

You and your buddy may be able to schedule your tests for the same time. Big mistake. Two of my students from the same class took the exam at the same time, side by side, and both told me afterward that rather than providing support, the distraction was almost unbearable. Fortunately, they both scored well, but I wonder how different their results would have been had they tested separately. If you want to rely on your friend for support, study with him or plan a celebration afterwards, but don't buddy up to take the test.

Changing Your Morning Routine

The GRE is stressful enough. The last thing you need to do is add more anxiety to the whole nerve-racking experience by changing your morning routine.

If you normally have one cup of coffee, should you have an extra cup for more energy or only half a cup to reduce anxiety? Should you have an omelet for more protein or just have toast to avoid the food crash later? Here's a suggestion: Do what you normally do. It works every other day, and it'll work just as well the day of the test. Don't change your routine.

If you're tempted to try an energy drink or something unusual for an enhanced test-taking experience, try it first on a practice test! Make sure your new concoction doesn't upset your stomach, give you a headache, or cause you to zone out.

Chapter 24

Ten Ways to Take Advantage of Online Practice

Sure, you can answer the questions on the GRE. You've mastered the manipulation of decimals, the measurement of a quarter circle, and the elimination of wrong verbal answer choices. This, however, does you no good if you can't handle the test-taking experience. The GRE challenges two things: your ability to answer the questions and your ability to take the exam. Most students focus on the former while ignoring the latter, but being able to answer the questions is only half of what you need. The other half requires that you hone your test-taking skills, and the best way to do that is to take GRE practice tests. Here are ten suggestions on how to optimize the benefits of taking the GRE practice tests online. (See Chapter 3 for details on ETS's Powerprep software that simulates a real-life GRE test.)

Take an Exam in One Sitting to Build Stamina

How well you can answer the questions doesn't matter if you can't maintain your energy for the length of the exam. Your brain accounts for up to 20 percent of the body's total energy consumption, and when you're taking a challenging standardized exam such as the GRE, your brain is in overdrive. It needs to get used to working intensely for four hours at a stretch so you can go the distance on exam day.

For extra credit, at the end of the practice exam, take a short break then work two more sections of another practice exam (or two quizzes that you can create online at learn.dummies. com). If you're used to working at the GRE level for six hours, then the actual exam at five hours will be easy. (Imagine that! "GRE" and "easy" in the same sentence.) For one thing, the real GRE has that unscored extra section, so the real exam is longer anyway. Also, on test day, you're likely to be amped and then burn out faster, so having extra stamina under your belt only does you good.

Recognize the Wrong Turns You Make Under Pressure

Did you get stuck on an early question and not reach the second half of a section? Did you leave a bunch of questions unanswered, intending to return to them, but forget? Did you get lost in the software, unable to find the questions that you wanted to return to? This happens to everyone, but you can work out the bugs on the practice exam, where it doesn't matter.

Only by falling in a trap do you figure out how to avoid it so that you don't make a fatal mistake on exam day. Make the mistake at home, where it's an *oops,* not on the real deal, where it's a tragedy.

Get Accustomed to the Presence of Other Test-Takers

Nothing is more distracting on your GRE than hearing someone typing, working, cursing, or (if she used *GRE For Dummies*) chuckling confidently while she works her GRE. Get used to distractions by taking your practice exams in a roomful of people, perhaps along with any friends who are also taking their practice exams. The sounds as they work and sigh and groan and perhaps pat themselves on the back (because they also got *GRE For Dummies*) become less of a distraction as your brain acclimates to the background audio.

Some testing centers offer earplugs. If your plan is to use earplugs, try them out on a full-length practice test *before* test day. Some people can't stand earplugs for ten seconds, let alone five hours. You, however, might be okay with them. Maybe not. Either way, if this is your plan, make sure it's a good plan by trying them out first.

Make It a Dress Rehearsal

Play by the rules of the testing center. No cellphone, hat, drink, snack, or anything that brings a modicum of comfort is allowed within reach in the exam room. Your breaks are short, and your scratch paper is rationed. If this is not something you're used to, it will be distracting, so practice under these same conditions, and you'll get used to it.

Do you get thirsty? Hungry? Uncomfortable? What do you wish you had: water, sandwich, power bar, coffee, aspirin? Keep these in mind and plan accordingly on test day. You have access to your personal belongings during the breaks, so bring these things in a bag and grab a quick refreshment during your break.

Make It Personal

The practice test doesn't matter, so why try hard? In the third hour of the exam, you're exhausted, and you just want to get through it. One student said she begins favoring Choice (C) because it's right in the middle. Naturally, this is not an effective test-taking strategy.

On the real exam, finding yourself flagging is fatal; but on the practice test, it's okay, right? Wrong. If you've never worked at full capacity for the duration, you won't do it on exam day. You may intend to, but fading after 90 minutes is a hard habit to break.

One way to get around this is by recording your scores and trying to beat your last performance. Another way is to bring a test-taking friend in the room for competition. It's like running a race by yourself versus running a race against someone else: You try harder when others are in the game. Foster in yourself a competitive edge, and you'll bring this edge to the real exam.

Practice Your Strategies

As you study for and practice the GRE, you develop strategies for taking the exam. Maybe you try to answer all the easy questions first and then go back to the tougher questions if time allows. Perhaps you prefer reading comprehension over text completion and want to work the reading comprehension questions first. Or on the math section, maybe you want to complete the quantitative comparison questions before moving on to the others. And you always want to make educated guesses of answers you're unsure of so you have all the questions answered before time expires.

As you answer GRE practice questions, practice your strategies, too. You may discover that what you imagined would be a great strategy doesn't work as well as you thought it would. The time to choose the strategies that work best is before the test, not on test day.

Go through a practice exam that you've already worked so that the questions are familiar to you. Now you can focus on the overall strategies rather than the individual questions.

Discover How the Software Works

If you placed Hemingway in front of a computer running Microsoft Word, would he be able to write anything? Probably not, even though he's one of the most noted authors of our time. For him, the problem wouldn't be the writing; it would be the software. The same applies to you: You can answer the questions, but can you work the software? How do you mark answers you want to return to? How do you return to those answers later? How do you call up the calculator and check the clock? Can you go back to check your answer? Does that button cancel the exam? The software is easy to learn, but you have enough on your mind during the exam. Learn the software *before* the exam.

Take the ETS GRE practice tests. The ETS software looks and feels exactly like the actual GRE, providing you with a more genuine simulation.

Get Used to Writing the Essays First

Essays can wear you out, especially if you're not used to writing them. Focusing on 100 math and verbal questions is far more challenging after writing two 30-minute essays. Make sure this is something you're used to by actually writing the essays on the practice exam. Don't just skip them, as non-Dummies-prepared test-takers do. They'll learn a hard lesson.

Gauge Your Skill Level

Do you miss more reading comprehension or text completion questions? Do you handle triangles better than you do exponents? Does your performance drop significantly by the third section? By taking practice tests, you can get a sense of your skill level on various tasks and at different points in the exam before taking the actual exam.

People tend to be good at what they enjoy, but when you're taking the exam, you need to be good at answering all the question types, whether you enjoy them or not. If your mind wanders when you're reading a passage, you're probably not so good at answering reading comprehension questions. So what do you do? You get good at it, or at least better at it. Raise your skill level in your weakest areas. The more you improve, the more you'll start to enjoy — or won't mind as much — tackling those challenging question types, and in turn, you'll improve even more.

Review the Answers and Explanations

After taking a four-hour practice test, the last thing you probably want to do is spend time reviewing answers and explanations, so take a well-deserved break and look at the answers and explanations later. When you're rested, take the following steps to review:

1. **Have your English teacher or a friend who's skilled at writing score and comment on your essays.**

2. **Identify which questions you answered correctly and incorrectly.**

3. **Read the answer explanation for each question you answered incorrectly and review any relevant material so you can answer a question of that type correctly next time.**

4. **Read the answer explanation for each question you answered correctly so you fully understand how to approach questions of this type and why the wrong answer choices are incorrect.**

Read the answer explanations for all questions, regardless of whether you answered correctly, so you have a clearer understanding of how to approach different question types and recognize common traps. As you review questions and answers, you begin to understand how the GRE designers think, which gives you a major advantage for answering questions.

About the Authors

Ron Woldoff completed his dual master's degrees at Arizona State University and San Diego State University, where he studied the culmination of business and technology. After several years as a corporate consultant, Ron opened his own company, National Test Prep, where he helps students achieve their goals on the GMAT, GRE, and SAT. He created the programs and curricula for these tests from scratch, using his own observations of the tests and feedback from students. Ron has also taught his own GMAT and GRE programs as an adjunct instructor at both Northern Arizona University and the internationally acclaimed Thunderbird School of Global Management. Ron lives in Phoenix, Arizona, with his lovely wife, Leisah, and their three amazing boys, Zachary, Jadon, and Adam. You can find Ron on the web at testprepaz.com.

Joe Kraynak is a freelancer who specializes in team writing with professionals in various fields. He holds a BA in creative writing and philosophy and an MA in English literature from Purdue University and has co-authored numerous *For Dummies* titles, including *Bipolar Disorder For Dummies* with Candida Fink, MD; *Food Allergies For Dummies* with Robert A. Wood, MD; and *Flipping Houses For Dummies* with real-estate mogul Ralph R. Roberts. Joe lives in Crawfordsville, Indiana, with his wonderful wife, Cecie, three cats, and numerous forest critters. You can find Joe on the web at joekraynak.com.

Dedication

Ron Woldoff: This book is humbly dedicated to the many hundreds of students who have passed through my test-prep programs on their way to achieving their goals. You have taught me as much as I have taught you.

Authors' Acknowledgments

Ron Woldoff: I would like to thank my friend Elleyne Kase, who first connected me with the *For Dummies* folks and made this book happen. I would also like to thank my friends Ken Krueger, Lionel Hummel, and Jaime Abromovitz, who helped me get things started when I had this wild notion of helping people prepare for standardized college-admissions tests. And more than anyone else, I would like to thank my wife, Leisah, for her continuing support and for always being there for me.

Both authors would like to thank agent Bill Gladstone of Waterside Productions in Cardiff, California, for giving us the opportunity to revise this book. Special thanks to the technical editor, Karen Berlin Ishii, for meticulously checking the manuscript, ferreting out errors, and generously offering her own GRE expertise and insight. Also, much thanks to Vicki Adang for her patience and persistence in shepherding the manuscript, figures, and equations through editing and production. And thanks to copy editor Danielle Voirol, who carefully edited the manuscript to ensure clarity and root out errors. Finally, a shout out to Erin Calligan Mooney, our acquisitions editor, who was ultimately responsible for choosing us to revise this edition and for dealing with all the minor details to get it going and keep it on track.

Publisher's Acknowledgments

Acquisitions Editor: Erin Calligan Mooney

Senior Project Editor: Victoria M. Adang

Copy Editor: Danielle Voirol

Technical Editor: Karen Berlin Ishii

Project Coordinator: Sheree Montgomery

Cover Image: ©iStock.com/Andrew Rich

Index

capricious, 293–294
Carnegie (Krass), 281
carp, 76
carping, 37
castigate, 294
catalyst, 289, 293
Causes of War (Levy and Thompson), 271
central angles, 144
chaos, 37, 76
cheating, 341
chicanery, 76
choking, 343
choleric, 326
chords, 142
churl, 43, 76
cigarette, 72
circadian rhythms, 7
circles
    characteristics of, 141–142
    example questions, 142–143, 145–149
    formulas for, 143–148
    shaded-area problems, 149
circular reasoning, 62
circumferences
    defined, 141
    example question, 143
    formula for, 143
clothes, 19
coda, 76
codify, 76
coerced, 251
cognizant, 76
cohort, 43, 76
colloquial, 76
combinations
    defined, 168
    example questions, 168–169
commensurate, 38, 76, 293
common denominators, 97
commutative properties, 94–95
compelling, 290
complacency, 76
complacent, 330
complaisant, 330
complementary angles, 129
composite numbers, 92
concede, 293
conciliatory, 43, 77, 330
conclusions
    in Argument Analysis essays, 60–61,
        211–212
    defined, 60
    in Issue Analysis essays, 206
conclusive, 290
concrete, 41, 77
concurrent, 328

confidante, 77
confidence-building, in exam preparation, 23–24
congregation, 73
congruent polygons, 131
congruous, 77
consecutive integers, 156
consecutive probabilities
    example question, 165
    general discussion, 164
consternation, 77
constrained, 257
consummate, 43, 77
consummately, 326
contentious, 41, 77, 294
contra- (prefix), 70
contraindicated, 70
contravene, 70
contrite, 43, 77
contumacious, 77
convoluted, 294
coordinate geometry
    defined, 118
    example questions, 120–121, 123–125
    key formulas in, 119–121
    linear algebraic equations, 122
    simultaneous equations, 123–124
coordinate plane, 118
coquette, 72
correlate, 257
correlations
    defined, 290
    example question, 180–181
    in scatter plots, 180
corroborate, 77, 290, 293
countenance, 77
counter, 40, 77
counterpart, 77
counting methods
    counting principle, 166–167
    example questions, 167–169
    general discussion, 166
    permutations, 167
courteous, 294
coy, 43
craven, 77, 294
cred (root), 73
credible, 73
credulity, 77
credulous, 73
cronyism, 77
cross-multiply, 100
cubes
    defined, 150
    surface area of, 151
    volume of, 150
culp (root), 70

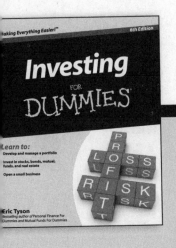
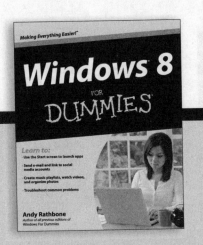

Anatomy and Physiology For Dummies, 2nd Edition
978-0-470-92326-9

Astronomy For Dummies, 3rd Edition
978-1-118-37697-3

Biology For Dummies, 2nd Edition
978-0-470-59875-7

Chemistry For Dummies, 2nd Edition
978-1-118-00730-3

1001 Algebra II Practice Problems For Dummies
978-1-118-44662-1

Microsoft Office

Excel 2013 For Dummies
978-1-118-51012-4

Office 2013 All-in-One For Dummies
978-1-118-51636-2

PowerPoint 2013 For Dummies
978-1-118-50253-2

Word 2013 For Dummies
978-1-118-49123-2

Music

Blues Harmonica For Dummies
978-1-118-25269-7

Guitar For Dummies, 3rd Edition
978-1-118-11554-1

iPod & iTunes For Dummies, 10th Edition
978-1-118-50864-0

Programming

Beginning Programming with C For Dummies
978-1-118-73763-7

Excel VBA Programming For Dummies, 3rd Edition
978-1-118-49037-2

Java For Dummies, 6th Edition
978-1-118-40780-6

Religion & Inspiration

The Bible For Dummies
978-0-7645-5296-0

Buddhism For Dummies, 2nd Edition
978-1-118-02379-2

Catholicism For Dummies, 2nd Edition
978-1-118-07778-8

Self-Help & Relationships

Beating Sugar Addiction For Dummies
978-1-118-54645-1

Meditation For Dummies, 3rd Edition
978-1-118-29144-3

Seniors

Laptops For Seniors For Dummies, 3rd Edition
978-1-118-71105-7

Computers For Seniors For Dummies, 3rd Edition
978-1-118-11553-4

iPad For Seniors For Dummies, 6th Edition
978-1-118-72826-0

Social Security For Dummies
978-1-118-20573-0

Smartphones & Tablets

Android Phones For Dummies, 2nd Edition
978-1-118-72030-1

Nexus Tablets For Dummies
978-1-118-77243-0

Samsung Galaxy S 4 For Dummies
978-1-118-64222-1

Samsung Galaxy Tabs For Dummies
978-1-118-77294-2

Test Prep

ACT For Dummies, 5th Edition
978-1-118-01259-8

ASVAB For Dummies, 3rd Edition
978-0-470-63760-9

GRE For Dummies, 7th Edition
978-0-470-88921-3

Officer Candidate Tests For Dummies
978-0-470-59876-4

Physician's Assistant Exam For Dummies
978-1-118-11556-5

Series 7 Exam For Dummies
978-0-470-09932-2

Windows 8

Windows 8.1 All-in-One For Dummies
978-1-118-82087-2

Windows 8.1 For Dummies
978-1-118-82121-3

Windows 8.1 For Dummies, Book + DVD Bundle
978-1-118-82107-7

Available in print and e-book formats.

Available wherever books are sold. **For more information or to order direct visit www.dummies.com**

Take Dummies with you everywhere you go!

Whether you are excited about e-books, want more from the web, must have your mobile apps, or are swept up in social media, Dummies makes everything easier.

Leverage the Power

For Dummies is the global leader in the reference category and one of the most trusted and highly regarded brands in the world. No longer just focused on books, customers now have access to the For Dummies content they need in the format they want. Let us help you develop a solution that will fit your brand and help you connect with your customers.

Advertising & Sponsorships

Connect with an engaged audience on a powerful multimedia site, and position your message alongside expert how-to content.

Targeted ads • Video • Email marketing • Microsites • Sweepstakes sponsorship

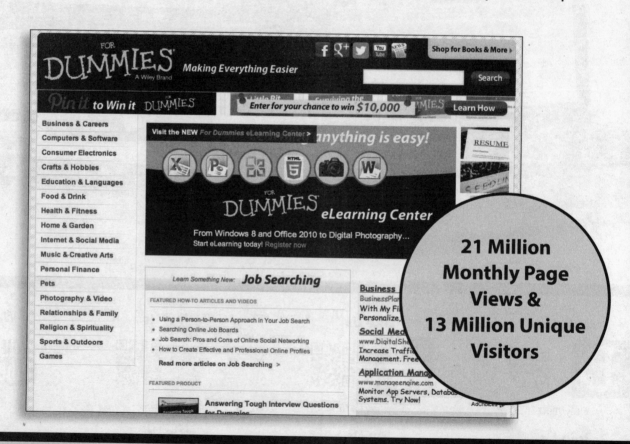